The Philokalia and the Inner Life

# The Philokalia and the Inner Life

*On Passions and Prayer*

Christopher C.H. Cook

PICKWICK *Publications* • Eugene, Oregon

THE PHILOKALIA AND THE INNER LIFE
On Passions and Prayer

Copyright © 2012 Christopher C. H. Cook. All rights reserved. Except for brief quotations in critical publications or reviews, no part of this book may be reproduced in any manner without prior written permission from the publisher. Write: Permissions, Wipf and Stock Publishers, 199 W. 8th Ave., Eugene, OR 97401.

This edition published by Wipf and Stock Publishers by arrangement with James Clarke & Co. First published in the United Kingdom, 2011.

Pickwick Publications
An imprint of Wipf and Stock Publishers
199 W. 8th Avenue, Suite 3
Eugene OR, 97401
www.wipfandstock.com

ISBN 13: 978-1-62032-520-9

Manufactured in the U.S.A.

# Contents

*Acknowledgements*   vii

*Names & Abbreviations*   ix

*Prologue*   xiii

1: Influences and Foundations   1

2: The Passions   47

3: Remedies for the Passions   99

4: Mental Well-Being   151

5: Psychotherapy   203

6: On Thoughts and Prayer   257

*Epilogue*   299

*Appendix 1: Constituent Works of the Greek Philokalia*   301

*Appendix 2: Authors of the Works included in the Greek Philokalia*   307

*Notes*   317

*Bibliography*   361

Index   367

*For* Joy

A loyal wife brings joy to her husband

(Sirach chapter 26, verse 2a)

# Acknowledgements

I am indebted to many people who have helped me with my research into the *Philokalia*. First and foremost, I must acknowledge my enormous debt to Andrew Louth. It was he who conceived this project, who recognised its links with my previous work and interests, and who invited me to work with him on it. Subsequently he undertook to be my PhD supervisor when we agreed that the project would involve my submission of a dissertation as well as preparing a book for publication. He has offered invaluable comments on all of the manuscripts, including the very earliest drafts. I have learned so much from his gentle but incisive wisdom and spirituality and his encyclopaedic knowledge of Christian theology.

Most of the writing, including almost all of the initial chapter drafts, was undertaken on Holy Island, whilst staying in Cambridge House as a guest of the Marygate Community. They have made me warmly welcome, even amidst some severe Northumbrian weather, and I have appreciated the rhythm of daily prayer at St Mary's Church during my stays there. This has helped me to remember that thoughts and prayer really are linked inextricably, and that it is not possible to write on a subject like this with integrity without also being immersed in a community of prayer. The work was finished at St Deiniol's Library in North Wales, with the support of a Richard L. Hills scholarship, and I am therefore also grateful for their generous hospitality.

The Leventis Foundation and the Society of the Sacred Mission have kindly supported my work on this project with generous grants, for which I am most grateful. It would not have been possible to undertake this work without their support.

I am very grateful to Kallistos Ware and to Renos Papadopoulos for their helpful comments on the PhD dissertation which became the basis for this book. I am grateful also to Andrew Powell for his comments on an early draft of the chapter on psychotherapy.

My thanks are extended to Faber and Faber Ltd for allowing me to quote extensively from *The Philokalia: The Complete Text compiled by St Nikodimos of the Holy Mountain and St Makarios of Corinth*, translated from the Greek and edited by G.E.H. Palmer, Philip Sherrard and Kallistos Ware (Volume 1: 1979, Volume 2: 1981, Volume 3: 1984, Volume 4: 1995).

I am grateful to Liturgical Press for allowing me to quote material from *The Sayings of the Desert Fathers,* translated by Benedicta Ward: Copyright Sister Benedicta, 1975. Revised edition 1984. A Cistercian Publications title published by Liturgical Press, Collegeville, MN. Reprinted with permission.

Material from *Evagrius of Pontus: The Greek Ascetic Corpus* by Robert E. Sinkewicz (2003) has been used by permission of Oxford University Press, Inc.

Finally, I must thank my family for their love and support throughout the period of my work on this project, and especially my wife, Joy, who has often been in my thoughts and prayers. This book is dedicated to her.

# Names & Abbreviations

Many of the names of authors of the *Philokalia* are susceptible to differing transliteration. The spellings employed in the English translation of the *Philokalia* have been used throughout in this book, except where quoting from other published work.

Many of the authors of the *Philokalia* are saints of the Christian Church, and are referred to as such in the text of the *Philokalia*. For simplicity, and to avoid making distinctions in the present context, they have been referred to here without the prefix of "Saint" or "St". This also avoids the difficulty, as in the case of Evagrios, of deciding what to do when the person is recognised as a saint of one part of the Church but not another.

[Name] The use of square brackets around a name indicates that a text is attributed to the named author but that it is in fact no longer considered to have been actually written by that author. Unless otherwise indicated, this means that the true author of the text is now unknown.

Titles of works included within the English translation of the *Philokalia* have been abbreviated according to the list of abbreviations provided at Appendix 1.

**Abbreviations used for titles of the works of Evagrios**

*Foundations*  The Foundations of Monastic Life: A Presentation of the Practice of Stillness (included in the English Philokalia as *Outline teaching on asceticism and stillness in the solitary life*)

*To Eulogius*  To Eulogius. On the Confession of Thoughts and Counsel in their Regard

*Eight Thoughts* *On the Eight Thoughts*
*Praktikos*   *The Monk: A treatise on the Practical Life*
*On Prayer*  *Chapters on Prayer* (included in the EGP as *On Prayer: 153 Texts*)

Other works of Evagrios, where mentioned, are referred to using their full title.

## Other abbreviations

| | |
|---|---|
| AL1 | Andrew Louth (1996) |
| AL2 | Andrew Louth (2003) |
| BDEC | *Blackwell Dictionary of Eastern Christianity* (Parry et al., 1999) |
| C&C | Refers to the tabulation of versions of the *Philokalia* provided by Conticello and Citterio, 2002 |
| DB | David Balfour (1982) |
| DS | Refers to the entry on the *Philokalia* in *Dictionnaire de Spiritualité* (K. Ware, 1984) |
| EGP | English translation of the Greek *Philokalia* (Palmer et al., 1979, 1981, 1984, 1995) |
| IH | Irénée Hausherr (1978) |
| LTN | *Letter to Nicolas* |
| MEC | *A Monk of the Eastern Church* (1987) |
| NCE | *New Catholic Encyclopedia* (Mcdonald et al., 1981) |
| NGP | Notes by Nikodimos in the Greek *Philokalia* (Andrew Louth, personal communication) |
| No. | Number |
| NRSV | New Revised Standard Version |
| ODCC | *Oxford Dictionary of the Christian Church* (Cross and Livingstone, 1997) |
| OTSL | *On the Spiritual Law* |
| RBW | *Righteous by Works* |
| Ref | Reference |

| | |
|---|---|
| TR | Theophan the Recluse. Biographical notes from the *Dobrotolubiye* (Kadloubovsky and Palmer, 1979) |
| Vol | Volume Number |

### References to the *Philokalia*

Where possible, references to works in the *Philokalia* are given citing the name of the author, the name of the work (using the abbreviated title in Appendix 1) and the paragraph number (preceded by #), followed by the volume and page references to the English translation in brackets. For example:

> Mark the Ascetic in *On the Spiritual Law*, #85 (EGP 1, 116)

Where paragraph numbers are not provided (e.g. in the works of Peter of Damaskos), the name of the author and the titles of the work and portion of the work are given, followed by volume and page references to the English translation in brackets. For example:

> Peter of Damaskos in *Book II* in *VI. Hope* (EGP 3, 227)

# Prologue

> As sheep to a good shepherd, the Lord has given to man intellections of this present world.
>
> Evagrios of Pontus
> *Texts on Discrimination*, #16 (EGP 1, 48)

Thoughts, like sheep, given the chance, are prone to wander aimlessly. Sheep follow one another, without any necessary sense of direction or purpose. They are often found gathered together in flocks, but each individual creature presents its own image of vulnerability and individuality. They get lost, and become sick or lame or hungry. But they can also be shepherded, thus gaining direction, and may be cared for, fed, and protected. A good shepherd will search out the lost, feed the hungry and care for the sick.

Such an image, particularly for those familiar with rural life, offers countless metaphorical and parabolic possibilities. Thus, most famously in the Christian tradition, Jesus is the good shepherd and we are the sheep of his pasture.[1] Evagrios of Pontus (345/346-399), however, suggests that we are all shepherds and that God has given us thoughts – or here "intellections" – as sheep to be cared for.

It is a much neglected, and somewhat disconcerting, facet of the extended metaphor of sheep and shepherd, at least in relation to the New Testament of Christian scripture, that the sheep are, at the end of the day, there for the shepherd, or for the one whom the shepherd serves, and not primarily the other way around. In ancient times, as now, sheep were kept for their wool and lambs for meat. Then, although less commonly now, lambs were killed for sacrifice. Unless they are the victims of sickness, or of marauding wolves, sheep and lambs are eventually put to death. Perhaps this reality betrays an intended irony when the Jesus of John's gospel expresses his willingness to lay down his life for his sheep? However, returning to the metaphor of thoughts as sheep that human beings shepherd in their minds, can we say that these sheep are there for the benefit of those who think them, or for those whom the thinker serves, rather than for their own sake?

The answer to this question will depend upon theology and philosophy for it could well be argued, amongst other things, that the thoughts are simply there for no purpose or that they are there for the benefit of those who think them, or that they are ultimately there for the glory of God. Perhaps it is a little more helpful, however, to ask what the purpose might be of shepherding these thoughts? Surely most people shepherd their thoughts with a purpose in mind? That purpose might be to serve their own advantage, or to serve the benefit of others, or to serve God, or perhaps it might be for some other purpose. However, the fact is that we do shepherd our thoughts and that we perceive ourselves as doing so for a reason. No matter how much they wander randomly, become sick, follow the wrong leader, or otherwise misbehave, it is a feature of the inner life of human beings that we do keep trying to shepherd our thoughts in particular ways with particular purposes in mind. The writing and the reading of this text are but one example of this amongst an infinite number of possible examples that could be taken from the thoughts that humans have, whether communicated in speech or writing or remaining secret within our own minds and souls.

Furthermore, the shepherding of thoughts is something which we perceive as uniquely and characteristically human and as deeply intimate. To talk about the ways in which we shepherd thoughts within our own inner space is to talk about something which gets to the heart of what it means to be human and also – at the individual level – to the heart of what it means to be "me". Thoughts are very personal and yet, because they wander like sheep, going to places to which we perhaps wish they hadn't gone, we may be ashamed of them and not want other people to know about them. Undoubtedly most of us, most of the time, only share with others those thoughts that we feel pleased with, or at least which are not embarrassing. We talk about the ones that are shepherded in ways that we think others will approve of, but not about the ones that get lost, or the ones that we took to prohibited places. Our conversation about the shepherding of our thoughts, if not the actual business of shepherding, is strongly determined by a sense of what is socially acceptable.

In a post-Freudian world, we are aware that much of what we "think" is unconscious and that the unconscious world – of which we are generally not explicitly aware, but about which we are generally uneasy – has characteristic ways of making itself felt: in dreams, in slips of the tongue, in humour and so on. Indeed, so familiar are we now with this concept that we feel less ashamed than we used to of confessing thoughts that Freud has led us to believe we need not be ashamed about. Or, at least, we are less ashamed of some such thoughts some of the time, for we now seem to spend much more time in western society talking about sex, but much less time talking about death, for example.

Applying this Freudian knowledge to our metaphor of thoughts as sheep and ourselves as shepherds, we might say that we don't always know where our sheep have gone, but we are often vaguely aware that there are some missing. Or else we might be more ready to admit pasturing sheep in some places than in others. But, still, the process of tending this flock is very important to us and we spend much – if not all – of our waking life giving it our attention.

Where, then, does this extended metaphor take us?

It is used here primarily for two reasons. Firstly, it facilitates an introduction to talking about why our inner world is important to us as human beings and yet why we also often do not speak about it. Secondly, however, the quotation with which it began is taken from one of the earlier contributions to a collection of texts known as the *Philokalia* – an anthology of spiritual writings from the Eastern Christian tradition, spanning the fourth to the fifteenth centuries C.E.

*Philokalia* means literally "love of the beautiful", but is usually understood in Greek as referring to an anthology of works.[2] Today, reference to the *Philokalia* is usually taken, unless specified otherwise, to denote a particular anthology assembled by two Greek monks in the eighteenth century, which was first published in Venice in 1782.[3] The compilers, Nikodimos of Mount Athos (1749-1809) and Makarios of Corinth (1731-1805) apparently chose their texts with a view to making more widely available that which would be helpful in the spiritual life, drawn from the hesychastic tradition. This tradition, broadly understood, seeks to find an inner stillness of the soul – away from the distractions of thoughts and desires – within which contemplation of God might be undertaken and, eventually, union with God found. In other words, it is a tradition of Christian prayer which emphasises attention to the inner life, the life of thoughts, with a view to the purpose of contemplating God himself. To quote from another contributor to the *Philokalia*, Maximos the Confessor, and following the same metaphor used by Evagrios, within this tradition: 'sheep represent thoughts pastured by the intellect on the mountains of contemplation'.[4]

The intention here, then, is to explore the ways in which this collection of texts might help with the process of shepherding thoughts or, to be less allegorical, the ways in which the tradition expressed within this collection of texts might assist in developing a Christian understanding of the inner life of thoughts and of nurturing mental well-being. Necessarily, this exploration does not confine itself to the inner life – the *Philokalia* talks of virtue in Christian living and not only of thoughts and desires. However, it does emphasise the life of prayer as the only basis on which Christians can properly understand the inner life or conceive of mental well-being. It thus assumes from the outset that the central, primary and underlying purpose for which Christians will properly and beneficially shepherd their thoughts is that of loving, serving and worshipping God. It also assumes that the shepherding of thoughts for other purposes – such as human happiness as an end in itself – will always be more or less unsatisfactory. However, whilst these are fairly major assumptions, which atheist shepherds of thoughts such as Freud would undoubtedly disagree with, it is not intended that they should hide this exploration away from a critical encounter with other shepherds and other traditions. On the contrary, such encounters are exactly what is intended here.

These assumptions do recognise, however, that complete objectivity is not attainable, either in the inner life or in academic discourse. An observer must occupy a particular position in order to observe and an awareness of the subjectivity of the space which one occupies is, it is contended here, not a weakness but rather a strength. There may, then, be other reasons for my use of the metaphor of sheep and shepherd as an introduction to this work. In fact, perhaps there is a necessity – rather than merely the possibility – of other reasons for my beginning in this way. If I approach this work from an academic perspective, I must also necessarily approach it as an exploration of my own inner world from within the Christian tradition to which I belong. This will surely reveal that there must be other reasons for my choice of this particular metaphor – reasons which are either concerned with my own conscious sense of vocation to be a shepherd of thoughts, or else perhaps my own unconscious thoughts around this theme (the "sheep" that I am only vaguely aware have "gone missing" from the fold of my consciousness). Perhaps – as I hope – these reasons concern my sense of purpose in combining a vocation to the priesthood with a training in clinical psychiatry and academic study, all of which seem to me to have this theme in common. Or perhaps – although I consciously deny it – they concern an attempt to find connections where there are none, to cover up the aimlessness of the mental wandering of my own thoughts like lost sheep. The point is not so much that either of these reasons is necessarily correct as that there are various possible reasons which are more concerned with the subjectivity of my vocation to write than the actual purpose of writing this particular text for others to read.

This subjectivity of writing is not eliminable from this text, but neither is it entirely unhelpful. Because of it, I approach the *Philokalia* with a view to being challenged by its discourse as to the ways in which my own thoughts may better be shepherded. If I do not allow the texts of the *Philokalia* to challenge me in this and other ways, as I also myself challenge them with a spirit of critical academic enquiry, the encounter is false. Indeed, to talk about a subject such as this and to remain entirely unaffected, or to avoid altogether any examination of its impact upon the understanding of one's own thoughts, would seem rather dishonest. This is, after all, itself primarily an attempt to shepherd thoughts for a particular purpose – that of understanding better how the inner life may be understood and developed. Although the circularity of this process might seem to some to be undermining of objectivity, it is the reality of the process in which the compilers and authors of the *Philokalia* themselves engaged and in which they invite us to join them. Whilst I will not be uncritical of these fellow authors, I trust that I will show enough respect to take seriously what they have said to me.

I have wondered (my thoughts wandering like lost sheep perhaps?) what other metaphors might have been used to introduce this subject. As much of the writing was undertaken on Holy Island, in Northumberland, I looked across the beach and saw rocks scattered across the sea shore like sheep scattered across a pasture. I considered my own walks across these beaches and the way in which one's attention is divided between an intended destination across the beach and the immediate task of finding a firm footing for one's next step. It is easy to go astray from the former goal because of the necessity of the latter task. Rocks on the beach, like thoughts in the mind, are necessary as a basis for moving forward, but can easily also lead away from the place to which one intended to travel. But the need to find a firm footing does not invalidate the destination or refute the evidence of the eyes. It speaks only to human limitation.

Do such images assist in the examination of a subject which, since Freud, has become the subject of a vast and diverse technical literature? The possible answers to that question will be left for later consideration, but an unprejudiced examination of a pre-Freudian and pre-modern literature and the wisdom that it contains cannot avoid examining the possibility that they do assist in reaching a final destination; whereas, perhaps, the more technical tools of our contemporary academic discourse may confine themselves more to finding the next rock on which to stand.

The writers of the *Philokalia* sought a final destination by means of taking individual steps with care. To the best of my ability I have sought to follow that example in my writing on this subject. This book may therefore be considered as comprising six steps towards the goal of understanding what the *Philokalia* has to tell us about mental well-being and the shepherding of thoughts. These steps are:

1. In Chapter One I give consideration to influences that have helped to shape the writing of the *Philokalia*, its compilation, its teachings on the inner life of thoughts, and the foundations upon which it has been built. I do not feel that the teaching of the *Philokalia* on the inner life can be properly appreciated without this contextual information.

2. In Chapter Two, I focus on the teaching of the *Philokalia* on thoughts of a particularly troublesome kind, which the *Philokalia* refers to as "passions". I have started here partly because this is such a central theme of the *Philokalia*, but also because it is where human beings start in trying to order their thoughts. It is a study in the unruliness of human thoughts, their tendency to go astray, and the nature of the challenge that they present to those who wish to shepherd them.

Prologue                                                                 xix

3. In Chapter Three, my controlling metaphor turns from rural life to the world of medicine, and I consider the remedies for the passions that the *Philokalia* prescribes.

4. Chapter Four might be considered a glance towards my final destination, rather than a step forward. However, if it is a step forward, it is the step of understanding how the *Philokalia* conceives mental well-being. In the medical terms of the previous chapter, it is concerned with better understanding health in order to be better equipped to treat the disease of the passions.

5. Chapter Five steps aside from the *Philokalia* in order to give consideration to the contemporary world of psychotherapy. What is psychotherapy, how does it conceive mental well-being, and what does it aim to achieve? The possibility of understanding the as providing a kind of psychotherapy is then considered. This raises questions about the nature of the soul, or self, and human concerns with inwardness and reflexivity.

6. Chapter Six attempts to explore the relationship between thoughts and prayer. When the *Philokalia* is consulted as a source of reference on thoughts, or the inner life, it always turns the focus onto prayer. When it is consulted as a source of guidance on prayer, it turns the reader's attention towards a careful examination of their thoughts. This relationship therefore seems to be central to the *Philokalia*. It is studied here with reference to the preceding discussion on psychotherapy, and also by way of a brief exploratory engagement with some other western strands of thought, on philosophy (Paul Ricoeur on hermeneutics) and spirituality (Denys Turner and *The Darkness of God*).

In the Epilogue, reflecting briefly on the steps that have been taken, we shall return to the theme of shepherding thoughts and ponder where our journey has taken us.

I will close this introduction with one final quotation from the *Philokalia* on the theme of sheep and shepherds, this time from Ilias the Presbyter:

> Where fear does not lead the way, thoughts will be in a state of confusion, like sheep that have no shepherd.

Where fear leads the way or goes with them, they will be under control and in good order within the fold. Fear is the son of faith and the shepherd of the commandments. He who is without faith will not be found worthy to be a sheep of the Lord's pasture.[5]

Here, then, is the question to be addressed. How does the *Philokalia* teach us that we can control and order thoughts that are confused, difficult to control and in disorder?

# 1

# Influences and Foundations

Explorations of the inner world of human beings might reasonably be expected to be dependent upon the outer world in which they live: its culture, its history, traditions, assumptions, language and beliefs. Such things influence the way in which we perceive ourselves and thus, at least potentially, the way in which we think. If we are to understand properly what the authors and compilers of the *Philokalia* had to say about the inner life it would therefore seem to be important to consider the nature of their outer world, and especially its anthropological assumptions and beliefs. However, this immediately presents a problem, for the *Philokalia* is the work of about 40 authors, and two compilers, whose lives span well over a thousand years. Can anything be said about "their world" which might go beyond vague generalities or spurious over-generalisations?

It might be tempting to emphasise the importance of tradition to Byzantine civilisation and Orthodox Christianity as reason for expecting continuity of fundamental assumptions across even a thousand years and more of writing. However, it has famously been suggested that "to represent Byzantium as immutable over a period of eleven centuries is to fall into a trap set by Byzantium itself".[1] We must also remember that, during the period in question, some very significant events took place – not least the seven universally agreed ecumenical church councils and the great schism of 1054. The doctrinal, and especially the Christological, controversies that raged during this period variously affect different works within the *Philokalia*. For example, one work attributed to Neilos the Ascetic in the original Greek *Philokalia* is now known to have been by Evagrios of Pontus (345/346-399), but transmitted under the name of Neilos because of the tainting of reputation of Evagrios by his association with Origenist heresy. Almost at the other end of the chronological span of the *Philokalia*, the writings of Gregory Palamas (1296-1359) show evidence of his concern to defend the hesychast tradition itself from its critics. Maximos the Confessor (580-662), the single biggest contributor of texts, was exiled and tortured for his defence of the doctrine of the divine and human wills in Christ, in keeping with the Council of Chalcedon. He was only vindicated at the 6th Ecumenical Council, almost 20 years after his death. The historical contexts and doctrinal preoccupations that emerge from place to place within the *Philokalia* are thus varied indeed, and in some places represent fierce controversies of their time.

In an introduction to the English translation of the *Philokalia*, the translators and editors suggest that there is an inner unity to the *Philokalia* which is conferred more than anything by recurrent reference to invocation of the name of Jesus (or the Jesus Prayer as it is now known). They argue that this is "one of the central forms of the art and science which constitute hesychasm" and that this is evident even in some of the earliest texts.[2] It is again tempting to draw from this a reassurance as to common underlying assumptions within the *Philokalia*, but that would certainly be premature. The Jesus Prayer is but one theme amongst many to be found in these texts and it is hardly clear that it is a major theme in the earlier texts, even if it might be argued that evidence of it is to be found in them. It would seem in any case unlikely that a tradition of spirituality dating back to the fourth century would not have undergone at least some changes in emphasis and development of ideas – especially in view of the vicissitudes of its history. Thus, for example, the later texts would seem to show evidence of the influence of the Syrian spirituality introduced in the thirteenth/fourteenth century revival, an influence which exerts its own distinctive emphasis on these later texts.

A glossary provided in the English translation to the *Philokalia* also implies that there is a consistency of terminology throughout its span of writings. There is no doubt that this glossary provides helpful clarification for the reader who is new to the *Philokalia* and its world of thought, and that there is a terminology with which a reader gradually becomes familiar when reading and re-reading the *Philokalia*. However, greater familiarity begins to suggest that the appearance of consistency is almost as much confusing as it is helpful. Thus, for example, the glossary helpfully points out that even such a fundamental term as "passion" refers on the part

## Chapter 1: Influences and Foundations

of some writers to something intrinsically evil, but on the part of others to something fundamentally good, something which may be redeemed.[3] Again, the helpful analysis of the process of temptation[4] refers to various sources, both from within the *Philokalia* itself and also John Climacus's *Ladder of Divine Ascent*, but careful study of these sources shows a heterogeneity of understandings, albeit with some core terms (such as "provocation" or "assent") which are used more or less consistently.

It is not, however, necessary to be completely nihilistic as to the possibility of grasping something of an understanding of the common assumptions that have formed the understanding of life in the inner world that is such a central theme of the *Philokalia*. Firstly, there have been historical, philosophical and theological influences, which appear to have provided something of an enduring source of reference to its authors. Secondly, there is evidence of internal consistency in regard to certain significant fundamental assumptions and themes – of which the Jesus Prayer is but one.

It would therefore appear helpful here to give some further consideration to the following:

1. The compilation and history of the *Philokalia* as an anthology of texts
2. The anthropology of the *Philokalia*
3. The tradition of the Desert Fathers
4. The work of Evagrios of Pontus
5. The use of scripture by the authors of the *Philokalia*

To some extent these might be considered as external influences that helped to shape the *Philokalia*, but to some extent (especially in the case of Evagrios) they are internal to its fabric. They are therefore considered together here, partly as formative external influences and partly as foundational stones upon which the *Philokalia* was erected.

### 1. Compilation, Translation and Evolution of the *Philokalia*

The hesychastic tradition, from within which the *Philokalia* emerged, has a long history. From as early as the fourth century C.E. the term "hesychia" was used by Christian monastic writers to refer to a state of inner quietness to be achieved in prayer as preparation for communion with God. From the sixth to the eleventh centuries in the Byzantine world a "hesychast" was simply a monk or ascetic, and hesychasm referred simply to a broadly contemplative approach to prayer. In the thirteenth and fourteenth centuries there was something of a spiritual revival, centred on Mount Athos, in which Gregory of Sinai (1258-1346) and Gregory Palamas took a leading role. This gave birth to a movement now known as the "Hesychast Tradition", which drew upon traditions of Christian spirituality both from Syria and the Egyptian desert fathers.

The hesychastic tradition came under fierce attack in the fourteenth century, primarily because of an assertion that prayer of the heart can lead to a vision of Divine Light; a light which, it was asserted, can be seen even in this life, and by human eyes in a literal physical sense. This light, it was further asserted, is identical to that which surrounded Christ on Mount Tabor in his transfiguration. Gregory Palamas, a contributor to the *Philokalia*, was a leading – and eventually successful – defender of the tradition against these attacks. Hesychasm was formally adopted at the Councils of Constantinople (1341, 1347 and 1351) and subsequently became an accepted part of Orthodox spiritual tradition.[5]

The compilation and dissemination of the *Philokalia* in the eighteenth century represented a significant component of a renaissance of the hesychastic tradition.[6] The *Philokalia* was compiled by Nikodimos of the Holy Mountain and Makarios of Corinth, both of whom belonged to the spiritual renewal movement of the "Kollyvades". This movement was traditional and conservative, critical of liberal teaching of the enlightenment, and enthusiastic for the spirituality and theology of the Fathers of the Eastern Church. However, Nikodimos at least was not so conservative as to prevent his drawing upon western sources in his own writings.[7]

Makarios was born in 1731 in Corinth and was named Michael at his baptism. He was educated in Corinth and eventually became a teacher there himself. In 1764 the Archbishop of Corinth died, and Michael was elected his successor. In 1765, in Constantinople, he was ordained Archbishop and renamed Makarios. As Archbishop he began a series of reforms, including prohibition of clergy from holding political office, and measures to ensure that the clergy were properly educated. The outbreak of the Russo-Turkish war

Chapter 1: Influences and Foundations                                    5

in 1768 forced Makarios to leave Corinth and although peace was restored in 1774 another Archbishop was appointed in his place and he never resumed his position there. In 1783 Makarios anonymously published *Concerning Frequent Communion of the Divine Mysteries*, in which he argued the case of the Kollyvades in favour of more frequent reception of communion than the two or three times each year that had become customary. The book was hastily condemned by the Ecumenical Patriarch but later (in 1789) approved and recommended by a new Patriarch. The last years of his life, from 1790 to 1805, were spent almost entirely in a hermitage on Chios where, according to Cavarnos, he "[subjected] himself to severe ascetic struggle, practicing interior prayer, writing books, confessing and counselling people, instructing them in the true Faith, inciting them to virtue, and offering material help to those in need".[8]

Nikodimos was born in 1749 on Naxos, one of the Aegean islands. He was educated initially on Naxos, and from the age of 15 years at Smyrna, where he learnt Latin, Italian and French. In 1775 he went to Mount Athos and became a monk. It was in 1777 that Makarios visited Athos and gave him the task of editing the *Philokalia*, and also two other works,[9] although in fact the two men had first met some years earlier on the island of Hydra. Nikodimos went on to become a prolific author, editor and translator of other theological works.[10] Nikodimos' last years were spent in writing, and it is as an author, translator and compiler that his life most stands out. However, there is also no reason to doubt the testimony that he practiced mental prayer assiduously throughout his 34 years on Mount Athos.[11] It would not seem unreasonable to speculate that his introduction to the *Philokalia* by Makarios in 1777 exerted a lifelong influence upon him.

Clearly the selection of texts for inclusion in the *Philokalia* is a very significant matter, but we know surprisingly little about how the selection was made. Constantine Cavarnos first reports a traditional view that it was compiled by monks on Mount Athos in the fourteenth century, but then goes on to assert that Makarios himself was the real compiler.[12] Certainly it is clear that Makarios was the more senior editor and that the initiative for the work came from him and not from Nikodimos.[13] We might speculate that the selection was not actually made by Nikodimos and Makarios, but rather already existed in some way as a collection of texts revered by tradition, or else already assembled by earlier compilers. Alternatively, Ware has suggested, there may have been a policy of including rare or unpublished texts.[14]

We do know that the texts were drawn from the libraries of Mount Athos. The introduction by Nikodimos refers to "manuscripts which had been lying inglorious and motheaten in holes and corners and darkness, cast aside and scattered here and there".[15] In this introduction, Nikodimos also describes the purpose of the *Philokalia* as being the provision of a "mystical school" of mental (or "inward") prayer[16]:

> This book is a treasury of inner wakefulness, the safeguard of the mind, the mystical school of mental prayer.... an excellent compendium of practical spiritual science, the unerring guide of contemplation, the Paradise of the Fathers, the golden chain of the virtues.... the frequent converse with Jesus, the clarion for recalling Grace, and in a word, the very instrument of theosis."[17]

The full title of the original Greek *Philokalia* is:

> The Philokalia of the Neptic Saints gathered from our holy Theophoric ["God-bearing"] Fathers, through which, by means of the philosophy of ascetic practice and contemplation, the intellect is purified, illumined, and made perfect.[18]

The English translators of the *Philokalia*, commenting on the title and subtitle, suggest that it is through "love of the beautiful" that the intellect is "purified, illumined and made perfect", and that it was this purpose of purification, illumination and perfection that governed the choice of texts.[19] The texts of the *Philokalia* are thus, they argue, "guides to the practice of the contemplative life".[20]

Kallistos Ware,[21] one of the English translators of the *Philokalia*, has suggested that reflection on its contents enables us to deduce something about its scope, its aim and the means that it recommends to those who wish to achieve its aim. The scope of the *Philokalia* he understands as being defined by its focus on the inner life, characterised especially by the concepts of nepsis (watchfulness) and hesychia (stillness). The aim of the *Philokalia* he identifies as deification. The means to this end he identifies as being a life of unceasing prayer from the depths of the heart, exclusive of all images and thoughts, in which the name of Jesus is invoked, and in which particular physical techniques (see, for example, Chapter 3, p.147) may or may not be employed.

Ware further suggests that the spirituality that emerges from the *Philokalia* has four characteristics:

1. A predominant influence of Evagrios and Maximos
2. A basic antinomy between the knowability and unknowability, the immanence and transcendence, of God which might be regarded as "Palamite", although preceding the time of Gregory Palamas
3. An absence of western influence
4. A relevance to all Christians

Whilst questions remain about exactly what guided the inclusion and exclusion of particular texts, the overall thrust of the *Philokalia* would therefore seem fairly clear. This is an anthology of eastern Christian texts designed to assist in the inner life of prayer.

All the texts included in the *Philokalia* by Nikodimos and Makarios were originally written in Greek, except for two by John Cassian, which were translated from Latin into Greek during the Byzantine period. We may count 62 texts included in the *Philokalia* (see Appendix 1).[22]

The authors were undoubtedly all men (although the actual authorship of some texts remains in dispute) and all belonged to the monastic tradition. Cassian is the only "western" author included. The single biggest contributor was Maximos the Confessor, followed by Peter of Damaskos. About some of the authors we know much; about others, however, we know little or nothing with any certainty. We may calculate that there were approximately 40 or more authors in all (see Appendix 2). Attributions of authorship of some texts in the original Greek edition are now known to be incorrect. In several cases we know that contributions were made to particular texts by two or more authors.

The *Philokalia*, as a compilation of the original Greek texts, prepared by Makarios and Nikodimos, with an overall introduction and with notes to introduce the texts associated with each author, was published in a single volume in Venice in 1782 at the expense of John Mavrogordatos, Prince of Moldo-Wallachia.[23] A second edition was produced in Athens in 1893, including some additional texts by

Patriarch Kallistos. A third edition was produced in five volumes, also in Athens, in 1957-1963.[24]

The first translation of the *Philokalia*, into Slavonic, was made by Paisius Velichkovsky (1722-1794),[25] and was published in Moscow in 1793 under the title *Dobrotulubiye* and under the sponsorship of Metropolitan Gabriel.[26] Velichkovsky was a Ukrainian monk who lived on Mount Athos from 1746-1763. He was later abbot of large monasteries at Dragomirna (1763-1775) and Niamets (1779-1794) in Romania and was the initiator of a spiritual renaissance there within the hesychastic tradition.

During his time on Mount Athos, Velichkovsky developed a concern to find, copy, collect and translate patristic texts. Initially this seems to have arisen out of an inability to find a suitable spiritual instructor (or starets). Starchestvo (or eldership) was a key element in the hesychastic tradition.[27] However, as Velichkovsky was unable to find someone suitable as his own starets, he seems to have turned to patristic writings as an alternative source of instruction.[28] The concern for patristic texts that he acquired in this way early in life continued during his later life as an abbot in Romania, by which time he seems to have had literally hundreds of monks working on the tasks of copying and translation.

Velichkovsky's *Dobrotulubiye* was not a complete translation of the Greek *Philokalia*. Only 27 of the 62 works comprising the latter were included in copies of the first edition, although a few additional texts by Patriarch Kallistos were included.[29] A second edition was published in 1822 (almost 30 years after Velichkovsy's death). A further 13 works from the Greek *Philokalia* were included in the second edition and in at least some copies of the first edition.[30]

It is clear that Velichkovsky's interest in patristic works was one that he shared with the compilers of the Greek *Philokalia* and also that he knew of their interest. In a letter of uncertain date to Archimandrite Theodosius of Sophroniev, Velichkovsky wrote of Makarios' fervour and care in the process of seeking out and copying patristic books on Mount Athos, a process that led to the publication of the *Philokalia*.[31] It is also clear that Velichkovksy's interest in these texts predated by many years the assignment by Makarios to Nikodimos in 1777 of the task of compiling and editing the Greek *Philokalia*. Whether we may accept the conclusion of the editors of the biography of Velichkovsky (written by his disciple Schema-monk Metrophanes) that in fact it was Velichkovsky who imparted to Makarios the knowledge of what to look for, the purpose of the search, and awareness of the value of the texts would seem much more debatable.[32] However, it is clear that Velichkovsky's translation work began very many years before the *Philokalia* was published in 1782. We might speculate that a loose collection of texts existed prior to the interests of both Velichkovsky and Makarios.

Subsequently, the *Philokalia* was translated into Russian. There are widespread references in the literature to an alleged Russian translation by Ignatii Brianchaninov (1807-1876), published in 1857.[33] However, according to Kallistos Ware it would seem that this translation does not in fact exist.[34] A Russian translation by Theophan the Recluse (1815-1894) was published in Moscow from 1877-1889 in five volumes, also under the title *Dobrotolubiye*.

Theophan[35] studied at Kiev Academy and entered monastic orders in 1837. After two months he was ordained priest and subsequently became a schoolteacher. Like Makarios, he demonstrated an openness to western scholarship and was widely read. In 1850 he was appointed as a member of the Russian Official Commission to Jerusalem. In the course of this work he travelled widely and was able to visit a series of ancient libraries, which he found to be neglected and unappreciated. He developed a knowledge of French, Arabic, Greek and Hebrew which enabled him to read and catalogue the rare manuscripts that he found. It would seem that it was at this stage in his life that he developed an interest in early ascetic Christian literature.

In 1859 Theophan became Bishop of Tambov, and then in 1863 Bishop of Vladimir. In 1866 he became Prior of Vysha monastery. Three months later he was released from his responsibilities as superior in order to become a recluse and in 1872 he entered almost complete seclusion. During his time in seclusion Theophan engaged in a prolific correspondence and also published a number of important works, including *Unseen Warfare* (a revision and translation of an earlier Greek translation of Lorenzo Scupoli's *Spiritual Combat and Path to Paradise* made by Nikodimos) and the Russian *Dobrotolubiye*.

Theophan's *Dobrotolubiye* represented a considerable expansion of the Greek *Philokalia*, from 1,200 to 3,000 pages, published in five volumes.[36] Whilst it included a number of additions not to be found in the Greek *Philokalia* it also omitted a number of texts.[37]

The *Philokalia* was later translated into Romanian by Father Dumitru Stăniloae (1903-1993), and published between 1946 and

1991 in twelve volumes under the title *Filocalia sau culegere din scrierile sfintsilor Parintsi*. The additions to the Romanian *Filocalia* are even more numerous and extensive.[38]

Stăniloae was born and lived his whole life in Romania but received theological education in Athens and Munich. He became a professor of theology in Bucharest and published 90 books, 275 theological articles and numerous other translations, reviews, lectures and other items over a period of some 60 years.[39] Stăniloae had a particular interest in the works of Gregory Palamas. Along with many other clergy, he was imprisoned from 1958 to 1963 by the communist authorities as a political criminal. Four volumes of his translation of the *Philokalia*, based on the first two volumes of the Greek *Philokalia*, were published prior to this imprisonment, during the period 1946 to 1948. The fifth volume did not appear until 1976. However, after the translation of the Greek *Philokalia* was completed (with the publication of the eighth volume in 1979)[40] Stăniloae continued to work on four more volumes, incorporating works by a number of authors not included in the original Greek version.[41]

Modern translations of the Greek texts of the *Philokalia* have also appeared in English, French, German, Italian, Spanish, Finnish and Arabic, and the Greek text may now be consulted in a modern fifth edition.[42]

If our speculation that a loose collection of texts already existed prior to 1777 is correct, then the apparently free additions of texts to Russian and Romanian translations might be taken to suggest something of a living tradition. Within this tradition, additions to a core *Philokalia* were apparently either not considered inappropriate, or else were thought necessary because of unavailability of the supporting texts that would originally have been found alongside the *Philokalia* in the library of Mount Athos.[43]

## 2. Anthropology

In his *Republic*, Plato (*c*.347-247 B.C.E.) argues for a tripartite understanding of the human soul or mind (ψυχή).[44] Both in the course of Plato's argument, and also in our own experience, two of these elements are easier to understand than the third. All three are more akin to motives than to "parts" in any anatomical sense. The first is reason, a reflective and rational element (λογιστικόν).

## Chapter 1: Influences and Foundations

The second is irrational appetite (ἐπιθυμητικόν) – which includes desires such as hunger, thirst and sexual drive, orientated towards satisfaction and pleasure. The third (θυμικόν), including apparently varied motives such as anger, indignation, ambition and a sense of what is "in the heart", the so-called "incensive" power, might be translated "spirited" – although the use of such a theologically loaded word in the present context would inevitably be confusing. For Plato, the immortal soul was understood as being imprisoned, during this life, in its physical body.

The Platonic understanding of the soul has been very influential upon Christianity in general, and in particular the tripartite model of the soul appears to have influenced the *Philokalia*, almost from beginning to end. However, before we give consideration to this in more detail, it is important to say something about the relationship between body and soul.

The *Philokalia* not infrequently, but perhaps mainly in its earlier texts, refers to an apparently tripartite model of human beings, usually as body, soul and spirit, or as body, soul and intellect. Thus, for example, in the text attributed to Antony the Great (but probably actually of Stoic origin), and placed as the first text in the original Greek *Philokalia*, we find:

> Life is the union and conjuncture between intellect, soul and body, while death is not the destruction of these elements so conjoined, but the dissolution of their inter-relationship; for they are all saved through and in God, even after this dissolution.[45]

Again, in Evagrios:

> Let the virtues of the body lead you to those of the soul; and the virtues of the soul to those of the spirit; and these, in turn, to immaterial and principial knowledge.[46]

However, this impression of a tripartite anthropology appears to be either unrepresentative or illusory as there seem to be many more references to human beings as simply body and soul (or, sometimes, body and intellect),[47] and it is clear that this is because the spirit, or intellect, is seen as being merely a part of the soul. Thus, for example, in the aforementioned text attributed to Antony we find:

> The body, when it is united with the soul, comes from the darkness of the womb into the light. But the soul,

> when it is united with the body, is bound up in the body's darkness. Therefore we must hate and discipline the body as an enemy that fights against the soul.[48]

In fact, although it was clearly believed by the original compilers to be an authentic work of Antony, the English translators of the *Philokalia* have placed this work in an appendix on the basis that there is no evidence of Christian authorship, but rather that it appears to be a collection of Stoic and Platonic texts written between the first and fourth centuries C.E. (The negative Platonic view of the soul as imprisoned in the body is clearly evident here.) However, the understanding of human beings as body and soul seems to provide the generally pervading anthropology of the *Philokalia*, and the tension between the body and soul is often evident. For example, in *Theoretikon*, [Theodoros the Great Ascetic] writes:

> What, then, is the nature of our contest in this world? The intelligent soul is conjoined with an animal-like body, which has its being from the earth and gravitates downwards. It is so mixed with the body that though they are total opposites they form a single being. Without change or confusion in either of them, and with each acting in accordance with its nature, they compose a single person, or hypostasis, with two complete natures. In this composite two-natured being, man, each of his natures functions in accordance with its own particular powers. It is characteristic of the body to desire what is akin to it. This longing for what is akin to them is natural to created beings, since indeed their existence depends on the intercourse of like with like, and on their enjoyment of material things through the senses. Then, being heavy, the body welcomes relaxation. These things are proper and desirable for our animal-like nature. But to the intelligent soul, as an intellective entity, what is natural and desirable is the realm of intelligible realities and its enjoyment of them in the manner characteristic of it. Before and above all what is characteristic of the intellect is an intense longing for God. It desires to enjoy Him and other intelligible realities, though it cannot do this without encountering obstacles.[49]

Elsewhere, the tension between body and soul is even more marked, as in the reference by Theognostos to "war between body and soul",⁵⁰ or else more positively construed, as in Peter of Damaskos:

> We should marvel, too, at how the body, that is not its own animating principle, is, at God's command, commixed with the noetic and deiform soul, created by the Holy Spirit breathing life into it (cf. Gen. 2:7).⁵¹

Here, and in other places,⁵² the relationship between body and soul is seen as parallel to that between God and human beings. God/soul provides the "animating principle" or life to that which would otherwise be inanimate or lifeless. Similarly, in Gregory Palamas, the divine quality of the soul, albeit set in contrast to the material nature of the body, is emphasised in the context of the doctrine of creation:

> So great was the honour and providential care which God bestowed upon man that He brought the entire sensible world into being before him and for his sake. The kingdom of heaven was prepared for him from the foundation of the world (cf. Matt. 25:34); God first took counsel concerning him, and then he was fashioned by God's hand and according to the image of God (cf. Gen. 1:26-27). God did not form the whole of man from matter and from the elements of this sensible world, as He did the other animals. He formed only man's body from these materials; but man's soul He took from things supracelestial or, rather, it came from God Himself when mysteriously He breathed life into man (cf. Gen. 2:7). The human soul is something great and wondrous, superior to the entire world; it overlooks the universe and has all things in its care; it is capable of knowing and receiving God, and more than anything else has the capacity of manifesting the sublime magnificence of the Master-Craftsman. Not only capable of receiving God and His grace through ascetic struggle, it is also able to be united in Him in a single hypostasis.⁵³

This vision of the divine soul in union with a physical body created by God is in tension, however, with the condition of the soul and body as they exist after "the fall". Thus, Gregory of Sinai writes:

> When God through His life-giving breath created the soul deiform and intellective, He did not implant in it anger and desire that are animal-like. But He did endow it with a power of longing and aspiration, as well as with a courage responsive to divine love. Similarly when God formed the body He did not originally implant in it instinctual anger and desire. It was only afterwards, through the fall, that it was invested with these characteristics that have rendered it mortal, corruptible and animal-like. For the body, even though susceptive of corruption, was created, as theologians will tell us, free from corruption, and that is how it will be resurrected. In the same way the soul when originally created was dispassionate. But soul and body have both been denied, commingled as they are through the natural law of mutual interpenetration and exchange. The soul has acquired the qualities of the passions or, rather, of the demons; and the body, passing under the sway of corruption because of its fallen state, has become akin to instinct-driven animals. The powers of body and soul have merged together and have produced a single animal, driven impulsively and mindlessly by anger and desire. That is how man has sunk to the level of animals, as Scripture testifies, and has become like them in every respect (cf. Ps. 49:20).[54]

Much of what the *Philokalia* has to tell us about the inner life depends upon this basic anthropology of body and soul created by God in union with each other, but also in tension with each other; fundamentally good, but also fundamentally distorted and corrupted by the fall. Whilst, as we have seen already, there are variations in emphasis amongst different contributors to the *Philokalia*, which is only as one would expect, this basic understanding seems to pervade the texts. Sometimes the emphasis is more on the goodness of creation, sometimes more on its corruption as a result of the sin of Adam. The sense of tension between body and soul, and within the soul, is however more or less ubiquitous.

As for the soul itself, the tripartite Platonic model is adopted throughout, almost completely without any deviation or dissent.[55] In English translation, these parts are usually rendered as the "intellect" or "intelligence", the "desiring" or "appetitive" power, and the "incensive" power. The latter two are often referred to as the "passible", or irrational, aspects of the soul, implying greater vulnerability to passion (πάθος – about which, more later). However, this does not imply that the intellect or intelligence is not also susceptible to passion, and the passions are sometimes classified according to which of these three parts of the soul they primarily affect.

At this point, various clarifications are required, for things are not quite as simple as has been portrayed so far. In particular, the nature and terminology of Plato's "rational" element of the soul, as understood by the authors of the *Philokalia*, requires some further elaboration. According to the glossary in the English translation of the *Philokalia*, this part of the soul is to be referred to as the "intelligent" (λογιστικόν) aspect or "intelligence" (λογικόν). However, in practice, the authors of the *Philokalia* often also refer to it as the "intellect" (νοῦς).[56] Furthermore, both of these terms are clearly distinguished from "reason" (διάνοια), a term which is never used by authors of the *Philokalia* as a name for this part of the soul.[57]

Reason is clearly distinguished from intellect and intelligence. As the translators and editors of the English edition make clear in their glossary, it is:

> the discursive, conceptualizing and logical faculty in man, the function of which is to draw conclusions or formulate concepts deriving from data provided either by revelation or spiritual knowledge (q.v.) or by sense-observation. The knowledge of the reason is consequently of a lower order than spiritual knowledge (q.v.) and does not imply any direct apprehension or perception of the inner essences or principles (q.v.) of created beings, still less of divine truth itself. Indeed, such apprehension or perception, which is the function of the intellect (q.v.), is beyond the scope of the reason.[58]

This becomes clear in, for example, usage of the term by Ilias the Presbyter:

> By means of intellection the intellect attains spiritual realities; through thought the reason grasps what is rational. Sense-perception is involved with practical and material realities by means of the fantasy.[59]

The intellect, however, is described in the English glossary as the "highest faculty" possessed by human beings, through which they may perceive spiritual realities. Rather than operating through use of rational or abstract processes, it discerns Divine truth by direct experience or "intuition". It is the means by which human beings may engage in contemplation.[60]

In distinction from this, the Greek root of the word for intelligence betrays its even closer association with Divine reality – with the Λόγος himself. It is used with reference to the possession of spiritual knowledge. It is the "ruling aspect" of the intellect.[61]

Thus, for example, Maximos the Confessor writes, in *Various Texts: C2*:

> Every intellect girded with divine authority possesses three powers as its counselors and ministers. First, there is the intelligence. It is intelligence which gives birth to that faith, founded upon spiritual knowledge, whereby the intellect learns that God is always present in an unutterable way, and through which it grasps, with the aid of hope, things of the future as though they were present. Second, there is desire. It is desire which generates that divine love through which the intellect, when of its own free will it aspires to pure divinity, is wedded in an indissoluble manner to this aspiration. Third, there is the incensive power. It is with this power that the intellect cleaves to divine peace and concentrates its desire on divine love. Every intellect possesses these three powers, and they cooperate with it in order to purge evil and to establish and sustain holiness.[62]

Here, intelligence, desire and the incensive power represent the three powers of the intellect, where "intellect" appears effectively to be synonymous with "soul".[63] Elsewhere, the intellect is distinguished from the soul,[64] or else described as being in various other relationships to it. It is referred to as being in the depths of the soul,[65] as being the "eye of the soul",[66] as being "the pilot of the soul",[67] as being "consubstantial" with the soul,[68] the illumination of the soul,[69] and as capable of being united with the soul.[70] The relationship is therefore not a simple one, and the descriptions of it, at least in the *Philokalia*, do not appear to be entirely consistent.

The place of intelligence, however, is to restrain the intellect and the passions,[71] to contemplate virtue,[72] and to cleave to God himself.[73] But this purpose can only be fully understood in the context of the incarnation of the Λόγος who has created, and re-created, all things, including the human λογικόν:

> The Logos of God, having taken flesh and given our nature subsistence in Himself, becoming perfect man, entirely free from sin, has as perfect God refashioned our nature and made it divine. As Logos of the primal Intellect and God, He has united Himself to our intelligence, giving it wings so that it may conceive divine, exalted thoughts. Because He is fire, He has with true divine fire steeled the incensive power of the soul against hostile passions and demons. Aspiration of all intelligent being and slaker of all desire, He has in His deep-seated love dilated the appetitive aspect of the soul so that it can partake of the blessings of eternal life. Having thus renewed the whole man in Himself, He restores it in an act of re-creation that leaves no grounds for any reproach against the Creator-Logos.[74]

The Platonic tripartite model of the soul is thus very much in evidence in the *Philokalia*, but it is also clear that it has been utilised for a Christian purpose – that of understanding the inner life of human beings in the context of the incarnation of God in Christ.

### 3. The Desert Fathers

For three centuries Christians suffered persecution. At first (until about 64 C.E.) this was at the hands of Jewish authorities, then at the hands of the Roman empire. Christianity seems widely to have been disapproved of in the Roman world, and Christians were referred to as "atheists" because of their failure to believe in the Roman gods. At times this disapproval was associated with mob violence. Successive emperors and governments made it a capital offence to be a Christian, banished Christians, confiscated their property, sent them into the arena to fight as gladiators, tortured and imprisoned them. Churches and copies of scripture were burned. Periods of respite were brief, until in 311 Galerius, Caesar of the east, issued an Edict of Toleration. Although his successor Maximinus attempted to counteract this edict, his efforts were largely ineffective and in 313 he also issued notices of toleration. Emperors in the west, first Maxentius and then Constantine, followed suit and in 313 the latter drew up an edict of toleration similar to that of Galerius.[75]

It is perhaps hard for many Christians today to imagine what it must have been like to live, and die, under the persecution experienced by Christians during these first three centuries, although it is also easy to exaggerate. For example, persecution of Christians in Russia in the twentieth century might arguably have been much worse. Nonetheless, many died, and some renounced their faith. Many, but not all, lived on the social edges of society. For them, the injunction of Jesus that they should deny themselves and take up their crosses and follow him can hardly have seemed metaphorical.[76] It would seem also that such Christian communities lived in eager anticipation of the expected return of Christ. In this context, there is evidence that from the early third century C.E. onwards some Christians, although at this stage they should not be considered to have adopted a "monastic" life, deliberately chose a poor, celibate and ascetic lifestyle in order that they may devote themselves more fully to their Christian vocation as they understood it.[77]

At the beginning of the fourth century C.E., with the edicts of toleration, and then the adoption of Christianity by Constantine, everything changed. Christianity was now a legal and acceptable part of the fabric of society. Undoubtedly, many Christians found this difficult to accommodate. Increasingly, some – perhaps many – chose to retreat into the deserts of Syria, Palestine, and especially Egypt, where they could devote themselves to prayerful waiting for the return of Christ.[78] One contemporary account states:

> One can see them in the desert waiting for Christ as loyal sons watching for their father.... There is only the expectation of the coming of Christ in the singing of hymns.... There is no town or village in Egypt and the Thebaid which is not surrounded by hermitages as if by walls.[79]

Many of these Christians lived as solitary hermits – perhaps most famously Antony of Egypt, whose subsequently highly influential life was written by Athanasius.[80] Others lived in coenobitic communities, and from this developed a Christian tradition of monasticism which eventually, at least partly through the influence of John Cassian (*c*.365-*c*.433), had an important influence upon the whole western European monastic tradition.[81]

Amongst the desert hermits, coenobites and monks of the fourth and fifth centuries C.E., there developed a focus on the inner life – upon the presence of sin in the human heart, the need for forgiveness, virtue in human living, and prayer. Many, perhaps most, of these Christians were not learned. Their focus was upon a simple, practical, life of prayer and certainly not on writing or academic study. Indeed, the impression is sometimes given that writing and study were positively frowned upon.[82] However, various kinds of literature did emerge from this tradition.[83] In particular, there are the "*Lives*" of various saints (especially that of Antony of Egypt by Athanasius, *c*.355-362), accounts of travels to the Egyptian desert (especially the *Lausiac History*, *c*.419/420, and the *History of the Monks of Egypt*, *c*.394/395), various kinds of instructional literature (notably that by Evagrios and Cassian), and letters from various authors (including seven by Antony of Egypt and 14 by Ammonas). The pinnacle of traditional monastic literature, however, is to be found in the sayings, proverbs and anecdotes of those who lived in the Egyptian desert, which were recorded, edited and passed on. Collections of these sayings appeared in the late fifth century and in the sixth century, which are now known as the "*Sayings of the Desert Fathers*" or the *Apophthegmata Patrum*.[84]

The life of the Desert Fathers was severe. They lived in small huts or caves and undertook basic manual work such as rope or basket making. They ate and drank extremely little, they forsook sleep in favour of prayer and, of course, they gave up the possibilities of marriage and family life. Renouncing of material possessions was a fundamental step, and most did not even have a copy of the Bible, but would rely for prayer and meditation on such passages as they had committed to memory. Most of their time would be spent alone, and remaining alone in ones cell was often emphasised as being of fundamental importance to the spiritual life.[85]

Sayings that have been handed down frequently take the form of a question – usually posed by a visitor or by a more junior brother to an older and wiser "Abba" or, in some cases, "Amma". The responses given to such questions vary between the obscure, profound, apparently rude, and extremely harsh. Because they are usually located in particular circumstances, many of which were not be recorded, different sayings can also appear contradictory of each other. However, they also reflect extreme humility, compassion, wisdom and, at least sometimes, humour.

In some ways, the *Philokalia* and the sayings of the Desert Fathers are worlds apart. A five-volume anthology hardly compares with a largely oral tradition that had a suspicion of books and learning. However, possession of the *Philokalia* potentially avoids the need to own, or have access to, a large library.[86] Some of the "centuries" of texts in the *Philokalia* also have a literary quality about them which is not dissimilar to that of the *Apophthegmata Patrum*. They have similar ascetic concerns, they both appear to be intended as a basis for prayer and living, rather than academic study, and they employ a not dissimilar terminology of the inner life of thought and prayer and virtue.

Thus, for example, we might compare Abba Theonas and Hesychios the Priest on prayer and the passions:

> Abba Theonas said, "When we turn our spirit from the contemplation of God, we become the slaves of carnal passions."[87]

Whereas, in *Watchfulness & Holiness* by Hesychios, we find:

> Contemplation and spiritual knowledge are indeed the guides and agents of the ascetic life; for when the mind is raised up by them it becomes indifferent to sensual pleasures and to other material attractions, regarding them as worthless.[88]

Such common ground should, of course, not be surprising. Apart from the general observation that the Desert Fathers might be considered the founders of Christian monasticism or, if this is debated, at least that they influenced its subsequent course very considerably, and that the *Philokalia* emerged from that same monastic tradition, there are also more direct links to be found.

At least three of the earlier authors of the *Philokalia* had in fact lived in the Egyptian desert themselves. Isaiah the Solitary was probably not the contemporary of Makarios of Egypt that Nikodimos considered him to be, but probably did live at Sketis in Egypt in the fifth century C.E., before moving to Palestine, and therefore can be said to represent firsthand experience of the tradition of the Desert Fathers.[89] Evagrios of Pontus went to Egypt in 383 C.E. and spent the remaining 16 years of his life first at Nitria and then at Kellia.

During this time he was a disciple of Makarios the Great (also known as Makarios of Egypt) and also had contact with Makarios of Alexandria.[90] John Cassian lived in Egypt from c.385/6 to 399, during which time he was a disciple of Evagrios. He subsequently travelled to Constantinople and then spent the remainder of his life in the west. He founded two monasteries in Marseilles and wrote two books, *The Institutes* and *The Conferences*, based upon his experiences in the Egyptian desert, abbreviated parts of which are included in the *Philokalia*.[91] Although between them these three authors contribute a little less than a third of only the first volume of the *Philokalia*, they are the first three books in the English translation and are the earliest contributors.

In addition to Isaiah, Evagrios and Cassian, it seems likely that Mark the Ascetic also spent some time living as a hermit in the desert, although in fact we know very little about him.[92] The *Philokalia* also includes a paraphrase by Symeon Metaphrastis of homilies that purport to be by Makarios the Great, whose sayings feature prominently in the *Apophthegmata Patrum*. However, it would now seem highly unlikely that Makarios was in fact the author of these homilies.[93] Similarly, it is of note that the opening work of the original Greek *Philokalia* was one attributed to Antony the Great. Although this is now known not to have been written by Antony of Egypt, it would seem reasonable to assume that it may have suited the compilers of the *Philokalia* very well to place first in their work a text by this most famous of the Desert Fathers.

In addition to the contributions to the *Philokalia* by those who had firsthand experience of the desert tradition, it is clear that there is a more pervasive influence. For example, Peter of Damaskos (whose works effectively provide a "mini-Philokalia" within the *Philokalia*) quotes the Desert Fathers some 30 times,[94] and Nikiphoros the Monk quotes from the lives of a number of the Desert Fathers in *Watchfulness & Guarding*.[95] The Desert Fathers also exerted an indirect influence on writers such as Maximos the Confessor, the single largest contributor to the *Philokalia*, although this is not always explicitly acknowledged.[96] But perhaps the most important direct and indirect influence comes from the perceptiveness of Evagrios of Pontus. There can be little doubt that his spirituality and psychology influenced all the subsequent writers whose works were included in the *Philokalia*.[97] It is therefore to Evagrios that we must turn next.

## 4. Evagrios of Pontus

> If you are a theologian, you will pray truly; and if you pray truly, you will be a theologian.[98]

Evagrios was born in Pontus, in Cappadocia, but moved in 379 to Constantinople where he studied under Gregory Nazianzen.[99] By this time he was possibly already a monk. Although, up until this time, he appears to have shown much promise as a theologian, he left the city in 382 having begun an affair, albeit perhaps unconsummated, with the wife of a prominent local figure. Fleeing to Jerusalem he came close to abandoning his monastic vocation altogether, but was persuaded not to by Melania the Elder, a prominent Roman widow and foundress of a double monastery. Perhaps also with her encouragement, Evagrios left Jerusalem in 383 for the Egyptian desert, where he was to remain (apart from brief excursions to Alexandria and elsewhere) until his death.

Evagrios spent his first two years in Egypt in the desert at Nitria, one of the major monastic centres of the time. He then retired to the even more remote centre of Kellia, where he became a pupil of Makarios the Great, one of the most famous of the Desert Fathers. During his time here he subjected himself to a severe regime, which probably damaged his health. He would sleep only four hours each night, walking back and forth and keeping himself occupied in order to remain awake during the day. When subject to sexual temptation he once spent an entire night in mid-winter praying naked standing in a cistern of water.[100] He ate only once a day, and then only very limited foods.

He remained at Kellia until his death in *c*.399. During this time he became a respected teacher and, unusually, also the author of a series of important works. Amongst these were instructions on the monastic life (*The Foundations of Monastic Life: A Presentation of the Practice of Stillness*,[101] and *The Monk: A treatise on the Practical Life*[102]), numerous commentaries on scripture (including *Scholia* on Proverbs, Ecclesiastes, Job, and Psalms), various letters and most importantly for the present purpose some works on prayer and the inner life (*Chapters on Prayer*[103], *On the Eight Thoughts*,[104] *On Thoughts*[105], *Antirrhetikos*, *Gnostikos*, and the *Kephalaia Gnostica*). Some of these works[106] survive only in Latin, Armenian or Syriac translation.

During his lifetime, Evagrios remained a respected theologian and teacher on the spiritual life. After his death, as the works of

Origen were increasingly scrutinised and condemned as heretical, Evagrios' reputation began to suffer by association. Despite this, his works were widely circulated and translated into Latin, Coptic, Syriac, Arabic and various other languages. Eventually, Origen was condemned at the Second Ecumenical Council in 553, as were a series of beliefs held by Evagrios, and many copies of his works were subsequently destroyed.[107] Despite this, Evagrios' insights into prayer, the inner life and asceticism were still widely appreciated and were read and developed by others. That it was possible that this could happen was partly because his so-called theological works were separated from his ascetic and spiritual works, partly because of wide dissemination and translation, and also because some works were transmitted under other names (as indeed originally happened with one of his contributions to the *Philokalia*).

### i. *Foundations*

Taught by Makarios, Evagrios shared with the Desert Fathers a belief that inner stillness, hesychia, was facilitated by avoiding frequent or inappropriate social contacts, or any other external circumstances which might provide unnecessary agitation or distraction.[108] In *Foundations* he sets out the basics: celibacy, poverty, a frugal diet, living either alone or with like-minded brothers in the desert, avoidance of cities, infrequent contact with family and friends, undertaking basic manual labour so as not to be a burden on others, but avoidance of buying and selling where at all possible, and sleeping little and only on the ground. All these matters were, however, merely preliminary. His real concern was with the inner world of thoughts and it is here that he showed himself to be highly psychologically insightful and original. These "foundations" of the monastic life are put in place in order to attain and preserve an inner state of "stillness"[109] (ἡσυχία) and this in turn is preparatory to other things, which he deals with in his other works.

### ii. *Eight Thoughts*

In *Eight Thoughts*, Evagrios deals in turn with eight thoughts, or kinds of thoughts, each of which presents to the Christian a point of potential struggle or temptation. The material is presented as a series of brief paragraphs, often only one sentence long, under each heading. These paragraphs take the form of proverbs, aphorisms, or wise sayings, or else admonitions and instructions. Allegory and metaphor are used liberally. Reference to, and quotation of, scripture is used to illustrate and justify, but some whole sections of the discourse (specifically on fornication and acedia) do not explicitly refer to scripture at all. Whilst the texts have a certain quality reminiscent of the sayings of the Desert Fathers, and presumably must have been derived, at least in part, from the same underlying oral tradition, the Fathers are not explicitly quoted. The texts appear to be offered for contemplation and reflection – to be prayed over and lived out rather than studied systematically in an academic fashion. One is left with the impression that they arise in turn from Evagrios' own reflections, and those of his mentors.

The list, which appears elsewhere in Evagrian work and is original to Evagrios, has been highly influential upon other authors – including authors of the *Philokalia*. Elsewhere, Evagrios states that "All the generic types of thoughts fall into [these] eight categories in which every sort of thought is included."[110] The list comprises the following:

1. Gluttony
2. Fornication
3. Avarice
4. Anger
5. Sadness
6. Acedia
7. Vainglory
8. Pride

The title of this work refers to these items as being "thoughts", but in other works (e.g. *On the Vices opposed to the Virtues*) they are referred to as vices, and in each case there is at least some reference here to an opposing virtue. In places the thoughts are also referred to as "passions" (e.g. Gluttony, #3; Fornication, #12; Avarice, #1). In other works (e.g. *Praktikos*), but interestingly not here, Evagrios refers to demons using the same names.

Gluttony, fornication and avarice are all concerned with desires that affect the concupiscible or appetitive aspect of the soul.[111] Anger is concerned with "a boiling over"[112] of the irascible part of the soul. Elsewhere, Evagrios makes clear that sadness, vainglory and pride arise in the intelligent aspect of the soul, and that acedia arises from both the passible and intelligent aspects of the soul.[113]

Table 1.1 (pages 26-29) summarises Evagrios' teaching on the eight thoughts. In each case, Evagrios proves to be a perceptive and diligent student, who has analysed the root causes, nature and consequences of the particular kind of thought. Gluttony is a fire fuelled by food, fornication is a wind that throws the ship of the soul off course, and avarice sinks that ship by weight of possessions. Anger is a form of madness, impairing the intellect, and sadness, which arises from frustration of anger or desire, is all consuming and all encompassing, like a devouring lion, or a prisoner's bonds. Acedia is a wind that bends a delicate plant, but Evagrios notes that a wind also has the potential to strengthen a growing plant. Vainglory is the bindweed that saps away life, and the rock which causes shipwreck. Pride is a wound or infection that requires treatment by cautery or a scalpel if it is to be cured. Each of these thoughts, if not treated correctly, leads to its own particular consequences. They are inter-related and mutually reinforcing.

It is perhaps helpful here to say a little more about sadness and acedia, as these might represent more unexpected items in the list, at least to contemporary western minds. Evagrios refers to sadness as arising as a result of frustration of desire, or else closely following anger.[114] It is thus closely related to the other passions, but also similar to contemporary accounts of depression.[115] Acedia is "a relaxation of the soul which is not in accord with nature".[116] It thus represents a lack of commitment to, or perseverance with, the vocation of the ascetic life and/or the life of prayer. These thoughts are therefore more significant in terms of where they arise from, and what they lead to. Like desire for food or sexual fulfilment, it is not so much that these thoughts are sinful in themselves – for they are most often uninvited – but rather they present temptations to something else.

Evagrios also proves perceptive in his analysis of various trains of thought and sequences of events. Thus, for example, in his section on fornication he includes a much longer than usual paragraph (2.8), in which he traces the typical course of a series of interactions of a monk and a woman. At first encounter, modesty and chastity prevail. At a second encounter, the gaze has changed subtly, and at a third encounter eye contact has been made. Eventually, the soul is

Table 1.1: Definitions, allegories and consequences of the thoughts described by Evagrios in *Eight Thoughts*

| Passion | Definition | Allegory and Metaphor | | Consequences |
|---|---|---|---|---|
| Gluttony | Not defined here, but: "gluttony is the mother of licentiousness" (2.1) | Wood as fuel for a fire (1.4-1.6, 1.27, 1.33) | Wood = food<br>Gluttony = fire | Disobedience (10)<br>Licentiousness/fornication (11, 34)<br>Darkens the mind (13, 15, 16)<br>Inhibits prayer (12, 14, 19)<br>Blunts the intellect (17)<br>Shameful thoughts (18)<br>Contrary to impassibility (25) |
| Fornication | Not defined here, but: "The demon of fornication compels one to desire various bodies." (*Praktikos* 8) | Oil lamp (2.2) | Oil = encounters with women<br>Flame = pleasure | Disregard for life (14)<br>Pleasure (17, 20)<br>Desire (20) |
| | | Ship without ballast battered by waves (2.3) | Waves = thought of fornication<br>Ship = intemperate | |
| | | Festering wound caused by poisoned arrow (2.6-2.7) | Arrow = sight of a woman<br>Wounded body = wounded soul | |
| | | Plant that flourishes near water (2.10) | Water = encounters with women<br>Plant = "passion of licentiousness" | |
| | | Pillar erected on a base (2.12) | Pillar = fornication<br>Base = satiety | |

| Passion | Definition | Allegory and Metaphor | | Consequences |
|---|---|---|---|---|
| Fornication (continued) | | Ship caught in a storm which hastens towards a harbour (2.13) | Ship = chaste soul<br>Waves = "forms of women"<br>Harbour = solitude | |
| Avarice | "Avarice is the root of all evils (1 Tim 6:10), and it nourishes the remaining passions like evil branches." (3.1) | Root and branch (3.1-3.2) | Root = avarice<br>Branch = other passions | Other passions (1)<br>Sadness (7)<br>Unsatisfied desire (8) |
| | | Heavily laden/leaky boat that easily sinks in a sea storm (3.3) | Boat = person (monk)<br>Load = possessions<br>Waves = concerns | |
| Anger | "Anger is a passion that leads to madness and easily drives those who possess it out of their senses; it makes the soul wild and moves it to shun all (human) encounter." (4.1) | Water driven by the wind (4.3) | Wind = "senseless thoughts"<br>Water = "the irascible person" | Madness (1)<br>Shunning human company (1)<br>Impairment of the intellect (5, 9)<br>Darkening of the mind (6)<br>Bloodshot eyes (10)<br>Separation from God (14)<br>Inhibits prayer (16, 18) |
| | | Mist that thickens the air (4.5) | Mist = "movement of irascibility"<br>Air = intellect | |
| | | Cloud that darkens the sun (4.6) | Cloud = thought of resentment<br>Sun = mind | |
| | | Lion rattling the hinges of its cage (4.7) | Lion = person (monk)<br>Hinges of cage = thoughts of anger | |
| | | A stone which troubles the water into which it falls (4.15) | Stone = an evil word<br>Water = the human heart | |

| Passion | Definition | Allegory and Metaphor | | Consequences |
|---|---|---|---|---|
| Sadness | "Sadness is a dejection of the soul and is constituted from thoughts of anger, for irascibility is a longing for revenge, and the frustration of revenge produces sadness." (5.1) In *Praktikos*, Evagrios also speaks of sadness as arising from frustrated desire (10) | A devouring lion (5.2) | Maw of the lion = sadness That which is devoured = person afflicted by sadness | Suffering (4) Loss of spiritual pleasure (5) Inhibits prayer (6, 7, 21, 22) Dulling of the mind (21) |
| | | A bound prisoner who cannot run (5.7-5.8) | Fetters/bonds = sadness Prisoner = person Running = contemplation | |
| Acedia | "Acedia is a relaxation of the soul, and a relaxation of the soul which is not in accord with nature does not resist temptations nobly." (6.1) | A north wind that nourishes young plants (6.2) | North wind = temptations Plants = Endurance of the soul | Wandering restlessness (5, 8, 10, 11, 13) Service undertaken for selfish motives (6, 7) Dissatisfaction with work (12, 16) Distraction (14, 15) Laziness in prayer (16) |
| | | A waterless cloud chased away by the wind (6.3) | Cloud = mind without perseverance Wind = acedia | |
| | | A light breeze that bends a feeble plant (6.8) | Breeze = fantasy about a trip away Plant = monk overcome by acedia | |
| | | A well rooted tree not shaken by the wind (6.9) | Tree = firmly established soul Wind = acedia | |
| | | A sick person not satisfied with a single type of food (6.12) | Sick person = monk afflicted by acedia Food = type of work | |

| Passion | Definition | Allegory and Metaphor | | Consequences |
|---|---|---|---|---|
| Acedia (continued) | | A pleasure loving man dissatisfied with one wife (6.13) | Man = monk given to acedia<br>Wife = cell | |
| | | A sick person who cannot carry a heavy burden (6.16) | Sick person = person afflicted by acedia<br>Burden = work of God | |
| Vainglory | "Vainglory is an irrational passion and it readily gets tangled up with any work of virtue." (7.1) | Bindweed entangled around a tree so that its roots are killed (7.2) | Bindweed = vainglory<br>Roots = virtues | Destroys virtues (2, 3, 5, 17)<br>Impairs prayer (8)<br>Makes enemies (15) |
| | | Wind that wipes out a footprint (7.7) | Wind = vainglory<br>Footprint = almsgiving | |
| | | A ship that loses its cargo when running against an underwater rock (7.9) | Underwater rock = vainglory<br>Cargo = virtues (implied) | |
| Pride | "Pride is a tumour of the soul filled with pus; when it has ripened, it will rupture and create a great disgusting mess." (8.1) | A flash of lightning which foretells thunder (8.2) | Lightning = vainglory<br>Thunder = pride | Ruins virtue (8)<br>Terrifying fantasies & attacks of demons (10)<br>Boasting (18)<br>Impairing of prayer (19) |
| | | A vine prop supporting a young branch weighed down with fruit (8.9 & 8.8) | Vine prop = fear of God<br>Branch = virtuous soul<br>Weight of fruit = pride | |
| | | A tree without roots which cannot withstand the wind (8.14) | Tree = proud person (monk) | |
| | | A long-standing infection/wound cured by cautery (& scalpel) (8.30 – 8.31) | Infection = habit of vainglory (& pride)<br>Cautery/scalpel = dishonour & sadness | |

besieged by the interaction; it has become "entangling", destructive and poisonous. Similarly, in the section on acedia (6.15), he provides an amusing account of a monk who is supposed to be reading. But this monk finds himself yawning, stretching, looking at the wall, counting pages, and jumping to the end. If he gives in to sleep, Evagrios observes, then he will find himself awakened by hunger.

Apparently innocent, or even good, thoughts and actions may thus lead to undesirable outcomes. Elsewhere, Evagrios goes further and suggests that beneath the apparently innocent thought or action there lays another motive. For example:

> A person afflicted with acedia proposes visiting the sick, but is fulfilling his own purpose.[117]

Evagrios is not specific here as to whether such a person consciously intends proposing visitation of the sick for ulterior purposes.[118] The possibility is left open that they might not have insight into their own motivation. Thus, being unaware of the dynamics of such thoughts, they may be deceiving themselves more than others as to their true purpose. However, once having read these passages, it is Evagrios' expectation that the monk will no longer be able to claim ignorance of what is really going on in his (or, we might add, her) own mind.

The context and purpose of considering each of these eight thoughts is clearly that of facilitating a life of virtue and of prayer. Thus, for example, in the section on gluttony we find:

> The smoke of incense sweetens the air, and the prayer of the abstinent person presents a sweet odour to God (cf. Rev. 8:4).[119]

Or again, in the section on vainglory:

> Vainglory advises you to pray in the streets, but he who wars against it prays in his chamber (cf. Matt. 6:5-6).[120]

However, the work does not treat of prayer itself, and is generally considered to be an introductory work for the monk who is in the early stages of monastic life.

### iii. *Praktikos*

*Praktikos* takes things on a further stage. It deals again with the eight thoughts, saying a little about the nature of each and then providing more or less brief suggestions for remedies against each of them. However, it then develops a more general discussion about the passions and the part that sense perceptions and demons play in provoking them. This provides the introduction to a series of instructions for dealing with these things including, for example, attentiveness to ones thoughts, that one might get to know better the tactics of the demons. It then moves on to a discussion of impassibility.

Impassibility (ἀπάθεια), or dispassion as it is usually translated in the *Philokalia*, is concerned with impartiality or detachment, with peace or tranquillity, but not with absence of suffering.[121] It is translated by Cassian as "purity of heart".[122] According to Evagrios, impassibility is encountered after victory is gained over the demons/passions.[123] It is the "blossom" of the practical life and, in turn, gives birth to love.[124] Although he does not develop the theme here, it is also the gateway to the first type of contemplative prayer – that of the contemplation of the essence of created beings.[125]

*Praktikos* closes with further practical advice about the ascetic life and then with some sayings of the Desert Fathers.

## iv. *On Thoughts*

*On Thoughts* takes things on a further stage and provides a more detailed account of the mental life and especially of the struggle against the demons. It is clear that this is all in aid of attaining "pure prayer", but again little is said about that in this work. The work rather appears to be preparatory for that end; it is written for the monk who is striving to achieve impassibility.[126]

In *On Thoughts*, three thoughts – those of gluttony, avarice and vainglory – are seen as being of fundamental importance. Demons are understood as being at work in these thoughts: as suggesting them, enticing human beings with them, and as being "entrusted" with them.[127] It is these thoughts/demons which open the way to all the others and it is these three with which Jesus is understood as having been tempted in the wilderness.[128] Further, all demonic thoughts are understood as entering the soul through "mental representations of sensible objects".[129] It is not all such mental images, or memories, that are necessarily demonic, but rather those that are associated with "irascibility or concupiscibility contrary to nature".[130] In other words, these thoughts arouse the desiring and incensive aspects of the soul in a way which is likely to lead to sinful behaviour and which prevents the intellect from perceiving the image of God. This may happen in sleep as well as in wakefulness.[131]

Thoughts are understood by Evagrios as originating from angels, from demons or from the human mind. He uses as an example thoughts of gold. Angelic thoughts may be about why God created gold, how it is referred to in the Bible and the holy purposes to which it may be put. Demonic thoughts will be about selfish acquisition of gold and the pleasures that this will bring. Human thoughts neither investigate divine purpose, nor indulge selfish passion, but rather appear to be a dispassionate imaging of gold by the intellect.[132]

Later, "mental representations", by which he appears to be referring to the neutral images that are human thoughts, are metaphorically referred to as sheep which have been entrusted to human beings as to a shepherd.[133] These sheep are vulnerable to wolves or other wild beasts. The extended metaphor becomes a little confusing as it is developed because he first refers to wolves as being another kind of mental representation (by implication associated inappropriately with passion), but then goes on to refer to sheep being snatched by wild beasts when inappropriately pastured – e.g. when the mental representation of a brother is "pastured with hatred". On the one hand it appears that he considers wolves to be impassioned mental representations, but on the other hand he appears to consider wild beasts to be the potentially ravaging activities of the respective parts of the soul – incensive, desiring or intellective. It is clear, however, that he considers that the incensive and desiring aspects of the soul do have fundamentally good purposes. The proper function of the incensive part is to chase off the wolves, and the function of the desiring part is to nurture the sheep. Although he does not explicitly say so here, it is also more or less implicit that the proper function of the intellect is prayer.

In *On Thoughts*, Evagrios also introduces some new demons. Amongst these are "vagabond" and "insensibility".[134] Each is attributed, as are all the demons, with purposeful motivation to lead the soul away from God. The former does this by means of wandering, purposeless and irrelevant thoughts which at first simply occupy the mental space which otherwise might have been taken by knowledge of God, and then lead on to other thoughts, or rather demons, which more directly lead away from virtue and from God. The latter acts by diminishing the soul's sense of the seriousness of sin and of the fear of God. Later in this work, Evagrios also develops an account of the strategies of the demons, especially giving consideration to the circumstances of the monk who has been in combat with them for some time. For example, he talks of the way in which they follow in succession in their assaults – stronger ones following on from weaker ones – and of how they may change their tactic from (for example) a temptation to gluttony to a temptation to excessive asceticism.[135] (Such a temptation is still put into the mind by the demon of gluttony; it is simply gluttony in another form.)

The purpose of Evagrios' account of the demons is to arm the monk to fight against them. Thus, for example, he encourages his reader to be self-reflective about where his thoughts are led by "vagabond", in order that he can more easily recognise his influence, expose it and resist it.[136] Similarly, if a demon introduces a thought of avarice, the reader is encouraged to analyse the way in which it is not the object itself, or the mind or the mental representation of the object that is sinful, but rather a hostile desire to put the object to an improper use.[137]

Impassibility is seen here as being more nearly attainable than it was in *Praktikos*. For example, advice is given about how to test whether or not it has been attained.[138] There is also a concluding account of the need for freedom from mental representations as a pre-requisite for contemplative prayer.[139] Contemplative prayer (or more correctly "pure" prayer) is the goal towards which Evagrios has been leading his pupils and which is now coming into sight. His treatment of this for his more advanced pupils is first contained in *On Prayer*, a work which was originally included in the *Philokalia* under attribution to Neilos of Ancyra.

### v. On Prayer

Prayer is defined by Evagrios as "a communion of the mind with God"[140] and as "the ascent of the mind towards God".[141] His vision of prayer is much broader than these succinct definitions might appear to imply. In fact, he sees it as taking in the whole breadth of the ascetic life. However, at its heart, "true prayer" or "pure prayer" is the goal of the ascetic life and is something that is not easily attained.

For Evagrios, "the way of prayer … is … twofold: it involves the practical on the one hand and the contemplative on the other".[142] The practical life, as understood by Evagrios, is concerned with overcoming the "thoughts" (or vices, or passions) that he has dealt with at some length in his other works, and especially in *Praktikos*, as described above.[143] It represents a struggle against the demons, the outcome of which is impassibility.[144] It paves the way for contemplative prayer.[145]

Contemplative prayer is understood by Evagrios as comprising natural contemplation and theological contemplation.[146] Although these kinds of contemplation are nowhere precisely defined in *On Prayer*, it is already fairly clear here that natural contemplation is concerned with contemplation of natural, or created, beings, and theological contemplation is concerned with contemplation of God himself. The distinction between these is very important. In comparison with the latter, the former hardly qualifies as prayer at all. Thus, for example, Evagrios warns that natural contemplation can lead the mind "far away from God".[147] Indeed, natural contemplation is eventually incompatible with the contemplation of God himself. Contemplation of God is free of the images and intellections associated with created things.[148] Natural contemplation is contemplation of the many, theological contemplation is contemplation of the One.[149]

*On Prayer* thus begins with a consideration of the practical life insofar as it relates directly to the subject of prayer. This includes a reminder of the need to attend to the virtues,[150] the merit of tears,[151] the need to avoid distractions[152] and anger,[153] and the likelihood that the demons will oppose the efforts of the monk to pray.[154] The reader is enjoined not to pray for his[155] own needs, but rather that God's will be done.[156] However, all of this is, yet again, merely preliminary to the task in hand.

Prayer, Evagrios tells us, is all about God. Prayer is about loving God, being in communion with God,[157] being near to God,[158] beholding the "place of God",[159] longing for God,[160] and journeying with God.[161] Prayer is bestowed by God.[162]

If God himself is the destination of a journey then the journey begins with pursuit of virtue, in order to get to the place of natural contemplation, which in turn leads to the contemplation of the Logos himself.[163] Prayer is a focus on God which is blind to all distractions. Initially, and most fundamentally, these distractions are from the passions, but as the soul draws nearer to God it becomes blind even to the distractions offered by natural contemplation of corporeal, or even incorporeal, beings.[164] And so, Evagrios turns at last to the focus of pure prayer, which is God himself.

He warns that God cannot be contemplated in the form of any image.[165] God is immaterial, without quantity or form. Attempts to approach God in this way are therefore either misguided human effort, or demonically inspired. On the other hand, for the soul that is receptive, God graciously bestows prayer, sending his angels to oppose demonic activity, to provide illumination and to instil "knowledge of true prayer".[166] Whilst this appears to be the climax of Evagrios' *On Prayer*, it can easily feel as though it is an anti-climax. Pure prayer remains an unimaginable and undescribed mystery for it is communion with God who is imageless, and the imageless cannot be imagined or described. Whilst there is much that can be done to make the soul receptive to God, pure prayer is ultimately the gift of God and so Evagrios urges patience.[167]

Perhaps this accounts for the shift of focus at this point to something that sounds at first as though it ought to have been in Lesson 1 – the matter of psalmody.[168] Psalmody, Evagrios urges, "puts the passions to sleep"[169] and prepares the mind for prayer. Although he implies here that it is a form of natural contemplation, he clearly sees this as being a good way to maintain a patient readiness for God to bestow theological contemplation or pure prayer.[170] But there is some ambiguity, for psalmody is both something which he urges his reader practise, and also something which, like pure prayer, is graciously bestowed by God.[171]

The structure of the work from this point on is curious. Sinkewicz, in his translation, groups together paragraphs 89 to 105 under the heading of "Trials", paragraphs 106 to 112 under the heading of "Apophthegmata" and then 113-153 as a concluding miscellany. The Apophthegmata might be taken as undergirding what has gone before with the authority of the Desert Fathers or, perhaps more likely, as providing examples to encourage patience and perseverance. The other paragraphs provide a return to earlier themes – such as the need to be wary of the attacks of the demons, and the imagelessness of true prayer. Perhaps these also are offered as encouragements to perseverance, even when the path towards prayer seems to be opposed by demons and when their proffered images of God might appear seductive. Whatever the intention may have been, the work ends on a positive note:

> When you have passed beyond every other joy in your prayer, then you have truly discovered the practice of prayer.[172]

After the battle with the passions is won, when the demons have been defeated, when patience has been rewarded by God's gracious bestowal of prayer, when the seduction of that which can be imagined and described has been rebuffed, the "theology" that is the contemplation of God in prayer offers more joy than anything else possibly could. It is clear, however, that this is still just the beginning.

### vi. *Gnostikos*

In *Gnostikos*, we learn more. It appears to have been intended as part of a trilogy – *Praktikos*, *Gnostikos*, and *Kephalaia Gnostika*.[173] It comprises 50 chapters, which are devoted largely to the subject of contemplative knowledge, for this is the primary concern of the "gnostikos", the "one who knows". However, this is not to say that the practical or ascetical life can now be forgotten. There are repeated reminders against such things as anger,[174] sadness,[175] avarice,[176] vainglory,[177] and gluttony.[178] Vice and virtue are still important concerns.[179] Knowledge cannot be acquired by one who is still immersed in the passions.[180]

According to *Gnostikos*, there are two kinds of knowledge: that derived by the senses from the external, material, world, and that derived interiorly by grace.[181] *Gnostikos* is concerned, however, not so much with these kinds of knowledge in themselves, as with what might be expected of the gnostikos. In addition to exhortations about vice and virtue, which have already been mentioned, advice is given on what may or may not be said to others,[182] and on what it is "necessary" or "good" to know.[183] Interestingly, speaking about God "without [careful] consideration" is warned against.[184] However, in contrast, Evagrios apparently considers it important to advise on "causes of abandonment" or reasons why God might withdraw from the soul for its own good. These include the revealing of virtue, punishment which leads to renewal of virtue, the salvation of others, humility, and hatred of evil.[185] Evagrios warns against going beyond one's knowledge, or imagining that one knows more than one actually does.[186]

Rather as *On Prayer* closes with a series of apophthegmata, drawing on the authority of the Desert Fathers, *Gnostikos* closes with a series of quotations from various authorities, including Basil of Caesarea, Athanasius, and Didymus the Blind.[187] Two final chapters tantalisingly suggest that the goal of the life of knowledge is merely a preparation for something else: theology, a restoring gaze upon God himself.

> The goal of the *praktike* is to purify the intellect and to render it free of passions; that of the *gnostike* is to reveal the truth hidden in all beings; but to distance the intellect from matter and to turn it towards the First Cause – this is a gift of theology.
>
> Gazing fixedly upon the archetype, I strive to engrave the images without neglecting anything which might accomplish the gaining [back] of the fallen-away.[188]

### vii. *Kephalaia Gnostika*

We are thus taken, eventually, to *Kephalaia Gnostika*, the final part of the trilogy, in the hope of learning more about exactly what Evagrios understands contemplative prayer to be. However, as David Bundy has commented, this work is "deliberately disjointed and cryptic, intended only for those who are already committed to an ascetic life and who have the intellectual background to read the 'encoded' instructions".[189] It is clearly intended to be read only by those who are advanced in the life of prayer, and have already achieved apatheia. Even then, it appears to be something intended as a basis for contemplation – not something which is to be read from beginning to end in a logical sequence of argument. It is, after all, offered as an aid to the person seeking God, who is beyond all words and images, and any encounter with whom is inevitably ineffable. All of this said, we find out some interesting things here about contemplative prayer.

Firstly, contemplation is a kind of vision of the soul:

> THE sense, naturally by itself, senses sensory things, but the mind [nous] always stands and waits [to ascertain] which spiritual contemplation gives it vision.[190]

Secondly, and connected with this metaphorical vision, contemplation is concerned with knowledge, of God, of Christ, and of created beings:

> THE light of the *nous* is divided into three:
> knowledge of the adorable and holy Trinity;
> and the incorporeal nature that created by it;
> and the contemplation of beings.[191]

Knowledge of created things is concerned with their λόγοι, their inner essences or meanings. It is apatheia that enables this knowledge, or vision, of the inner essences of things:

> THE *nous* that is divested of the passions and sees the *logoi* of beings does not henceforth truly receive the *eidola* that (arrive) through the senses; but it is as if another world is created by its knowledge, attracting to it its thought and rejecting far from it the sensitive world.[192]

Knowledge of God, however, is importantly different to the knowledge that is the concern of contemplation of created beings. God is "essential knowledge", never simply an "object" of contemplation.[193] Spiritual contemplation therefore remains, ultimately, a mystery.[194] Amongst many aspects of this mystery, however, Evagrios returns repeatedly to his vision of God as both Unity[195] and Trinity,[196] and of Christ as existing in unique relationship both to God and human beings.[197]

Thirdly, contemplation is transformative:

> JUST as the senses are changed through being receptive of different qualities, so also the *nous* is changed, [through] constant gazing at diverse contemplations.[198]

Contemplation is healing,[199] generative,[200] brings growth and life,[201] is restorative,[202] and even deifying.[203] Contemplation of the *logoi* of judgement and providence appear to assume a particular significance in this process. For Evagrios, "judgement" is a matter of God's progressive transformation of reasoning beings (λογικοί, a category which includes but is not confined to human beings) in order to assist their spiritual development, and "providence" is a matter of God's provision of what is required to return them to the union with God from which they are fallen.[204]

Fourthly, Evagrios provides us with a definition of contemplation:

> CONTEMPLATION is:
> spiritual knowledge of the things which have been and will be:
> it is this which causes the *nous* to ascend to its first rank.[205]

Contemplation is defined, therefore, in terms of knowledge and of salvation of the human soul. Commenting on this definition, Dysinger suggests that we should see here a Christological and soteriological basis for the Evagrian theology of contemplation. Because God in Christ has both descended and ascended, the contemplative who, by definition, has fallen from his primordial state is also enabled to ascend towards [knowledge of] God.[206]

Fifthly, there are different kinds of contemplation. We have already seen that "natural" and "theological" contemplation are to be distinguished. However, in *Kephalaia Gnostika*, the classification becomes much more complex and inconsistent. There appears to be an expectation of progress from "second" to "first" natural contemplation:

> VIRTUES cause the *nous* to see second natural contemplation; and the latter cause it to see first [natural contemplation]; and the first in its turn (makes it see) the Blessed Unity.[207]

Terminology of first and second natural contemplation occurs in Evagrian literature only in *Kephalaia Gnostika*, and nowhere else.[208] There are also references to up to five kinds of contemplation:

> FIVE are the principal contemplations under which all contemplation is placed. It is said that the first is contemplation of the adorable and holy Trinity; the second and third are the contemplation of incorporeal beings and of bodies; the fourth and the fifth are the contemplation of judgment and of providence.[209]

Elsewhere, a different five-fold order is presented:

> WITH God is said to be: first, the one who knows the Holy Trinity; and next after him one who contemplates the *logoi* concerning the intelligible [beings]; third, then, is one who also sees the incorporeal beings; and then fourth is one who understands the contemplation of the ages; while one who has attained apatheia of his soul is justly to be accounted fifth,'.[210]

And elsewhere again different two and three fold orders are presented.[211]

All of this is not easy to disentangle and the tangle is made no easier to unravel by the virtual interchangeability of the terms "contemplation" and "knowledge",[212] as well as an at times rather mystical use of the term "contemplation" in relation to Christ himself.[213] If the tangle can be unravelled, it is clear that Evagrios only expects us to unravel it in the practice of contemplative prayer itself.

What is finally clear is that contemplative knowledge of God, Unity and Trinity, is the aim of the Evagrian system.

## 5. Scripture

Scriptural quotations, allusions and references are pervasive within the text of the *Philokalia*. Scripture is used to justify, illustrate, explain and facilitate the themes which the authors take up. Again, with a work spanning so many centuries, it is not surprising to find that there are differences in frequency and style of reference, as well as in theological approach, to scripture. Thus, for example, there appears to be far more frequent explicit reference to scripture in the works of Peter of Damoskos than in any other author. However, the foundational importance of scripture to all of the authors of the *Philokalia* is evident[214] and so it deserves some further consideration here.

Scripture is used again and again as justification for the ideas that are expressed in the *Philokalia*, even to the point of appearing to a modern reader to be contrived. Thus, for example, in *Guarding the Intellect*, by Isaiah the Solitary, we find a series of quotations from the Psalms used as authority for the hesychastic concept of "guarding of the heart":

> Holy Scripture speaks everywhere about the guarding of the heart, in both the Old and the New Testaments. David says in the Psalms: 'O sons of men, how long will you be heavy of heart?' (Ps. 4:2. LXX), and again: 'Their heart is vain' (Ps. 5:9. LXX); and of those who think futile thoughts, he says: 'For he has said in his heart, I shall not be moved' (Ps. 10:6), and: 'He has said in his heart, God has forgotten' (Ps. 10:11).[215]

It is not at all evident to us that such examples show that scripture speaks anywhere, let alone "everywhere", about guarding of the heart in the sense understood within the hesychastic tradition. In order to understand this apparently curious use of scripture we must consider the nature of the hermeneutical tools employed within the *Philokalia*. However, what must first be affirmed is that the authors of the *Philokalia* share an understanding that scripture provides foundational authority for their theology, anthropology, psychology and spirituality. Even if we, or their contemporaries, might argue that their use of scripture is flawed, the important point for them appears to be that they are able to argue that what they believe about the inner life and prayer can be shown to be consistent with scripture and not alien to it. In this sense, even the later writers appear ultimately to rely not on tradition but rather on scriptural authority for what they teach.

We should not, however, allow this reliance on scripture as authority to mislead us into thinking that scripture was primarily either a source of theological concepts and ideas or the means of justifying such concepts and ideas when they were drawn from elsewhere. The *Philokalia* is concerned primarily with prayer, and with the virtuous life as an essential basis for prayer, and so the importance of scripture is primarily as an aid to prayer and a guide to virtue. Thus, for example, Hesychios the Priest warns against an approach to scripture that avoids confrontation with its implications for practical living:

> He who does not know the truth cannot truly have faith; for by nature knowledge precedes faith. What is said in Scripture is said not solely for us to understand, but also for us to act upon.[216]

Further, meditation on scripture provides a means of approaching God in prayer. For example John of Karpathos, in *For the Monks in India*, states that:

> nothing so readily renews the decrepit soul, and enables it to approach the Lord, as fear of God, attentiveness, constant meditation on the words of Scripture, the arming of oneself with prayer, and spiritual progress through the keeping of vigils.[217]

Scripture is thus understood not as an end in itself but as a means of assisting the soul in its approach to God. Maximos the Confessor therefore warns that, if used incorrectly, scripture can hinder rather than assist in this process.[218] On the other hand, correctly used, scripture provides an essential aid to the intellect in its ascent to God.[219]

On the one hand, then, the writers of the *Philokalia* understand scripture as interpreting the human condition[220] and leading the soul towards God. On the other hand, however, this process assumes that the human soul is also capable of properly interpreting scripture.

This reflexive hermeneutical process is largely implicit within the *Philokalia*, but it is an important one. Most frequently, it appears to assume the form of allegory.

Allegory is to be found everywhere in the Patristic interpretation of scripture, and is certainly not unique to the *Philokalia*. Both the European Reformation and the Enlightenment have left a deep distrust of such an approach, which is seen as lacking in objectivity both theologically (because it supposedly avoids encounter with the divinely revealed truth contained in scripture) and scientifically (because it is perceived as the antithesis of the historical-critical method, making almost no effort to discern the "original" meaning of the text).[221] However, to approach the *Philokalia* with this kind of distrust is to completely misunderstand the Patristic method and purpose of allegorical interpretation. It is also to ignore the way in which modern hermeneutical thinking and Patristic allegorical interpretation of scripture both recognise that in fact texts are capable of multiple meanings and that the "original" meaning (if indeed that is accessible at all) is not the only possible valid one. Most importantly, it fails to appreciate the mystery, richness and depth that the Fathers found in scripture. Allegorical interpretation, understood in this way, is not a flawed method for uncovering objective meaning, it is rather (at least in the present, Christian, sense) an exploration of the mystery of God in Christ. It is, in fact, prayer.

Examples of allegory abound within the pages of the *Philokalia*. For example, John Cassian interprets "the wicked of the earth" and "the children of Babylon", in Psalms 101 and 137 respectively, as being wicked thoughts.[222] The story of Ish-bosheth and his doorkeeper, in 2 Samuel 4:5-8, is interpreted by Neilos the Ascetic as referring to the intellect and reason.[223] Maximos interprets Jacob's well, in John 4:5-15, as a reference to scripture itself.[224] Nikitas Stithatos interprets the bread/food, the wine, and the oil, referred to in Psalms 104:15 and 23:5 as references to scripture, each in respect of a different stage of the spiritual life.[225]

Peter of Damaskos appears to be alone amongst the authors of the *Philokalia* in his expression of reservation at this hermeneutical method. Ironically, he expresses this reservation in the context of an approving reference in *Book II* to an allegorical interpretation of John 10:1 by Maximos the Confessor, and further uses the same allegory himself in the course of his argument:

If, however, a thief or robber tries to enter, not by the proper door, but by 'climbing up some other way', as the Lord puts it (John 10:1), then the sheep – that is, according to St Maximos, divine thoughts – pay no attention to him. For the thief enters only so that he can deceive by hearsay, and kill the Scriptures by turning them into allegory, since he is unable to interpret them spiritually. Thus through his presumption and his pseudo-knowledge he destroys both himself and the divine thoughts contained in the Scriptures. But the shepherd, as a good soldier of Christ, feels compassion for these thoughts; and by keeping the divine commandments he enters in through the narrow gate (cf. Matt. 7:13), the gate of humility and dispassion. Before receiving divine grace he devotes himself to studying and to learning about everything by listening to others; and whenever the wolf approaches in the guise of a sheep (cf. Matt. 7:15), he chases him off by means of self-criticism, saying, 'I do not know who you are: God knows.' And should a thought approach shamelessly and ask to be received, saying to him, 'If you do not watch over thoughts and discriminate between things, you are ignorant and lacking in faith', then he replies, 'If you call me a fool, I accept the title; for like St John Chrysostom I know that whoever is foolish in this world becomes wise, as St Paul puts it' (cf. 1 Cor. 3:18).[226]

The intent of this discourse, in which thoughts are allegorically understood as sheep in both John 10 and Matthew 7, appears not so much to be an injunction against the use of allegory altogether (for that would invalidate both his own use of allegory, and that of Maximos) but rather a warning against "presumption" and "pseudo-knowledge" which may be displayed in the inappropriate use of allegory by those unable to interpret the scriptures "spiritually".[227] Like Maximos, Peter therefore seems to be concerned about the possible misinterpretation of scripture by those who are not as wise as they would like to imagine. The solution – of "spiritual" interpretation[228] – appears to be a combination of humility and dispassion, obedience to scriptural commands, willingness to learn from others, and a preparedness to appear foolish, if necessary, in being ready to admit to not knowing how to interpret. In other words, proper interpretation relies – at least in part – upon acquisition of dispassion and virtue, but is ultimately a matter of the grace of God. A similar model is given expression elsewhere in the *Philokalia* by Diadochos of Photiki:

> Spiritual knowledge comes through prayer, deep stillness and complete detachment, while wisdom comes through humble meditation on Holy Scripture and, above all, through grace given by God.[229]

Here, interpretation of scripture begins to sound much more like contemplative prayer, and indeed other authors of the *Philokalia* also speak of it in this way. For example, we find Maximos the Confessor writing in *Various Texts: C5*:

> As soon as anyone practises the virtues with true intelligence, he acquires a spiritual understanding of Scripture. He worships God actively in the new way of the Spirit through the higher forms of contemplation, and not in the old way of the written, code (cf. Rom. 7:6), which makes man interpret the Law in an outward and sensual manner and, Judaic-like, fosters the passions and encourages sin.[230]

Spiritual interpretation of scripture thus appears to be itself a form of contemplative prayer.

In some ways, this hermeneutic might be regarded as a hermeneutic of suspicion, for it recognises that human beings have a capacity to deceive themselves and it encourages the interpreter of scripture to distrust his or her own interpretation until finding confirmation of it elsewhere in scripture, or from those who are holier and wiser.[231] However, perhaps the terminology of suspicion is anachronistic here, for it evokes an age of scriptural interpretation informed by Freud, Nietzsche and Ricoeur and this is clearly not the world in which Peter of Damaskos lived. Rather, we should consider this to be a hermeneutic of humility, which recognises that the interpretation of scripture depends upon the grace of God, that no single interpretation is likely to exhaust its meaning, and that there are always others holier and wiser against whose interpretations one's own thoughts must be tested.

This is not a completely pre-critical hermeneutical model. We have seen already that it is critical at the personal, subjective, level. Neither does it eschew academic study, although it does place this in a broader context of the virtuous life and of prayer. It is also capable of accommodating source-critical comments, such as when we find John Cassian making reference to the reliability of the "best manuscripts".[232] Indeed, it is a rich source of critical reflection, insofar as it values the criticism offered by the interpretations of tradition.[233] However, it is not critical in a modern academic sense. Thus, for example, Peter of Damaskos appears unwilling to countenance the possibility that St Paul did not write the epistle to the Hebrews, or that Dionysios did not write the texts attributed to him. Moreover, his arguments against alternative authorship of these texts appear to reflect his own contemplative intuition, presumably reinforced by a sense of what he understood that tradition had taught on such matters.

The hermeneutic most frequently encountered in the *Philokalia* thus appears to be a contemplative one. Any tendency towards extreme subjectivism is checked by the emphasis on humility and the appeal to the traditions of the Church. This might be criticised as making it inherently conservative. However, it is also radically reflective and reflexive. It emphasises scripture as a place of personal encounter with the Logos of God.

## 6. Conclusions

The influences upon, and foundations of, the *Philokalia* that have been considered here together reflect a focus on finding God within the human soul. Evagrios was himself a part of the tradition of the Egyptian desert, and the compilers of the *Philokalia* merely collated and passed on texts that they inherited. On this basis, one could argue that the three foundations of the *Philokalia* are actually scripture, tradition and reason, where the primary tradition is that of the Desert Fathers, and the primary appeal to reason is that of Plato. However, this would be to gloss over the enormous original contribution made by Evagrios, who translated and made sense of the Christian traditions of the Egyptian desert in a highly perceptive way. If the anthropology of the *Philokalia* is fundamentally Platonic, then surely its psychology is fundamentally Evagrian.

# 2

# The Passions

PASSION (πάθος – *pathos*): in Greek, the word signifies literally that which happens to a person or thing, an experience undergone passively; hence an appetite or impulse such as anger, desire or jealousy, that violently dominates the soul.

From the glossary to the EGP

The passions (τὰ πάθη) represent a central concept in the psychology of the *Philokalia* and yet, with only one or two exceptions, its authors do not generally seem to consider that this concept requires definition. The definition helpfully provided by the editors of the English translation emphasises the passivity of that which is experienced by the soul.[1] However, for the present purpose, there is much more that needs to be said about the way in which the concept has been developed, employed and implicitly defined by the authors themselves.

Before proceeding to consider the way in which the concept is understood within the *Philokalia*, it may be helpful to look first at its use in the classical tradition, and then at the way in which it was employed by the Desert Fathers, and particularly by Evagrios.

## 1. The Classical Tradition

Whereas τὰ πάθη is rendered consistently by the English translators of the *Philokalia* as "the passions", translators of the works of classical literature have employed a variety of other terms. Thus, for example, in the glossary provided by one translator of Aristotle's *Nicomachean Ethics*, "pathos" is listed as meaning "susceptibility, feeling, emotion, experience, effect, affection, passion".[2] Richard Sorabji, in the introduction to his work on Stoic theory, *Emotion and Peace of Mind*, justifies use of the English word "emotions", in preference to "passions", on the basis that, in contemporary usage, the latter might be taken to indicate extreme emotions.[3] Not only does this difficulty of translation reflect the lack of a completely equivalent contemporary English word, but also it reflects the richness and variety of emphasis or understanding of the underlying term in classical thought.

The Platonic understanding of the division of the soul into rational and irrational parts has already been discussed in Chapter 1. According to this model, the passions are an expression of the irrational part of the soul, which is itself divided into desiring and incensive parts. In *Phaedrus*,[4] Plato likens the soul to a charioteer with two horses, each of which tends to pull in a different direction. The charioteer represents the rational part of the soul, and the two horses the irrational parts. According to this model, it is the task of the rational part to keep the irrational parts of the soul (and thus the passions) under control.

The Aristotelian understanding is somewhat different, and Aristotle appears to have defined the passions differently in different works. Thus, in *The Art of Rhetoric*, he defines τὰ πάθη as:

> those things by the alteration of which men differ with regard to those judgements which pain and pleasure accompany, such as anger, pity, fear and all other such and their opposites.[5]

He then goes on to consider in turn each of ten specific passions: anger, calm, friendship, enmity, fear, confidence, shame, favour, pity, indignation, envy and jealousy.

In *Nicomachean Ethics*, however, his definition is:

> desire, anger, fear, daring, envy, joy, friendliness, hatred, longing, jealousy, pity, and in general all conditions that are attended by pleasure or pain.[6]

Here we find that the examples listed differ, but also that whereas both definitions are concerned with pain and pleasure, the one and not the other is also concerned with altered judgement. Presumably, this is because the discourse in *The Art of Rhetoric* is concerned with the ways in which the emotions may influence or sway the judgement of those at whom a particular rhetorical discourse is aimed. However, it may also be significant that "desire" is referred to as one of the passions in *Nicomachean Ethics*, but not in *Rhetoric*. This terminology implies such things as hunger and thirst, and elsewhere in *Nicomachean Ethics* it is clear that sexual desire is also to be included.[7] This takes Aristotle's use of the term in *Nicomachean Ethics* well beyond anything that we would usually consider to be "emotion". In *De Anima*, the meaning is stretched still further.[8]

In his article on *Aristotle and the Emotions*, Stephen Leighton[9] concludes that Aristotle is not inconsistent, but rather that his use of the term τὰ πάθη varies according to context. Thus, in a broad sense, τὰ πάθη refers to various mental states – emotions and desires – which are defined by their association with pleasure or pain. Where he is being more specific, as in *Rhetoric*, he focuses more narrowly on states defined by an influence on judgement.

In the writings of Aristotle, it is possible to identify two inter-related components to passion: the feeling of pain or pleasure, and also the beliefs with which they are associated. Aristotle is not entirely explicit about whether the latter are sufficient, or merely necessary, for the former, but generally seems to write as though beliefs are sufficient conditions, at least where the passions in question are what we might refer to as emotions.[10] Further, these beliefs have in common that they ascribe value to objects in the external world, and Aristotle affirmed the rightness of this ascription. Thus, it is right and proper to feel grief at the death of a friend, or to fear disgrace, as long as these feelings are appropriate and proportionate to the circumstances in hand.[11] Not to feel grief, not to feel fear, would represent an undervaluing of things that are held to be important, and would thus represent a lack of integrity.

Stoicism offered yet another perspective. According to the Stoics virtue depended upon reason and the virtuous man is therefore also the wise man. The passions, although somewhat differently understood by different Stoic philosophers, therefore reflect a failure of reasoning.

According to Zeno of Citium (333/332-262 B.C.E.), founder of the Stoic school, the passions involve disobedience to reason.[12] In other words, they are cases of going against one's own better judgement. Zeno further introduced the concept of a rapid "fluttering" or "oscillation" of the soul between two opposed thoughts – that of reason, and that of passion. For Zeno, the passions were excessive impulses, which were, by definition, movements of the soul.[13] These movements are associated with the making of judgements, perhaps even caused by judgements, but it is the movements themselves that constitute the passions.

Chrysippus of Soli (*c*.280-*c*.204 B.C.E.), the greatest exponent of Stoic philosophy, understood the passions rather as *being* judgements.[14] In particular he understood two judgements as being involved: a judgement of something as being good or bad, and a judgement that it is appropriate to react. On the basis of present and future concerns, this allowed the Stoics to identify four generic passions: distress, pleasure, fear, and appetite:

1. Distress is the judgement of present bad, associated with the judgement that it is appropriate to feel an inner "contraction" or "sinking" of the soul.

2. Pleasure is the judgement of present good, associated with the judgement that it is appropriate to feel an inner "expansion" or "lifting" of the soul.

3. Fear is the judgement of expected bad, associated with the judgement that it is appropriate to avoid it.

4. Appetite is the judgement of expected good, associated with the judgement that is appropriate to reach out for it.

Chrysippus understood these judgements as being almost invariably false.[15] Firstly, the Stoics understood nothing as being inherently good or bad except moral character. Other things were to be treated as "indifferents". Only virtue really matters, and ultimately it is only our virtue that is really under our own control. Other things might be worth striving for, but having given our all to attain (or avoid) them, and having failed or succeeded, it does not ultimately matter that we failed or succeeded, whereas our virtue in the process of striving, and only this, does matter. If the judgement of goodness or badness is wrong, the judgement of appropriate reaction is inevitably also wrong. Even in respect of correct judgements of that which is good (i.e. virtue) or bad, the judgement of appropriateness of reaction is, in the Chrysippian view, usually false. However, because the passions are understood as being judgements, and because assent to any particular judgement can be given or withheld, Chrysippus understood them as being both voluntary and eradicable.

Posidonius (135-51 B.C.E.), in contrast, although a Stoic, adopted a seemingly more Platonic position in recognising irrational "capacities" of the soul which, although involuntary, he believed could be trained.[16] Thus, as education is necessary for the rational capacity of the soul as a means of gaining knowledge and understanding, so a process of "habituation" is necessary for the irrational capacities of the soul. This process began, in his understanding, with attention to the diet and lifestyle of the pregnant mother, and continued with such matters as the effect of music upon the irrational capacities of the soul. However, it also involved a more rational process of habituation, such as dwelling in advance on possible unpleasant things that might happen, so that if and when they happen they are not unfamiliar and may be associated with lessened passion, or even be experienced without passion.

Posidonius was not alone in the classical tradition in believing that the passions also depend upon physical bodily states. Galen (c.129-199 C.E.), a physician with Platonist sympathies, believed that both the soul and its capacities depended upon the balance or "blend" of hot, cold, wet and dry. This in turn depended, in his view, upon diet, lifestyle and climate.[17] In fact, the view that mental states were in some way or another dependent upon (or that they "followed") physical, bodily states seems to have been held by Plato, Aristotle, the Epicureans, and others.[18]

If this belief in the relationship between physical bodily states and the passions offers one area of fairly widespread agreement, there also appears to have been a wide degree of agreement that the passions are all concerned with beliefs about things external to the human agent, and especially beliefs about the value of things. Thus, love represents attachment to these externals (and especially to other persons), grief, pity and fear relate to their loss (by ourselves or others). Anger, which seems to be closely related to love, is concerned with our vulnerability to the actions of external agents – mainly other persons – towards us. The passions thus represent a valuing of things (including, but not only, other people) external to ourselves. For Aristotle, this was as it should be. To value things – especially other people – is appropriate as a recognition of their importance. But for Plato, and especially for the Stoics, this was not the way it should be at all. In their estimation, only virtue was held to be of value, and this is something that is located within. In comparison, externals are of no great consequence. For them, the passions therefore concern faulty beliefs, an over-estimation of the value of externals, which simply makes us vulnerable to things that are outside our own control.[19]

Martha Nussbaum[20] has identified four theses in the classical tradition which are concerned with the relationship between belief (or judgement) on the one hand, and passion on the other. It is on the basis of these that the differences between the various philosophical schools become clear. They are:

a) **Necessity** of belief for passion
b) Belief as a **constituent element** of passion
c) **Sufficiency** of belief for passion
d) **Identity** of belief with passion

Affirmations of these theses may be summarised thus:

|  | Plato | Aristotle | Epicurus | Zeno | Chrysippus |
|---|---|---|---|---|---|
| **Necessity** | ✓ | ✓ | ✓ | ✓ | ✓ |
| **Constituent Element** | ? | ✓ | ? | × | ✓ |
| **Sufficiency** | × | ? | ? | ✓ | ✓ |
| **Identity** | × | × | × | × | ✓ |

The Stoic view, and especially Chrysippus' influential account of it, is thus the extreme one, insofar as these theses are concerned. Furthermore, according to the Stoics, the passions have an in-built propensity to tend towards uncontrollable excess, and they are inter-related in such a way that each one tends to lead to others. Love leads to hate and anger, joy leads to fear and grief, pity to rage, and so on.[21]

The classical tradition therefore incorporated two views of the passions. On the one hand, there was a very negative strand, finding expression in Stoicism, and on the other there was a more favourable view, discernible in Plato but more fully developed in Aristotle.[22]

## 2. The Desert Fathers

The Desert Fathers also had much to say about the passions. Passions that are specifically named in the *Apophthegmata* include:

"an uncontrolled tongue",[23] fornication,[24] avarice,[25] vain-glory,[26] anger,[27] slander,[28] and accidie.[29] We do not find (at least not within the *Apophthegmata Patrum*) any attempt on the part of the Desert Fathers to define exactly what the passions are. However, a number of things become clear from a reading of references to the passions within the *Apophthegmata*.

Firstly, the passions are closely related to thoughts – but are not necessarily the same thing as thoughts. Thus, Abba Abraham challenges an old man who claims that he has "destroyed fornication, avarice and vain-glory in [him]self".[30] When the old man explains that he struggles against his *thoughts* so as not to act wrongly, Abba Abraham points out that "the passions continue to live; it is simply that they are controlled by the saints".[31] In this way, Abba Abraham appears to imply that the passions are in fact thoughts. However, in a fashion which is typical of the way in which the sayings of the Desert Fathers can be contradictory of each other, a saying of Abba Arsenius seems to imply that the passions are an "exterior" affair, to be contrasted with the "interior activity" of thoughts:

> A brother questioned Abba Arsenius to hear a word of him and the old man said to him, 'Strive with all your might to bring your interior activity into accord with God, and you will overcome exterior passions.'[32]

Secondly, as both of the examples just quoted show, the passions are something with which the godly person is expected to struggle or strive inwardly. Whether or not they are actually thoughts, they are at least something which seems to exert a strong grip upon the inner self in such a way as to make it hard to resist. They are thus also closely related to concepts of temptation and desire:

> A brother asked Abba Sisoes, 'What shall I do about the passions?' The old man said, 'Each man is tempted when he is lured and enticed by his own desire' (James 1.14).[33]

Thirdly, the passions are (like much else that we find in the *Apophthegmata*) ambiguous and contradictory, thus eluding definition. Perhaps the closest that we come to finding a definition of the passions amongst the *Apophthegmata* is in the parable of the governor and the courtesan, attributed to John the Dwarf:

> There was in a city a courtesan who had many lovers. One of the governors approached her, saying, 'Promise me you

will be good, and I will marry you.' She promised this and he took her and brought her to his house. Her lovers, seeking her again, said to one another, 'That lord has taken her with him to his house, so if we go to his house and he learns of it, he will condemn us. But let us go to the back, and whistle to her. Then, when she recognises the sound of the whistle she will come down to us; as for us, we shall be unassailable.' When she heard the whistle, the woman stopped her ears and withdrew to the inner chamber and shut the doors.' The old man said that this courtesan is our soul, that her lovers are the passions and other men; that the lord is Christ; that the inner chamber is the eternal dwelling; those who whistle are the evil demons, but the soul always takes refuge in the Lord.[34]

Here, the lovers of the courtesan are allegorically understood as the passions and they remain outside of the soul – at least unless or until the soul chooses to let them in.[35] They are therefore not inner thoughts, although they clearly evoke desire within the soul. They are also in this parable, at least when they attempt to entice the soul, demonic. However, the relationship between the passions and the demons is also complex and it is interesting that the parable allows a degree of ambiguity about this. On the one hand the lovers (and other men) are the passions. On the other hand "those who whistle" are the demons. John seems to deliberately distinguish here between the passions and the demons, whilst allowing the possibility that the two are the same.[36]

In general, then, we might discern within this tradition a negative tendency towards the passions, but this is in the context of apparently deliberate ambiguity and paradox.

## 3. Evagrios of Pontus

Evagrios also used the concept of the passions in his works as though it would automatically be understood what he meant by it. However, it is clear from his writings that he understands the passions as closely related to thoughts (λογισμοί). Passions and thoughts are in places referred to almost interchangeably[37] and elsewhere are referred to as though there is an intimate causal relationship between them.[38] To complicate things somewhat, he also clearly understands a close causal relationship between the passions and sense perception.[39]

Chapter 2: The Passions    55

Thus memories of sensory objects can also evoke the passions, and vice versa.[40] And, further, there is a close relationship between the passions and the activity of demons.[41]

The passions are referred to by Evagrios as subjecting us to warfare,[42] slavery,[43] imprisonment,[44] burning,[45] and sickness.[46] Their effects are to lead us away from stillness,[47] to impede prayer,[48] and to cause sadness.[49]

Passions that are specifically named by Evagrios include: malicious talk,[50] contention,[51] vainglory,[52] pride,[53] jealousy,[54] gluttony,[55] fornication,[56] licentiousness,[57] avarice,[58] anger,[59] pleasure,[60] greed,[61] sadness,[62] and resentment.[63] Thus, all of the "eight thoughts" are specifically understood as being passions,[64] as well as various other behaviours, emotions and attitudes more or less directly related to them. Concupiscibility[65] and irascibility[66] are also referred to as passions, although perhaps this might better be understood as a way of referring to groups of passions rather than specific passions. Elsewhere, Evagrios classifies the passions into passions of the soul and passions of the body.[67]

The concept of "the passions" is thus not without considerable ambiguity in the Evagrian literature. Although, subjectively, it is usually possible to understand exactly what he means by it, on the other hand, objectively, the concept is elusive and difficult to define. There is a tension between the extent to which the passions are external – or at least externally imposed – and the extent to which they are an internal feature of human experience which human beings must own. It is also not entirely clear whether they are thoughts, emotions, motives, powers of the soul, or possibly something else; although it does seem fairly clear that whilst they may be manifested as outward behaviour, it is more with the internal phenomena from which the behaviour arises that Evagrios is fundamentally concerned.

Perhaps the closest that we get to an Evagrian definition of a passion is where, in reference to the passion of avarice, he writes that this is:

> a pleasure hostile to humanity, born of free will, and compelling the mind to make improper use of the creatures of God.[68]

If this may be considered a definition, it clearly has limitations. If the passions are "pleasures" then this definition requires us to understand anger and sadness as pleasurable, which is certainly contrary to what we would usually expect, if not fundamentally contradictory. However, it might be argued that the definition is, after all, particular to avarice and that in the case of sadness and anger we are dealing with frustration of pleasure rather than pleasure itself.[69]

The definition, if it is a definition, certainly encapsulates some of the ambiguity of the concept. Whilst the passions are "hostile to humanity" and put the mind under compulsion, they are also here "born of free will" and engage the mind as an active participant in the improper use of God's creatures. They are thus, in a sense, both external and internal. However, it is not entirely clear what "born of free will" means here. It is true that Evagrios sometimes sees the passions as arising as a result of human decision. For example, the decision to eat more than is needful, in the Evagrian schema, is likely to give birth to the passion of fornication.[70] But, elsewhere, he talks about the demons as "presiding" over,[71] "mobilising",[72] or even "producing",[73] the passions. There is, in any case, something of an internal contradiction between that which is both born of free will and yet which results in compulsion of the mind.

This definition does, however, also have its value. It understands the passions not merely as pleasures, but rather as "hostile pleasures". Within this tension is conveyed the sense of something desirable which is nonetheless not fundamentally in our own best interests. It also introduces the idea that the passions make "improper" use of creatures of God which are fundamentally good and which do, therefore, have their proper uses. The passions are thus concerned with a tendency which is contrary to divine purpose. In this sense, they are intimately concerned with what it means for human beings to be subject to temptation.

There would seem to be little doubt that Evagrios understood the passions as being potentially set in motion by heterogeneous factors, some of which would appear to be more or less completely outside of human control and some of which are more or less within human influence.[74] We might also note, in passing, that Evagrios even understood human thoughts, let alone passions, as arising from a variety of origins and thus, in a sense, not always belonging to the person who thought them.[75] Given the complexity of his understanding of the relationships between thoughts, memories, sense perceptions and passions we should therefore not be surprised if we find within the Evagrian corpus various, or even diverse, understandings of what we might call the phenomenology of the passions.

Despite this complexity and diversity, perhaps there are still some conclusions which can be drawn here in respect of the Evagrian understanding of the passions. Firstly, the concept would appear to encompass two tensions: that of pleasure with hostility to human good, and that of human free will with the experience of being acted upon. Secondly, it is concerned with Divine purpose in the created order, particularly as it affects the relationship of human beings to objects encountered in their internal and external worlds. Beyond this, it is perhaps wise to allow the concept something of the ambiguity and flexibility which Evagrios himself appears to have allowed it.

## 4. The *Philokalia*

Before proceeding to a more careful study of what the *Philokalia* has to say about the passions, and at risk of jumping too soon to a conclusion, it is worth noting Kallistos Ware's general observation that the Greek Fathers have tended to adopt the more negative stance of Stoicism in respect of their approach to the passions.[76] It will be seen that the *Philokalia* is not exceptional in this regard. However, the *Philokalia* is also not exceptional in regard to its inclusion of a minority viewpoint which is discernibly more Aristotelian and affirmative. Ware identifies as particular exponents of this position Abba Isaias (d?491) and Theodoret of Cyrus (393-?460), but goes on to find evidence of similar thinking in Dionysios the Areopagite, Maximos the Confessor and Gregory Palamas. According to this view, the passions may be understood as in accordance with nature when properly directed, and thus the Christian task is not to eliminate them but to redirect them. However, this is moving ahead to the subject matter of the next chapter. What must be noted here is that Isaias, or rather Isaiah the Solitary as he is here identified, Maximos, and Gregory Palamas are all authors of works included within the *Philokalia* and that we may therefore need to listen carefully for an affirmative whisper about the passions amidst the hubbub of a more negative conversation.

### i. Definitions

Only two authors of the *Philokalia*, Maximos the Confessor and Philotheos of Sinai, provide any kind of definition of the passions. Briefly taking the second of these first, in *Forty Texts on Watchfulness*, Philotheos of Sinai writes that:

> Passion, in the strict sense, they define as that which lurks impassionably in the soul over a long period.[77]

This "definition" is somewhat circular, in that it defines "passion" by reference to that which "lurks impassionably" in the soul, and thus begs the question as to what exactly impassionable lurking might be. The answer to that question is at least partly provided by a consideration of the context within which Philotheos offers the definition: that of a consideration of the strategy of the demons, and of the process by which human beings are subject to temptation. We shall return to a consideration of the latter process shortly. First, however, it may be helpful to give somewhat more detailed consideration to the definition(s) offered by Maximos the Confessor.

In the first of his four centuries of texts *On Love*, Maximos helpfully explains that:

> A culpable passion is an impulse of the soul that is contrary to nature.[78]

By way of amplification and clarification, Maximos offers in his second century of these texts some examples of what such impulses contrary to nature might be:

> Passion is an impulse of the soul contrary to nature, as in the case of mindless love or mindless hatred for someone or for some sensible thing. In the case of love, it may be for needless food, or for a woman, or for money, or for transient glory, or for other sensible objects or on their account. In the case of hatred, it may be for any of the things mentioned, or for someone on account of these things.[79]

The two defining criteria thus appear to be that a passion is both an "impulse of the soul" and also "contrary to nature". Nature is clearly here understood, as in most of the texts of the *Philokalia*, not in the sense of the natural way that things are found to be in the world, but rather in the sense of the way that things were divinely intended to be. In the second of the above quotations, this is further seen as being evidenced by the "mindless[ness]" and "needless[ness]" of the impulses in question. There also appears to be an implication that contrariness to nature might be evidenced by motivation for transient and selfish pleasure, rather than eternal and Divine purpose. This general model is further affirmed in the third century

Chapter 2: The Passions                                    59

of these texts, where it is stated that "a passion is mindless affection or indiscriminate hatred for ... things".[80]

The references here to mindlessness in relation to love and hatred appear to suggest that Maximos sees the rational part of the soul as that part which, properly, directs the desiring and incensive parts towards their proper purpose. Passions are thus, effectively, those impulses of the desiring and incensive parts of the soul which are not conformed by the rational part of the soul to Divine purpose. Elsewhere, in the first century of *Various Texts*, he writes:

> When the intelligence dominates the passions it makes the senses instruments of virtue. Conversely, when the passions dominate the intelligence they conform the senses to sin. One must watchfully study and reflect how the soul can best reverse the situation and use those things through which it had formerly sinned to generate and sustain the virtues.[81]

He further explains:

> Every passion always consists of a combination of some perceived object, a sense faculty and a natural power – the incensive power, desire or the intelligence, as the case may be – whose natural function has been distorted. Thus, if the intellect investigates the final result of these three inter-related factors – the sensible object, the sense faculty and the natural power involved with the sense faculty – it can distinguish each from the other two, and refer each back to its specific natural function. It can, that is to say, view the sensible object in itself, apart from its relationship to the sense faculty, and the sense faculty in itself, apart from its connection with the sensible object, and the natural power – desire, for example – apart from its impassioned alliance with the sense faculty and the sensible object. In this way, the intellect reduces to its constituent parts whatever passion it investigates, in much the same way as the golden calf of Israel in Old Testament days was ground into powder and mixed with water (cf. Exod. 32:20): it dissolves it with the water of spiritual knowledge, utterly destroying even the passion-free image of the

passions, by restoring each of its elements to its natural state.[82]

Here it becomes clear that Maximos understands the passions as actually comprising a complex pathology of one of the three powers of the soul in combination with a perceived object and the sense faculty responsible for perception of that object. However, the root of the pathology lies clearly in one or another of the powers of the human soul, not in the object itself or the process of sensory perception. In his third century of his texts *On Love*, Maximos distinguishes more clearly between objects and perceptual images of objects, on the one hand, and passions on the other.[83] The pathology thus lies within the soul – not in the world of perception or of that which is perceived.

It also becomes clear in this text that Maximos understands the intelligence as being equally capable of pathology as the incensive and desiring parts of the soul. However, he also understands the "intellect" (by which he at first appears here to mean the rational function of the soul in a more originally Platonic sense) as capable of analysing its own pathology in a rational way. Furthermore, this rational analysis appears, in itself, to be understood as being in some way therapeutic – capable of breaking the "impassioned alliance" and restoring everything to its proper purpose and function. This process only makes sense insofar as the intellect and intelligence are here distinguished, or else the intelligent part of the soul would have to be seen as capable of understanding and restoring its own pathology. But the reference to "spiritual knowledge" (γνῶσις) perhaps also implies the need for a form of knowledge imparted by Divine grace as necessary to enable this self-reflective and restorative process.

### ii. Lists

There are many and various lists of the passions in the *Philokalia*. These vary from apparently ad hoc groupings of two or three particular passions through to the magisterial listing of 298 passions by Peter of Damaskos.[84] However, it is clear that the "eight thoughts" first identified by Evagrios provide a common point of reference to at least four other authors, over a period of almost a millennium, even if the order or nomenclature varies slightly from place to place (see Table 2.1, pages 62-63).

Within this list of eight passions, although not always consistently, and sometimes adding to the list, various authors attempt to identify a smaller number of "principal", "main", or "worst" passions (see Table 2.2, pages 64-66). Within these shorter lists, gluttony, avarice, and self-esteem may be seen to occur especially frequently.

The legacy of Evagrios in the *Philokalia* is therefore clear. The eight thoughts provide an apparently enduring directory of the particular passions that may be identified in human experience, even if numerous variations might be added, or various contractions of it might be made. The passions which are found in these lists might all find their roots in the inner world of human thought, but it is clear that they are a varied group of phenomena, including emotions, desires, behaviours and attitudes.

### iii. Vocabulary and Metaphor

A rich, colourful and diverse vocabulary is employed by the authors of the *Philokalia* in reference to the passions. This vocabulary employs metaphor extensively, stretching the meaning of words well beyond their normal limits in an attempt to bring to life the nature of what is essentially an abstract concept. So stretching is this process that it is at times difficult to know to what extent personification and metaphor are being used, and to what extent the concept has been reified and the passions objectively understood as personal demonic entities. However, there is no doubt that the language employed offers considerable material for characterisation of the way in which the passions are to be understood within the tradition of the *Philokalia*.

As a preliminary exploration of the language of the passions, lists of adjectives, nouns and verbs encountered in reference to the passions in the English translation of the *Philokalia* have been compiled by the author[90] In Table 2.3 (pages 68-71) these words are presented, grouped according to theme.[91] From this table, it is clear that the language of the passions in the *Philokalia* is highly metaphorical and symbolic, diverse, and at times contradictory or paradoxical. Thus, for example, the passions are portrayed as being both "inner" phenomena, but also "outer" in relation to the human subject. They are portrayed as being both "fire" and "frost". These oppositions appear to operate in such a way as to convey something of a dialectical tension in respect of certain aspects of the passions, or perhaps in such a way as to overcome a certain inherent ineffability.

Table 2.1: Names given to the [major groupings of] Passions in the *Philokalia*

| Author/Work | Date | Terminology | Names given to the Passions/Thoughts/Vices | | | | | | | |
|---|---|---|---|---|---|---|---|---|---|---|
| Evagrios of Pontus *Eight Thoughts*[85] | b. 345/346 d. 399 | Eight thoughts | gluttony γαστριμαργία | fornication πορνεία | avarice φιλαργυρία | anger ὀργή | | | | |
| | | | sadness λύπη | acedia ἀκηδία | vainglory κενοδοξία | pride ὑπερηφανία | | | | |
| John Cassian *Eight Vices* (EGP 1, 73) | b. c.360 d. c.435 | Eight vices | gluttony γαστριμαργία | unchastity πορνεία | avarice φιλαργυρία | anger ὀργή | | | | |
| | | | dejection λύπη | listlessness ἀκηδία | self-esteem κενοδοξία | pride ὑπερηφανία | | | | |
| [John of Damaskos] *On Virtues & Vices* (EGP 2, 337) | ?7th c. | Impassioned thoughts | gluttony γαστριμαργία | unchastity πορνεία | avarice φιλαργυρία | anger ὀργή | | | | |
| | | | dejection λύπη | listlessness ἀκηδία | self-esteem κενοδοξία | pride ὑπερηφανία | | | | |
| Peter of Damaskos *Book I, Introduction* (EGP 3, 79)[86] | 11th/12th c. | Ruling passions | gluttony γαστριμαργία | unchastity πορνεία | avarice φιλαργυρία | anger ὀργή | | | | |
| | | | dejection λύπη | listlessness ἀκηδία | self-esteem κενοδοξία | pride ὑπερηφανία | | | | |

| Author/Work | Date | Terminology | Names given to the Passions/Thoughts/Vices | | | |
|---|---|---|---|---|---|---|
| Gregory on Sinai *On Commandements & Doctrines, #91* (EGP 4, 231) | b.c.1265 d.1346 | Eight ruling passions | gluttony γαστριμαργία | avarice φιλαργυρία | self-esteem κενοδοξία | unchastity πορνεία |
| | | | anger ὀργή | dejection λύπη | listlessness ἀκηδία | arrogance ὑπερηφανία |
| Gregory of Sinai *On Commandments & Doctrines, #104* (EGP 4, 235) | | Six universal passions | insolence παρρησία | gluttony γαστριμαργία | talkativeness πολυλογία | distraction περισπασμός |
| | | | pretentiousness φυσίωσις | self-conceit οἴησις | | |

Table 2.2: [Shorter] lists of principal passions provided in the *Philokalia*

| Author/Work | Date | Terminology | Names given to these Passions/Thoughts/Vices/Demons | | |
|---|---|---|---|---|---|
| Evagrios of Pontus *Texts on Discrimination*[87], #1 & #23 (EGP 1, 38 & 52) | b. 345/346 d. 399 | Demons in the front line | Gluttony | Avarice | Esteem in the eyes of others |
| Mark the Ascetic *Letter to Nicolas* (EGP 1, 157) | Early 5th c. | Oppressive & deep seated passions[88] | Forgetfulness | Laziness | Ignorance |
| [Antony the Great] *On the Character of Men*, #79 (EGP 1, 341) | 1st to 4th cc. | Four passions | Self-esteem | Levity | Anger | Cowardice |
| Theodoros the Great Ascetic *Spiritual Texts*, #10 (EGP 2, 16) | ?9th c. | Three principal passions | Love of sensual pleasure | Love of riches | Love of praise |
| Theodoros the Great Ascetic *Spiritual Texts*, #61 (EGP 2, 26) | | Three groups of demons in the front line | Gluttony | Avarice | Self-esteem |

| Author/Work | Date | Terminology | Names given to these Passions/Thoughts/Vices/Demons | | | | |
|---|---|---|---|---|---|---|---|
| [Theodoros the Great Ascetic] *Theoretikon* (EGP 2, 42) | | Main passions | Self-indulgence | Avarice | Love of praise | | |
| Maximos the Confessor *On Love: C2*, #59 (EGP 2, 75) | 580-662 | Three first and most general impassioned thoughts | Gluttony | Avarice | Self-esteem | | |
| Maximos the Confessor *On Love: C2*, #79 (EGP 2, 78) | | Principal vices | Stupidity | Cowardice | Licentiousness | Injustice | |
| Maximos the Confessor *On Love: C2*, #56 (EGP 2, 92) | | Three principal thoughts of desire | Gluttony | Avarice | Self-esteem | | |
| Thalassios the Libyan *For Paul: C3*, ##19-20 (EGP 2, 320) | 7th c. | Four prevalent passions | Distress ↔ | Sensual pleasure | Fear of punishment ↔ | Desire | |
| [John of Damaskos] *On Virtues & Vices* (EGP 2, 335) | ??7th c. | Roots or primary causes of all passions of body & soul | Love of sensual pleasure | Love of praise | Love of material wealth | | |
| Ilias the Presbyter *Gnomic Anthology: 4*, #125 (EGP 3, 63) | Late 11th/ early 12th c. | Source of all unholy passions | Gluttony | Bad temper | Malice | | |

| Author/Work | Date | Terminology | Names given to these Passions/Thoughts/Vices/Demons | | | | |
|---|---|---|---|---|---|---|---|
| Nikitas Stithatos *On Virtues: 100 Texts*, #12 (EGP 4, 82) | 11th c. | Three major principalities & powers of the mustered passions[89] | Avarice | Self-indulgence | Love of praise | | |
| Gregory of Sinai *On Commandments & Doctrines*, #91 (EGP 4, 231) | b. c.1265 d. 1346 | Three principal passions | Gluttony | Avarice | Self-esteem | | |
| Gregory of Sinai *On Commandments & Doctrines*, #121 (EGP 4, 241) | | Five passions hostile to obedience | Disobedience | Contentiousness | Self-gratification | Self-justification | Self-conceit |

↔  The double-headed arrow is used in this table to indicate the way in which Thalassios understands the four prevalent passions as set "one against the other" (#19). He writes that "Distress checks sensual pleasure; the fear of punishment withers desire." (#20).

Chapter 2: The Passions    67

Doubtless different observers might see different patterns emerge from this lexicon of the passions, or else might want to emphasise a lack of any consistent pattern in the way that the passions are characterised in the *Philokalia*. However, Table 2.3 is offered here as one way of attempting to bring some order and to suggest some major themes that emerge:

1. A large number of terms are employed which might be seen as pertaining to six inter-related themes, here labelled as "destructive/ attacking", "controlling/ enslaving", "influence/ temptation", "evil/ defiling", "dark/ obscuring" and "subtle/ cunning". The passions are thus seen as evil forces which assail and otherwise influence human beings in such a way as to bring them into slavery and imprisonment. In general, this language affirms a sense of passivity of the human subject in the face of attack. However, there are clear references to human agency (e.g. words like "reprehensible" and "culpable" imply human guilt in succumbing or co-operating in some way). The language of darkness and cunning also conveys a sense of the human subject being taken unawares by an invisible and crafty enemy who propagates obscurity, or perhaps generates a kind of "fog of war", as a means of gaining victory through inadvertent co-operation of the deceived and confused human subject with the powers of darkness.

2. The passions are characterised as being both living things (be it "plant" or "animal" or "human"), a part of the natural order, but also as "unnatural", pathological and a source or kind of death. Thus, the passions grow, have roots and come to life, but they are also an incurable malady, a disease or plague, a kind of "death". The passions are almost always seen as unnatural, in the sense that they are contrary to the Divinely instituted natural order of things, even if they are occasionally understood as "natural" in the sense that they are a part of the natural order of things in a fallen world, or else that they have a proper natural purpose if employed as servants of the human subject rather than being themselves served.

## Table 2.3: The language of the passions

| Theme | Adjectives | Nouns | Verbs | |
|---|---|---|---|---|
| *Group 1: Evil Forces that Assail Human Beings* | | | | |
| Destructive/ Attacking | Anarchic Deadly Destroying Destructive Hostile Rebellious Savage Violent | Armies, hostile Assaults Attack(s) Blasts Enemies Slaying Violence | Attack Beset Besiege Bring injury Conquer Debilitate Destroy Fight Harass Induce suffering Kill Oppose Overcome | Overpower Overwhelm Pierce Prevail Revolt Shake Shatter Shipwreck (faith) Slay War Weaken |
| Controlling/ Enslaving | Dominant Ruling Tyrannising | Bonds Burden Clutches Domination Egypt of the spirit Fetters Grip Lordship Princes Prison(s) Red Sea Slave(ry) Sway Tyranny Yoke | Carry away Constrain Dominate Drag down Encompass Enslave Ensnare Get a hold Govern Hold back Imprison Keep from (prayer) Master Oppress | Prevent Stifle Tie Tyrannise |
| Influence/ Temptation | Culpable Taking advantage | Imprint Influence Mediators (of eternal punishment) | Distract Drag Generate images Generate other passions Induce a state Involve Lead (astray) Motivate Persuade Prompt Stimulate Suggest | |
| Evil/ Defiling | Abominable Accursed Corrupting Degrading Demonic Evil Foul(est) | Corruption Crooked paths Defilement(s) Depravity Dunghill Evils Fall | Become (evil) Corrupt Defile Give (entry to demons) Impel (towards evil) | Intoxicate Precede (demons) Produce licentiousness Rot |

| Theme | Adjectives | Nouns | Verbs |
|---|---|---|---|
| Evil/ Defiling (continued) | Foul-smelling<br>Frightful<br>Gross(er)<br>Hateful<br>Ignoble<br>Impure<br>Noxious<br>Reprehensible<br>Ridiculous<br>Shameful<br>Shameless(ly)<br>Sinful<br>Unclean<br>Unholy | Filthy, soiled, garment<br>Fumes<br>Putrescence<br>Soot<br>Stench<br>Stink<br>Ugliness | Seek (our perdition)<br>Smut<br>Stain |
| Dark/ Obscuring | Dark<br>Behind<br>Hidden<br>Secret<br>Unnoticed<br>Unseen | Cloak<br>Cloud(s) of cares<br>Fantasies<br>Storm clouds<br>Engulfing clouds<br>Darkening<br>Darkness<br>Murk<br>Night<br>Obscurity<br>Veil | Befuddle<br>Blind<br>Darken<br>Delude<br>Induce darkness<br>Produce obfuscation<br>Produce obscurity |
| Subtle/ Cunning | Subtle(st) | Cunning | Creep<br>Lie<br>Lurk |
| *Group 2: Unnatural Forces, Death and Disease* ||||
| Living (plant) | Grown<br>Rooted | Herbs of the soul (evil)<br>Root(s)<br>Seeds<br>Suckers | Grow<br>Put down (roots)<br>Take root |
| Animal | Bestial<br>Brute-like | Camels | Make (like domestic animals) |
| Life v *Death* | | *Death*<br>Life | Come to life<br>*Deaden* |
| Natural v *Unnatural* | According (to nature)<br>*Contrary to nature*<br>Natural<br>*Unnatural* | | Belong to nature |
| Disease | Incurable<br>Unhealed | Malady<br>Paralysis<br>Plague<br>Sickness<br>Weals<br>Wounds | Afflict<br>Cause disease<br>Enervate<br>Wound |

| Theme | Adjectives | Nouns | Verbs | |
|---|---|---|---|---|
| *Group 3: Affect and Storm* | | | | |
| Affective | Affecting<br>Dreadful<br>Full (of sorrow)<br>Stirring | Provocations | Affect<br>Agitate<br>Deject<br>Disturb<br>Grieve | Humiliate<br>Produce disturbance<br>Provoke<br>Trouble |
| Storm | | Storm<br>Tempest<br>Torrents<br>Tumult<br>Turbulence<br>Turmoil | | |
| *Group 4: Matter and Energy* | | | | |
| Material/<br>Sensual<br>v<br>*Without existence* | Bodily<br>Carnal<br>Earthly<br>Fleshly<br>*Insubstantial*<br>Material<br>Sensual<br>Wordly | *Existence (without)*<br>Material, raw<br>Materiality<br>Matter<br>Matter/inflammatory<br>Sensuality | Attach (to a sensible thing)<br>Come into being<br>Induce to descend to the realm of the senses<br>Consist<br>Produce diffusion of blood around the heart | |
| Energy/<br>Power<br>v<br>*Impotent* | *Impotent*<br>Powerful<br>Strong | Burning energy<br>Energy<br>Impulse(s)<br>Impulsion<br>Power | | |
| *Group 5: Movement and Continuity* | | | | |
| Active<br>v<br>*Inactive* | Active<br>*Inactive*<br>*Quiescent* | Action<br>Activity<br>Acts<br>Movement<br>Operations<br>*Quiescence*<br>Working(s) | Operate<br>Work | |
| Coming & going<br>v<br>*Continuously present* | *Adherent*<br>*Continuous*<br>Emerging<br>*Habitual*<br>*Inveterate*<br>*Present* | *Dispositions*<br>Eruption<br>Infancy<br>*Presence*<br>Resurgence<br>*State*<br>Waves | Arise<br>Arouse<br>Decrease<br>Disperse<br>Increase<br>Return<br>Spring | Stay<br>Subside<br>Visit |

| Theme | Adjectives | Nouns | Verbs |
|---|---|---|---|
| *Group 6: Inwardness & Exteriority* ||||
| Inner v *Outer* | Deep-seated<br>In us<br>Indwelling<br>Inherent (in thought)<br>Innate<br>Inner<br>*Outer* | *Woven garment*<br>*Old garment* | Belong to soul/body<br>Establish within |
| *Group 7: Humoural Forces* ||||
| Dry v *Wet* | | Aridity<br>*Moisture*<br>*Sea*<br>*Springs*<br>*Waters* | |
| Hot v *Cold* | | Fire<br>Flame<br>*Frost*<br>Heat<br>Heat, arid<br>*Winter* | |
| *Group 8: Magnitude and number* ||||
| Many | Innumerable<br>Many<br>Prevalent<br>Swarming in | Swarm | |
| Great | Enormous<br>Great<br>Serious | Mountains | |
| *Group 9: Other* ||||
| Remaining (not elsewhere classified) | Coarse(r)<br>Contrary to the intelligence<br>Human<br>Linked (with images)<br>Mindless<br>Opposing (one another) | Company<br>Desires<br>Form<br>Rawness<br>Servants<br>Sphere<br>Stone<br>Trace<br>World | Assume (form)<br>Become (good)<br>Contribute<br>Intercommunicate<br>Support (other passions) |

3. The affective character and expression of the passions receives surprisingly little explicit attention, although it is frequently implied in metaphor, such as the metaphors of storm, tumult and turbulence, and of course several of the named passions (see below) are affective states. An affective dimension is also implied in, or associated with, metaphors such as those of violence, dragging down, darkness, degradation and intoxication.

4. The passions are referred to in various places as having almost material existence, or at least as being some kind of power or energy with physical effects. However, there are also references by Maximos the Confessor to their being without existence, and thus impotent.

5. The passions are both continuously present, but also come and go. They are active, but may also (at least for a time) remain inactive or lay quiescent.

6. The passions both exist within the human subject, but also assail him or her from without.

7. The passions are desert like – in being arid, hot or cold – but are also described in terms of water (moisture, sea, springs, etc.). There is almost certainly a reference here, at least in some places, to humoural theories of disease (based upon a balance between "hot" and "cold" or "wet" and "dry").[92] However, it would appear likely that these metaphors operate at various levels and in different ways. A "sea", for example, might also evoke images of drowning, being adrift, of great expanse, and of being at the mercy of the elements.

8. The passions are consistently quantified, where any quantification is offered, as being both numerous and great.

The passions are thus clearly seen in the *Philokalia* as a formidable, personal, active and evil foe. There may be ambiguity about whether they attack from within or without or as to the nature of their ontology. They may come and go, or they may be always present. They may be redeemable, or not. But there must clearly be no underestimating the power of the passions to assail the inner life

Chapter 2: The Passions                                                  73

of human beings, to deny human beings their full potential, and to draw them into utter darkness, at least as far as the authors of the *Philokalia* are concerned.

### iv. Processes

The passions are not viewed, within the tradition of the *Philokalia*, as has been seen, as merely static phenomena or states. They are active processes, or at least they are a part of an active process, and they are closely related to the activity of demons, the inner mental life of human beings, and the experience of temptation to sin.

Various processes of temptation, and other mental processes which involve the passions, are described in the *Philokalia*. These are summarised in Tables 2.4a to 2.4g. In Table 2.5 an overall summary is provided.

It is not clear that the identification of these processes originates with Evagrios, although certainly Evagrios does show an acute awareness of the way in which human beings are tempted and drawn into fruitless or seductive mental processes to the detriment of virtue and of prayer.[93] Rather, the earliest contributor to the *Philokalia* in whose writings such processes may be identified is Mark the Ascetic (see Table 2.4a, page 74). Importantly, Mark identifies and defines mental phenomena of "Provocation", "Entertainment" and "Assent" which are connected in a sequential process which, if not successfully resisted, culminates in morally culpable acts or thoughts (i.e. sin). The process is described in slightly different terms in each of two places in Mark's writings in the *Philokalia*. Given the apparent influence of these texts on later writers, some further detail here is warranted.

In *On the Spiritual Law*,[94] Mark describes provocation as "an image-free stimulation in the heart". This he distinguishes carefully from thoughts accompanied by images as a result of the giving of mental assent to them. This process is morally culpable. Elsewhere, in *Righteous by Works*,[95] he makes clear that provocation is initiated by the devil but that the giving of assent to provocations is facilitated by a human process of indulgence which he describes here as entertainment. The process is apparently thus: i) provocation of thoughts (initiated by the devil), ii) pleasurable entertainment of these thoughts (by a self-indulgent human mind), and iii) assent. However, there is some ambiguity. Why does Mark accord significance to the

Table 2.4a: Processes leading to passion, according to Mark the Ascetic (early 5th c.)

| Provocation | Momentary disturbance of the intellect | Entertainment | Assent | Prepossession | Passion |
|---|---|---|---|---|---|
| "A provocation is an image-free stimulation in the heart. Like a mountain-pass, the experienced take control of it ahead of the enemy." OTSL, #140 (EGP 1, 119) | "the mere thought of lust . . . without any movement and working of bodily passion" LTN (EGP 1, 153) | "the man, urged on by self-indulgence and self-esteem, begins to entertain this provocation with enjoyment" RBW, #224 (EGP 1, 145) | "Once our thoughts are accompanied by images we have already given them our assent; for a provocation does not involve us in guilt so long as it is not accompanied by images. OTSL, #141 (EGP 1, 119- 120) (See also #182 [EGP 1, 122])  "he takes pleasure in [the provocation] and accepts it" RBW, #224 (EGP 1, 145) | "Prepossession is the involuntary presence of former sins in the memory. At the stage of active warfare we try to prevent it from developing into a passion; after victory it is repulsed while still but a provocation." OTSL, #139 (EGP 1, 119) (See also #183 [EGP 1, 122]) | "When we have freed ourselves from every voluntary sin of the mind, we should then fight against the passions which result from prepossession." OTSL, #138 (EGP 1, 119 |
| "The devil initiates the whole process by testing a man with a provocation which he is not compelled to accept" RBW #224 (EGP 1, 145) | | | | "Those who are under the sway of passions must pray and be obedient. For even when they receive help, they can only just manage to fight against their prepossessions." RBW, #160 (EGP 1, 139)  "If you hate rebuke, it shows that the passion in which you are involved is due to your own free choice. But if you welcome rebuke, the passion is due to prepossession." OTSL, #151 (EGP 1, 120) | |

"When the intellect through rejection of the passions attains to unwavering hope, then the enemy makes it visualize its past sins on the pretext of confessing them to God. Thus he tries to rekindle passions which by God's grace have been forgotten, and so secretly to inflict injury. Then, even though someone is illumined and hates the passions, he will inevitably be filled with darkness and confusion at the memory of what he has done. But if he is still befogged and self-indulgent, he will certainly dally with the enemy's provocations and entertain them under the influence of passion, so that this recollection will prove to be a prepossession and not a confession." RBW, #152 (EGP 1, 138) linking of thoughts with images in *On the Spiritual Law*, whereas in *Righteous by Works*, it is the pleasurable entertainment and then acceptance of thoughts that distinguishes provocation from a morally culpable state of assent?

Elsewhere, Mark describes other mental phenomena and processes, suggesting that things might work differently at different times and/or in different people. Thus, in the passage immediately preceding the one just described in *On the Spiritual Law*, he refers to "the passions" as being the result of "prepossession".[96] The passions are not here defined, but prepossession is defined as "the involuntary presence of former sins in the memory". It is also made clear here that a provocation can develop into prepossession. The more experienced monk will repulse a provocation before it develops into a prepossession. The monk who is still engaged in the stage of "active warfare" however will be concerned principally with preventing a prepossession from developing into a passion. The sequence for the novice is thus provocation, prepossession, passion. For the more advanced monk, however, the provocation may be promptly repelled at source.

It is implicit, although not entirely clear, that Mark intends us to understand an overall sequence, of provocation, entertainment, assent, prepossession, passion. This certainly seems to be what the English translators of the *Philokalia* think, as their glossary describes a sequence of this sort, apparently based largely or entirely on the pattern outlined by Mark (see Table 2.4g, page 89).[97] Here, they emphasise the transition from entertainment to assent as being distinguished by resolution to act or, in other words, the intention of the heart. The transition from assent to prepossession, according to their understanding, is made as a result of "repeated acts of sin". As a result, "force of habit" makes it more difficult to resist temptation. Neither of these distinctions is necessarily completely clear in the text of the passages from Mark that have just been considered.[98] However, they would certainly appear to be reasonable interpretations of them.

It is implicit, both in the Markan texts and in the Glossary to the English translation, that the actual committing of sin represents a step in the sequence intermediate between assent and prepossession. However, for both, it is the giving of assent, and thus not the act of sin itself, that is morally culpable. In fact, in this context, it is clear that the commission of sin actually occurs within the mind; assent is, in effect, a sinful act (even if only an "act" of thought).

It is not entirely clear, either in the Markan texts or in the English Glossary, what distinguishes a prepossession from a passion. The emphasis in both places is upon the struggle to prevent a prepossession from becoming a passion. However, it would appear clear that they are not the same thing – even if only differing in degree – and that, according to Mark, passions do not only arise as a result of prepossession. Thus, in *On the Spiritual Law*, he distinguishes between passions resulting from free choice and those due to prepossession, on the basis of whether or not rebuke is welcomed (which it is in the latter case, but not the former).

Before moving on to the processes described by other authors in the *Philokalia*, we must consider just one more complication in the Markan account. This concerns the phenomenon of "momentary disturbance of the intellect" (παραρριπισμός). This is referred to by Mark in only one place in the *Philokalia*, in his *Letter to Nicolas*,[99] where he encourages his reader "to put to death every trace and stirring of passion itself". In this context, a momentary disturbance of the intellect is a simple thought of lust, occurring without any "movement or working of bodily passion". As the English translators aptly comment,[100] this cannot be the same thing as a provocation, since Mark clearly expects that freedom from such momentary disturbances is possible, whereas provocations must be experienced even by the most advanced monk. It must, therefore, be something more than simply provocation, but presumably rather less than entertainment?

Whatever the remaining ambiguities of the process(es) described by Mark the Ascetic, they clearly provide a perceptive and helpful theological and psychological account of the mental phenomena of temptation and passion. The value of this approach was obviously recognised by other authors, amongst whom, we may assume, was John Climacus ("John of the Ladder"; *c.*579 – *c.*649), abbot of the monastery of the Burning Bush (later St Catherine's) on Mount Sinai, and the author of *The Ladder of Divine Ascent*.

*The Ladder* was one of the most influential works of early Christian spirituality, being widely translated and disseminated. Although not included in the Greek *Philokalia*, extracts were included in the *Dobrotolubiye*, and the full text was included in the Romanian *Filocalia*. Addressing the contemplative and "active" aspects of Christian life, *The Ladder* offers thirty steps which lead from renunciation of the world, through the practice of the virtues and the struggle with the passions, to union with God.[101] In Step 15, which deals with chastity, or the struggle against the passion of lust, John quotes the "discerning Fathers" as authority and source for his account of distinctions between "provocation, coupling, assent, captivity, struggle, and ... passion".[102] Whilst he does not explicitly refer to Mark the Ascetic, the terminology and descriptions bear a remarkable similarity to Mark's account.[103]

John's account is somewhat more detailed and logically ordered than that of Mark, and is also less ambiguous (see Table 2.4b, pages 78-80). What Mark refers to as entertainment, John refers to as "coupling", which is defined as "conversation" with the word or image encountered in the provocation. John does not make distinctions here based upon the linking of thoughts with images,[104] but rather assent is a "delighted yielding of the soul to what it has encountered". John does not refer to prepossession at all, but between assent and passion he introduces "captivity" and "struggle". The former refers to "forcible and unwilling abduction of the heart" and the latter to the counter-attacking force, which may win or lose the battle "according to the desires of the spirit". Finally, passion is here described as "something that lies hidden for a long time in the soul and by its very presence it takes on the character of a habit, until the soul of its own accord clings to it with affection".

John also identifies a phenomenon of disturbance (παραρριπισμός), which appears to be more or less similar to Mark's category of the same name, but which again carries a slightly more detailed description. This description includes more of an emphasis on the speed of the disturbance than is found in the Markan account, it also includes reference to its appearance "by a simple memory" (such that it appears to overlap somewhat with the Markan category of prepossession), and finally it describes a movement directly from sense perception to commission of a sin of unchastity without intervening thought.

The causal sequence of the process is made fairly explicit by John. Provocation is a word or image encountered, coupling is conversation with what has been encountered, assent is yielding of the soul to what has been encountered, and so on. However, he does remain open to the possibility that passions may generate thoughts, as well as thoughts generating passions.[105]

John's more detailed account of these processes seems to have influenced at least some subsequent authors of the *Philokalia*. In particular, Philotheos of Sinai (?ninth/tenth century) and Peter of

Table 2.4b: Processes leading to passion, according to John Climacus, and authors in the *Philokalia* who follow a similar pattern

| | Provocation | Disturbance of the mind | → Coupling | → Assent | → Captivity | → Struggle | → Passion |
|---|---|---|---|---|---|---|---|
| John Climacus b. 579 d. c.649<br><br>*Ladder of Divine Ascent*, Step 15 (Luibheid et al., 1982, pp.182-183) | "simple word or image encountered for the first time, which has entered into the heart" | "In a moment, without a word being spoken or an image presented, a sudden passionate urge lays hold of the victim." | "conversation with what has been encountered, whether this be passionately or otherwise" | "delighted yielding of the soul to what it has encountered" | "Forcible and unwilling abduction of the heart, a permanent lingering with what we have encountered and which totally undermines the necessary order of our souls" | "force equal to that which is leading the attack…this force wins or loses according to the desires of the spirit" | "something that lies hidden for a long time in the soul and by its very presence it takes on the character of a habit, until the soul of its own accord clings to it with affection" |
| | "free of sin" | | "sometimes" free of sin | The "condition of soul" determines whether or not it is sinful | Judged differently depending upon prayer, importance or context of evil thoughts | "can earn a crown or punishment" | "unequivocally denounced in every situation and requires suitable penitence or future punishment" |

| | Provocation → | Coupling → | | Assent → | Captivity → | Struggle | Passion |
|---|---|---|---|---|---|---|---|
| Philotheos of Sinai ?9th/10th c. *Forty Texts on Watchfulness*, ##34-36 (EGP 3, 29) | "a thought still free from passion, or an image newly engendered in the heart and glimpsed by the intellect" | "to commune with this thought or image, in either an impassioned or a dispassionate way" | | "pleasurable acceptance of the soul of the thing seen" | "the forcible and enforced abduction of the heart, or persistent intercourse with the object, disrupting even our best state" | | "that which lurks impassionably in the soul over a long period" |
| | "sinless" | "not altogether free from sin" | | "sinfulness... depends upon our inner state" | "one thing at the time of prayer, another when we are not engaged in prayer" | "the struggle itself brings us either punishment or crowns of victory" | "incontestably leads either to a corresponding repentance or to future chastisement" |

| | Provocation → | Coupling → | Wrestling → | Assent → | Seduction or Captivity | Passion |
|---|---|---|---|---|---|---|
| Peter of Damaskos 11th/12th c. Book I (EGP 3, 207) | "conceptions of either good or evil" | "to entertain a particular thought and parley with it" | "our intellect wrestles with the thought, and either conquers it or is conquered by it" | "a pleasurable inclination of the soul towards what it sees" | "the heart is induced forcibly and unwillingly to put the thought into effect" | "When the soul dallies for a long time with an impassioned thought there arises what we call a passion. This in turn … becomes a settled disposition… compelling the soul … towards the corresponding action" |
| | | "this leads us either to give assent to it or to reject it" | "brings the intellect either credit or punishment when the thought is put into action" | | | |
| | | "Our reaction to the thought, if in accordance with God's will, is praiseworthy, though not highly so; but if it accords with evil, then it deserves censure." | | | | |
| | "neither commendable nor reprehensible" | | | | | "must either repent proportionately or else undergo punishment in the age to come" |

→ The arrows in this table represent the causal relationships between terms and the directionality of the processes described.

Damaskos (eleventh/twelfth century) produce very similar accounts (see Table 2.4b), albeit the latter inexplicably moves the category of struggle from its place between captivity and passion, back to a new location between coupling and assent.[106] Peter also explicitly acknowledges John Climacus as his source.[107]

Returning for a moment to the seventh century, Maximos the Confessor (580-662), a contemporary of John Climacus, describes in his texts *On Love* a similar but different account of the process of the passions (see Table 2.4c, page 82). This account is based initially, in the first century of texts, on a quotation from Colossians 3:5:

> Put to death therefore whatever is earthly in you: unchastity, uncleanness, passion, evil desire and greed.[108]

Maximos interprets Paul's references to "earth" as "the will of the flesh", "unchastity" as "the actual committing of sin", "uncleanness" as "assent to sin", "passion" as "impassioned thoughts", "evil desire" as "the simple act of accepting the thought and the desire", and "greed" as "what generates and promotes passion". From this interpretation he derives a sequence of memory, passion free thought, lingering of the thought, arousal of passion, failure to eradicate passion, assent, and the committing of sin.[109]

In the second century of texts *On Love*, Maximos describes the process slightly differently.[110] Here, the sequence is that of demonic activity, which acts upon the "passions lying hidden in the soul", which in turn generates impassioned thoughts, to which assent is given, leading to sin in the mind, and then sin in action.

The processes described by Maximos in the first and second centuries of *On Love* differ in various minor ways, notably that one begins with memory, and the other with demonic activity. However, they are clearly not completely different, and a composite model is proposed in Table 2.4c. Neither are these processes completely different than those proposed by Mark the Ascetic and, after him, John Climacus. Both begin with a provocation (although Maximos does not call it this), both involve a stage of lingering with or entertaining thoughts, both recognise the giving of assent to these thoughts as crucial to moral responsibility, and both allow a place for the committing of sin in the mind as prelude to the committing of sin in action. What is perhaps most different, apart from the largely differing terminology, is that passion appears to be the outcome of the process described by Mark and John, whereas it makes an appearance

**Table 2.4c: Processes leading to passion, according to Maximos the Confessor (580–662)**

| Source | Process/Terminology | | | | | |
|---|---|---|---|---|---|---|
| *On Love: C1*, #83 (EGP 2, 62) (Col 3:5)[iii] | "what generates and promotes passion" (St Paul: greed) | "act of accepting the thought and the desire" (St Paul: evil desire) | Impassioned thoughts (St Paul: passion) | | Assent to sin (St Paul: uncleanness) | Committing of sin (St Paul: unchastity) |
| *On Love: C1*, #84 (EGP 2, 62-63) | Memory → | Passion free thought → | Lingering in intellect → | Passion aroused → | Intellect assents | Sin |
| | | | | Passion not eradicated → | | |
| *On Love: C2*, #31 (EGP 2, 70) | Demons → | | "passions lying hidden in the soul" → | Arouse impassioned thoughts → | Assent to sin → | Sin in the mind ↓ Sin in action |
| Proposed Composite | Memory/ Demons → | Thought → | Passion(s) → | Impassioned thoughts → | Assent to sin → | Sin in the mind ↓ Sin in action |

→ The arrows in this table represent the causal relationships between terms and the directionality of the processes described.

## Chapter 2: The Passions

much earlier on in the process described by Maximos. In particular, in the second of the two Maximian accounts described here, it is the "passions lying hidden in the soul" upon which the demons initially act, and it is these passions which allow the possibility of the arousal of "impassioned thoughts".[112]

It would perhaps be making too great an assumption to conclude either that the processes described by Mark the Ascetic and John Climacus on the one hand, and Maximos on the other, are completely separate traditions or that they must have common historical origins. However, other authors of the *Philokalia* would appear to have drawn on either or both of them, or to have developed new descriptions of similar processes.

Thus, we find that the (?seventh century) text attributed to John of Damaskos uses similar terminology to Mark and John, but with addition of a new term of "actualisation" (for the putting of impassioned thoughts into effect), and removal of "passion" to an earlier stage in the process, more akin to the approach of Maximos (see Table 2.4d, page 84).[113]

Hesychios the Priest (?eighth or ninth century) retains the terminology of provocation, coupling and assent, but almost completely without reference to the passions.[114] Here the mental process described is one of temptation to sin, rather than drawing on the terminology of the passions (see Table 2.4e, page 85-86).

Theodoros the Great Ascetic (?ninth century) describes a sequence of "forbidden desire", assent, passion, and sin.[115] Symeon Metaphrastis (late tenth/early eleventh century) describes perhaps the simplest process of all, but without any terminology, in which simple self examination, and an inward bias of love towards God or the world, determine outward action.[116] Finally, Ilias the Presbyter (late eleventh/early twelfth century) describes a sequence of imaging evil, desiring evil, feeling pleasure or pain in respect of evil, becoming conscious of evil, and then inwardly or outwardly uniting with evil.[117] (See Table 2.4e for a summary of these processes.)

Table 2.4f (page 88) summarises an altogether more complicated series of processes described by Gregory of Sinai (c.1245-1346) in *On Commandments and Doctrines*.[118] It is clear that Gregory intends us to realise that the processes are complex and can move in different directions. For example, the prompting of demons gives rise to passion, but passion can also give entry to demons. At risk of over-simplifying things, it would seem that the basic sequence

**Table 2.4d: Processes leading to and following from passion, attributed to John of Damaskos (?7th c.)** *On Virtues & Vices* (EGP, 2, 337-8)

| Provocation → | Coupling → | Passion → | Wrestling → | Assent → | Actualisation → | Captivity |
|---|---|---|---|---|---|---|
| "a suggestion coming from the enemy" (Mat 4:3) | "acceptance of the thought suggested by the enemy. It means dwelling on the thought and choosing deliberately to dally with it in a pleasurable manner" | "letting the imagination brood on the impassioned thought continually" (Gal 5:17) | "resistance offered to the impassioned thought" (→ destruction of impassioned thought or assent) | "giving approval to the passion inherent in the thought" | "putting the impassioned thought into effect" | "forcible and compulsive abduction of the heart already dominated by prepossession and long habit" |

→   The arrows in this table represent the causal relationships between terms and the directionality of the processes described.

Table 2.4e: Processes leading to and following from passion, according to Hesychios the Priest, Theodoros the Great Ascetic, Symeon Metaphrastis, and Ilias the Presbyter

| | | Provocation → | Coupling → | Assent → | Concrete action |
|---|---|---|---|---|---|
| Hesychios the priest (?8th or 9th c.) *Watchfulness & Holiness* | #46 (EGP 1, 170) | | "the mingling of our thoughts with those of the wicked demons" | "both sets of intermingling thoughts contriving how to commit the sin in practice" | "the sin itself" |
| | ##143-144 (EGP 1, 186-7) | Provocation may take the form of a "mental image of a sensory object" | "impassioned fantasy"? - potential to consort with, conform to, become intimate with, be distracted by, or give assent to | "our thoughts…give assent to it" | "evil actions" |
| | | Forbidden desire→ | Assent→ | Passion→ | Sin |
| Theodoros the Great Ascetic (?9th c.) *Spiritual Texts* | #19 (EGP 2, 17-18) | "first the thought begins to darken the intellect through the passible aspect of the soul" | "submission to self-indulgence…. the soul submits to the pleasure, not holding out in the fight. This is what is called assent, which…is a sin." | "When assent persists it stimulates the passion in question" | "Then little by little it leads to the actual committing of the sin." |

| | | | | | |
|---|---|---|---|---|---|
| Symeon Metaphrastis (late 10th/ early 11th c.)<br><br>*Paraphrase of Makarios* | #55 (EGP 3, 308–9) | A man examines himself and finds doubt & hesitancy about what to do → | "the measure and balance in his conscience make it clear inwardly whether the bias inclines to love for God or love for the world" → | Outward action | |
| Ilias the Presbyter (late 11th/ early 12th c.)<br><br>*Gnomic Anthology: 4* | #123 (EGP 3, 63) | "First the soul imagines evil" → | "then desires it" → | "then feels pleasure or pain with respect to it" → | "then becomes fully conscious of it" → | "and finally unites with it either outwardly or inwardly" |

→  The arrows in this table represent the causal relationships between terms and the directionality of the processes described.

here is of distractive thoughts giving rise to fantasies, which in turn gives rise to the passions. But passions can then give rise to further distractive thoughts (apparently with or without the involvement of demons) and so the whole cycle can repeat itself.

Table 2.5 (pages 90-91) provides an overall summary of the above processes. It will be seen that "assent" provides the almost universal reference point in the processes summarised here; only Symeon Metaphrastis and Ilias the Presbyter avoid this term completely. The triad of provocation, coupling (or entertainment) and assent is employed by five out of the nine authors of the *Philokalia* included in the table. Passion, where it appears, usually appears towards the end of the sequence described by each author, but Maximos the Confessor, and the text attributed to John of Damaskos, find a place for the passions somewhat earlier in their processes.

What does this review of passion as process in the *Philokalia* reveal?

Firstly, and most importantly, it is clear that the passions are viewed as important by the authors of the *Philokalia*[119] not for abstract theological reasons, but because they represent a key aspect of the phenomenology of temptation and sin. This is not to say that the concept of the passions does not draw both on classical philosophy and also Christian theology, but it is above all a concept which arises out of the lived experience of a tradition of spirituality which dates back to the Egyptian desert, or at least to the writings of Mark the Ascetic. It draws on a collective wisdom which is based, it would seem, upon self-reflection and subjective experience. Passion is a key part of the understanding, within this tradition, of how thoughts lead to sins. It is true that there are various starting and ending points in the processes described. In some places passion appears as a root cause, and in others as a final state of captivity. However, it is passion which removes temptation, virtue and prayer from a merely rational arena into the realm of feelings, emotions and desires which exert a power over human beings to draw them in a direction which they might otherwise not choose to take. It is this which makes the life of virtue and prayer so challenging.

Secondly, although the passions are to be viewed in the context of the inner world, as primarily subjective experiences of what it is to be human in the presence of the realities of evil and sin, they are also relational phenomena. Quite apart from reference to demonic provocation of the processes which culminate in the passions, these

**Table 2.4f: Processes leading to passion, according to Gregory of Sinai (c.1265-1346)**
*On Commandments & Doctrines, ##62-75 (EGP 4, 223-225)*

| Text | Processes/terms | | | | | | | | | | |
|---|---|---|---|---|---|---|---|---|---|---|---|
| #62 | Sinful acts → | Passions → | | | | | | | | | |
| #62 | "mindless desire for evil and a strong attachment to the senses and to sensory things" → | Sinful acts → | | | Misdirected directions → | Lustful appetites → | Laziness → | Ignorance → | Forgetfulness → | Fragmentation of the memory → | Multiplicity of ideas |
| #67 | Promptings of demons → | Distractive thoughts (= precursors of passions) → | | Passions → | | | | | | | |
| #67 | Promptings of demons → | Mental images → | | Particular actions | | | | | | | |
| #70 | Occasions (material, demonic, natural and supernatural; see #69) → | Distractive thoughts → | Fantasies → | Assent (to passion) → | Passions → | Entry to demons | | | | | |
| #71 | Demons → | Image (corresponding to passion) → | Distractive thoughts → | Fantasies → | Passions → | Demons | | | | | |
| #74 | Distractive thoughts → | Passions → | | Demons | | | | | | | |
| #74 | Passions → | | | | | | | | | | |
| #75 | Bias of the Will (tested by demonic provocation) → | Perversion of character → | Misuse of things → | | | | | | | | |

**Key:**

→ The arrows in this table represent the causal relationships between terms, and the directionality of the processes, described by Gregory.

Distractive thoughts | Fantasies/Images | Passions | Demons

Table 2.4g: Processes leading to passion, according to the Glossary of the EGP (Palmer, Sherrard & Ware, 1979)

| Terminology | (i) Provocation | (ii) Momentary disturbance | (iii) Communion or coupling | (iv) Assent | (v) Prepossession | (vi) Passion |
|---|---|---|---|---|---|---|
| Definition/ Description | "initial incitement to evil" | "more than the 'first appearance' of a provocation described in stage (i) above; for, at a certain point of spiritual growth in this life, it is possible to be totally released from such 'momentary disturbance', whereas no one can expect to be altogether free from demonic provocations" | "Without as yet entirely assenting to the demonic provocation, a man may begin to 'entertain' it, to converse or parley with it, turning it over in his mind pleasurably, yet still hesitating whether or not to act on it" "The provocation is no longer 'image-free' but has become a logismos or thought" | "a person now resolves to act upon [the evil suggestion]" | "results from repeated acts of sin which predispose a man to yield to particular temptations. In principle he retains his free choice and can reject demonic provocations; but in practice the force of habit makes it more and more difficult for him to resist." | "If a man does not fight strenuously against a pre-possession, it will develop into an evil passion" |
| Attribution of moral responsibility | "so long as the provocation is not accompanied by images, it does not involve man in any guilt. Such provocations, originating as they do from the devil, assail man from the outside independently of his free will, and so he is not morally responsible for them." | | "a person is morally responsible for having allowed this to happen" (i.e. the provocation to become a logismos) | "There is now no doubt as to his moral culpability: even if circumstances prevent him from sinning outwardly, he is judged by God according to the intention in his heart." | | |

Table 2.5: Summary of processes of passion/temptation in the *Philokalia* and in the *Ladder of Divine Ascent*

| Author | Date | Process/Terms | | | | | | |
|---|---|---|---|---|---|---|---|---|
| Mark the Ascetic | Early 5th c. | Provocation | Momentary disturbance | Entertainment | Assent | Prepossession | Passion | |
| John Climacus[121] | c.579–c.649 | Provocation | Disturbance of the mind | → Coupling | → Assent | → Captivity | → Struggle | → Passion |
| Maximos the Confessor[120] | 580-662 | Memory/ Demons → | Thought → | Passions → | Impassioned thoughts → | Assent to sin → | Sin in the mind → | Sin in action |
| [John of Damaskos] | ?7th c. | Provocation→ | Coupling→ | Passion→ | Wrestling→ | Assent→ | Actual-isation→ | Captivity |
| Hesychios the priest | ?8th or 9th c. | Provocation → | Coupling → | Assent → | Concrete action | | | |
| Theodoros the Great Ascetic | ?9th c. | Forbidden desire→ | Assent→ | Passion→ | Sin | | | |
| Philotheos of Sinai | ?9th /10th c. | Provocation→ | Coupling→ | Assent→ | Captivity→ | Passion | | |
| Symeon Metaphrastis | Late 10th/ early 11th c. | Self-examina-tion → | Doubt & hesitancy → | Inclination towards God/world | | | | |
| Peter of Damaskos | 11th /12th c. | Provocation→ | Coupling→ | Wrestling→ | Assent→ | Seduction or Captivity→ | Passion | |

| Author | Date | Process/Terms | | | | | |
|---|---|---|---|---|---|---|---|
| Ilias the Presbyter | Late 11th/ early 12th c. | Imagination → | Desire → | Pleasure or pain → | Conscious awareness ↑ | Outward/inward uniting | |
| Gregory of Sinai | c.1265-1346 | Distractive thoughts → | Fantasies → | Passions → | Demons ↑ | Distractive thoughts → | Etc. → |
| Philokalia Glossary | 1979 | (i) Provocation | (ii) Momentary disturbance | (iii) Communion or coupling | (iv) Assent | (v) Prepossession | (vi) Passion |

→  The arrows in this table represent the causal relationships between terms and the directionality of the processes described.

processes display concern with relationship with the self, with others and with God. They recognise an implicit division within the self which presents choices – for good or evil. We may be drawn powerfully in one direction or another, and we can choose to be self-indulgent or we can choose to deny ourselves. They recognise also an implicit division from others, and a tendency to misuse that which we perceive with our senses – a tendency which will, by default and but for the grace of God, be biased always towards self-indulgence and pleasure rather than the good of others or the proper use of created things. They recognise, more explicitly, a division of ourselves from God. And it is union with God in prayer that is the goal offered by both the *Philokalia* and the *Ladder of Divine Ascent*.

Thirdly, however, a recognition that the passions are a process, or at least a part of a process, guards against naïve optimism that they are a thing of the past, or that they need no longer be taken seriously. As was noted in the last section, the passions are dynamic and active phenomena that may appear to come and go, to become quiescent or to re-emerge. This being the case, complacency is dangerous, even for the more experienced, let alone for the spiritual novice. Given the right provocation, or momentary disturbance, for all except the most advanced in the spiritual life, there will always be the danger of re-emergence of the passions.

### v. Physiology and Pathology

It has been noted that, amongst diverse metaphors employed for the passions, the *Philokalia* includes a reference to medical terms. There is a degree of diversity within this realm of medical reference, with the passions being referred to as maladies, paralysis, plague, sickness and wounds, amongst other things (see Table 2.3, pages 68-71). Whilst, on the one hand, this appears to be just one of a number of (largely metaphorical) themes identifiable within the vocabulary employed (as discussed above) it does seem to play an important role in acknowledging that the passions comprise pathological processes with physical, as well as spiritual and psychological, aspects. To this extent, it is rather more than metaphorical. Normally in the *Philokalia* the emphasis is upon the spiritual and psychological dimensions of the process, as described in the last section, but where the physical is mentioned, it is seen to be in a dynamic interaction with the spiritual and psychological.

The vocabulary of the *Philokalia* betrays a humoural understanding of the physical nature of human beings. Humoural theories are found in the writings of Plato and the Hippocratic corpus.[122] Although there is some variation amongst humoural theories, the Hippocratic account given in *The Nature of Man*, refers to four substances or humours: blood, phlegm, yellow bile and black bile. Health depends upon the balance of these humours in strength and quantity. These humours differ in terms of two binary pairs of qualities: hot and cold, moist and dry. These four qualities are also referred to, at least in this work, as "elements". Understanding of causation and treatment of disease, according to this system, thus depends upon imbalance and restoration of balance, respectively. Medical theories based upon such understandings remained popular for many centuries and were transmitted to the Arabic world, and later to Latin America. Although they were disproved by modern scientific medicine, they continue to form the basis for much folk medicine in various parts of the world.[123]

Specific humours are referred to only very infrequently in the *Philokalia*. However, for Mark the Ascetic, sensual desire needs to be cooled and dried and therefore, presumably, represents excess heat and moisture. Overeating and the drinking of wine are understood by him to cause heating of the blood.[124] Bile is understood by Hesychios the Priest to be associated with the incensive power of the soul,[125] whereas for Gregory of Sinai this power is associated with overheating of the blood.[126] Philotheos of Sinai refers to the "will of the flesh" as a compound of blood and phlegm,[127] Ilias the Presbyter refers to reduction in hot-bloodedness and drying up of the sexual organs in the elderly,[128] and Nikitas Stithatos refers to the creation of human beings with "gastric fluid" (presumably bile) that is dry and cold like the earth, blood that is warm and moist like air and fire, and phlegm that is moist and cold like water.[129]

In a rather more complex reference,[130] Maximos the Confessor refers to desire as producing a "diffusion" of blood around the heart and the incensive power as causing the blood to boil. His concern here appears to be to show that the intelligence should "stand alone", or that it should be in command of the whole human being. Where this does not happen, physical influences, such as the imbalances of diffused or boiling blood, appear to work to reinforce the enslavement of the intelligence to the passions. Where it does happen, such physical imbalances are eliminated. This text may also reflect an awareness on the part of Maximos of a Platonic anatomy which associated the rational part of the soul with the brain, the incensive part with the heart, and the desiring part with the liver.[131] However, anatomical associations of this sort appear to be quite rare in the *Philokalia*.[132]

General references to the body's humours, and to temperament as the balance or blend of the body's humours,[133] are somewhat more commonly found. In these references, the humours are seen both as a cause of the passions, but also as a point at which demons may exert an effect upon human beings so as to cause passion. Thus, Evagrios refers to thoughts from which the intellect should withdraw, out of its longing for God, as having their source in sense perception, memory, or soul-body temperament.[134] However, having initially left the impression that these are purely natural phenomena that may distract from prayer, he goes on to suggest that Satan may in some way disturb the temperament of the body as a means of producing such thoughts.[135] Similarly, Diadochos of Photiki talks of Satan using the body's humours to "befog the intellect with the delight of mindless pleasures",[136] and of his exploitation of them so as to "seduce" the soul.[137]

Maximos the Confessor refers to "angels, demons, the winds and diet", as well as "memory, hearing and sight – namely when the soul is affected by joyful or distressing experiences", as being potential causes of change in the body's temperament, each of which may in turn thus lead to either impassioned or dispassionate thoughts.[138] Thalassios the Libyan similarly recognises both natural (diet and weather) and demonic influences as potential causes of disturbance in temperament.[139]

Gregory of Sinai sees "senseless anger and mindless desire" as arising from the body's humours, in contrast to the intrinsic incensive and desiring powers of the soul, which give rise to courage and divine love respectively.[140] By way of explanation of this rather dualistic understanding, Gregory argues that the body was created without humours. Exactly where the humours came from in Gregory's thought is unclear (at least insofar as the texts included in the *Philokalia* are concerned). However, in the Gregorian scheme of things, the humours are associated with corruptibility and materiality, and these were qualities which appeared at the time of the fall, thus rendering human beings more like (non-human) animals. Conversely, at the resurrection of the body, the destiny of human beings is to be free

Chapter 2: The Passions

of humours once again. For Gregory, this "almost bodiless" state is achievable for the dispassionate person even in this life.[141]

The *Philokalia* should, therefore, not be seen as painting a purely psychological and spiritual portrait of the passions. The passions are, rather, seen as being in dynamic interaction with the human organism, both caused or mediated by, and causing, physical changes in the body.

### vi. Affirmation of the Passions

The affirmative whisper, for which the reader was encouraged to listen carefully at the beginning of this section, has been very quiet indeed. Did we miss it amidst the noise of the more vocal negative views of the passions as pathology of the soul or as hostile demonic forces?

It was noted, when discussing the language and vocabulary of the passions, that they are sometimes understood as natural rather than unnatural. In places, this is merely because it is recognised that the "natural" order of the world is fallen and only redeemed by grace.[142] Sometimes there is a recognition that they are natural in a non-reprehensible sense, recognising their place in a created, God-given, order of things. However, this more affirmative voice is often qualified. Thus, for example, Maximos affirms that:

> Appetites and pleasures which are in accordance with nature are not reprehensible, since they are a necessary consequence of natural appetency. For our ordinary food, whether we wish it or not, naturally produces pleasure, since it satisfies the hunger which precedes a meal. Drink also produces pleasure, since it relieves the discomfort of thirst; so does sleep, since it renews the strength expended in our waking hours; and so, too, do all our other natural functions necessary for maintaining life and conducive to the acquisition of virtue.[143]

However, he immediately continues:

> But every intellect that is trying to escape from the confusion of sin transcends such passions, lest through them it remains a slave to passions which are subject to our control, contrary to nature and reprehensible; for

these have no ground in us other than the activity of the passions which are in accordance with nature, although not on that account destined to accompany us into immortal and everlasting life.[144]

The affirmative whisper is thus drowned out.[145]

Gregory Palamas offers a more developmental view, suggesting that passions in children are natural and "sustaining of nature", but that they arise later in the "passion-charged intellect". However, he also goes on to emphasise the need to deal radically with the passions lest they rage like an uncontrolled fire.[146]

One of the most positive notes that sounds from the pages of the *Philokalia* in support of the passions is the opening text of *Guarding the Intellect*, by Isaiah the Solitary. Ironically this is now the opening text in the first volume of the English translation (the text attributed to Antony having been relegated to an Appendix):

> There is among the passions an anger of the intellect, and this anger is in accordance with nature. Without anger a man cannot attain purity: he has to feel angry with all that is sown in him by the enemy.[147]

Sometimes, passions are themselves the remedies for the passions, a matter to which we shall return in the next chapter.

## vii. Conclusions

The understanding of the passions that is conveyed in the *Philokalia* is one of a pathology of the soul which distorts our relationships with God and the created order. The passions are a varied group of phenomena, including emotions, desires, thoughts, attitudes and behaviours. They transcend contemporary notions of affect or appetite, but they all involve processes of thought which are in some way "weighted" or biased towards self-indulgence, and thus away from God. In this sense, they are not "natural", they are not according to Divine purpose.

A predominant image of the passions in the *Philokalia* is one of an assailing and enslaving enemy, but the wealth and diversity of language employed should warn against simplistic understanding, and against any underestimation of the seriousness of the threat that the passions present to the person whose goal in life is one of pure prayer or union with God. The language of personification,

## Chapter 2: The Passions

metaphor and demonic activity should not lead towards a projection of the passions into a purely spiritual dimension of life, or to a denial of personal responsibility, for the passions are clearly identified as "inner" as well as "outer", as being intimately related to the material order of things and not simply "spiritual".

The understanding of the passions conveyed by the *Philokalia* is especially a dynamic one, which is concerned with processes of temptation to evil, human responsibility, and experience of the inner world of thought, desire and choice.

The *Philokalia* appears to draw upon Stoic, Platonic, and Aristotelian traditions of the passions, but is also influenced by the Desert Fathers, and especially Evagrios. In particular, it recognises that the passions are concerned with the inner world of thoughts, affect and desire, with important implications for personal moral responsibility and judgement. It recognises that the passions behave both as hostile external agencies, but also as an inner pathology of the human body and soul. They are both natural and unnatural, to be affirmed and (much more frequently) denied. However, the *Philokalia* has expanded considerably upon the vocabulary and understanding of the sources from which it has drawn.

The *Philokalia* is not always consistent in its understanding of the passions, but this is hardly surprising for an anthology of forty or so authors, writing over a period of more than a millennium. Neither is it necessarily the purpose of either the authors or compilers of the *Philokalia* to produce an entirely consistent account or terminology. Rather these texts are presented for meditation, reflection and prayer. Thus, the passions may be both the outcome and origin of inner mental processes, depending upon the purpose or terminology of any particular writer. Rather, the shared concern of these authors is with human reflection upon how the passions do operate against the pursuit of virtue and the life of prayer – both as the origin of thoughts which lead away from both of these objectives, and also as the result of processes of thought which result from perception, memory, and demonic provocation.

### 5. The Passions – Conclusions

Taking together the composite picture of the passions that emerges from the classical tradition, the Desert Fathers, Evagrios and the *Philokalia*, what overall conclusions may be offered here? It is clear that there are some inconsistencies, variations of understanding, and lack of clarity, but some over-riding themes do emerge.

Firstly, the passions represent a rich and complex understanding of the inner life of human beings which goes a long way towards providing a robust psychological framework for understanding the struggle for virtue. The passions provide a phenomenology of the inner life which incorporates perception, affect, cognition and appetite in support of explaining why people fail to adhere to the virtues that they espouse and make judgements which do not withstand the light of reason.

Following on from this, it is clear that the passions provide fertile theological ground for exploring the process of temptation. Although at times the role of the demons is ambiguous and open to possibly unhelpful literalist interpretation, or else a demythologisation which leads only to dismissal, the concept as developed by the Desert Fathers, Evagrios and the other authors of the *Philokalia* maintains the tension necessary to recognise both external influence and inner motivation; both the way in which human beings are acted upon, and also the way in which they must accept personal responsibility. The passions are both an aspect of the human soul, but also something external which influences from without. They are thus the focus of an inner struggle against an enemy that threatens to destroy and enslave.

The passions are, however, not merely hostile. They are rather "hostile pleasures". In a dynamic process, which invites comparison with the phenomenon of addiction, they both confer pleasure and pain, they attract and enslave, they seduce and destroy.

Secondly, the passions provide a framework for explorations of spirituality and prayer. If the pleasures that seduce human beings actually only enslave, the question arises as to what brings freedom? If the things that we think will make us happy don't, or if at best they obscure, befuddle and confuse, then the question arises as to how peace may be found and true happiness pursued. For Christian theology, this becomes a question of the quest for God in prayer, and an understanding of the passions provides a potential way of advancing in this quest; it is a way of overcoming some of the major obstacles. For the Desert Fathers, Evagrios and the other authors of the *Philokalia*, an understanding of the passions was only useful as a means, albeit a very important one, to this end.

# 3

# Remedies for the Passions

If the passions are "hostile pleasures", which threaten to enslave and debilitate human beings, then what remedies might be found to address them?

There is no doubt that remedies for the passions are on offer in the classical tradition, in the teachings of Evagrios and the Desert Fathers, and in the *Philokalia*. However, before moving on to consider these remedies, and to assess their efficacy, it may be well to consider briefly what is being suggested by the idea of a "remedy", or at least what might be implied in the use of that word in the present context.

A "remedy" might refer either to a cure or treatment for a medical condition, or else to something that puts right a problem or fault.[1] These two meanings are clearly similar, the main difference being in the explicitly medical allusion of the first, which is lacking in the second. As we have already seen, medical metaphor provides at least a part of the vocabulary of the passions as encountered in the *Philokalia* and "remedies" for the passions are referred to in various places within it pages.[2] However, it is not the only metaphor. The passions can also be viewed as hostile forces, enslaving powers, desert-like regions, confusing influences, and so on. According to which metaphors are preferred, defences, weapons, escape routes, evasion tactics, maps, guides, life supports, manifestos, or various other non-medical terms might be preferable to the word "remedy". One of the advantages of the word "remedy" over, say "therapy" or "treatment" is that it allows more ambiguity and greater scope for understanding such non-medical interpretations. But, as the medical sense does seem to be somewhat predominant, to what extent is it legitimate to allow medical terminology a hegemony in this account? Would completely non-medical terminology[3] be more appropriate here?

Firstly, it is important to note that the classical tradition, in its predominantly philosophical account of the passions, also recognised that the philosopher is a physician who seeks to bring healing to the suffering human soul. Martha Nussbaum has traced out this medical model carefully in her book *The Therapy of Desire*.[4] Recognising that ancient Greece also had available other models of ethical enquiry, she argues that the medical model offered certain advantages. It provided pragmatic and compassionate help to its patients, taking into account the realities of their lives and the views of patients about their own condition, their needs and desires. It listened to its patients, it engaged them in their treatment and it sought their well-being. In short, it was a patient-centred approach.

Classical philosophy thus sought both to immerse itself in the reality of its patients' lives and circumstances, but also to find the critical objectivity and perspective that comes with professional distance. Like a good physician, the philosopher therefore sought both to make contact with patients by means of empathy and a good "bedside manner", but also to apply critical skills to interpretation of the history and findings thus obtained. In order to try and sort out the material presented by its patients, it then made use of some very medical ideas, such as diagnosis of disease, reference to norms of health, and appropriate methods of investigation.[5]

Perhaps more controversially, there were other implications of the medical model of philosophy.[6] For Nussbaum, medicine is directed mainly towards the health of the individual. Whilst this neglects contemporary medical perspectives on public health, and the role of the public health physician, it is certainly a potential danger that a focus on the needs of an individual will lead to a neglect of the wider community. Medicine is also usually associated with an asymmetry of roles. The doctor is the expert, and the patient is expected to be obedient and compliant. Notwithstanding the contemporary trend towards empowerment of "service users", patients are also traditionally discouraged from seeking alternative or conflicting therapies.

The medical model therefore offered classical philosophy certain advantages and, at least potentially, disadvantages of perspective upon its proffered remedies for the passions. Arguably, the former outweigh the latter but, even if they do not, at least this model reminds us that we should not be neglectful of the latter. Thus, for example, in any critique that we bring to bear upon particular remedies that are offered for the individual, it might be well to ask what help they offer to a community. Or, again, does a particular remedy that might be helpful for one patient prevent another patient from seeking (possibly – for them) more effective help elsewhere? In a similar way, it would seem, medical terminology might offer a useful vocabulary and framework for studying the responses to the passions that are to be found in the pages of the *Philokalia*.

Secondly, medical metaphors are familiar to Christian theology. In the synoptic gospels,[7] Jesus famously identifies sinners as being those who are sick (κακῶς ἔχοντες) and thus in need of a physician (ἰατροῦ). Luke Dysinger notes that, by the end of the fourth century there was a well established tradition of using medical analogies as illustrations of Christian principles.[8] In *On Thoughts*, Evagrios refers to Christ as the "physician of souls", in *Praktikos* he refers to ascetic practices as [medicinal] "remedies" (φάρμακα), and in *Thirty-Three Ordered Chapters*, he lists sixteen biblical afflictions which are allegorically interpreted as spiritual vices.[9] In the *Apophthegmata* there are references to healing from blasphemous thoughts[10] and to anger as sickness,[11] and prayer is likened to medicine.[12] Amongst others, Ignatius of Antioch, Clement of Alexandria, Origen, and (to a lesser extent) Athanasius all employed medical imagery in their writings.[13] In the *Philokalia*, references are made to Jesus as physician[14] or doctor,[15] and to God as physician[16] or doctor.[17] Maximos the Confessor refers to the person who is able to use the passions as a remedy against evil as being a physician,[18] and, similarly, Thalassios the Libyan refers to the "physician like intellect".[19] Nikitas Stithatos refers to God as the "Healer of our souls",[20] and Gregory Palamas understands Christ as the "soul's Healer".[21]

Thirdly, medical terminology offers a bridge across different perspectives, academic disciplines, and professional boundaries. Nussbaum notes that the challenges confronting classical philosophy in its day were not unlike those encountered by psychological medicine today, and that its concerns in many ways anticipated those of modern psychoanalysis.[22] Galen, in the second century C.E., was able to talk about passions as "diseases of the soul" as both a physician and philosopher.[23] Modern psychoanalysis, and other psychodynamic therapies, have important historical roots in the work of physicians such as Sigmund Freud (1856-1939) and Carl Jung (1875-1961).[24] Even where psychotherapy is offered in a completely non-medical setting, medical terminology (such as "therapy", "pain" and "pathology") still tends to creep into the conversation. The long tradition of using medical language as illustration, metaphor and allegory in the Christian tradition also enables a connection to be made here.

Fourthly, although medical science is sometimes criticised as being reductionistic, and the "medical model" is perceived by some as being unduly preoccupied with the biological aspects of physical disease, medicine at its best offers an holistic understanding of the problems encountered by a patient in context. This understanding now commonly refers to the "bio-psycho-social" model of complex disorders such as addiction, and increasingly also recognises a spiritual dimension to the problems that people encounter, and the remedies that are offered for them.[25] An holistic medical model of this kind is therefore integrative of the physical, psychological, social and spiritual. Given the way in which the *Philokalia* easily switches between talking about the passions in physical, psychological and spiritual terms, medical language would therefore appear to offer a promising vocabulary and conceptual framework.

For these reasons, the word "remedy" with its implication of, but not exclusive reference to, a medical dimension of things will be used in this chapter in relation to various proposed responses to, or solutions for, the problem of the passions. Whilst the medical inferences of this term will be taken up where appropriate, they will not be allowed to exclude other (at times more helpful) metaphorical images of the forms that these remedies might take.

This chapter will be devoted, then, to a consideration of the remedies offered for the passions, first within the classical tradition, then by Evagrios and the Desert Fathers, and finally by the *Philokalia* itself.

## 1. The Classical Tradition

Plato appears not to have expected that the passions could, or even should, be eliminated, but rather that restraint should be exercised in their expression, in order not to impede the process of deliberation necessary as a basis for rational action.[26]

For Aristotle, the remedy to the passions was to be found in learning to respond to particular situations in a rationally appropriate way. To some extent this learning depends upon processes which are outside individual control – it is something which takes time

## Chapter 3: Remedies for the Passions

(it is not often observed in the young), it depends upon upbringing and family environment in childhood, and it is dependent upon the wider social environment of the community. The task of philosophy is therefore not only concerned with individuals learning to manage their passions, but of creating good homes and a more just society.[27] Insofar as it is concerned with the individual, however, it is concerned with moderation of the passions.[28]

Moderation of the passions for Aristotle was a matter of finding the mean – being neither completely wanting nor excessive in respect of any particular passion. However, this was not simply a matter of quantity, it was also concerned with the nature and context of the passion:

> It is possible, for example, to feel fear, confidence, desire, anger, pity, and pleasure and pain generally, too much or too little; and both these are wrong. But to have these feelings at the right times on the right grounds towards the right people for the right motive and in the right way is to feel them to an intermediate, that is to the best, degree; and this is the mark of virtue.[29]

This understanding of moderation thus allows that some passions (e.g. malice, shamelessness and envy) are always wrong. Similarly, some actions based upon passion (e.g. adultery) will always be wrong.[30]

For Aristotle, the remedy for the passions, the means of achieving the therapeutic goal of moderation, depends upon their responsiveness to reason – at least to some degree.[31] Engagement in therapy for the passions will involve self-scrutiny, reflection and critical review.[32] It is thus possible to learn moderation – albeit within certain limits imposed by age, upbringing and social circumstances. This intellectual learning process is morally complemented by practice and the development of good habits.[33] Aristotle (taking in this respect a contrary position to Plato) also recognised a value in emotional catharsis[34] induced, for example, by music or drama. This therapy, which by very use of the word catharsis implies an analogy with medical catharsis, appears to have been based upon the idea that induction of emotion in a safe and appropriate context is helpful in getting rid of "excess" or unhealthy emotion that might otherwise cause problems.

For the Stoics, the necessary remedy was understood as being much more severe. Nothing short of complete elimination of the passions would do. The wise person (even if wise people were rarely to be found) was one who is completely free of the passions. Events that would be painful for others are, for the wise person, merely like a grazing of the skin.[35] According to Epictetus, the spirit of such a person is "like the country on the other side of the moon: it is always calm there".[36] This state of freedom from the passions, or apatheia, could be envisaged as a happy and god-like state of contemplation.[37]

Why did the Stoics believe that such a radical remedy was indicated? Their arguments seem to have been along the following lines:[38]

1. The passions are false judgements. They are concerned with external objects which, *pace* Aristotle, are of no real value.

2. The passions are not necessary, *pace* Aristotle, to motivate virtuous action.

3. The passions are experienced as a state of illness. They are associated with often severe (emotional) pain, weakness and disability. This is true even of positive passions, such as joy or love, as well as negative states such as anger or fear.

4. The passions represent vulnerability to an uncontrollable and changeable world.

5. The passions are uncontrollable: they tend to excess, and indulgence in one makes us liable to others.

The Stoics did allow for certain affective states, called eupatheiai, which did not need to be eliminated. These were "prudent caution", will or "rational wish", and a kind of joy or "rational uplift".[39] However, they were keen to emphasise that these are not passions, and they give the appearance more of being an apologetic against Aristotelian criticisms of Stoic apatheia as being a loss of all that is emotionally valuable, rather than in any way undermining the radical nature of the Stoic indictment of the passions.

The remedies that the Stoics prescribed for the passions were adopted from various sources, including the Pythagoreans and the Cynics, as well as apparently innovating their own practices. The nature and practice of these remedies included, amongst other things, the following:[40]

- A daily review each morning of what might be expected or achieved that day, and/or an evening review of one's reactions to the day's events

## Chapter 3: Remedies for the Passions

- Observing one's own angry face in a mirror, so as to appreciate the ugliness of anger
- Ascetic discipline: not eating meat, sleeping on a hard bed, avoiding hot baths
- Meditation on suicide. (Seneca understood the possibility of suicide as always providing, in extreme circumstances, a possible final alternative to unvirtuous action that might otherwise be imposed by force of circumstances or by an evil dictator.)
- Reflection on what is or is not within one's power. (Things that are outside of one's own power, in Stoic terms, are merely indifferent.)
- Conscious and regular remembering of the impermanence of things (including the mortality of family and other loved ones) and anticipation of misfortune.[41]
- Exercise of patience in waiting by not projecting ones thoughts forward to what is anticipated
- Self-distraction from emotional states
- Inviting and exercising self-criticism
- Learning to want only with reservation (e.g. "if Zeus wills").
- Relabelling: e.g. if caught up in a crowd, imagine it to be a festival, if thinking of a dead son imagine him as merely absent,[42] or if thinking of an attractive woman imagine her as smelling unpleasant.[43]
- Considering the lot of others (which might either offer an example to follow, or else a reminder that things could be worse)
- Living each day as if it is your last
- Delay before acting on anger

## 2. The Desert Fathers

As has already been seen in Chapter 2, the *Apophthegmata* offer a completely unsystematic approach to the passions. However, there does seem to be a general sense that, although perhaps the passions should be entirely eliminated, in practice they are controlled or subdued rather than completely destroyed. Thus, for example, we find Abba Abraham demonstrating to a man who claims to have destroyed the passions that in fact he has only brought them under control, and that they still live within him.[44] In a rather cryptic story about Abba Bessarion, his disciples relate that, although he passed his life in solitude "without trouble or disquiet", seeming "entirely free from all the passions of the body", in company and in relatively more comfortable surroundings, he would weep and lament.[45]

Where the possibility of eliminating the passions entirely is raised, it is never entirely clear that this is a possibility that can be realised in practice.[46] Thus, for example, we find Abba Poemen talking about instruction of others as the proper task of the man who is "whole and without passions".[47] But this saying is clearly a warning against giving instruction to others when the passions still linger within. It is not clear that Poemen imagines that there are many, or even any, such passion free people about.

In various places, reference is made to "struggle" with the passions, or to the passions being brought under control. In addition to the story of Abba Abraham, already related (above), we find Abba Arsenius referring to the inner struggle that is needed in order to bring exterior passions under control:

> A brother questioned Abba Arsenius to hear a word of him and the old man said to him, 'Strive with all your might to bring your interior activity into accord with God, and you will overcome exterior passions.'[48]

Similarly, Abba Joseph talks of "reigning" over the passions,[49] and Abba Pityrion, although he speaks of "banishing" demons, speaks only of "subduing", "mastering", or "controlling" the passions themselves.[50]

An interesting saying by Abba Poemen suggests that remedies for the passions were identified as operating at different possible levels, according to a four stage process through which the passions were understood to operate:

> Another brother questioned him in these words: 'What does, "See that none of you repays evil for evil" mean?' (1 Thess. 5.15) The old man said to him, 'Passions work in four stages – first, in the heart; secondly, in the face; thirdly, in words; and fourthly, it is essential not to render

> evil for evil in deeds. If you can purify your heart, passion will not come into your expression; but if it comes into your face, take care not to speak; but if you do speak, cut the conversation short in case you render evil for evil.'[51]

Apatheia, or complete elimination of the passions, can be understood here as being a state of purity of heart, although it is still not clear to what extent it was expected that this might ever be realised in practice. If passions linger in the heart they can still be prevented from exerting an influence, according to Abba Poemen, upon non-verbal or verbal communication with others, and upon actions.

A rather different model appears to be implied in a saying by Abba Sisoes:

> Abba Joseph asked Abba Sisoes, 'For how long must a man cut away the passions?' The old man said to him, 'Do you want to know how long?' Abba Joseph answered, 'Yes.' Then the old man said to him, 'So long as a passion attacks you, cut it away at once.'[52]

Here, it would appear that apatheia might never be attainable – for the passions are portrayed as autonomous agents capable of continuing, or presumably also renewing, their attacks for as long as they choose. The remedy is to respond swiftly to "cut away" the passion as soon as possible in the face of each new attack. On the basis of this saying alone, it might be presumed that Abba Sisoes and Abba Poemen had rather different understandings of how the passions operate, with the former seeing them as external assailants, and the latter understanding them as situated within the human heart. However, in another saying attributed to Abba Sisoes, it is clear that he also understood them as forces operating from within, responsibility for which must be owned by the human agent:

> A brother asked Abba Sisoes, 'What shall I do about the passions?' The old man said, 'Each man is tempted when he is lured and enticed by his own desire' (James 1.14)[53]

Elsewhere, in a saying which suggests that remedies should be varied according to the maturity of strength of the individual concerned, Abba Joseph talks of the need for some to resist attacks of the passions, and "cut them off", thus not allowing them entry within, whereas others may allow them "entry" and then fight against them within. Indeed, the latter course of action is described as one which brings about a strengthening of the person concerned. Remedies may thus be understood as operating on the basis of both interior and exterior models of agency.

In that rather enigmatic fashion which is so typical of the *Apophthegmata*, the brother enquiring of Abba Sisoes, in the last quoted saying (above) who effectively asks what remedies he might use against the passions, is here told simply that they dwell within him – that they have their roots in his own desires. Whilst this implies that remedies must therefore be employed at this level, that is interiorly, it hardly gives any practical advice about exactly what to do. Perhaps the implied remedy is simply to be reflective upon what exactly his own luring and enticing desires actually are? Even then, the brother is not told what he should do once he identifies them.

In fact, very few specific or direct instructions are given in the *Apophthegmata* as to what remedies should be employed against the passions. Control of the tongue is clearly considered to be important, and is mentioned more than once. Thus, Abba Agathon says:

> No passion is worse than an uncontrolled tongue, because it is the mother of all the passions.[54]

Again, Abba Hyperechius says:

> He who does not control his tongue when he is angry, will not control his passions either.[55]

However, these sayings are rather circular and unspecific. If the problem is lack of control of the tongue, and the remedy is to control the tongue, we are told nothing about how to implement the remedy.

Abba John the Dwarf offers more specific advice about the benefit of fasting as a means of weakening the passions.[56] Abba Cronius, offering a remedy for "invisible" passions, talks of "seek[ing] after God" and "remember[ing] the eternal judgement".[57] Abba Makarios offers the remedy (perhaps more prophylactic than curative) of not criticising others.[58] Elsewhere, in a passage reminiscent of Stoic teaching on indifferents, he suggests that slander and praise, poverty and riches, deprivation and abundance should be accepted alike.[59]

Another passage reminiscent of Stoicism, this time making use of the technique of relabelling, is found in the story of an anonymous brother who was tempted by lustful thoughts. In this story, the brother

# Chapter 3: Remedies for the Passions

is said to dig up the corpse of his dead wife and smear her blood onto his cloak. When he returned to his cell, the cloak eventually began to smell. He would then say to himself:

> 'Look, this is what you desire. You have it now, be content.' So he punished himself with the smell until his passions died down.[60]

Again, the story of a hermit who burned all his fingers in order to overcome the temptation of lust is explicitly a Christian reminder of the fate of eternal torment for those who consent to passion, but it might also be taken as a Stoic reminder of one's own mortality, or else as a form of self-distraction.[61]

We might conclude that remedies for the passions may be found amongst the sayings of the Desert Fathers, that they operate at various levels and in different ways, but that they are often enigmatic and unspecific. We are left with a clear impression that finding such remedies is important, but that in the end, they need continuing application. To continue with our medical imagery, we might say that these remedies are more like an ointment for a chronic skin condition than an antibiotic that will definitively eliminate an acute infection.

## 3. Evagrios of Pontus

In *Praktikos*, Evagrios identifies love and abstinence as the principal preventive remedy for the passions.

> The passions are naturally set in motion by the senses. When love and abstinence are present, they will not be set in motion; when they are absent, they will be set in motion.[62]

In the *Kephalaia Gnostika*, he identifies knowledge as that which heals the nous, love as that which heals the thumos, and chastity as that which heals the epithumia.[63] This corresponds with the general advice that he gives in *Praktikos* as an introduction to a more detailed consideration of particular remedies for each of the eight thoughts in turn:

> When the mind wanders, reading, vigils, and prayer bring it to a standstill. When desire bursts into flame, hunger, toil, and anachoresis extinguish it. When the

irascible part becomes agitated, psalmody, patience, and mercy calm it.[64]

Each part of the soul, then, has its own remedies.

In *On the Vices Opposed to the Virtues*, he considers the virtue opposed to each vice:

1. Gluttony v Abstinence
2. Fornication v Chastity
3. Avarice v Freedom from Possessions
4. Sadness v Joy
5. Anger v Patience
6. Acedia v Perseverance
7. Vainglory v Freedom from Vainglory
8. Jealousy v Freedom from Jealousy
9. Pride v Humility

In each case, he lists a series of consequences, descriptions and metaphors applicable to the practice of the vice or virtue concerned. Here, then, the remedy for each vice/passion is its corresponding virtue.

In *Eight Thoughts*, and in *Praktikos*, more specific or practical advice is given. Evagrios identifies practical remedies for dealing with each of the eight thoughts in turn (see Table 3.1). Whilst there are some parallels with Stoic methods (e.g. ascetic discipline and meditation on death) and measures based on the principles of humoural medicine (e.g. a dry diet) this would not appear to be an approach that is primarily attributable to the classical tradition. In part, it shows evidence of Judeo-Christian reasoning, as in the suggestion that hospitality provides a remedy for anger, based upon the story of Jacob and Esau.[65] However, much of what is proposed here appears to be based upon Evagrios' own analysis of the eight thoughts. Thus his radical approach to avoiding contact with women, or even thinking about fornication, reflects his underlying philosophy that fornication is fed by such things in the way that oil fuels a lamp, or water feeds a plant. More originally, we find here his observation that one passion may be used to drive out another (e.g. vainglory as a remedy for fornication) or that anger may be turned back and used as a weapon against the demons.

**Table 3.1: Remedies against the Passions in *Eight Thoughts* and *Praktikos***

| Passion | Remedies | | |
|---|---|---|---|
| | | *Eight Thoughts* | *Praktikos* |
| Gluttony | Abstinence/fasting | 1.1, 1.9, 1.14, 1.15, 1.20, 1.24, 1.26, 1.31 | |
| | Dry diet | 1.13 | |
| | Avoiding heavy consumption | 1.5, 1.16 | |
| | Avoiding satiety | 1.17, 1.28, 1.33 | 16 |
| | Avoiding banquets | 1.21 | |
| | Avoiding rich foods | 1.34 | |
| | Avoid variety of foods | | 16 |
| Fornication | Abstinence | 2.1 | |
| | Avoid encounters with women | 2.2, 2.6, 2.8-10, 2.13, 2.15 | |
| | Avoid satiety | 2.4, 2.11-12 | |
| | Avoid crowds | 2.5, 2.7 | |
| | Avoid prolonged thinking about women | 2.19-20 | |
| | Avoid thinking about fornication | | 23 |
| | Restrained use of water | | 17 |
| | Vainglorious thoughts | | 58 |
| Avarice | Freedom of possessions | 3.3-7, 3.10-13 | |
| | Avoid thinking about possessions | 3.7 | |
| | Charity | | 18 |
| Anger | Avoid resentment | 4.6, 4.14, 4.16, 4.19, 4.21 | |
| | Avoid angry thoughts | 4.7, 4.16 | 23 |
| | Compassion & gentleness | | 20 |
| | Resist temptation to withdraw | | 21 |

| Passion | Remedies | | |
|---|---|---|---|
| | | *Eight Thoughts* | *Praktikos* |
| Anger (continued) | Turn anger against the demons | | 24 |
| | Avoid provoking others to anger | | 25 |
| | Hospitality | | 26 |
| Sadness | Abstinence | 5.12 | |
| | Impassibility | 5.8-15 | |
| | Avoid worldly pleasure | | 19 |
| Acedia | Perseverance | 6.3, 6.5, 6.17 | |
| | Stay in your cell | 6.5 | 28 |
| | Avoid distracting activity | 6.8, 6.14 | |
| | Work | 6.17-18 | |
| | Prayer | 6.18 | |
| | Tears | | 27 |
| | Thoughts of death | | 29 |
| | Abstinence | | 29 |
| Vainglory | Prayer in private | 7.12 | |
| | Keep virtue secret | 7.13, 7.18-19 | |
| | Avoid boasting | 7.15 | |
| | Do not seek the esteem of others | 7.20-21 | |
| | Dishonour & sadness | 8.30, 8.31 | |
| | Keep in mind purpose and goal of spiritual contemplation | | 32 |
| Pride | Avoid confidence in own strength | 8.5-6, 8.31 | |
| | Give credit to God | 8.12 | 33 |
| | Avoid presumption | 8.16, 8.21 | |
| | Avoid boasting | 8.18 | |
| | Welcome instruction | 8.23-26 | |

Chapter 3: Remedies for the Passions                                    113

In *Praktikos*, and *On Thoughts*, as well as in other works, Evagrios also offers some more general remedies for the passions:

1. **Observation** of thoughts involves attention to the varying intensity, incidence, and inter-relationships of thoughts so as to better understand how they operate and thus be able to identify and rebuff them earlier.[66]

2. **Ascetic lifestyle**[67] is a remedy which is basic to the Evagrian system and is therefore discussed in virtually all his works (see also Table 3.1, where it is invoked as a remedy for most of the eight thoughts individually, although not for vainglory and pride, as it can easily become a new focus for these passions).

3. **Examination of thoughts**, so that the sinful element(s) within them may be identified and dissipated.[68]

4. **Natural contemplation**, especially of the relationship between incorporeal beings and the material world. This is only recommended for relatively advanced (or intermediate) practitioners.[69]

5. **Transfer of the mind** from an impure thought to a pure one.[70]

6. The importance of **scripture** as an Evagrian remedy for the passions is reflected in his writing of an entire book containing scriptural texts to be used against each of the eight thoughts. *Antirrhetikos* contains 492 such texts, arranged in eight chapters (one for each thought), with a brief introduction to each, indicating the kind of thought against which it is considered useful.[71] Luke Dysinger notes that some of these verses are directed against the demons, as a kind of exorcism, some are directed as prayers to God, and others (the majority) are directed at the tempted soul, as a kind of encouragement.[72]

7. **Psalmody** is understood by Evagrios as having an important role in preparing the mind for prayer, part of which is achieved by its effect of calming the passions.[73] This will be discussed further, below, when psalmody is considered as a remedy for the passions in the *Philokalia*.

8. Evagrios describes **prayer** as invigorating and purifying the mind for the struggle against the passions/demons.[74] However, as has already been seen in Chapter 1, for Evagrios, prayer is much more than simply a remedy for the passions. It is the goal of the Christian life, and the reason for which a remedy for the passions is sought in the first place.

Evagrios, then, left details of a more systematic and detailed store of remedies for the passions than may be found in the sayings of the Desert Fathers. Elements of this therapeutic armamentarium show points of close contact with Stoic thinking. However, this should not be allowed to obscure the specifically Christian methods that he employed, nor that he was in places highly original. More especially, his remedies were radical. If the passions were a kind of disease, then Evagrios saw this disease as life threatening, and he was prepared to take all measures necessary in order to address it.

## 4. The *Philokalia*

Many and varied remedies for the passions are provided by many and different authors within the pages of the *Philokalia*. These include, for example, tears for sins,[75] meditation on death,[76] the "commandment of love",[77] patient endurance,[78] trials and sufferings,[79] and obedience,[80] as well as the almost ubiquitous injunctions to ascetic lifestyle, virtue and prayer. There is warning from Evagrios that a remedy for passion can itself become a passion,[81] and instruction from Maximos the Confessor on how passions can be turned into remedies.[82] Maximos also urges that the remedies for different passions vary according to the cause of those passions,[83] and that some remedies may merely stop the passions from growing, whilst others may actually cause them to diminish.[84] Thalassios the Libyan warns that some remedies are more painful to bear than others and that if we do not avail ourselves of those that are easy to bear, God may impose that which is more painful.[85] Many more such examples could be given, for there is hardly an author or a work included within the *Philokalia* that does not touch on this subject in one way or another.

The *Philokalia* is, effectively, a compendium of remedies for the passions; this being an assertion which should perhaps be qualified by a reminder that, in the *Philokalia*, as in the works of Evagrios,

Chapter 3: Remedies for the Passions                                    115

overcoming the passions is merely a means to an end of a life of prayer and union with God. This pharmacopoeia of remedies for the passions is therefore only provided within the pages of the *Philokalia* insofar as it is a necessary tool to enable the achieving of that aim.

What, then, are the primary remedies included within this pharmacopoeia? Whilst many remedies are listed, it would seem that four deserve especial mention and that most of the rest fall under one or other of these headings:

1. A practical life of asceticism and virtue

2. Watchfulness

3. Psalmody

4. Prayer

These will now be considered in turn.

### i. The Practical Life

Running throughout the *Philokalia* is a basic assumption that victory over the passions depends upon an ascetic way of life. This emphasises both renunciation of basic comforts and pleasures, such as food, sleep and possessions, and also pursuit of a practical life of virtue. Whilst many of the works were clearly written primarily with monks in mind, references to life in the world make clear that a similar principle is expected of lay people as well.

As has already been noted in Chapter 1, the *Philokalia* opens within the tradition of the Desert Fathers which (as we have seen) strongly emphasised an ascetic way of life. The first four works included in the Greek edition were all originally considered to have arisen within this tradition.[86] The third text originally included in the Greek *Philokalia* (the second in the English translation) was Evagrios' *Foundations*[87], which, as we have also seen, provides an introduction to the basics of the ascetical life that Evagrios espoused for combating the eight thoughts and, eventually, finding inner stillness, or hesychia. This emphasis upon a practical life of asceticism and virtue, established at the outset, and drawn from the desert tradition, continues throughout the *Philokalia* although, unsurprisingly, emphases vary slightly from place to place. It may therefore be helpful to take just one example from each of the subsequent volumes of the *Philokalia*.

### a. Maximos the Confessor

Maximos urges obedience and practice of virtue as important for those who have "just begun to follow a holy way of life".[88] For the body "entangled in the defilements of the passions", he urges active pursuit of the virtuous life, and passive acceptance of the sufferings that God allows for our good.[89] He is a little more cautious about some aspects of asceticism. He sees it as unduly focussed upon the body and limited in value.[90] But this appears to be more reflective of a concern to ensure moderation and balance than of any suggestion that he disagrees with the underlying tradition. Like Evagrios (by whom he was strongly influenced) he warns, for example, that laxity about diet and encounters with women easily lead to thoughts of unchastity.[91]

For Maximos, ascetical practice is founded upon the theology of self-emptying (kenosis) of the Logos in Christ. Thus, in *On the Lord's Prayer*, writing of those who attain to the grace of deification, he writes:

> by emptying themselves of the passions they lay hold of the divine to the same degree as that to which, deliberately emptying Himself of His own sublime glory, the Logos of God truly became man.[92]

For Maximos, the aspects of asceticism concerned with renunciation are "virtues of the body" and those concerned with acquisition of virtue are "virtues of the soul":

> There are virtues of the body and virtues of the soul. Those of the body include fasting, vigils, sleeping on the ground, ministering to people's needs, working with one's hands so as not to be a burden or in order to give to others (cf. 1 Thess. 2:9, Ephes. 4:28). Those of the soul include love, long-suffering, gentleness, self-control and prayer (cf. Gal, 5:22).[93]

Although Maximos adopts much of the Evagrian schema of the spiritual life, a major difference is the great emphasis which he places upon the virtue of love. For Maximos, the remedy for the passions is not simply their elimination, but rather their complete transformation and reintegration.[94] For Maximos, apatheia is a state of love, and love is itself a passion – but a holy and blessed one:

# Chapter 3: Remedies for the Passions

> Just as passion-free thought of human things does not compel the intellect to scorn divine things, so passion-free knowledge of divine things does not fully persuade it to scorn human things. For in this world truth exists in shadows and conjectures. That is why there is need for the blessed passion of holy love, which binds the intellect to spiritual contemplation and persuades it to prefer what is immaterial to what is material, and what is intelligible and divine to what is apprehended by the senses.[95]

### b. Peter of Damaskos

Volume 3 of the *Philokalia* is dominated by *Book I* and *Book II* of the works of Peter of Damaskos (eleventh/twelfth century), which amount to a mini-Philokalia within the *Philokalia* itself. After the introduction to *Book I*, Peter begins by considering the *Seven Forms of Bodily Discipline*.[96] The first three of these forms of discipline are removal from the distractions of human society, moderate fasting, and moderate vigils. Later, in regard to fasting, he clarifies what is meant here by "moderation":

> It is abstention and dissipation that bring on illness, while self-control and a change of foods each day are conducive to health. The body then remains impervious to pleasure and sickness and co-operates in the acquisition of the virtues.[97]

Peter also includes in *Book I* a discourse on *The Bodily Virtues as Tools for the Acquisition of the Virtues of the Soul*.[98] Here, he links "excision of desires" with ascetic practice and other tools necessary for the acquisition of virtue. However, it is in a *Short Discourse on the Acquisition of the Virtues and on Abstinence from the Passions*[99] that we get a more detailed idea of the kinds of things that Peter expects his reader to engage in as remedies for the passions. In the space of only slightly more than two pages, he includes under this heading:

- Spiritual reading in stillness
- The thought of death
- Self-reproach

- The excising of our own will
- Solitary life
- Meditation
- Reflection on God's gifts
- Reflection on our own wickedness
- Trials and temptations
- Avoidance of excess and deficiency
- Humility
- Abandoning every personal thought and desire
- Pure prayer
- Endurance of affliction
- Trying for one day to do something good
- To bear with the neighbour who wrongs us
- Faith, hope and love

In *Book II*, under the title *Mortification of the Passions*,[100] Peter urges detachment from material things through mortification of the body. For Peter, overcoming the passions is inextricably linked with overcoming the attraction to sensory objects.[101] Desire for comfort from such things is "non-spiritual" and in conflict with the life of virtue.[102] But, it is not that these things are bad in themselves and, like Maximos, his view of the passions is not entirely negative. Indeed, for the one who has restraint and judgement, it is possible:

> to discern the intention of God hidden in the six passions that surround him – those, that is, above him and below, to his right and to his left, within him and without. Whether it relates to the practice of the virtues or to spiritual knowledge, there is some good purpose lying within the six passions that oppose him.[103]

### c. Gregory of Sinai: *On Commandments & Doctrines*

In Volume 4, a work of Gregory of Sinai (*c.*1265-1346) is included under the title *On Commandments and Doctrines, Warnings and Promises; on Thoughts, Passions and Virtues, and also on Stillness* *and Prayer: One Hundred and Thirty-Seven Texts*.[104] In this work, Gregory proposes for the would-be hesychast a demanding regime of fasting, night vigils and prayer, built upon a foundation of five virtues: silence, self-control, vigilance, humility and patience.[105] Thus, for example, he advises:

> A pound of bread is sufficient for anyone aspiring to attain the state of inner stillness. You may drink two cups of undiluted wine and three of water. Your food should consist of whatever is at hand – not whatever your natural craving seeks, but what providence provides, to be eaten sparingly. The best and shortest guiding rule for those who wish to live as they should is to maintain the threefold all-embracing practices of fasting, vigilance and prayer, for these provide a most powerful support for all the other virtues.[106]

Perhaps not surprisingly given the austerity of this regime, he notes that it is not uncommon for those on the spiritual path to find ascetic practice hard. For these, he recommends obedience as a virtue that will provide an effective remedy for the passions.[107] But the one who has achieved union with God, who is a "true friend of God", he understands as being one who will have undergone ascetic purification, as well as noetic contemplation.[108] For those who refuse ascetic discipline, the danger is that of delusion due to unchecked self-indulgence. Such individuals imagine that they are recipients of divine revelation when, in fact, they are "intoxicated and befuddled with passion".[109]

### d. Kallistos and Ignatius: *Directions to Hesychasts*

Finally, in Volume 5, we find that Kallistos (d.1397) and Ignatius (fourteenth century), in their *Directions to Hesychasts*,[110] in charting the path to pure prayer and passionlessness, emphasise (amongst other things) the need for ascetic practice and a practical life of virtue as more or less fundamental first steps. Divine grace remains present in all who have been baptised, they say, but is "buried under the passions".[111] The solution is to strive to keep the commandments, a striving which is met with God's grace to help us. In particular, Kallistos and Ignatius emphasise the importance of striving after three virtues within which, they argue, all the others are subsumed: faith, love, and peace. They also especially recommend complete obedience to a well-chosen spiritual guide, self-renunciation, silence and solitude, and an ascetic regime including a meagre diet and limited sleep.

### e. The Practical Life: Some Conclusions

Throughout the *Philokalia*, then, ascetic lifestyle and pursuit of a practical life of virtue are emphasised as fundamental remedies for the passions. At times, it can seem as though there is a circularity in the argument. People are not virtuous because of the passions – they must therefore be virtuous in order to defeat the passions. However, this apparent circularity overlooks both the grace of God and the importance of self-control. Thus, for example, Maximos writes:

> The person who has come to know the weakness of human nature has gained experience of divine power. Such a man, having achieved some things and eager to achieve others through this divine power, never belittles anyone. For he knows that just as God has helped him and freed him from many passions and difficulties, so, when God wishes, He is able to help all men, especially those pursuing the spiritual way for His sake. And if in His providence He does not deliver all men together from their passions, yet like a good and loving physician He heals with individual treatment each of those who are trying to make progress.[112]

There is, of course, a danger of passivity if we imagine, then, that there is nothing that we can do but hope and pray for God's grace. But Maximos argues that God heals those "who are trying to make progress". Similarly, in the *Introduction* to *Book I* of his *Treasury of Divine Knowledge*, Peter of Damaskos emphasises the importance of divinely bestowed knowledge, which reminds us of the divine commandments, and in addition:

> alongside this knowledge, there is our capacity to choose. This is the beginning of our salvation; by our free choice we abandon our own wishes and thoughts and do what God wishes and thinks. If we succeed in doing this, there is no object, no activity or place in the whole of creation that can prevent us from becoming what God from the

Chapter 3: Remedies for the Passions 121

> beginning has wished us to be: that is to say, according to His image and likeness, gods by adoption through grace, dispassionate, just, good and wise....[113]

Gregory of Sinai also recognises that a combination of human effort and divine grace is required. Appearing if anything to err towards a view that grace alone may be all that is needed in some cases, he warns against any shadows of virtue that lack that grace:

> The pursuit of the virtues through one's own efforts does not confer complete strength on the soul unless grace transforms them into an essential inner disposition. Each virtue is endowed with its own specific gift of grace, its own particular energy, and thus possesses the capacity to produce such a disposition and blessed state in those who attain it even when they have not consciously sought for any such state. Once a virtue has been bestowed on us it remains unchanged and unfailing. For just as a living soul activates the body's members, so the grace of the Holy Spirit activates the virtues. Without such grace the whole bevy of the virtues is moribund; and in those who appear to have attained them, or to be in the way of attaining them, solely through their own efforts they are but shadows and prefigurations of beauty, not the reality itself.[114]

The truly beautiful, then, is that virtue which arises where human choice and striving meld with the grace of God. In this is to be found the first remedy for the passions that the *Philokalia* recommends.

## ii. Watchfulness

Watchfulness (νῆψις) is another remedy for the passions which clearly builds upon the Evagrian tradition, and which permeates many, if not most, of the pages of the *Philokalia*. Indeed, the full title of the Greek *Philokalia* is "The Philokalia of the Niptic Fathers".[115] In other words, watchfulness ("nipsis") is almost a defining characteristic of the texts of the *Philokalia*, and one wonders whether the concept may not have been amongst the criteria that, by design or consensus, determined inclusion of particular texts within its pages.

Watchfulness is defined by the English translators of the *Philokalia* as:

literally, the opposite to a state of drunken stupor; hence spiritual sobriety, alertness, vigilance. It signifies an attitude of attentiveness (προσοχή – *prosochi*), whereby one keeps watch over one's inward thoughts and fantasies (q.v.), maintaining guard over the heart and intellect *(*φυλακὴ καρδίας νοῦ *– phylaki kardias/nou;* τήρησις καρδίας νου/ *– tirisis kardias/nou)*.[116]

The author of a thirteenth century text attributed in the *Philokalia* to Symeon the New Theologian[117] notes that essentially the same practices are variously referred to as:

- Attentiveness
- Guarding of the heart
- Guarding of the intellect
- Investigation of thoughts
- Rebuttal
- Stillness of the heart
- Watchfulness

Nikiphoros the Monk (thirteenth century)[118] produces a slightly different list of synonyms, and indicates that the list is not complete:

- Attentiveness
- Custody of the heart
- Guarding of the intellect
- Noetic stillness
- Watchfulness

Similarly, the English translators of the *Philokalia* suggest that watchfulness, inner attentiveness, and guarding of the intellect are "virtually synonymous".[119] However, there are hints in places that some of these terms should be distinguished.

Hesychios the Priest (?eighth or ninth century) hints that watchfulness and guarding of the intellect may be distinguished by absence of mental images associated with the latter.[120] More importantly, he also distinguishes between watchfulness and rebuttal:

> It is the task of unceasing watchfulness – and one of great benefit and help to the soul – to see the mental images of

# Chapter 3: Remedies for the Passions 123

> evil thoughts as soon as they are formed in the intellect. The task of rebuttal is to counter and expose such thoughts when they attempt to infiltrate our intellect in the form of an image of some material thing.[121]

Similarly, the English translators of the *Philokalia* define rebuttal (ἀντιλογία, ἀντίρρησις) as:

> the repulsing of a demon or demonic thought at the moment of provocation (q.v.); or, in a more general sense, the bridling of evil thoughts.[122]

It seems that rebuttal at least, then, might denote a process of countering, repulsing or bridling evil thoughts, rather than simply being attentive to, or being vigilant in observation of, such thoughts. However, differences between the other terms (especially watchfulness and guarding of the heart/intellect, the most commonly used) are less clear.

Four texts from the *Philokalia* on watchfulness will be considered here:

1. *Watchfulness & Holiness* by Hesychios the Priest (?eighth or ninth century)

2. *Forty Texts on Watchfulness* by Philotheos of Sinai (?ninth or tenth century)

3. *Three Methods of Prayer*, which is attributed to Symeon the New Theologian (942-1022) but is actually by an anonymous author (?tenth or eleventh century)

4. *Watchfulness & Guarding* by Nikiphoros the Monk (thirteenth century)

In passing, however, it is interesting to note that the *Extracts from the Texts on Watchfulness*, by Evagrios, included in the first volume of the *Philokalia*, is actually a compilation of texts taken from *Praktikos*.[123] These texts are, in fact, more about the practical and ascetic life than about watchfulness in the specific sense defined above. As we shall see, ascetic practice is, more or less, considered by other authors in the *Philokalia* as a foundation for watchfulness. We might speculate, therefore, that Nikodimos and Makarios wanted readers of the *Philokalia* to understand watchfulness broadly, and for it to be understood that the practical life is a foundation for watchfulness in the specific sense. Nonetheless, the selection of five paragraphs from the 100 paragraphs of *Praktikos*, and their reordering under this particular heading, is curious.[124]

### a. Hesychios the Priest: *Watchfulness & Holiness*

*Watchfulness and Holiness*, by Hesychios the Priest, is an important contribution to the *Philokalia* on the subject of watchfulness. Hesychios opens this work with a sweeping vista of the landscape that watchfulness surveys:

> Watchfulness is a spiritual method which, if sedulously practised over a long period, completely frees us with God's help from impassioned thoughts, impassioned words and evil actions. It leads, in so far as this is possible, to a sure knowledge of the inapprehensible God, and helps us to penetrate the divine and hidden mysteries. It enables us to fulfil every divine commandment in the Old and New Testaments and bestows upon us every blessing of the age to come. It is, in the true sense, purity of heart, a state blessed by Christ when He says: 'Blessed are the pure in heart, for they shall see God' (Matt. 5:8); and one which, because of its spiritual nobility and beauty – or, rather, because of our negligence – is now extremely rare among monks. Because this is its nature, watchfulness is to be bought only at a great price. But once established in us, it guides us to a true and holy way of life. It teaches us how to activate the three aspects of our soul correctly, and how to keep a firm guard over the senses. It promotes the daily growth of the four principal virtues, and is the basis of our contemplation.[125]

As the English translators note, this is a broad definition.[126] As Hesychios himself notes, it "is a way [of] embracing every virtue".[127] He clearly considers it fundamental to the whole monastic vocation, for he later says: "A true monk is one who has achieved watchfulness; and he who is truly watchful is a monk in his heart".[128] He sees watchfulness as beginning with ascetic practice, and as involving (or perhaps culminating in) hesychastic stillness.

> The fruit starts in the flower; and the guarding of the intellect begins with self-control in food and drink, the

> rejection of all evil thoughts and abstention from them, and stillness of heart.[129]

For Hesychios, watchfulness is a remedy for the passions, but it is also much more than this: it is the gateway to contemplative prayer and opens the way to a vision of the divine light.[130]

At the core, Hesychios describes watchfulness as a process of self awareness, and attentiveness to one's own thoughts:

> Watchfulness is a continual fixing and halting of thought at the entrance to the heart. In this way predatory and murderous thoughts are marked down as they approach and what they say and do is noted; and we can see in what specious and delusive form the demons are trying to deceive the intellect. If we are conscientious in this, we can gain much experience and knowledge of spiritual warfare.[131]

Although some attempts within the *Philokalia* to find a scriptural basis for this practice might seem very allegorical,[132] Hesychios appeals to Christ's temptation in the wilderness as the model for Christians to follow.[133] Hesychios identifies five methods of watchfulness:[134]

1. "closely scrutinizing every mental image or provocation"
2. "freeing the heart from all thoughts, keeping it profoundly silent and still, and in praying"
3. "continually and humbly calling upon the Lord Jesus Christ for help"
4. "always to have the thought of death in one's mind"
5. "to fix one's gaze on heaven and to pay no attention to anything material"

Hesychios later gives a more detailed account of how some of these methods might work:

> Now when the provocation has taken the form of a mental image of a sensory object, the evil thought behind it can be identified. For instance, if the image is of the face of someone who has angered us, or of a beautiful woman, or of gold or silver, it can at once be shown that it is the thought of rancour, or of unchastity, or of avarice that fills

our heart with fantasies. And if our intellect is experienced, well-trained and used to guarding itself, and to examining clearly and openly the seductive fantasies and deceits of the demons, it will instantly 'quench the fiery darts of the devil' (cf. Eph. 6:16), counter-attacking by means of its power of rebuttal and the Jesus Prayer. It will not allow the impassioned fantasy to consort with it or allow our thoughts passionately to conform themselves to the fantasy, or to become intimate with it, or be distracted by it, or give assent to it. If anything like this happens, then evil actions will follow as surely as night follows day.[135]

Watchfulness thus provides a mental remedy against the process of the passions. In this case, a number of stages might be identified:[136]

1. Awareness of a mental image, or "fantasy"
2. Recognition that, behind this image, there lays an evil thought, or passion
3. Response by way of "rebuttal", or mental rejection of the thought/image – including a resistance to dwelling on it, being distracted by it, giving assent to it, or in any other way engaging with it
4. Response by way of prayer (in this case, the Jesus Prayer – which we will consider later)

Hesychios later emphasises that following the first three of these stages alone would be insufficient. He considers invocation of the name of Jesus to be vital to the whole process.[137]

### b. Philotheos of Sinai: *Forty Texts on Watchfulness*

Whilst Philotheos of Sinai, like Hesychios, recognises watchfulness as being a remedy for the passions, he sees it as much more than just this. Like Hesychios, he finds its beginnings in ascetic practice, and its end in a vision of contemplative prayer:

> If, then, we seek – by guarding our intellect and by inner watchfulness – to engage in the noetic work that is the true philosophy in Christ, we must begin by exercising self-control with regard to our food, eating and drinking as little as possible. Watchfulness may fittingly be called

> a path leading both to the kingdom within us and to that which is to be; while noetic work, which trains and purifies the intellect and changes it from an impassioned state to a state of dispassion, is like a window full of light through which God looks, revealing Himself to the intellect.[138]

It is this vision of contemplative prayer, or to use Philotheos' own terminology this "noetic vision" or "perfect remembrance of God in [the] heart", with which he opens his *Forty Texts* and this is, for him, the goal of watchfulness.[139]

Philotheos[140] identifies three "gateways" to watchfulness:

1. "Silencing of [the] tongue" ("Nothing is more unsettling than talkativeness and more pernicious than an unbridled tongue, disruptive as it is of the soul's proper state."[141])

2. "balanced self-control in food and drink"

3. "ceaseless mindfulness of death"

Although he does not refer to it as a "gateway", Philotheos also considers humility to be a fundamental requirement. In order to engender this, he encourages the remembrance of sins, mindfulness of death, remembrance of Christ's passion, and review of God's blessings.[142]

Philotheos also shares with Hesychios a Christological emphasis, and he combines this with a vivid depiction of the mental turmoil that watchfulness seeks to address:

> Be extremely strict in guarding your intellect. When you perceive an evil thought, rebut it and immediately call upon Christ to defend you; and while you are still speaking, Jesus in His gentle love will say: 'Behold, I am by your side ready to help you.' When this whole detachment of the enemy has been put out of action through prayer, again turn your attention to your intellect. There you will see a succession of waves worse than before, with the soul swimming among them. But again, awakened by His disciple, Jesus as God will rebuke the winds of evil (cf. Matt. 8:23-27). Having found respite for an hour perhaps, or for a moment, glorify Him who has saved you, and meditate on death.[143]

It has been suggested that Philotheos has a greater emphasis on bodily ascetic practice in his account of watchfulness, as compared with that of Hesychios.[144] However, the similarities between these two accounts are much greater than any differences.

### c. [Symeon the New Theologian]: *Three Methods of Prayer*

The author of *Three Methods of Prayer*[145] offers a somewhat different account to Hesychios and Philotheos. The first two methods of prayer described by the author of this work fail to address the need to guard the heart. The first method turns the focus of the intellect heavenwards and, in the opinion of the author, leads inevitably to pride and delusion. The second turns the focus of the intellect inward and away from sensory things. Here, the author sees again the danger of self-esteem, but with no peace or end to the mental conflict that is entailed, for it fails "to observe the enemies who attack from within".[146]

The third method of prayer, which the author of this work enthusiastically endorses, begins with obedience to a spiritual guide and attention to purity of conscience. Having addressed these rather important preliminaries, the author turns to a description of the characteristics of attentiveness:

> True and unerring attentiveness and prayer mean that the intellect keeps watch over the heart while it prays; it should always be on patrol within the heart, and from within – from the depths of the heart – it should offer up its prayers to God. Once it has tasted within the heart that the Lord is bountiful (cf. Ps. 34:8. LXX), then the intellect will have no desire to leave the heart, and it will repeat the words of the Apostle Peter, 'It is good for us to be here' (Matt. 17:4). It will keep watch always within the heart, repulsing and expelling all thoughts sown there by the enemy. To those who have no knowledge of this practice it appears extremely harsh and arduous; and indeed it is oppressive and laborious, not only to the uninitiated, but also to those who, although genuinely experienced, have not yet felt the delight to be found in the depths of the heart. But those who have savoured this delight proclaim with St Paul, 'Who will separate us from the love of Christ?' (Rom. 8:35).[147]

## Chapter 3: Remedies for the Passions

The scriptural basis for this approach is built upon references to the teaching of Christ in Matthew's gospel – particularly on the evil thoughts that proceed from the heart (Matthew 15:19-20) and Jesus' injunction to the Pharisees on the need for inner cleanliness (Matthew 23:26). On the basis of this teaching, he claims, the holy fathers:

> abandoned all other forms of spiritual labour and concentrated wholly on this one task of guarding the heart, convinced that through this practice they would also possess every other virtue, whereas without it no virtue could be firmly established.[148]

This author thus places guarding of the heart[149] as the necessary precondition for attaining virtue. It is not simply one remedy for the passions, but rather *the* remedy, or at least the remedy which must be applied before any other remedies can be expected to produce any real or lasting benefit. Accordingly, at the end of the work, when the author describes four stages of the spiritual life, guarding of the heart is the first and fundamental stage:[150]

1. Curtailment of the passions (guarding of the heart) – the stage of beginners

2. Practice of psalmody – referred to as growing up "spiritually from adolescence to youth"

3. Persevering in prayer – "the spiritual transition from youth to manhood"

4. Undeviating absorption in contemplation – the stage of "the old man with grey hairs"

As a means of facilitating guarding of the heart, the author describes a technique of prayer that gives attention to bodily posture, breathing, and an inner searching with the intellect, "so as to find the place of the heart, where all the powers of the soul reside".[151] Once this state has been achieved, distractive thoughts are driven away and destroyed by invocation of Jesus Christ.

### d. Nikiphoros the Monk: *Watchfulness & Guarding*

Our fourth example of a text in the *Philokalia* that is dedicated to watchfulness begins with a collection of extracts from writings of the saints, including an extract from Athanasius' *Life of Antony the Great*, other lives and writings of the desert fathers, a brief compilation of extracts from John Climacus' *Ladder of Divine Ascent*, and also extracts of several other works included in the *Philokalia*.[152] These writings generally endorse the importance of watchfulness, rather than providing much detail about what exactly it entails. There then follows a brief account "From Nikiphoros Himself".[153]

Nikiphoros describes attentiveness[154] as follows:

> Attentiveness is the sign of true repentance. It is the soul's restoration, hatred of the world, and return to God. It is rejection of sin and recovery of virtue. It is the unreserved assurance that our sins are forgiven. It is the beginning of contemplation or, rather, its presupposition, for through it God, descrying its presence in us reveals Himself to the intellect. It is serenity of intellect or, rather, the repose bestowed on the soul through God's mercy. It is the subjection of our thoughts, the palace of the mindfulness of God, the stronghold that enables us patiently to accept all that befalls. It is the ground of faith, hope and love. For if you do not have faith you cannot endure the outward afflictions that assail you; and if you do not bear them gladly you cannot say to the Lord, 'Thou art my helper and my refuge' (Ps 91:2).[155]

This is clearly a very broad picture of what watchfulness entails. It provides none of the detail about the inner experience of watchfulness that is found in Hesychios or Philotheos, but rather speaks in metaphors of "the palace of the mindfulness of God" and "the stronghold that enables us patiently to accept all that befalls". It would appear that Nikiphoros expects that details will be filled in by face to face instruction from a teacher, and this is confirmed by his subsequent reference to the importance of finding such a spiritual guide.

Nikiphoros goes on to describe (apparently for the benefit of those who cannot find a suitable guide or teacher) a psychosomatic technique of prayer which is not dissimilar to that described by the author of *Three Methods of Prayer* (see above). However, Nikiphoros is rather more anatomically specific. After describing the function of

## Chapter 3: Remedies for the Passions

the heart (according to humoural theory) in maintaining homeostasis of body temperature, he continues:

> concentrate your intellect, and lead it into the respiratory passage through which your breath passes into your heart. Put pressure on your intellect and compel it to descend with your inhaled breath into your heart. Once it has entered there, what follows will be neither dismal nor glum. Just as a man, after being far away from home, on his return is overjoyed at being with his wife and children again, so the intellect, once it is united with the soul, is filled with indescribable delight.[156]

Once the intellect is "firmly established in the heart", Nikiphoros recommends repetition of, and meditation on, the Jesus Prayer (which we shall discuss further, below).[157] This, he says, will protect the intellect from distraction, protect it against attacks of the demons, and increase its love for God.[158]

This process is clearly more similar to that of the author of *Three Methods of Prayer* than it is to either of the accounts of Hesychios or Philotheos. As the English translators of the *Philokalia* speculate, it is likely that the method had a long history on Mount Athos prior to being written down first by Nikiphoros and then others (including the author of *Three Methods of Prayer*).[159]

The scriptural support adduced by Nikiphoros is (cf. Luke 17:21) "the kingdom of heaven is within us". The emphasis in the process that he describes is correspondingly more on the location of the intellect in the heart, and by this means finding God within, than it is on mental vigilance and guarding against distractive thoughts (although these elements are not entirely lacking).

The text as a whole clearly still understands watchfulness as a remedy for the passions. However, this is largely expressed in the anthology of other writings with which it begins. Nikiphoros himself does not speak of this aspect, except to refer to it (in only one place, in the introduction) as a means to achieve dispassion.[160] Rather, one is left with the impression that the (very long) opening sentence summarises the primary purpose of watchfulness in Nikiphoros' understanding:

> to attain the wondrous divine illumination of our Saviour Jesus Christ; to experience in your heart the supracelestial fire and to be consciously reconciled with God....[161]

### e. Watchfulness: Some Conclusions

What conclusions may we draw, then, in regard to these four different accounts of watchfulness?

Firstly, we must note the holistic understanding that each of these authors brings. Bodily concerns are not neglected. For Hesychios and (especially) Philotheos this is found in the ascetic context within which watchfulness is firmly located. For the author of the *Three Methods of Prayer*, and for Nikiphoros, the somatic elements of their methods of prayer (posture and breathing in particular) ensure that this is not seen as a purely psychological or spiritual exercise. All four authors also emphasise psychological processes. Although this is more evident in the first three as a process of mental vigilance over thoughts, it is represented by Nikiphoros as a concern with bringing the intellect to reside in the heart. But none of these authors describe a purely psychosomatic process. In each case, prayer is seen as a vital component of watchfulness, and this receives a particular Christological emphasise from Hesychios and Philotheos.

Secondly, watchfulness is clearly described in various ways, and with varying emphasis by different authors within the *Philokalia*. This is evident in the theological and scriptural under-pinning of the process, in descriptions of it, and in methods prescribed for its realisation. Doubtless, had more examples been considered here, we might have identified even greater variety.

Thirdly, watchfulness is clearly an important remedy for the passions. This is set in the context of a vision or goal of contemplative prayer, and is not an end in itself. However, there is no doubt that watchfulness is perceived as a powerful remedy, which the *Philokalia* highly commends.

### iii. Psalmody

We have already noted in passing (above) that psalmody was one of the remedies for the passions prescribed by Evagrios. Evagrios listed psalmody (along with longsuffering and compassion) as being of particular value as a remedy for passions associated with the incensive power of the soul (the thumos), and one of the texts in which he makes this link is included in the *Philokalia*.[162]

Apart from some quotations from Psalms by Isaiah the Solitary, Evagrios is the first contributor to the *Philokalia* to address psalm-

## Chapter 3: Remedies for the Passions 133

ody as a remedy for the passions. Given also the importance of the Evagrian tradition generally as formative of the authors of the *Philokalia*, it will therefore be helpful to give some further consideration to what Evagrios has to say on this subject.

Five principal texts by Evagrios on psalmody are extant, and four of these, from *On Prayer*, are included in the *Philokalia*.[163] The relevant passage in which these four texts appear (taken here from the English translation of the *Philokalia*) is as follows:

> 82. Pray gently and calmly, sing with understanding and rhythm; then you will soar like a young eagle high in the heavens.
>
> 83. Psalmody calms the passions and curbs the uncontrolled impulses in the body; and prayer enables the intellect to activate its own energy.
>
> 84. Prayer is the energy which accords with the dignity of the intellect; it is the intellect's true and highest activity.
>
> 85. Psalmody appertains to the wisdom of the world of multiplicity; prayer is the prelude to the immaterial knowledge of the One.
>
> 86. Spiritual knowledge has great beauty: it is the helpmate of prayer, awakening the noetic power of the intellect to contemplation of divine knowledge.
>
> 87. If you have not yet received the gift of prayer or psalmody, persevere patiently and you will receive it.[164]

The immediately preceding chapters of *On Prayer* are concerned with the importance of imageless prayer (66-73) and the assistance offered by angels to those who pray (74-81). The chapters in question (82-87, and particularly 82, 83, 85 and 87) then turn to the relationship between psalmody and prayer. The theme of prayer is continued in Chapter 88. Chapters 89-105 are concerned with various kinds of trials and sufferings, including attacks of the demons.[165]

Dysinger's helpful commentary on this passage[166] concludes that it shows how Evagrios understood psalmody and prayer as mutually supportive. He argues that it shows psalmody as preparing the whole person (body, soul and nous) for prayer. One aspect of the support that psalmody provides for prayer (although by no means the only consideration here) is its remedial effect against the passions.

A key word here, in Chapter 82, is "rhythmically" (εὐρύθμως). This adverb has been variously translated as "with rhythm" (as here, in the *Philokalia*), "with good rhythm", "with attention to the requirements of music", "in a well ordered way", or "well rhythmed".[167] Whilst the primary reference is to the proper cadence and rhythm of chanting the psalms, it seems possible (if not likely) that Evagrios is also hinting at an inner harmony of psalmody which parallels the calmness of prayer.

In Chapter 83, Evagrios uses the verb κατευνάζω to indicate the calming effect of psalmody on the passions. This can mean "to put to bed", "to lull [to sleep]", "to quiet or calm", or (in theological usage) "to appease". It can also refer to the soothing of a wound or physical disorder, the soothing of emotions, and the soothing effect of music.[168] There would appear to be allusions here to an ancient pagan understanding of the soothing effects of music on animals, and on the irrational part of the human soul, which was taken up by the Christian tradition. Evagrios' use of the term in this way is consistent with similar usage by Basil of Caesarea and Gregory of Nyssa.

Another key term in Chapter 83 is ἀκρασία. This may variously be translated "uncontrolled impulses" (as here), "intemperance", or "imbalance". In the Septuagint and New Testament it invariably refers to lack of self-control or self-indulgence. It is thus the vice opposed to the virtue of temperance, a vice of indulgence or excess. However, there is an alternative possible meaning, which is less common and more specific. Here, in a more physiological, psychological or medical sense, it can mean "bad mixture", "failure of mixture", "disharmony" or "imbalance". This imbalance would then be taken to refer to an imbalance of the four humours, or incomplete digestion of food. This usage is not common in Christian texts. However, given Evagrios' proclivity for medical metaphors, it cannot be ruled out. Thus, psalmody may be understood as exerting either a moral or a physical/psychological restoration of balance, or perhaps both.[169]

Evagrios understood anger as a "boiling up" of the thumos, or incensive power,[170] a definition which draws on elements of definitions previously offered by Plato, Aristotle and Galen.[171] In various places, Evagrios links psalmody specifically with calming of the thumos.[172] In *Antirrhetikos*, Evagrios specifically describes the effect of psalmody as an effect on temperament (that is κρᾶσις or humoural balance, in this translation "condition of the body"):

> Against the soul that does not know that the melody that accompanies the Psalms alters the condition of the body and drives away the demon that touches it on the back, chills its sinews, and troubles all its members:
> And it happened that when the evil spirit was upon Saul, David took his harp and played with his hand, and Saul was refreshed, and it was good with him, and the evil spirit departed from him (1 Kgdms 16:23).[173]

Psalmody thus appears to have been understood by Evagrios as exerting a remedial effect, at least on passions of the incensive part of the soul, via a soothing influence which restored humoural balance. The remedy for passions of the thumos that Evagrios found in the practice of psalmody was important not only because of its direct effect on these passions, but also because a restored thumos itself has a part to play in combating the passions. Anger, properly directed against the demons, used "in accordance with nature", is thus itself a remedy for the passions.[174]

However, Evagrios perceived the Psalms as being a remedy for the passions in at least two further ways. The first of these is hinted at in Chapter 85 of *On Prayer*. Here, psalmody is associated with the multiplicity of the created order, and prayer with the divine unity. The multiplicity (ποίκιλος), or diversity, of the created order is understood by Evagrios as a manifestation of divine wisdom (cf. Ephesians 3:10: ἡ πολυποίκιλος σοφία τοῦ θεοῦ). In Dysinger's translation of this chapter, this is referred to as "multiform wisdom".[175] Multiform wisdom appears to be understood by Evagrios as denoting the opportunity that the Psalms afford for contemplation of God through the logoi (meanings) concealed behind the appearance of created things. However, created things also have the potential to provide distractions during prayer. Pure prayer, for Evagrios, is without any images of such things.

In *Praktikos* 69-71, Evagrios writes in more detail of the importance of undistracted psalmody:[176]

> 69. To pray without distraction is a considerable achievement, but greater still is the ability to practise psalmody also without distraction.

> 70. The person who has established the virtues within himself and has become wholly mingled with them no longer remembers the law or the commandments or punishment, but says and does those things which this excellent state dictates to him.
>
> 71. The demonic songs set our desire in motion and cast the soul into shameful fantasies, but psalms, hymns, and spiritual songs (Eph 5:19) call the mind to the constant remembrance of virtue, cooling our boiling irascibility and extinguishing our desires.[177]

The problem that he appears to be grappling with here is that undistracted prayer requires a laying aside of images, but that the Psalms present a multiplicity of images and can thus be distracting. However, in Chapter 70 he goes on to speak of the person who is "entirely permeated" with the virtues. The word that is used for this is ἀνάκρασις. This is strongly reminiscent of his reference to the power of psalmody to affect a restoration of the κρᾶσις of humoural balance. In Chapter 71, he goes on to write of the beneficial effect of psalmody on all three parts of the soul: thumos, epithumia, and nous. Thus, meditation on the content of the Psalms, according to Evagrios, has the potential to bring about a mingling or permeation of the soul with virtues.

A fuller understanding of what undistracted psalmody entails is to be found in his *Scholia on Psalms* where, commenting on verse 1 of Psalm 137, he writes:

> To chant psalms before the angels is to sing psalms without distraction: either our mind is imprinted solely by the realities symbolised by the psalm, or else it is not imprinted. Or perhaps the one who chants psalms before the angels is he who apprehends the meaning of the psalms.[178]

Undistracted psalmody can thus mean three things:

1. The mind is passively imprinted with the inner meaning of the psalm

2. The mind receives no such impression (presumably because it is attentive to God)

3. The mind actively searches for the meaning of the psalm

Dysinger suggests that Evagrios intends that undistracted psalmody requires the ability to move backwards and forwards between these different meanings.[179] It is a form of contemplative prayer which is impressionable, focussed on God, and actively searching, all at the same time – or at least in a dynamic interplay, one after the other. Whilst this is another way in which psalmody provides a remedy for the passions, by bringing about a "mingling" of the soul with virtue, this is clearly not its most important function. Rather, it is a reflection of the way in which psalmody merges with contemplative prayer. The focus here is on contemplation of the inner meanings of things, and on God himself.

However, Evagrios also understood the Psalter, if not also the practice of psalmody,[180] as a remedy for the passions in yet another way. Here, the metaphor that Dysinger employs is one of a spiritual weapon, rather than a medical remedy.[181] However, as we have seen, multiple metaphors may be applied in this arena, and we may return to the medical imagery shortly.

The Psalter provided Evagrios with a spiritual weapon in various ways. Most fundamentally, it could be used for ἀντίρρησις (antirrhesis), that is "refutation" or "contradiction" of demons, thoughts, people, and sinful tendencies or behaviours. It also provided him with a source of spiritual comfort, and prayers.[182] In all these ways, it could be used similarly to many other biblical texts. We have already seen (above) that the book of *Psalms* was cited more frequently by Evagrios in his *Antirrhetikos* (a collection of biblical texts to be used for antirrhesis) than any other book of scripture. Interestingly, the *Psalms* are used most often not in the section devoted to anger (where five such quotations appear) but in the sections on sadness (22 quotations) and acedia (18 quotations).[183] Antirrhetic texts are found in Evagrios' *Scholia on Psalms*, as well as in *Antirrhetikos*.[184]

Returning to our theme of psalmody as a remedy for the passions, this "spiritual weapon" might better be understood in medical terms as being an antidote, a prophylactic medicine, or perhaps a form of cognitive psychotherapy.

To review what has been said here on the Evagrian understanding of psalmody as a remedy for the passions, we are left with at least three models or processes:

1. Psalmody as restorative of a balance in the thumos, perhaps primarily through the calming effect of the rhythm of psalmody

2. Psalmody as bringing about a merging of the soul with the virtues, through a complex process of both active and passive contemplative prayer

3. Psalmody as a cognitive and spiritual "antidote" for the passions

Only the first of these might properly be said to be evident in texts included in the *Philokalia*, the second is merely hinted at, and the third is only to be found elsewhere in the Evagrian corpus. We must therefore now proceed to consider how other authors whose works are included in the *Philokalia* understand this remedy for the passions.

Firstly, it must be said that there are surprisingly few references to psalmody (as opposed to references to the *Psalms*) in the *Philokalia*. Only 37 references are listed in Stapakis' master index to the first four volumes of the English translation.[185] This is surprising not only because of the length of the *Philokalia* (there being over 1500 pages in these four volumes) but also because the Psalter occupied a central place in monastic life by the end of the fourth century. Psalmody was virtually a universal practice amongst the Desert Fathers, and occupied many of their waking hours.[186] Nor was the practice discontinued. Gregory of Sinai (*c.*1265-1346), for example, describes a daily routine in which psalmody occupied three hours each day.[187]

Secondly, it is evident that there is a heterogeneity of views on the subject of psalmody represented and addressed within the pages of the *Philokalia*. This is evident within one text by Gregory of Sinai, where he specifically addresses himself to the question:

> Why do some teach that we should psalmodize a lot, others a little, and others that we should not psalmodize at all but should devote ourselves only to prayer and to physical exertion such as manual labour, prostrations or some other strenuous activity?[188]

However, it is not simply a question of varying views on quantity. Maximos the Confessor writes of psalmody as a means of acquiring love and cleaving to God.[189] Thalassios the Libyan refers to psalmody

## Chapter 3: Remedies for the Passions

along with moderate fasting and vigils as a means of "achieving a balance in the body's temperament" (presumably reflecting a humoural understanding similar to that of Evagrios).[190] Ilias the Presbyter understands prayer as better than psalmody, and natural contemplation as better still.[191] Nikitas Stithatos, who addresses himself to the problems of distraction in psalmody, emphasises psalmody as prayer of the intellect, and itself a form of contemplation.[192]

Evagrios is not alone amongst contributors to the *Philokalia* in understanding psalmody as a remedy for the passions. John of Karpathos (?fifth to seventh century), quoting Ephesians 5:19, refers to the use of psalms to destroy the passions within.[193] Maximos the Confessor, although making more references to psalmody in relation to love of God, does also refer to it as a means of repelling impassioned thoughts.[194] Thalassios the Libyan refers to psalmody as a means of preventing delusion of the intellect by the passions. Given his reference also to the effect of psalmody upon the temperament of the body (see above), or in other words the humoural balance of the body, we may wonder whether he shared an Evagrian sense of the capacity of psalmody to subdue the passions via a mediating effect at this level.

We noted (above) that the *Seven Forms of Bodily Discipline* considered by Peter of Damaskos begin with three measures focussed on the development of the practical life. The fourth measure is the recital of psalms, which Peter understands as being directed at "purification of the intellect".[195]

The author of *Three Methods of Prayer*[196] appears to take a different view. As we saw above, he proposes four stages of the spiritual life, of which the second stage is concerned with the practice of psalmody. However, according to this schema of the spiritual life, this second stage can only be reached after the passions have been curtailed (in the first stage) by guarding of the heart:

> For when the passions have been curtailed and laid to rest, psalmody brings delight to the tongue and is welcomed by God, since it is not possible to sing to the Lord in a strange land (cf. Ps. 137:4), that is to say, from an impassioned heart. This is the mark of those who are beginning to make progress.[197]

So, not all texts in the *Philokalia* that refer to psalmody and the passions understand the former as being a remedy for the latter. However, as we have seen in the section on watchfulness (above) the

*Three Methods of Prayer* does provide a somewhat different view of watchfulness as well. The *Philokalia* is not a uniform collection of texts that have been edited so as to be in complete agreement with each other, but rather they provide a variety of views around a central concern with the purification, illumination and perfection of the Christian soul.

Psalmody cannot be understood as playing such a central role in the pharmacopaeia of remedies for the passions provided by the *Philokalia* as, for example, ascetic practice or watchfulness does. On the other hand, practice of psalmody was probably as universally observed as either of these practices were, at least in the fourth or fifth centuries.[198] If we assume (*pace* the question on varied practice addressed by Nikitas Stithatos nearly a millennium later) that psalmody remained a fairly universal monastic practice more or less consistently during the period covered by the *Philokalia*, we must ask what argument can reliably be made from silence? Either psalmody was not considered by most writers to be a remedy for the passions, but rather was understood as something else (a form of contemplative prayer, for example) or else it might have been so widely understood that psalmody was a remedy for the passions that nothing need be said about it. Neither of these hypotheses would seem very secure. However, where the subject of the relationship between psalmody and the passions is directly addressed within the *Philokalia* it would seem to support the latter rather than the former.

### iv. Prayer

Like watchfulness, prayer is so much at the heart of what the *Philokalia* is all about that it permeates almost every page. In fact, Stapakis' master index to the English translation of the *Philokalia* includes almost 250 references to prayer.[199] That the number is not even higher than this presumably relates only to the specificity of the use of the word "prayer". It is difficult to find any page of the *Philokalia* that does not have something to do with prayer, either directly or indirectly.

The *Philokalia* also has a diverse and broad understanding of what prayer might include, or how it might be defined. Thus, for example, it includes Evagrios' definition that "Prayer is communion of the intellect with God",[200] Maximos the Confessor's definition of prayer as "petition for the blessings given by the incarnate Logos",[201]

## Chapter 3: Remedies for the Passions 141

and Gregory Palamas' definition (quoting Isaac of Nineveh) that "prayer is purity of the intellect".[202]

Most contributors actually recognise a variety of kinds or levels of prayer. Thus, for example, Peter of Damaskos writes:

> For it is said of God that He 'gives prayer to him who prays' (1 Sam. 2:9. LXX); and indeed to one who truly prays the prayer of the body God gives the prayer of the intellect; and to one who diligently cultivates the prayer of the intellect, God gives the imageless and formless prayer that comes from the pure fear of Him. Again, to one who practises this prayer effectively, God grants the contemplation of created beings. Once this is attained – once the intellect has freed itself from all things and, not content with hearing about God at second hand, devotes itself to Him in action and thought – God permits it to be seized in rapture, conferring on it the gift of true theology and the blessings of the age to be. [203]

Peter seems to understand five stages of prayer:

1. "prayer of the body"
2. "prayer of the intellect"
3. "imageless and formless prayer"
4. "contemplation of created beings"
5. complete devotion to God "in action and thought", a "gift of true theology"

We might imagine that the higher stages of this schema correspond approximately to Evagrios' "pure prayer" (which is imageless and formless) and his categories of natural contemplation (of created beings) and theological contemplation (of God), although things cannot be quite that simple as, for Evagrios, pure prayer is imageless and natural contemplation is not.[204] However, the idea that the prayers of beginners will be different to those of people advanced in prayer is common to both Evagrios and Peter.[205]

Presumably, therefore, the first two stages of Peter's hierarchy would relate to the kind of prayer that Evagrios would have expected of the readers of *Praktikos* – that is, those engaged in establishing the practical life. For Peter, "prayer of the body" seems to have been psalmody.[206] As we have already seen, Peter understood psalmody as having a purifying effect upon the intellect. We might imagine, therefore, that he understood psalmody as purifying the intellect in preparation for the second stage of prayer, "prayer of the intellect".

If prayer is to be understood as a remedy for the passions, we might then expect those prayers that effect this remedial action to be those most needed by beginners engaged with the issues and struggles of the practical life. In the Evagrian schema, those advanced in prayer, who are engaged in "pure prayer" or theological contemplation, have largely left the passions behind. This is not to say that they are immune or need not be aware of further attacks from the thoughts/passions/demons, but rather that they are more proficient in dealing with such things, and that having more or less achieved apatheia, their primary concern is now with contemplation of God.

What kind of prayer, then, is required of beginners as a remedy for the passions? Both Evagrios and Peter seem to understand psalmody as playing an important part here. For Evagrios, as we have seen, psalmody has a bridge like quality, which takes prayer from concern with the multiform created order into the imagelessness of the divine unity. Its role for Peter (although we have not considered this in depth) would appear to be somewhat similar – in purifying the intellect in preparation for imageless prayer. Not that either Evagrios or Peter prescribe psalmody alone. Rather, as we have seen above, each of them emphasises the broader context of the need for engagement with the practical life.[207]

But does the *Philokalia* offer any other kinds of prayer that exert this remedial efficacy against the passions? One in particular requires further consideration here, for it has become very important in the spiritual tradition with which the *Philokalia* is associated, and this is "the Jesus Prayer".

The Jesus Prayer, in its full form, consists of the words "Lord Jesus Christ, Son of [the living] God, have mercy upon me [a sinner]". However, it may be abbreviated in various ways (e.g. "Lord Jesus Christ, have mercy", etc.) and in its simplest form may involve only the name of "Jesus". It is repeated many times, sometimes using a prayer rope with knots, which acts rather like a rosary, and it is usually recommended that repetition of the prayer be synchronised with breathing. For example, the first half of the prayer might be recited during inspiration, and the second half during expiration.[208]

The repetition of this prayer is an ancient practice. Diadochos of Photiki (*c*.400-*c*.486), in *On Spiritual Knowledge*, a work included in the *Philokalia*,[209] attaches some importance to unceasing "remembrance" of "the Lord Jesus" although he does not invoke the precise formula of the Jesus Prayer in its fully developed form. Neilos the Ascetic (d *c*.430) also refers to invocation of the name of Jesus in his writings, although not in the text on *Ascetic Discourse* included within the *Philokalia*.[210] Dorotheos of Gaza (*c*.506-*c*.560) is known to have used a prayer of the form "Lord Jesus Christ our God, have mercy on me! Son of God, save me!".[211]

The anonymous *Discourse on Abba Philimon* (sixth to seventh century), which is included in the *Philokalia*, is the earliest source to cite the precise formula "Lord Jesus Christ, Son of God, have mercy upon me".[212] The author cites Diadochos as authority for this prayer.[213] Hesychios (?eighth or ninth century), in a work included in the *Philokalia* (*Watchfulness & Holiness*), seems to have been the first to refer to "the Jesus Prayer".[214]

The Jesus Prayer provides a bridge from prayer expressed in words to the silence of prayer that is listening to God. It also provides a bridge between formal times of prayer and prayer undertaken during the course of everyday amidst the routine of work and other activities. It is thus a means of making it possible to "pray without ceasing".[215] It can be undertaken (more commonly) alone, or in groups. It provides a means to focus thoughts in prayer, in the present moment, "laying aside" other thoughts and distractions,[216] in the presence of God. It provides a bridge between oral prayer and prayer "of the heart", between "our" prayer and the prayer of Jesus "in us".[217]

The Jesus Prayer is linked with the *Philokalia* in the popular nineteenth century Russian story (or, more correctly, series of stories) commonly known as *The Way of the Pilgrim*.[218] In these narratives a wandering pilgrim, who carries with him a copy of the *Dobrotolubiye* which he reads devotedly, recites the Jesus Prayer continuously. The text of the *Philokalia* is quoted and alluded to frequently within the text of *The Way of the Pilgrim*. The "pilgrim" provides a model for the spiritual life of every Christian.

The English translators of the *Philokalia* suggest that "it is the recurrent references to the Jesus Prayer which more than anything else confer on [the *Philokalia*] its inner unity".[219] Although the Jesus Prayer is undoubtedly an important theme running through the *Philokalia*, this assertion would seem to go too far. Depending upon exactly how one might define references to the Jesus Prayer, it would seem that less than half of the contributing authors might be considered to make any kind of reference to the Jesus Prayer.[220] However, in places it does indeed assume particular importance, and one aspect of this importance is its place as a remedy for the passions. To that we must now turn. As the use of the Jesus Prayer is closely related to the subject of watchfulness, we shall consider again here the same four texts that we studied, above, under that heading.

### a. Hesychios the Priest: *Watchfulness & Holiness*

We have already seen that Hesychios considers watchfulness and the Jesus Prayer to be closely related considerations. "[C]ontinually and humbly calling upon the Lord Jesus Christ for help" was, in fact, the third of his five methods of watchfulness. Not only this, but he considered invocation of the name of Jesus to be a vital component of the overall process. He writes:

> Watchfulness and the Jesus Prayer, as I have said, mutually reinforce one another; for close attentiveness goes with constant prayer, while prayer goes with close watchfulness and attentiveness of intellect.[221]

And again:

> The Jesus Prayer requires watchfulness as a lantern requires a candle.[222]

The Jesus Prayer is not only a part of watchfulness in Hesychios' view of things. It is, rather, a form of prayer which reinforces, and is reinforced by, watchfulness, and which requires watchfulness, just as watchfulness requires the Jesus Prayer.

The Jesus Prayer is, however, also a remedy for the passions in its own right. In fact, Hesychios goes so far as to say that:

> it is impossible to cleanse our heart from impassioned thoughts and to expel its spiritual enemies without the frequent invocation of Jesus Christ.[223]

And again:

> Just as snow will not produce a flame, or water a fire, or the thorn-bush a fig, so a person's heart will not be freed

Chapter 3: Remedies for the Passions 145

> from demonic thoughts, words and actions until it has first purified itself inwardly, uniting watchfulness with the Jesus Prayer, attaining humility and stillness of soul, and eagerly pressing forward on its path.[224]

Elsewhere he refers to invocation of the name of Jesus as making the mind "invulnerable" to its enemies.[225] He refers to calling upon the name of Jesus as a means of conquering demonic fantasy.[226] He refers to the "venerable name of Jesus" as a means of breaking and routing the devil,[227] and to invocation of Jesus Christ by the intellect as a means of routing the demons and putting them to flight.[228] Invocation of Jesus Christ is also a cure for forgetfulness,[229] and a means of dispersing evil thoughts.[230] Although many of the metaphors used here are military rather than medical, it is clear that Hesychios sees the Jesus Prayer as a powerful and uniquely effective remedy for the passions.

### b. Philotheos of Sinai: *Forty Texts on Watchfulness*

Like Hesychios, Philotheos of Sinai also perceives a close connection between watchfulness and calling on Jesus Christ in prayer. After introducing his "noetic vision" in the first of his *Forty Texts on Watchfulness*, he links watchfulness and the Jesus Prayer in his second text as means of achieving this vision:

> From dawn we should stand bravely and unflinchingly at the gate of the heart, with true remembrance of God and unceasing prayer of Jesus Christ in the soul; and, keeping watch with the intellect, we should slaughter all the sinners of the land (cf. Ps. 101:8. LXX). Given over in the intensity of our ecstasy to the constant remembrance of God, we should for the Lord's sake cut off the heads of the tyrants (cf. Hab. 3:14. LXX), that is to say, should destroy hostile thoughts at their first appearance.[231]

Already, the nature of the relationship that Philotheos understands between watchfulness and the Jesus Prayer is hinted at here. The "true remembrance of God and unceasing prayer of Jesus Christ" hints both at the vision of the preceding paragraph, and also that such prayer is a weapon to be used in guarding that vision. In fact, Philotheos later employs a phrase which is uniquely his within the *Philokalia* – "to guard the heart with Jesus".[232] This is both a watching with and a fighting with. Jesus is vision, companion and weapon at the gateway to our hearts.

Later this relationship between watchfulness and prayer is spelled out in a little more detail:

> You must direct your wrath only against the demons, for they wage war upon us through our thoughts and are full of anger against us. As regards the manner of the hourly warfare within us, listen and act accordingly. Combine prayer with inner watchfulness, for watchfulness purifies prayer, while prayer purifies watchfulness. It is through unceasing watchfulness that we can perceive what is entering into us and can to some extent close the door against it, calling upon our Lord Jesus Christ to repel our malevolent adversaries. Attentiveness obstructs the demons by rebutting them; and Jesus, when invoked, disperses them together with all their fantasies.[233]

Watchfulness perceives the approach of the demons or evil thoughts and "to some extent" is effective in rebutting them. The incensive power of the soul, "wrath", is also a weapon that Philotheos encourages us to use against them. But it is only invocation of the name of Jesus that effectively repels and disperses them.

In addition to repulsion and dispersal of demons/thoughts, Philotheos of Sinai refers to the use of "unceasing prayer of Jesus Christ" to "destroy hostile thoughts at their first appearance",[234] and to "remembrance of Jesus Christ" to "concentrate your scattered intellect".[235] We saw (above – in the section on watchfulness) that he also speaks of the enemy being "put out of action". Later he writes:

> The blessed remembrance of God – which is the very presence of Jesus – with a heart full of wrath and a saving animosity against the demons, dissolves all trickeries of thought, plots, argumentation, fantasies, obscure conjectures and, in short, everything with which the destroyer arms himself and which he insolently deploys in his attempt to swallow our souls. When Jesus is invoked, He promptly burns up everything. For our salvation lies in Christ Jesus alone. The Saviour Himself

made this clear when He said: 'Without Me you can do nothing' (John 15:5).[236]

As with Hesychios, the primary metaphors used here are military rather than medical but, again, it is clear that Philotheos sees invocation of the name of Jesus as a powerful remedy for the passions. This remedy is applied as a means to an end of contemplative prayer, but in the process of its application that end is in part achieved, for it sees us standing side by side with Jesus. Conversely, the end in sight – perfect remembrance of God in the heart – is itself also a large part of the remedy.

### c. [Symeon the New Theologian]: *Three Methods of Prayer*

When considering the understanding of watchfulness offered by the author of *Three Methods of Prayer* (above) we noted that the method recommended concludes with invocation of Jesus Christ. Here, watchfulness seems to precede the use of the Jesus Prayer, and the latter is referred to mainly as a means of dealing with distractive thoughts. Here is the full description of the method:

> Then sit down in a quiet cell, in a corner by yourself, and do what I tell you. Close the door, and withdraw your intellect from everything worthless and transient. Rest your beard on your chest, and focus your physical gaze, together with the whole of your intellect, upon the centre of your belly or your navel. Restrain the drawing-in of breath through your nostrils, so as not to breathe easily, and search inside yourself with your intellect so as to find the place of the heart, where all the powers of the soul reside. To start with you will find there darkness and an impenetrable density. Later, when you persist and practice this task day and night, you will find, as though miraculously, an unceasing joy. For as soon as the intellect attains the place of the heart, at once it sees things of which it previously knew nothing. It sees the open space within the heart and it beholds itself entirely luminous and full of discrimination. From then on, from whatever side a distractive thought may appear, before it has

come to completion and assumed a form, the intellect immediately drives it away and destroys it with the invocation of Jesus Christ. From this point onwards the intellect begins to be full of rancour against the demons and, rousing its natural anger against its noetic enemies, it pursues them and strikes them down. The rest you will learn for yourself, with God's help, by keeping guard over your intellect and by retaining Jesus in your heart. As the saying goes, 'Sit in your cell and it will teach you everything.'[237]

Although the Jesus Prayer does appear to be a part of this method, the emphasis is more on the location of the intellect in the heart, as a way of guarding the heart, and less on the invocation of the name of Jesus. The latter also occurs after the former has been established, rather than (as with Hesychios) being integral and mutually reinforcing. After his description of the method of prayer, the author returns to the theme of his four stages of prayer. Here, in the third stage,[238] "invocation of the Lord Jesus Christ" is used to rout the evil spirits that cause further "blasts of passion".

### d. Nikiphoros the Monk: *Watchfulness and Guarding*

We saw, above, that Nikiphoros the Monk recommends a psycho-somatic form of guarding of the heart similar to that of the author of the *Three Methods*, and that he also refers to use of the Jesus Prayer only after the establishing of the intellect in the heart as the method of guarding the heart:

> Moreover, when your intellect is firmly established in your heart, it must not remain there silent and idle; it should constantly repeat and meditate on the prayer, 'Lord Jesus Christ, Son of God, have mercy on me', and should never stop doing this. For this prayer protects the intellect from distraction, renders it impregnable to diabolic attacks, and every day increases its love and desire for God.[239]

The emphasis here is already more clearly on establishing the intellect in the heart so as to pray – rather than an end in itself. The role of the Jesus Prayer is also expanded here (in comparison with the description in *Three Methods*) to defend against diabolic attacks

# Chapter 3: Remedies for the Passions

and to increase love for God. However, more importantly, it also assumes a role where the initiate experiences difficulty with the method of establishing the intellect in the heart:

> If, however, in spite of all your efforts you are not able to enter the realms of the heart in the way I have enjoined, do what I now tell you and with God's help you will find what you seek. You know that everyone's discursive faculty is centred in his breast; for when our lips are silent we speak and deliberate and formulate prayers, psalms and other things in our breast. Banish, then, all thoughts from this faculty – and you can do this if you want to – and in their place put the prayer, 'Lord Jesus Christ, Son of God, have mercy on me', and compel it to repeat this prayer ceaselessly. If you continue to do this for some time, it will assuredly open for you the entrance to your heart in the way we have explained, and as we ourselves know from experience.[240]

The Jesus Prayer therefore appears to assume greater importance here than it is given by the author of *Three Methods*.

### e. The Jesus Prayer: Some Conclusions

In conclusion, the Jesus Prayer clearly plays an important part in the *Philokalia*. Its use is closely related to the also important process of watchfulness, and the authors studied here generally seem to understand a mutually supportive relationship between the two. The nature of that relationship varies, with some accounts emphasising more the process of watchfulness (e.g. as in *Three Methods of Prayer*), and others the Jesus Prayer (e.g. Hesychios). However, in general, it must be concluded that the Jesus Prayer represents another important remedy provided within the therapeutic repertoire of the *Philokalia*.

## 5. Remedies for the Passions – Conclusions

The classical world, the Desert Fathers (including Evagrios), and the other authors of the *Philokalia* all sought remedies for the passions. In various ways, they understood the passions as enslaving, as hostile pleasures, which should at least be curbed if not completely eliminated.

Classical philosophy emphasised the importance of reason, and so tended to find reasonable remedies, although it has to be said that the Stoics were so radical in this quest that some readers may feel that the extremity of some of their measures, and of the quest to eliminate even human emotions that our society would value, might make them seem unreasonable.

Evagrios and the Desert Fathers were also extreme. Whilst the influence of classical philosophy is evident, especially in the writings of Evagrios, their motivation for elimination of the passions was clearly different. For them, the passions were a part of a world in which evil thoughts and demonic entities were not always easy to distinguish, and the quest to eliminate the passions was as much (perhaps more) theologically motivated than it was concerned with human flourishing, although of course they would not have distinguished between these aims. Radical evil called for radical measures, and some of the remedies that they applied would clearly be judged harmful, psychologically or physically, by our society. But this is to overlook an equally radical vision of prayer, which, for them, was so inspiring as to make all other sacrifices worthwhile.

These are the traditions that the authors of the *Philokalia* inherited and interpreted, each for their own day. If we are correct in assuming that the *Philokalia* was compiled as a "guide to the practice of the contemplative life", then the remedies that it sought to provide for the passions were each included with a view to the fundamental vision of prayer which made great sacrifice worthwhile. But the *Philokalia* also spans such a broad swath of history that it is not surprising that it also includes considerable reflection and variation upon the inherited influences of the classical world and, more importantly, the Christian traditions that emerged from the Egyptian desert in the fourth century.

The remedies for the passions that are found within the *Philokalia* are based upon perceptive psychological insights, and a depth of theological reflection. They are holistic, taking into account physical, psychological and spiritual aspects of what it means to be human. They are not cures which will simply make the problem go away, but they offer a way of life which may subdue and overcome the hostile pleasures that are the passions.

# 4
# Mental Well-Being

If the *Philokalia* provides a pharmacopoeia of remedies for the passions, then a little more needs to be said about the goal of the programme of treatment in support of which they are applied. Or, to put things a little differently, what does it mean to be a healthy and flourishing human being? In particular, what understanding of mental well-being does the *Philokalia* convey?

As in previous chapters, it will be helpful first to consider what the traditions of understanding were in the classical world and amongst the Desert Fathers, especially Evagrios. However, at this point some complicating problems of language, philosophy and history can no longer be avoided. Firstly, the overarching title of this work has been *The Philokalia and the Inner Life,* but what does it mean to speak of an "inner" life?

Charles Taylor[1] has pointed out that there is a language of inwardness in relation to the self which we imagine to be universal but which is actually a specific feature of self understanding in modern western civilisation. This is not to say that there are not universal ways in which human beings understand "inner" and "outer" dimensions to their lives, but rather that these universals are always embedded in historically and culturally richer and more specific understandings which rarely share many of the other features of our own sense of an inner "self".

There is a sense of "inside" which designates the thoughts or desires or intentions which we hold back for ourselves, as against those which we express in speech and action. When I refrain from saying what I think about you, the thought remains inner; when I blurt it out, then it is in the public domain. This distinction seems to be a common theme to many different cultures which is woven into a richer notion of what "inner" and "outer" mean, which expresses in each case the specific moral/spiritual vision of the civilization.²

For Taylor, the richer understanding of what "inner" and "outer" mean in our society has been formed by such processes as disengagement, radical reflexivity and expressivism. However important an understanding of these processes might be to the hermeneutical enterprise of applying the insights of the *Philokalia* to contemporary western life, we must beware any uncritical tendency towards finding them in its pages.

The history of inwardness which Taylor traces begins with Plato, but we should immediately notice that he chooses this starting point because it is clearly different to our own. Further, the next step in Taylor's history is concerned with Augustine of Hippo, to whom he attributes a major part in developing the language of inwardness that we know and use today. But Augustine of Hippo did not influence the history or thought of the *Philokalia*. The inner life of which the *Philokalia* speaks is therefore not necessarily the same in all respects, indeed is quite probably not at all the same in many respects, as the inner life of which we are used to speaking.

The second problem that we face is the use of the word "mental" in relation to well-being. This word, which has a fifteenth century Latin etymology, may now be defined as:

> of or involving the mind or an intellectual process.³

We have already seen (in Chapter 1) that the "intellect" (or νοῦς) has a specific meaning to the authors of the *Philokalia* which is significantly different than that of common contemporary western usage. "Mind" is also a word which does not have a direct equivalent in the *Philokalia*, but rather overlaps with the fields of meaning of words such as intellect (νοῦς), reason (διάνοια) and soul (ψυχή). Furthermore, contemporary western understandings of the mind are overlaid with further strata of philosophical meaning, notably those of René Descartes and his later critics, all of which are completely alien to the *Philokalia*. This behoves us to be careful in our terminology.

It might be argued that well-being of the soul, or spiritual well-being, would be better terms to use here, but this would simply shift the ground of debate, rather than avoid confusion altogether. In any case, it is already clear that the spiritual and psychological aspects of human well-being (not to mention also the physical and social) are so closely intertwined that no discussion of one can avoid discussion of the other without loss of something important to an overall understanding of what human well-being is all about.

The third problem that needs to be identified here is with the use of the word "well-being" itself. Here, the dictionary definition refers to

> the condition of being contented, healthy, or successful; welfare.[4]

Health is in turn somewhat difficult to define. Definitions in terms of the absence of disease are generally considered to be inadequate. The standard contemporary definition of the World Health Organisation, which somewhat controversially does not recognise a spiritual dimension to the concept, defines it in a rather circular fashion in terms of well-being.[5] Contemporary academic notions of well-being have in turn taken rather subjectivist, psychological and economic perspectives which would be largely anachronistic to ancient authors (although some interesting parallels with Epicureanism might be explored).[6]

It is interesting that our contemporary dictionary definition of well-being does not refer to happiness (although arguably contentment is not unrelated to happiness), or virtue, or the "good life". Previous generations of philosophers might find this completely incomprehensible. For example, Darrin McMahon[7] has traced a history of *The Pursuit of Happiness* which shows, amongst other things, that thinking about happiness and well-being have been inextricably linked since ancient times. Furthermore, the Greek word εὐδαιμονία is capable of translation as either happiness or well-being (although arguably the latter is more appropriate than the former).

The approach taken here, in regard to discussions of mental well-being, will therefore be one of exploring a range of terminology and concepts which appear to be characteristic of the literature concerned (firstly that of the Classical world, then that of the Desert Fathers and then, most importantly, that of the *Philokalia* itself). It will become apparent that well-being is a somewhat chameleon like concept (if indeed it might be regarded as a concept with any coherent or consistent meaning at all) that reflects the values, philosophies and theologies of the individuals and communities that have sought to find it. The aim in this chapter is not so much to critique those values and philosophies as to understand what they might have been.

## 1. The Classical Tradition

In the classical tradition health was understood as being concerned with appeals to natural norms and to a balance or blending of the qualities (moist and dry, hot and cold).[8] However, the philosopher Democritus of Abdera (fl. 420 B.C.E.), for example, noted that lifestyle was also important to an understanding of health, and that desires of the soul (e.g. for wine) could impair the health of the body.[9] Furthermore, human happiness does not depend upon physical health alone. What was (and is) more important than health in a narrowly medical sense therefore came to be recognised as human flourishing, or "eudaimonia" (εὐδαιμονία).[10] Eudaimonia, although it is sometimes translated as "happiness", actually implies activity rather than a passive state or feeling. It also carries a sense of the "completeness" of life, and thus cannot properly be assessed until a human life has been lived from birth through to death.

In Herodotus' *The History*,[11] the story is recounted of (an almost certainly fictional) encounter between the fabulously rich king of Lydia, Croesus, and the sage Solon. Croesus wished to know who the happiest man in the world might be, although it is clear that he thought he must be that man himself. He is shocked when Solon suggests that the happiest man is a dead father from Athens, killed in battle in the prime of life. Solon's suggested equal contenders for second place are also dead: two brothers who died in their sleep. Croesus concludes that Solon is "assuredly a stupid man"[12], but lives to repent of this and, having lost his son and a battle, and thinking that he is about to lose his own life as well, asserts that "No one who lives is happy".[13]

The story of Croesus and Solon is a reminder that none of us know what turn our lives will take in the future, and that the ways in which we negotiate tragedy and death are important components of well-being or "happiness". Important to note here, however, is that Herodotus employs at least three Greek words in order to refer to what it was that Croesus desired. Eudaimonia was to become the centrally important term in Greek philosophy, but here it is used alongside two words which might be translated "blessed": olbios (ὄλβιος) and makarios (μακάριος). All three of these words might be translated as "happiness". Olbios and makarios might also be rendered as "fortunate"[14] although in the latter case (as we shall see later) considerable theological reflection has subsequently been added by Christians to its original classical sense.

For Plato, eudaimonia was a matter of the harmony of the soul.[15] As health was to the body, eudaimonia was to the soul. This healthy, or harmonious, functioning of the soul was concerned with the ruling of the appetitive and incensive parts by the rational part. It was therefore not primarily a matter of feelings, but of the exercise of reason and self-mastery, and thus of virtuous living. Taylor[16] notes that this is not to be understood as mastery of the inner world over the outer (although undoubtedly Plato did think it better to live according to virtue, and to suffer for it, than to act contrary to virtue and be successful). Rather it was an affirmation of the soul over the body, the immaterial over the material, and the eternal over the changing. More importantly, the Platonic conception of reason was not one of the autonomously exercised reason of an individual, so much as conformity with a universal order of reason. It was about a vision of a cosmic order of reason. It was concerned with accession to an order of things outside oneself.

For Aristotle, eudaimonia was defined in terms of both a life of virtue and adequate availability of external goods.[17] As we have already seen in Chapter 3, Aristotle (like Plato) did not imagine that this required elimination of the passions – but rather their moderation. Aristotle also placed an emphasis on practical wisdom (phronesis) exercised by the individual in particular circumstances, but this was combined with an appreciation (common to Plato and Aristotle) of the importance of contemplation (θεωρία) of the eternal order. Contemplation brought human beings closer to the divine order, it was concerned with a striving for perfection. And because human beings are uniquely endowed with reason, the exercise of reason was understood as being a particularly important part of this striving.

For the Epicureans and Skeptics, eudaimonia was concerned with freedom from disturbance by the passions or "ataraxia". For the Skeptics this was concerned with eschewing commitment to particular beliefs.[18] For the Epicureans, it was held important to see through the illusions of divine order in order to appreciate the pleasures of present reality.[19]

For the Stoics, complete elimination of the passions was necessary for eudaimonia, which was defined in terms of the right activity of reason, or wisdom and virtue in thought.[20] The Stoics retained a vision of a cosmic order but (in distinction to Plato and Aristotle) not of contemplation of this order for its own sake.[21] For the Stoics, virtue was everything.

Classical notions of human flourishing were therefore diverse, but generally included an important place for the proper use of reason to eschew, or adopt, proper beliefs as a basis for behaviour.

## 2. The Desert Fathers

In the *Apophthegmata* human flourishing, happiness, health and well-being do not seem to be predominant concerns. In fact, any understanding of such that might be found here is rather turned upside down. Things are actually often said to be well when they appear to be quite the opposite. Thus, for example, Abba Nilus says:

> Happy is the monk who thinks he is the outcast of all.[22]

However, other related themes do emerge as important. Thus, inner peace (or hesychia) is highly prized. For example, Antony the Great warns against losing it,[23] Abba Doulas urges that it should be protected[24], and Abba Joseph exhorts a brother to go wherever his soul will most be at peace.[25] Abba Rufus, in response to a brother's question, says that inner peace is:

> sitting in one's cell with fear and knowledge of God, holding far off the remembrance of wrongs suffered and pride of spirit. Such interior peace brings forth all the virtues, preserves the monk from the burning darts of the enemy, and does not allow him to be wounded by them.[26]

He goes on not only to urge the brother to acquire it, but to exhort him to keep in mind his future death. In Rufus's estimation it is therefore clearly not an easy accommodation with comfortable feelings, but rather a challenging confrontation with one's own contingency upon God. It is also not singled out as an unique goal. For example, Abba Poemen sees it as an equivalent work to giving thanks to God despite illness, or serving God with purity of mind.[27]

Similarly, the thematic collection of sayings has a whole section on progress in perfection. As is so typical of the *Apophthegmata*, perfection does not appear to be understood here in any consistent fashion. We find Antony telling us how to please God,[28] Zacharias telling us what makes a monk,[29] John the Short imagining a man with all the virtues,[30] Sisois telling us how to find peace,[31] and an anonymous hermit urging us to seek inner grief and humility,[32] amongst a variety of other sayings. Perfection may be found here in various, and often paradoxical, ways. Perhaps this is not surprising if we recall that these sayings emerged from a tradition which had sought peace and perfection by a living martyrdom in the Egyptian desert. Here, health and well-being are found only when they are lost.[33]

## 3. Evagrios of Pontus

Evagrios generally seems to regard health as being the antithesis of the passions. Thus, for example, in *Gnostikos* he states:

> Those, therefore, who are still afflicted with the passions and who peer into the *logoi* of bodies and incorporeal [beings] resemble invalids who [carry on] discuss[ions] concerning health.[34]

Here, he refers to those who are afflicted by the passions as resembling "invalids". More usually, he refers metaphorically, analogically, or otherwise to passions as states of sickness or disease, and occasionally to wounds or injuries.[35]

Elsewhere, virtually all of the eight thoughts are explicitly contrasted to a state of health. Thus, for example, he refers to gluttony as "unbridled madness, a receptacle of disease, envy of health" and abstinence he associates with health.[36] Similarly, anger, fornication, sadness, acedia, vainglory and pride are all contrasted with health of the soul.[37]

As the passions are contrasted with health, it is no surprise to discover that Evagrios associates impassibility with health. In *Praktikos*, he even goes so far as to say that impassibility *is* the health of the soul.[38] In Chapter 1 we noted that Evagrios understood demonic thoughts as entering the soul through mental representations or images,[39] and so it is also no surprise to find that he understands the formation of images in sleep as an indication of ill health.[40]

There are occasional hints that Evagrios does not necessarily see health of the body and health of the soul as always going together. Thus, for example, we find him saying (at the beginning of a series of chapters on acedia) that "what is food for the healthy body constitutes a temptation for the noble soul".[41] He also acknowledges that illness and health do not distinguish between the just and the unjust.[42] However, elsewhere (and perhaps more commonly), he appears to see what is healthy for the soul as being good also for the body.[43]

Whilst the health of the soul is an important concept in the Evagrian literature, it is not the only one of relevance to our exploration of mental well-being or human flourishing. In particular stillness (hesychia), peace and blessedness are important.

Stillness is the fruit of the ascetic life[44] and psalmody.[45] Its preservation requires guarding of the senses, a "war on thoughts",[46] and perseverance.[47] It confers blessings and is "full of joy and beauty".[48] It is the "criterion for testing the value of everything".[49]

Evagrios urges that peace is to be sought in body, soul and spirit.[50] Peace with God is found through tears of penitence.[51] Peace is related both to impassibility and also to pure prayer, or contemplation.[52]

In at least two places in the *Philokalia*, dispassion is referred to by Evagrios as a blessing.[53] Prayer is also referred to as a blessed gift and a blessed path.[54] In *To Eulogios*, but not included in the *Philokalia*, Evagrios allegorically applies one of the beatitudes from Jesus' sermon on the mount ("Blessed are the peacemakers for they shall be called sons of God", Matthew 5:9) to the need for bringing about peace of body, spirit and soul.[55] In particular he urges his reader to apply ascetic discipline in the task of bringing about peace between body and spirit, and contemplative prayer to achieve peace and joy in the intellect.

An interesting set of seven beatitudes are included in *On Prayer* (see Table 4.2) which appear to be original to Evagrios.[56] The first four of these beatitudes are concerned with the blessedness of the intellect in relationship to God in prayer, a blessedness which is associated with a series of freedoms: from forms (or mental images), from distractions, from material things, and from sensations. Positively these freedoms (or at least the second of them) are associated with a greater desire for God. The remaining three of these beatitudes are concerned with blessedness of the monk in relation to self and others. Respectively, they are concerned with the ability of the monk to see God in others, to rejoice in the spiritual progress of others as though it were his own, and to regard himself as "the off-scouring of all things".[57] Positively these three beatitudes (or at least the first of them) are associated with an encounter with God in others.

The Evagrian beatitudes invert our understanding of happiness and well-being in a similar way to the sayings recorded in the

*Apophthegmata* or the beatitudes attributed to Jesus in two of the synoptic gospels (Matthew 5:3-11 and Luke 6:20-22), all of which Evagrios was presumably very familiar with. Perhaps most especially they are evocative of Mathew 5:8, "Blessed are the pure in heart, for they will see God".

As we saw in Chapter 1, for Evagrios, the goal in life was "pure prayer" or contemplative knowledge of God. Impassibility and inner peace, or hesychia, were merely preparatory for this. In a very real sense, for Evagrios, human flourishing was not so much about health, peace, or impassibility but rather about contemplative prayer and, ultimately, union with God. In Chapter 1 we considered the Christological context of this. Because God, in Christ, has both descended and ascended, so the contemplative who has (like all human beings) fallen from a state of health[58] is enabled to ascend to contemplative knowledge of God, a state of perfect health[59] and well-being.

## 4. The *Philokalia*

For Evagrios, then, human well-being was ultimately "pure prayer" or contemplative knowledge of God. This is, more or less, the tradition that the *Philokalia* adopted. Remedies for the passions are understood in the *Philokalia* as being applied with a view to attaining a state of contemplative prayer, or union with God, which is desirable above all other things. Even hesychia or apatheia are only objectives which are necessary as a means of achieving this goal. However, the exact nature of human well-being in the *Philokalia* is complex and multi-faceted and needs to be considered in more detail.

### i. Deification

We have noted that Nikodimos understood the *Philokalia* as being "an instrument of theosis".[60] Theosis, or deification,[61] was a key doctrine of Byzantine theology. It has been defined as:

> the doctrine that the destiny of humankind, or indeed of the cosmos as a whole, is to share in the divine life, and actually to become God, though by grace rather than by nature.[62]

The explicit scriptural foundation for this doctrine is arguably more or less limited to 2 Peter 1:4:

> Thus he has given us, through these things, his precious and very great promises, so that through them you may escape from the corruption that is in the world because of lust, and may become participants of the divine nature.

However, much wider implicit support is found in the Old and New Testaments, such as references to the intimate relationship between God and his people (e.g. Deuteronomy 4:7), the sonship of the people of God (e.g. Exodus 4:22, Romans 8:14-17), the transformation of the people of God into the divine likeness (e.g. 2 Corinthians 3:18, 1 John 3:2), and the eventual gathering together of all things in Christ (Ephesians 1:10). Early support for the doctrine is found in the writings of Irenaeus (*c*.130-*c*.200) and Clement of Alexandria (*c*.150-*c*.215), possibly influenced by the Platonic ideal of assimilation to God: ὁμοίωσις θεῷ.

The central idea is that as God in Christ became human so, by grace, human beings are called to participate in Christ's divinity. Athanasius writes:

> "For the Word became flesh" (Jn 1:14) in order that he may offer it for the sake of all and so that we, receiving from his Spirit, may be enabled to be divinized.[63]

Christ is the epitome of human deification and the model of perfect humanity. The doctrine thus rests on an essential Christological foundation, without which it does not make sense. John Meyendorff writes that deification is:

> a Christocentric and eschatological concept, expressed in Platonic language but basically independent of philosophical speculation.[64]

The definitive formulation of the doctrine was to be established by Gregory Palamas. In the hesychast controversy of the fourteenth century, it was alleged that the doctrine of deification blurred the boundaries between creator and created beyond that which was acceptable. Gregory defended the doctrine as referring to a participation in the divine energies (which are uncreated but knowable), but not the divine essence (which is unknowable).[65]

# Chapter 4: Mental Well-Being

The topic of deification is in fact treated explicitly by relatively few authors of the *Philokalia*, and specifically only by the author(s) of the text attributed to Antony the Great, Theodoros the Great Ascetic, Maximos the Confessor, Thalassios the Libyan, Theognostos, Ilias the Presbyter, Nikitas Stithatos, Theoliptos, Gregory of Sinai, and Gregory Palamas. Of these Maximos has much the most to say.

Deification is a characteristic theme of Maximos, for whom it represents the only proper goal of human existence.[66] In *On the Lords' Prayer*, he grounds the doctrine in an understanding of the self-emptying (kenosis) of Christ. Although deification comes only by grace,[67] it depends on human acceptance, an acceptance which is accomplished by the discipline of an ascetic life, which is itself a form of human self-emptying:

> The Logos bestows adoption on us when He grants us that birth and deification which, transcending nature, comes by grace from above through the Spirit, The guarding and preservation of this in God depends on the resolve of those thus born: on their sincere acceptance of the grace bestowed on them and, through the practice of the commandments, on their cultivation of the beauty given to them by grace. Moreover, by emptying themselves of the passions they lay hold of the divine to the same degree as that to which, deliberately emptying Himself of His own sublime glory, the Logos of God truly became man.[68]

A little further on, he also grounds the basis for deification in sacramental life,[69] in the movement of the intellect towards God,[70] and in the life of prayer.[71] Here and elsewhere Maximos' argument is deeply Christological, being rooted in the incarnation of God in Christ,[72] and the eventual perfection of the "person created according to Christ" is manifested thus:

> he is not in the least perturbed by any of the things that afflict the body, nor does he stamp his soul with any trace of distress, thereby disrupting his joy-creative state. For he does not regard what is painful in the senses as a privation of pleasure: He knows only one pleasure, the marriage of the soul with the Logos. To be deprived of this marriage is endless torment, extending by nature through all the ages. Thus when he has left the body and all that pertains

to it, he is impelled towards union with the divine; for even if he were to be master of the whole world, he would still recognize only one real disaster: failure to attain by grace the deification for which he is hoping.[73]

Deification is thus supremely desirable and inverts the natural understandings of pain and pleasure.

Elsewhere, in *Various Texts: C4*, Maximos grounds deification in a soteriological framework that makes reference to the divine "energy" to which Gregory Palamas would appeal in his defence of the doctrine some seven centuries later. Faith, Maximos concludes, brings about an ineffable union of the believer with his or her origin and consummation in God. The argument by means of which Maximos reaches this conclusion refers to an "inexpressible interpenetration of the believer with the object of belief" which is both the consummation of faith and a return to the believer's origin in God. This interpenetration brings about a fulfilment of the desire of the believer, an "ever-active repose in the object of desire", which in turn is an "eternal uninterrupted enjoyment" of this object and entails "participation in supra-natural divine realities".[74] This participation results in the believer becoming like that in which he participates and, as far as is possible, an identity of energy between the believer and that in which he participates. The argument concludes with a definition of deification which takes in, in one broad sweep, all of creation and the beginning and end of all things in God.

This identity with respect to energy constitutes the deification of the saints. Deification, briefly, is the encompassing and fulfilment of all times and ages, and of all that exists in either. This encompassing and fulfilment is the union, in the person granted salvation, of his real authentic origin with his real authentic consummation. This union presupposes a transcending of all that by nature is essentially limited by an origin and a consummation. Such transcendence is effected by the almighty and more than powerful energy of God, acting in a direct and infinite manner in the person found worthy of this transcendence. The action of this divine energy bestows a more than ineffable pleasure and joy on him in whom the unutterable and unfathomable union with the divine is accomplished. This, in the nature of things, cannot be perceived, conceived or expressed.[75]

Deification thus has an eschatological dimension for Maximos, as well as being Christological. It is ultimately ineffable and unfathomable, but is also fulfils the deepest human desire for God.

A text attributed to Maximos in the *Philokalia*, but thought by the editors of the English translation to have been written by an anonymous scholiast,[76] even refers to the "passion of deification". Rejection of passions which are superficial, false and alien to human nature lays open the way for a deeper, more authentic and fulfilling passion for God in Christ:

> Thus the intelligence, after rejecting everything alien, discovers what is desirable according to our true nature; and the intellect, after passing beyond the things that are known, apprehends the Cause of created things that transcends being and knowledge. Then the passion of deification is actualized by grace: the intelligence's power of natural discrimination is suspended, for there is no longer anything to discriminate about; the intellect's natural intellection is brought to a halt, for there is no longer anything to be known; and the person found worthy to participate in the divine is made god and brought into a state of rest.[77]

Although there is a degree of ambiguity in some passages, it is clear from the broad sweep of Maximos' eschatological arguments that he understands deification as something which is to be hoped for in this world and realised fully only in the world to come. Nonetheless, deification is a process,[78] something towards which we may be led by God in this life.[79]

Nikitas Stithatos suggests that there are three stages to attaining deification:

> When through the practice of the virtues we attain a spiritual knowledge of created things we have achieved the first stage on the path of deification. We achieve the second stage when – initiated through the contemplation of the spiritual essences of created things – we perceive the hidden mysteries of God. We achieve the third stage when we are united and interfused with the primordial light. It is then that we reach the goal of all ascetic and contemplative activity.[80]

The first two of these stages, the ascetic life and contemplative prayer, are clearly anchored in life in this world. It might be supposed that the third stage refers to a goal achieved only after death. However, the hesychasts believed that the vision of Divine light could be achieved in this life, and in the following paragraph Nikitas refers to the way in which, "by means of these three stages", intellects may provide illumination to others. Then, in the next paragraph, he writes:

> Deification in this present life is the spiritual and truly sacred rite in which the Logos of unutterable wisdom makes Himself a sacred offering and gives Himself, so far as is possible, to those who have prepared themselves.[81]

Here, then, deification is anchored "in this present life". Nikitas goes on, later in the same paragraph, to speak of these individuals as becoming "gods to other men on earth".

In contrast, Gregory of Sinai appears to distinguish between stages of spiritual perfection in this life and the corresponding state of deification to be achieved in the life to come:

> 55. A person is perfect in this life when as a pledge of what is to come he receives the grace to assimilate himself to the various stages of Christ's life. In the life to come perfection is made manifest through the power of deification.

> 56. If by passing through the different stages of spiritual growth you become perfect in virtue during this life, you will attain a state of deification in the life hereafter equal to that of your peers.[82]

Gregory also refers to "degree[s] of deification",[83] which appear to correspond to the degrees of spiritual progress made in this life.

Deification therefore appears as a broad and somewhat varied doctrine within the *Philokalia*. Maximos the Confessor has by far the most to say on the subject and, although it re-emerges in writings contemporary to the fourteenth century hesychast controversy, it is not as prominent as one might have expected even here.

## ii. Health & Well-Being

Returning to our themes of health and well-being, relatively little may be found explicitly on these subjects. Health of the soul is associated with the ascetic life by John Cassian and Ilias the Presbyter,[84] and with dispassion by Thalassios the Libyan.[85] Ilias the Presbyter warns that outward appearances of health can be deceptive and that sickness may lay hidden within, "in the depths of consciousness".[86] Evidence of health of the powers of the soul, he says, may be found in its absorption in the Jesus Prayer, in "opportune speech", and in "simplicity in taste".[87] Similarly, Peter of Damaskos finds evidence of health of the soul in contrition and humility.[88] Gregory Palamas finds the source of illness of the incensive power of the soul in unsatisfied desire, and the source of illness of the intelligence in distractions caused by sickness of the incensive and appetitive powers. He therefore counsels that healing of the incensive power is required first, then of the appetitive power, and finally of the intelligence, in order that full health may be restored.[89]

Neilos the Ascetic urges that well-being of the soul should be pursued first by guarding against mental preoccupation with material things, then by ascetic lifestyle, and finally by devotion to God.[90] Diadochos contrasts "natural well-being" with a state of being "energised by the Holy Spirit". The former is associated with "delusory joy" and the latter with "spiritual tears" and "a delight that loves stillness".[91] For Nikitas Stithatos, the capacity for well-being is located in wisdom and spiritual knowledge.[92] However, it is (again) Maximos the Confessor who has most to say on this subject.

For Maximos, the source of all well-being is found in God, but human creatures are free to accept or reject the gracious gift of well-being.[93] Maximos distinguishes between being, well-being and eternal being. Creatures with intellect and intelligence may participate in God in each of these kinds of being. The capacity for well-being is found in goodness and wisdom. Eternal being is a matter of grace alone.[94] In an allegorical interpretation of the first Genesis account of creation, in which he moves beyond the seven days explicitly referred to in the text and adds an "eighth day" of his own, Maximos argues that the sixth day represents fulfilment of the ascetic life and the attaining of virtue, the seventh day represents the contemplative life, and an end to natural thoughts about spiritual knowledge, and the eighth day represents the transformation which results in deification. Again, the sixth day represents the being of created things, the seventh day the well-being and the eighth day eternal well-being.[95] In this way, Maximos seems to suggest that a state of well-being is one of contemplative prayer. A state of eternal well-being, however, is one of deification.[96]

At this point we might conclude that both health and well-being in the *Philokalia* are concerned with achieving a life of dispassion and virtue. Well-being, however, appears to be the broader concept of the two, and it connects in turn with the doctrine of deification. Deification is a state of well-being, but it is much more than just this. It is an eternal, largely eschatological, but also very present and real, participation in God through Christ.

### iii. Purification, Illumination and Perfection of the Intellect

The full title of the *Philokalia* refers to it as being that "through which, by means of the philosophy of ascetic practice and contemplation" the purification, illumination and perfection of the intellect may be achieved. What does this tell us, if anything, about the nature of well-being that it envisages?

#### a. Purification of the Intellect

Purification of the intellect, which appears not to receive much explicit attention from most authors of the *Philokalia*, is achieved through ascetic discipline,[97] and tears of penitence, grief or fear.[98] Purity of intellect is evidenced by visions,[99] union with God in prayer,[100] spiritual perception and contemplative knowledge.[101] Presumably the compilers of the *Philokalia* understood a broader, implicit, sense in which its instructions on "ascetic practice and contemplation" would bring about purification of the intellect. The authors of the *Philokalia*, however, appear more often to have addressed matters of purity and purification not so much specifically in relation to the intellect but rather more broadly (e.g. to purity of the heart,[102] purity of conscience,[103] or purity of prayer[104]). In general, these references would seem to support what has already been said, that is, that well-being is concerned with dispassion and contemplation of God in prayer.

#### b. Illumination of the Intellect

With regard to illumination of the intellect, however, some rather different, and often somewhat obscure, things seem to be said. Firstly, Evagrios refers in various places to visions of light,[105] although he also warns against something that might sound like "illumination of the intellect" as a deceit of demons.[106] In fact, this appears to be a warning against pride associated with mental or perceptual images taken as evidence of spiritual progress. Diadochos provides similar warnings and, like Evagrios, seems to preserve an understanding of an illumination of the intellect by Divine light which in some way enables the intellect to "see" its own light.[107] It is not exactly clear how this should be understood. Nevertheless, Diadochos (unlike Evagrios) appears to see this as occurring at a relatively early stage of spiritual progress and expects it to be followed by experiences of abandonment by God, which he expects will prevent arrogance and instil hope.[108]

John of Karpathos urges continued struggle "to preserve unimpaired the light that shines within your intellect".[109] In contrast to Diadochos, he appears to see any subsequent withdrawal of this light (now referred to as darkness of the intellect) as indicating a resurgence of passion. Something similar seems to be implied by Maximos the Confessor. First he refers to "continual participation in the Divine radiance", which leads to the intellect being "totally filled with light".[110] Later, however, he implies that failure to keep the passions at bay by means of love and self-control might lead to a diminishing or darkening of this light.[111] A not dissimilar dynamic is also described by the author of *Abba Philimon*.[112]

Exactly how these references to "illumination" should be understood is somewhat unclear. However, Thalassios the Libyan mixes a similarly mysterious reference to the "light" of the intellect with more obviously metaphorical and analogical references to light.[113] Ilias the Presbyter helpfully distinguishes between sensible and spiritual (or intelligible) light in a passage[114] which seems to suggest that the latter is not to be understood by way of visionary or sensory experience, but rather that this language is being used to contrast sensory/physical and spiritual experiences. Perhaps more important than considerations of the phenomenology of the experiences referred to are their meaning. Illumination of the intellect in the passages referred to above generally appears to be associated with control over the passions. It is also associated with perception of the love of God, meditation on the name of Jesus, and the action of grace (in Diadochos), intense longing for God, unceasing love and contemplation of God (in Maximos), natural contemplation and holy knowledge (in Thalassios), the revealing of hidden mysteries (Abba Philimon), and preoccupation with prayer (Ilias the Presbyter).

In the writings of Nikitas Stithatos, greater care seems to be taken to qualify exactly what is meant by illumination of the intellect. Thus, in *On Virtues: 100 Texts*, Stithatos draws an explicit analogy between the outer senses and "their inner counterparts". Within this framework the intellect is referred to as "beholder of the light of divine life". The pure intellect is then characterised as giving assent only to thoughts that are divine. Finally, the whole process (including those parts relating to the other "senses" of the soul) culminates in the transcending of sense perception, the attainment of what lies beyond the senses, and the savouring of the "delight of things unseen".[115] Again, in *On the Inner Nature of Things*, Stithatos refers to the way in which the pure intellect "illumines the soul with lucid intellections", and is itself enlightened with divine knowledge.[116]

Gregory of Sinai also makes explicit reference to the illumination of the intellect in pure prayer. Not only is the vision of the intellect free from mental images, but the light within it draws it away from sensory images and towards an ineffable spiritual union with God:

> According to theologians, noetic, pure, angelic prayer is in its power wisdom inspired by the Holy Spirit. A sign that you have attained such prayer is that the intellect's vision when praying is completely free from form and that the intellect sees neither itself nor anything else in a material way. On the contrary, it is often drawn away even from its own senses by the light acting within it; for it now grows immaterial and filled with spiritual radiance, becoming through ineffable union a single spirit with God (cf. 1 Cor. 6:17).[117]

The subject of illumination of the intellect is dealt with at some length by Gregory Palamas in *To Xenia*.[118] The illumination of the intellect that Gregory describes is referred to as ineffable, and presumably therefore it is neither a vision involving the senses nor a mental image of any usual kind. (In fact, in #59, Gregory appears specifically to exclude both possibilities.) Rather it perfects the "inner being" and confers miraculous vision of "supramundane" things. Gregory provides supportive quotations from Saints Neilos, Diadochos and Isaac, presumably to reinforce the orthodoxy of his own position. However, he appears to differ from most of the earlier writers in the *Philokalia* by asserting that, rather than being vulnerable to any recrudescence of the passions, this illumination of the intellect confers stability of virtue and disinclination to sin. It is also associated with perception of the inner essences (the logoi) of created things, the apprehension of supernatural realities, and visionary insight into past, present and distant things. In conclusion of this passage Gregory writes:

> But their main concern is the return of the intellect to itself and its concentration on itself. Or, rather, their aim is the reconvergence of all the soul's powers in the intellect – however strange this may sound – and the attaining of the state in which both intellect and God work together. In this way they are restored to their original state and assimilated to their Archetype, grace renewing in them their pristine and inconceivable beauty. To such a consummation, then, does grief bring those who are humble in heart and poor in spirit.[119]

Such a consummation of the relationship between God and the soul begins to sound very similar to the doctrine of deification.

Finally, although he does not appear to use the term "illumination of the intellect" in a narrow sense, any account of light mysticism in the *Philokalia* would be incomplete without reference to Symeon the New Theologian.[120] At the age of 20 years, Symeon had the first of a series of visions of divine light. Writing in the third person, his initial vision appears to have incorporated light of various kinds, physical and immaterial, earthly and heavenly. His account of this experience, *On Faith*, is included in the *Philokalia*:

> One day, as he stood repeating more in his intellect than with his mouth the words, 'God, have mercy upon me, a sinner' (Luke 18:13), suddenly a profuse flood of divine light appeared above him and filled the whole room. As this happened the young man lost his bearings, forgetting whether he was in a house or under a roof; for he saw nothing but light around him and did not even know that he stood upon the earth. He had no fear of falling, or awareness of the world, nor did any of those things that beset men and bodily beings enter his mind. Instead he was wholly united to non-material light, so much so that it seemed to him that he himself had been transformed into light. Oblivious of all else, he was filled with tears

and with inexpressible joy and gladness. Then his intellect ascended to heaven and beheld another light, more lucid than the first. Miraculously there appeared to him, standing close to that light, the holy, angelic elder of whom we have spoken and who had given him the short rule and the book.[121]

Symeon went on to write extensively about God, the Trinity and Christ in terms of light, and his experiences are clearly those of a kind of union with God which was deeply transformative. It is not difficult to see in them the kind of direct and unmediated participation in the Divine energies that Gregory Palamus would speak about three centuries later, but Symeon does not make the distinctions that Palamus makes between the Divine essence and the Divine energies. Symeon's account is emotive, experiential, ineffable and radically engaging.

### c. Perfection of the Intellect

As with purification (above), references are very often made to perfection in a more general sense, and in regard to related but different or overlapping concepts, rather than specifically and explicitly to perfection of the intellect itself. For example perfection of the soul,[122] spiritual perfection,[123] perfection in love,[124] perfection of the saints,[125] perfection of people,[126] a state of perfection,[127] or simply perfection (unspecified)[128] are all addressed in various places in the *Philokalia*. The relationship of these more general, or different, forms of perfection to the intellect is varied and interesting. For example, John Cassian tells of how he and his friend Germanos begged Abba Moses to tell them how they might approach perfection. In his reply, Abba Moses speaks of the ascetic life as a means towards achieving purity of heart (which he appears to understand as being perfection). In conclusion he says:

> Whoever has achieved love has God within himself and his intellect is always with God.[129]

For Abba Moses, perfection is a matter of purity of heart and of love of God and these in turn are affairs of the intellect.

Maximos the Confessor, in *For Thalassios: C2*, speaks of the soul that has reached perfection and deification as "ceasing from all activity of intellect and sense".[130] Elsewhere he speaks of the intellect being on a journey to God which culminates in perfection and deification, a state that is "not subject to change or mutation".[131] Yet, in *On the Lord's Prayer*, he speaks of the intellect of the "person created according to Christ" as moving "incessantly towards God".[132] This person is described both as having achieved perfection (constituted by humility and gentleness of heart) and as still hoping for deification.

Nikitas Stithatos, in *On the Inner Nature of Things*, describes a process beginning with repentance, which leads to extinguishing of the passions, and then Divine illumination:

> God, who is above nature, descends with light and ineffable joy into the soul and sits on the heights of its intellect as upon a throne of glory, bestowing peace on all its inner powers[133]

This peace brings healing of the three powers of the soul, perfection of the soul, and union with God.

In *On Spiritual Knowledge*, Stithatos gives an allegorical interpretation of the transfiguration, within which perfection in love (along with advancement in faith and restoration of hope) provides the basis for a vision of the Divine light. This Divine light is manifest as "intellections of [God's] unutterable wisdom".[134] Intellections, within the vocabulary of the *Philokalia*,[135] are not abstract concepts but rather represent the active apprehension of spiritual realities by the intellect.

A very similar dynamic to this second example from the writings of Nikitas Stithatos is found in the *Texts* of Theoliptos. Here it is continual prayer that arouses love for God, and then the intellect, united with love, gives birth to wisdom. In response to the cry of prayer, the divine Logos:

> lays hold of the noetic power of the intellect as though it were Adam's rib and fills it with divine knowledge; and in its place, bringing to perfection your inner state, he confers the gift of virtue.[136]

Here again, then, love for God leads to a kind of transfiguration of the intellect with divine knowledge. Neither is explicit reference to illumination of the intellect completely absent for, later in the same paragraph, Theoliptos refers to love as "light generating". Here, however, perfection (of "inner state") is the outcome of the process. This appears to be similar to the first example taken from Nikitas Stithatos (*On the Inner Nature of Things*, see above), where perfection (of the soul) is the outcome of the descent of the light of God upon the intellect. In the second example from the writings of Stithatos (taken from *On Spiritual Knowledge*) perfection (in love) appears to be what starts the process off.

In *To Xenia*, Gregory Palamas describes another dynamic of love, illumination of the intellect and perfection. Here, he concludes that:

> no one can acquire spiritual love unless he experiences fully and clearly the illumination of the Holy Spirit. If the intellect does not receive the perfection of the divine likeness through such illumination, although it may have almost every other virtue, it will still have no share in perfect love.[137]

Here, then, illumination seems to be the basis for acquiring love, rather than the other way around. Perfection (of the divine likeness and of love) is again the result of, rather than the starting point for, this illumination of the intellect.

It would appear, then, that perfection and the intellect are related in some complicated and varied ways, with very different approaches being taken by different authors of the *Philokalia*, and even by the same author in different places. But what about explicit and specific references to perfection of the intellect? Again, there are diverse relationships to other concepts that have already been discussed, and especially to purity and illumination of the intellect. In *Abba Philimon*, for example, Philimon is quoted as saying:

> Let us, then, do all we can to cultivate the virtues, for in this way we may attain true devoutness, that mental purity whose fruit is natural and theological contemplation. As a great theologian puts it, it is by practising the virtues that we ascend to contemplation. Hence, if we neglect such practice we will be destitute of all wisdom. For even if we reach the height of virtue, ascetic effort is still needed in order to curb the disorderly impulses of the body and to keep a watch on our thoughts. Only thus may Christ to some small extent dwell in us. As we develop in righteousness, so we develop in spiritual courage; and when the intellect has been perfected, it unites wholly with God and is illumined by divine light, and the most hidden mysteries are revealed to it.

> Then it truly learns where wisdom and power lie, and that understanding which comprehends everything, and 'length of days and life, and the light of the eyes and peace' (Baruch 3:14). While it is still fighting against the passions it cannot as yet enjoy these things. For virtues and vices blind the intellect: vices prevent it from seeing the virtues, and virtues prevent it from seeing vices. But once the battle is over and it is found worthy of spiritual gifts, then it becomes wholly luminous, powerfully energized by grace and rooted in the contemplation of spiritual realities. A person in whom this happens is not attached to the things of this world but has passed from death to life.[138]

Here purity of the intellect (in this case translated as "mental purity") is the fruit of the ascetic life and leads in turn to contemplation, perfection of the intellect, union with God (cf. deification), and illumination by divine light. Elsewhere, Theognostos associates purification, perfection, inward illumination, and the raising of the intellect "to the heights of contemplation".[139] Theophanis identifies a sequence of purging of the intellect, illumination of the heart, and "perfection that is endless".[140] Symeon Metaphrastis seems to imply that perfection of the intellect results from purification of the intellect.[141] Doubtless many other similar links could be cited which connect not only purification, illumination, and perfection of the intellect, but also contemplation, deification and other aspects of well-being.

A final example from Gregory Palamas, taken this time from *On Prayer & Purity*, specifically tackles the relationship between purity, illumination and perfection of the intellect. Firstly, Gregory suggests that we consider someone who has purified their intellect through diligence in prayer and has, as a consequence, received at least partial illumination of the intellect. The dangers against which Gregory counsels at this point are those of delusion, presumption and pride. Rather, Gregory urges that this person should recognise the enduring impurity of the other powers of his soul, exercise humility, and grieve inwardly, in order that he might find healing of the other powers of his soul. He concludes this passage by writing:

> He will cleanse its moral aspect with the right kind of ascetic practice, its power of spiritual apperception with spiritual knowledge, its power of contemplation with

prayer, and in this way he will attain perfect, true and enduring purity of heart and intellect – a purity that no one can ever experience except through perfection in the ascetic life, persistent practice, contemplation and contemplative prayer.[142]

This is perhaps a helpful place to conclude this section on purity, illumination and perfection of the intellect, for it is a reminder that these aspects of well-being are all inter-related, and also that (in this world at least) great caution should be exercised against assuming that final perfection has been achieved in any of them, or that there is no longer any need for the ascetic life or for prayer.

### iv. Hesychia

The English translators of the *Philokalia* define hesychia (ἡσυχία), or stillness, as:

> a state of inner tranquillity or mental quietude and concentration which arises in conjunction with, and is deepened by, the practice of pure prayer and the guarding of heart (q.v.) and intellect (q.v.). Not simply silence, but an attitude of listening to God and of openness towards Him.[143]

In their introduction,[144] they also note that the word bears a sense of being "seated" or "fixed". This meaning is reflected in the sense of mental "concentration" that they include in their definition. However, they also note that the spiritual path of hesychasm cannot be followed in a vacuum. It is anchored in the doctrine, ecclesiology, soteriology, sacramental and liturgical life of the Eastern Church, and also (although not exclusively) within a monastic tradition located within the wider life of that church. Hesychia also involves a bodily dimension, as well as being a state of mind, the inner tranquillity being mirrored by an outer state of withdrawal from the world.[145]

How is this term, hesychia, used in the pages of the *Philokalia*?

Firstly, this term is used extremely widely in the *Philokalia*. In fact, it is employed by every author of the *Philokalia*,[146] except the author(s) of the text attributed to Antony the Great, the author of the text attributed to Theognostos, Theophanis, and Symeon the Studite (in a text attributed to Symeon the New Theologian).

Secondly, although it is in the nature of these things that there can be no surveys or statistics to quantify the matter, hesychia is a state which is almost certainly attained by very few people.[147]

Thirdly, hesychia is closely related to a number of other subjects of importance. For example it is related to the practice of theology (in the strict hesychastic sense of participation in divine realities and prayer), which presupposes attainment of hesychia. It also overlaps with the practice of watchfulness.[148]

Fourthly, hesychia is achieved by a variety of means, variously described by different authors of the *Philokalia*. These include: watchfulness,[149] detachment,[150] obedience,[151] courage,[152] inner grief, patience and humility,[153] attentive waiting on God,[154] prayer,[155] and psalmody.[156]

Fifthly, hesychia frees the intellect from impure thoughts,[157] destroys hidden passions,[158] and removes "impassioned craving" from the soul.[159]

Sixthly, hesychia opens the intellect to divine knowledge,[160] is full of wisdom and benediction,[161] brings about fear and love of God,[162] is the pathway to heaven,[163] initiates the soul's purification,[164] is associated with dispassion,[165] leads towards perfection,[166] and gives birth to an "unceasing aspiration towards [God]",[167] to contemplation,[168] and to prayer.[169]

It may be helpful to examine a few passages a little more closely.

Peter of Damaskos, who includes hesychia as the first of his list of seven forms of bodily discipline, understands it as:

> living a life without distraction, far from all worldly care.[170]

This is unusual, in that it emphasises the bodily aspect (referred to above) without any reference to the soul (unless this is implied by the reference to "worldly care"). The definition provided by Nikitas Stithatos is more typical, in that it defines hesychia in terms of the intellect, but is much fuller than most other accounts. He writes that hesychia is:

> an undisturbed state of the intellect, the calm of a free and joyful soul, the tranquil unwavering stability of the heart in God, the contemplation of light, the knowledge of the mysteries of God, consciousness of wisdom by

virtue of a pure mind, the abyss of divine intellections, the rapture of the intellect, intercourse with God, an unsleeping watchfulness, spiritual prayer, untroubled repose in the midst of great hardship and, finally, solidarity and union with God.[171]

The extent of overlap with, and relationship to, other concepts is apparent here, including notably prayer, illumination of the intellect, watchfulness, and deification (or at least union with God). Elsewhere, Nikitas describes hesychia (here translated as stillness) as a state of centring on God:

> Souls whose intelligence has been freed from material preoccupation, and in whom the self-warring appetitive and incensive aspects have been restored to harmony and harnessed to their heaven-bound well-reined chariot, both revolve around God and yet stand fixedly. They revolve incessantly around God as the centre and cause of their circular movement. They stand steadfast and unwavering as fixed points on the circumference of the circle, and cannot be diverted from this fixed position by the sense-world and the distraction of human affairs. This is therefore the perfect consummation of stillness, and it is to this that stillness leads those who truly achieve it, so that while moving they are stationary, and while steadfast and immobile they move around the divine realities. So long as we do not experience this we can only be said to practise an apparent stillness, and our intellect is not free from materiality and distraction.[172]

These passages from Nikitas Stithatos both emphasise that hesychia is about a certain kind of relationship towards God as much as, if not more than, being anything to do with tranquillity and concentration. This orientation towards the Divine, as well as the relationship with other important concepts such as illumination of the intellect, is also brought out in a passage from *On Commandments & Doctrines*, by Gregory of Sinai:

> Noetic prayer is an activity initiated by the cleansing power of the Spirit and the mystical rites celebrated by the intellect. Similarly, stillness is initiated by attentive

waiting upon God, its intermediate stage is characterized by illuminative power and contemplation, and its final goal is ecstasy and the enraptured flight of the intellect towards God.[173]

It is clear here that hesychia is closely related to contemplative prayer. In *On Stillness*, Gregory also emphasises that it is apophatic in form, involving a "shedding" of all thoughts, even those which might normally be considered helpful in prayer:

> For stillness means the shedding of all thoughts for a time, even those which are divine and engendered by the Spirit; otherwise through giving them our attention because they are good we will lose what is better.[174]

In this chapter, our interest has been in the extent to which hesychia might be considered an aspect of health or well-being of the soul. With this in mind, it may be helpful to close with a quotation relevant to this theme. In *Abba Philimon*, Philimon tells Paulinos (another monk) that it is impossible to "conform to God" without hesychia, and that hesychia:

> gives birth to ascetic effort, ascetic effort to tears, tears to awe, awe to humility, humility to foresight, foresight to love; and [that] love restores the soul to health and makes it dispassionate, so that one then knows that one is not far from God.[175]

Hesychia, then, is the basis for health of the soul.

## v. Blessedness

The word "blessed" (μακάριος) and its derivatives are also extremely widely used in the *Philokalia*. In fact, it is virtually ubiquitous. We have already noted its classical usage, and have seen some of the ways in which it is used by Evagrios in his contributions to the *Philokalia* and elsewhere. How is it employed by other authors of the *Philokalia*? In this section, the following answers to this question will be explored:

- The *Theoretikon* provides us with a definition of blessedness

- God, or the attributes of God, are referred to as blessed in numerous places
- Virtues, qualities and practices are described as blessed
- People, souls, lives or ways of life are described as blessed
- Eternal life or heaven or the "age to come" are described as blessed
- There are comments on, or interpretations of, beatitudes taken from scripture
- The *Philokalia* has some beatitudes of its own

### a. Blessedness according to the *Theoretikon*

In the *Theoretikon*, attributed to Theodoros the Great Ascetic, the purpose of human life is defined as blessedness. The following account provides us with a significant insight into his understanding of the nature of blessedness:

> To come to another point: everything may be understood in terms of its purpose. It is this that determines the division of everything into its constituent parts, as well as the mutual relationship of those parts. Now the purpose of our life is blessedness or, what is the same thing, the kingdom of heaven or of God. This is not only to behold the Trinity, supreme in Kingship, but also to receive an influx of the divine and, as it were, to suffer deification; for by this influx what is lacking and imperfect in us is supplied and perfected. And the provision by such divine influx of what is needed is the food of spiritual beings. There is a kind of eternal circle, which ends where it begins. For the greater our noetic perception, the more we long to perceive; and the greater our longing, the greater our enjoyment; and the greater our enjoyment, the more our perception is deepened, and so the motionless movement, or the motionless immobility, begins again. Such then is our purpose, in so far as we can understand it.[176]

According to this text, we discover that blessedness is to be understood as "the same thing" as the kingdom of heaven/God. It is "to behold the Trinity" and to suffer deification. A dynamic is set up whereby "noetic perception" creates ever greater desire for God, which in turn leads to greater enjoyment of God, which in turn leads to even greater desire, and so on.

A little further on, a "characterisation" of blessedness is described, within which a little more detail is given:

> Blessedness – of which any significant life on earth is not only an overture but also a prefiguration – is characterized by both energies; by both intellection and willing, that is, by both love and spiritual pleasure. Whether both these energies are supreme, or one is superior to the other, is open to discussion. For the moment we shall regard both of them as supreme. One we call contemplative and the other practical. Where these supreme energies are concerned, the one cannot be found without the other, in the case of the lower energies, sequent to these two, each may be found singly. Whatever hinders these two energies, or opposes them, we call vice. Whatever fosters them, or frees them from obstacles, we call virtue. Energies that spring from the virtues are good; those that spring from their opposites are distorted and sinful. The supreme goal, whose energy, as we know, is compound of intellection and willing, endows each particular energy with a specific form, which may be used for either good or evil.[177]

Here, the "already but not yet" character of blessedness is emphasised by describing life on earth as being an overture and prefiguration of blessedness. By implication, blessedness will be fully realised only after death. Blessedness is then described as being characterised by two energies: intellection (or love), which is contemplative, and willing (or spiritual pleasure), which is practical. Where these energies occur in their supreme form (again, by implication, this is in heaven, after death) they are always found together. However, they also occur in lower and specific forms (by implication in life on earth) which may occur separately and which may be put to good or evil purposes.

Although this dynamic is somewhat complex and obscure, it appears to put blessedness in this world in the context of a perfect state of blessedness which (by implication) will be finally achieved in heaven. It also provides a model of the energies motivating the contemplative and practical life as of equal importance and each open to use or misuse, leading to virtue or vice respectively.

Other authors of the *Philokalia* also refer to a state of blessedness, but do not offer the detail of definition that is found in the *Theoretikon*. Sometimes, these references appear also to relate to deification, or something similar.[178] Maximos the Confessor refers to blessedness as being a work of God which has its origins outside of time – it has always existed[179] – which indicates at least that he did not understand blessedness as limited either to the Divine essence/energies or to human beings.

The overall picture here is one of scope for ever greater blessedness in this life, a process which is integrally related to, in fact virtually identical with, deification. The process is characterised by deepening love and pleasure, but it is not unopposed and it is anchored in the ascetic realities of a life of practical virtue.

### b. The Blessedness of God

The intimate relationship between blessedness and deification, as described in the *Theoretikon*, is hinted at elsewhere in the *Philokalia* by references to both God and people as being blessed. Perfect and uncontingent blessedness, however, is clearly found in God alone. Thus, for example, in *Holy Fathers of Sketis*, John Cassian records Abba Moses as saying that knowledge of God in his "blessed and incomprehensible being" is reserved for the saints in the age to come, but that he may still be known in indirect and lesser ways here and now, in the world of his creation.[180]

Similarly, the attributes (or energies) of God are blessed in a unique way, but in a way which may be apprehended (at least in part) by human beings, and which is related to the process of their deification. Thus, Hesychios the Priest, in *Watchfulness & Holiness*, refers to the "blessed light of the Divinity", which illuminates the human heart to the extent that it is freed from images and thoughts (i.e. "form" and "concepts").[181]

Maximos the Confessor refers to God's essence as blessed.[182] The person who achieves deification, in the life to come, experiences "the blessed life of God", which is the only true life.[183] Similarly, Nikitas Stithatos refers to God as the source of "blessed light" and to the "image of divine blessedness" which may appear in the one who is "commixed with God".[184] Gregory Palamas refers to God who "alone is blessed" but who makes others partakers in his blessedness.[185]

### c. Blessed Virtues, Qualities and Practices

We have already seen that Evagrios refers to dispassion and prayer as blessed. References to virtues, human qualities and spiritual practices as blessed are widely employed in the *Philokalia*. Thus ascetic practice,[186] aspirations,[187] attentiveness,[188] contemplation,[189] dispassion,[190] expectation of perfection,[191] goodness,[192] grief,[193] handiwork,[194] humility,[195] joy,[196] love,[197] mortification of the passions,[198] poverty,[199] prayer,[200] psalmody,[201] purity,[202] remembrance of God,[203] self control,[204] spiritual knowledge,[205] stillness,[206] transformation (of union with God),[207] truth,[208] wisdom,[209] and words (of God's wisdom)[210] are all referred to as blessed (or as blessings). These might, therefore, be taken as specific signs or indicators of what the blessed, or spiritually healthy, life might look like.

### d. Blessed People, Lives, and Ways of Life

Sometimes people are referred to as blessed by virtue of displaying a particular quality or virtue. Thus, for example, Hesychios refers to those who practice stillness as being blessed by the Holy Spirit,[211] and to those who force themselves to abstain from sin as being blessed by God, angels and men.[212] An extension of this form of reference is where a whole way of life is referred to as blessed, as for example where Neilos the Ascetic urges a return to the "blessed way of life followed by the first monks",[213] or where Symeon the New Theologian says that many have called the eremitic life blessed, but then indicates that he considers the life lived "for God and according to God" the most blessed.[214] A variation on this is where a person is called blessed for having achieved virtue or holiness of life of a wide ranging order.[215] This kind of reference sometimes becomes explicitly or implicitly a reference to deification.[216] A life free from the passions is also described as blessed.[217]

### e. Blessedness of Eternal Life

Christians believe that after death lies the hope of resurrection and eternal life. However, as has been discussed above, the distinction between life in this world and eternal life is not always so clear cut. Deification or blessedness might, at least partly, be realisable in this world, even if the full experience of their divine realities is not experienced until after the resurrection. The English translators of the *Philokalia*, in their glossary, point out that a distinction is frequently made in the *Philokalia* between the "present age" and the "age to come" (or the "new age"). But the realities of the age to come (τὰ μέλλοντα – the "blessings held in store") can, by grace, be experienced in the present age.[218]

It is not surprising, then, that the *Philokalia* understands the age to come, and eternal life, as blessed. Hesychios refers to the blessings of the age to come.[219] The author(s) of *On the Character of Men* (attributed to Antony the Great) refer(s) to the "eternal blessedness and peace" to be enjoyed "after death" by those who "detach themselves from worldly things".[220] In *Spiritual Texts*, Theodoros writes:

> Truly, when pure souls leave the body they are guided by angels who lead them to the life of blessedness.[221]

Later he talks of the purification of the novice, in order that he be made:

> fit for heavenly treasures, for a life of immortality and a blessed repose whence 'pain and sorrow have fled away' (Isa. 35:10. LXX), and where gladness and continual joy flourish.[222]

Again, [Theognostos] refers to the blessedness "held in store" for those who calm the passions, and which "awaits" those who engage in pure prayer.[223] Theoliptos speaks of living this present life "in the expectation of blessedness", so that "at death you will leave this world with confidence".[224]

However, where Diadochos speaks of Christ leading "back to the blessedness of eternal life all who live in obedience"[225] he is clearly speaking of a blessedness that is to be experienced in the present age. Eternal life is something into which Christians enter in this world, and not only in the age to come. Similarly, we noted above that the author of the *Theoretikon* understood "any significant life on earth" as being an "overture" and "prefiguration" of blessedness.

Speaking of the need for the intelligence to control the incensive and desiring parts of the soul, and for the latter two parts to be made to conform to their true nature, [John of Damaskos] writes:

> He who has acquired a spiritual understanding of this truth will share, even here on earth, in the kingdom of heaven and will live a blessed life in expectation of the blessedness that awaits those who love God. May we too be worthy of that blessedness through the grace of our Lord Jesus Christ. Amen.[226]

There is, then, a blessed life to be lived "here on earth" which is a sharing in the kingdom of heaven in the present, but also an "expectation of the blessedness that awaits". Ilias the Presbyter conveys a similar idea, by way of reference to the blessings of "the kingdom within us" as a "pledge and foretaste" of "the kingdom that is to come".[227]

Maximos the Confessor writes:

> If the divine Logos of God the Father became son of man and man so that He might make men gods and the sons of God, let us believe that we shall reach the realm where Christ Himself now is; for He is the head of the whole body (cf. Col. 1:18), and endued with our humanity has gone to the Father as forerunner on our behalf. God will stand 'in the midst of the congregation of gods' (Ps. 82:1. LXX) – that is, of those who are saved – distributing the rewards of that realm's blessedness to those found worthy to receive them, not separated from them by any space.[228]

There is considerable ambiguity here as to whether this passage refers only to the age to come, or also to those who are alive in the present age. The emphasis here is on the realm of blessedness as being that place "where Christ Himself now is", but this Christological emphasis is linked to a soteriological theme. The realm of blessedness is the realm of "those who are saved", "the congregation of gods". Blessedness is participation in God in Christ. This realm of eternity is the realm in which all Christians currently live – albeit they may not yet have been found worthy to be made gods or to receive its rewards.

A similar idea is conveyed by Nikitas Stithatos:

> The restitution that will be consummated in the age to come after the dissolution of the body becomes clearly evident even now, through the inspiration and inner

activity of the Spirit, in those who have truly striven, have traversed the midpoint of the spiritual path, and been made perfect according to 'the measure of the stature of the fullness of Christ' (Eph. 4:13). Their joy is eternal, in eternal light, and their blessedness is of that final state.[229]

Perfection is "the measure of the stature of the fullness of Christ", and the blessedness that is enjoyed by the perfect is of the "final state" to be consummated in the "age to come after the dissolution of the body". But the restitution to be effected in that age is "clearly evident even now". The blessedness of the age to come is, at least for the perfect, already here.

### f. The Beatitudes of Jesus in the *Philokalia*

As indicated in Chapter 1, the *Philokalia* draws extensively upon scripture, making reference or allusion to scripture on virtually every page. Amongst the verses of scripture quoted, referred or alluded to, the beatitudes recorded by the gospel writers as being spoken by Jesus are included. The comments made by the authors of the *Philokalia* in relation to these verses are illuminating for the present purpose. A summary of the references found in the *Philokalia* to these beatitudes is given in Table 4.1.[230]

It will be seen that twelve[231] authors of the *Philokalia* make a total of 44 references to the beatitudes. Maximos the Confessor and Peter of Damaskos are represented most frequently, as would be expected from the two largest contributors to the *Philokalia*. Peter of Damaskos is unique in commenting on all the Matthean beatitudes verse by verse, but Maximos also provides a succinct summary of the Matthean beatitudes in *On Love: C3*. Only Gregory Palamas comments on the Lukan beatitudes. Only John of Karpathos comments on the beatitude recorded in John 20:29. Only John Cassian comments on the beatitude recorded as a saying of Jesus in Acts 20:35. Most comments and references therefore relate to the Matthean beatitudes.

The verses most commonly referred to are Matthew 5:3 and 5:8, which are, respectively: "Blessed are the poor in spirit, for theirs is the kingdom of heaven" and "Blessed are the pure in heart, for they will see God". These verses lend themselves especially well to the

Table 4.1: References to the beatitudes of Jesus in the *Philokalia*

| Beatitude | | *Philokalia* | |
|---|---|---|---|
| | Author/Text | Ref | Extract from text |
| **Matthew 5** | | | |
| v3 Blessed are the poor in spirit, for theirs is the kingdom of heaven. | Peter of Damaskos *Book 1: The Seven Commandments* | EGP, 3, 93 | Our Lord Himself began his teaching by speaking of fear; for He says, 'Blessed are the poor in spirit' (Matt. 5:3), that is, those who quail with fear of God and are inexpressibly contrite in soul. For the Lord has established this as the basic commandment…. |
| | Peter of Damaskos *Book 1: Obedience & Stillness* | EGP, 3, 108 | [God] confers on [those wholly devoted to Him] the meditation that belongs to the first stage of contemplation, which enables them to acquire inexpressible contrition of soul and to become poor in spirit (cf. Matt. 5:3). Leading them in this way gradually through the other stages of contemplation, He will make it possible for them to keep the Beatitudes until they attain peace in their thoughts. This peace is the 'realm' or 'dwelling-place of God', as Evagrios says, referring to the Psalter: 'In peace is His dwelling-place' (Ps. 76 : 2. LXX). |
| | Symeon Metaphrastis *Paraphrase of Makarios* | EGP, #100 (3, 329) | The soul that is 'poor in spirit' (Matt. 5:3) is aware of its own wounds, perceives the encompassing darkness of the passions, and always calls upon the Lord for deliverance. |
| | [Symeon the New Theologian] *Three Methods of Prayer* | EGP, 4, 71 | Elsewhere He also says, 'Blessed are the poor in spirit' (Matt. 5:3); that is to say, blessed are those who are destitute of every worldly thought. |
| | Gregory Palamas *To Xenia* | EGP, #27 (4, 303) | The Lord blesses the opposite of what the world calls blessed, saying, 'Blessed are the poor in spirit, for theirs is the kingdom of the heavens' (Matt. 5:3). In saying 'Blessed are the poor', why did He add 'in spirit'? So as to show that He blesses and commends humility of soul. And why did He not say, 'Blessed are those whose spirit is poor', thus indicating the modesty of their manner of thinking, but 'Blessed are the poor in spirit'? So as to teach us that poverty of body is also blessed and fosters the kingdom of heaven…. By calling the poor in spirit blessed He wonderfully demonstrated what is the root, as it were, and mainspring of the outward poverty of the saints, namely, their humility of spirit. |

| Beatitude | Philokalia | | |
|---|---|---|---|
| | Author/Text | Ref | Extract from text |
| v3 (continued) | | EGP, #34 (4, 306) | But as the Lord says, 'Where your treasure is, there will your intellect be also' (Matt. 6:21). How, then, can you gaze noetically at Him who sits on the right hand of the divine Majesty (cf. Heb. 1:3) while you are still amassing treasure upon the earth? How will you inherit that kingdom which this passion entirely prevents you even from conceiving in your mind? 'Blessed', therefore, 'are the poor in spirit, for theirs is the kingdom of heaven.' Do you see how many passions the Lord has cut away with one beatitude? |
| | | EGP, #42 (4, 310) | Thus all the passions of the flesh are healed solely by bodily hardship and prayer issuing from a humble heart, which indeed is the poverty in spirit that the Lord called blessed. |
| | | EGP, ##43-44 (4, 311) | Then in truth you will be poor in spirit and will gain dominion over the passions and clearly be called blessed by Him who said, 'Blessed are the poor in spirit, for theirs is the kingdom of heaven.' [44.] How, indeed, can those not be called blessed who have absolutely no truck with material wealth and place all their trust in Him? Who wish to please only Him? Who with humility and the other virtues live in His presence? |
| v4 Blessed are those who mourn, for they will be comforted. | Peter of Damaskos *Book I: The Seven Commandments* | EGP, 3, 94 | So it is that God grants us the blessing of inward grief, which constitutes the second commandment. For, as Christ says, 'Blessed are those who grieve' (Matt. 5:4) – who grieve for themselves and also, out of love and compassion, for others as well. We become as one who mourns a dead person, because we perceive the terrible consequences that the things we have done before our death will have for us after we are dead…. |
| | Peter of Damaskos *Book I: Spurious Knowledge* | EGP,3, 201 | We pray that through the sacrament we may enter into communion with the Holy Spirit; for in this world and in the next the Paraclete Himself solaces those who are filled with godlike grief (cf. Matt. 5:4), and who with all their soul and with many tears call upon Him for help. |
| | Gregory Palamas *To Xenia* | EGP, ##47-48 (4, 312) | After first calling blessed those who gain imperishable wealth because of their poverty in spirit. God, who alone is blessed, next makes those who grieve partakers of His own blessedness, saying, 'Blessed are those who grieve, for they will be consoled' (Matt. 5:4). 48. Why did Christ thus join grief to poverty? Because it always coexists with it. But while sorrow over worldly poverty induces the soul's death, grief over poverty embraced in God's name induces the 'saving repentance that is not to be regretted' (2 Cor. 7:10). |

| Beatitude | | Philokalia | | |
|---|---|---|---|---|
| | Author/Text | Ref | Extract from text | |
| | Gregory Palamas *To Xenia* (continued) | EGP, #53 (4, 314) | Together with grief compunction crushes the passions and, having freed the soul from the weight that oppresses it, fills it with blessed joy. That is the reason why Christ says, 'Blessed are those who grieve, for they will be consoled' (Matt. 5:4). | |
| v5 Blessed are the meek, for they will inherit the earth. | Maximos the Confessor *On the Lord's Prayer* | EGP, 2, 292 | 'For on whom shall I rest,' says Scripture, 'but on him who is gentle and humble, and trembles at my words?' (cf. Isa. 66:2). It is clear from this that the kingdom of God the Father belongs to the humble and the gentle. For 'blessed are the gentle, for they will inherit the earth' (Matt. 5:5). | |
| | Peter of Damaskos *Book I: The Seven Commandments* | EGP, 3, 94 | In this way God's grace, our universal mother, will give us gentleness, so that we begin to imitate Christ. This constitutes the third commandment; for the Lord says, 'Blessed are the gentle' (Matt. 5:5). Thus we become like a firmly rooted rock. . . . . | |
| v6 Blessed are those who hunger and thirst for righteousness, for they will be filled. | Peter of Damaskos *Book I: The Seven Commandments* | EGP, 3, 96 | That is why man has been given the fourth commandment, that is, longing to acquire the virtues: 'Blessed are they that hunger and thirst after righteousness' (Matt. 5:6). He becomes as one who hungers and thirsts for all righteousness, that is, both for bodily virtue and for the moral virtue of the soul. | |
| | Symeon Metaphrastis *Paraphrase of Makarios* | EGP, #30 (3, 296) | Those who deny the possibility of perfection inflict the greatest damage on the soul in three ways. First, they manifestly disbelieve the inspired Scriptures. Then, because they do not make the greatest and fullest goal of Christianity their own, and so do not aspire to attain it, they can have no longing and diligence, no hunger and thirst for righteousness (cf. Matt. 5:6). | |
| | Nikitas Stithatos *On Virtues: 100 texts* | EGP, #60 (4, 94-95) | The sorrow prompted by God, however, is extremely salutary, enabling one patiently to endure hardships and trials. It is a source of compunction for those struggling and thirsting for God's righteousness (cf. Matt. 5:6), and nourishes their heart with tears. | |

# Philokalia

| Beatitude | Author/Text | Ref | Extract from text |
|---|---|---|---|
| v7 Blessed are the merciful, for they will receive mercy. | Maximos the Confessor *Various Texts: C1* | EGP, #45 (2, 173) | Because He wishes to unite us in nature and will with one another, and in His goodness urges all humanity towards this goal, God in His love entrusted His saving commandments to us, ordaining simply that we should show mercy and receive mercy (cf. Matt. 5:7). |
| | Peter of Damaskos *Book I: The Seven Commandments* | EGP, 3, 96 | The greater our devotion to the practice of the virtues, the more our intellect is illumined by knowledge. It is in this way that we are accounted worthy of mercy, that is, through the fifth commandment: 'Blessed are the merciful, for they will receive mercy' (Matt. 5:7). The merciful person is he who gives to others what he has himself. |
| v8 Blessed are the pure in heart, for they will see God. | Hesychios the Priest *Watchfulness & Holiness* | EGP, #1 (1, 162) | [Watchfulness] … is, in the true sense, purity of heart, a state blessed by Christ when He says: 'Blessed are the pure in heart, for they shall see God' (Matt. 5:8); and one which, because of its spiritual nobility and beauty – or, rather, because of our negligence – is now extremely rare among monks. |
| | | EGP, #52 (1, 171) | If because of pride, self-esteem or self-love we are deprived of Jesus' help, we shall lose that purity of heart through which God is known to man. For, as the Beatitude states, purity of heart is the ground for the vision of God (cf. Matt. 5:8). |
| | | EGP, #75 (1, 175) | Humility and ascetic hardship free a man from all sin, for the one cuts out the passions of the soul, the other those of the body. It is for this reason that the Lord says: 'Blessed are the pure in heart, for they shall see God' (Matt. 5:8). |
| | | EGP, #150 (1, 188) | For He has blessed the pure of heart and given the commandments; and so Jesus, who alone is truly pure, in a divine way readily enters into hearts that are pure and dwells in them. |
| | Theodoros the Great Ascetic *Spiritual Texts* | EGP, #86 (2, 33) | If a man's heart does not condemn him (cf. 1 John 3:21) for having rejected a commandment of God, or for negligence, or for accepting a hostile thought, then he is pure in heart and worthy to hear Christ say to him: 'Blessed are the pure in heart, for they shall see God' (Matt. 5:8). |
| | Maximos the Confessor *On love: C4* | EGP, #72 (2, 109) | It is for this reason that the Saviour says, 'Blessed are the pure in heart, for they shall see God' (Matt. 5:8). They shall see Him and the riches that are in Him when they have purified themselves through love and self-control; and the greater their purity, the more they will see. |

| Beatitude | | Philokalia | | |
|---|---|---|---|---|
| | Author/Text | Ref | Extract from text | |
| v8 (continued) | Maximos the Confessor *Various Texts: C2* | EGP, #58 (2, 199) | When through self-control you have straightened the crooked paths of the passions…… you will have become pure in heart. In this state of purity, through the virtues and through holy contemplation, you will at the end of your contest behold God, in accordance with Christ's words: 'Blessed are the pure in heart, for they shall see God' (Matt. 5:8). And because of the sufferings you have endured for the sake of virtue you will receive the gift of dispassion. To those who possess this gift there is nothing which reveals God more fully. | |
| | Peter of Damaskos *Book I: The Seven Commandments* | EGP, 3, 97 | It is through detachment that one is enabled to fulfil the sixth commandment: 'Blessed are the pure in heart' (Matt. 5:8). The pure in heart are those who have accomplished every virtue reflectively and reverently and have come to see the true nature of things. | |
| | Symeon Metaphrastis *Paraphrase of Makarios* | EGP, #2 (3, 285) | What is the will of God that St Paul urges and invites each of us to attain (cf. 1 Thess. 4:3)? It is total cleansing from sin, freedom from the shameful passions and the acquisition of the highest virtue. In other words, it is the purification and sanctification of the heart that comes about through fully experienced and conscious participation in the perfect and divine Spirit. 'Blessed are the pure in heart,' it is said, 'for they shall see God' (Matt. 5:8). | |
| | Symeon the New Theologian *Practical & Theological Texts* | EGP, #73 (4, 39) | 'Blessed are the pure in heart,' says God, 'for they shall see God' (Matt. 5:8). But purity of heart cannot be realized through one virtue alone, or through two, or ten; it can only be realized through all of them together, as if they formed but a single virtue brought to perfection. | |
| | [Symeon the New Theologian] *Practical & Theological Texts* | EGP, #126 (4, 53) | We should regard all as saints, and should strive through inward grief to be purified of our passions, so that, illumined by grace, we may look on all as equals and attain the blessing of those who are pure in heart (cf. Matt. 5:8). | |

| Beatitude | Philokalia | | |
|---|---|---|---|
| | Author/Text | Ref | Extract from text |
| v8 (continued) | [Symeon the New Theologian] *Three Methods of Prayer* | EGP, 4, 72 | In short, if you do not guard your intellect you cannot attain purity of heart, so as to be counted worthy to see God (cf. Matt. 5:18[232]). |
| | Gregory Palamas *In Defence of Stillness* | EGP, #2 (4, 333) | When through self-control we have purified our body, and when through divine love we have made our incensive power and our desire incentives for virtue, and when we offer to God an intellect cleansed by prayer, then we will possess and see within ourselves the grace promised to the pure in heart (cf. Matt. 5:8). |
| v9 Blessed are the peacemakers, for they will be called children of God. | Peter of Damaskos *Book I: Introduction* | EGP, 3, 84 | For if the flesh is not consumed and if a man is not wholly led by the Spirit of God, he will not do the will of God unless he is forced to. But when the grace of the Spirit rules within him, then he no longer has a will of his own, but whatever he does is according to God's will. Then he is at peace. Men like that will be called sons of God (cf. Matt. 5:9), because they will the will of their Father, as did the Son of God who is also God. |
| | Peter of Damaskos *Book I: The Seven Commandments* | EGP, 3, 97 | In this way they find peace in their thoughts. For, as the seventh commandment puts it, 'Blessed are the peacemakers' (Matt. 5:9), that is, those who have set soul and body at peace by subjecting the flesh to the spirit. |
| | Peter of Damaskos *Book I: The Third Stage of Contemplation* | EGP, 3, 115 | Where is dispassion and perfect love, the peace that excels all intellect (cf. Phil. 4:7), whereby I should have been called a son of God (cf. Matt. 5:9)? |
| v10 Blessed are those who are persecuted for righteousness' sake, for theirs is the kingdom of heaven. | Peter of Damaskos *Book I: The Seven Commandments* | EGP, 3, 98 | the flesh no longer rises against the spirit (cf. Gal. 5:17). Instead, the grace of the Holy Spirit reigns in their soul and leads it where it will, bestowing the divine knowledge whereby man can endure persecution, vilification and maltreatment 'for righteousness' sake' (Matt. 5:10). |

| Beatitude | | Philokalia | |
|---|---|---|---|
| | | Author/Text | Ref | Extract from text |
| vv11-12 | Blessed are you when people revile you and persecute you and utter all kinds of evil against you falsely on my account. Rejoice and be glad, for your reward is great in heaven, for in the same way they persecuted the prophets who were before you. | Peter of Damaskos *Book 1: The Seven Commandments* | EGP, 3, 98 | the grace of the Holy Spirit reigns in their soul and leads it where it will, bestowing the divine knowledge whereby man can endure persecution, vilification and maltreatment 'for righteousness' sake' (Matt. 5:10), rejoicing because his 'reward is great in heaven' (Matt. 5:12)…. For the Beatitudes are gifts from God and we should thank Him greatly for them and for the rewards promised: the kingdom of heaven in the age to be, spiritual refreshment in this world, the fullness of all God's blessings and mercies, His manifestation when we contemplate the hidden mysteries found in the Holy Scriptures and in all created things, and the great reward in heaven (cf. Matt. 5:12). |
| vv3-12 | | Maximos the Confessor *On love: C3* | EGP, #47 (2, 90) | There are many people in the world who are poor in spirit, but not in the way that they should be; there are many who mourn, but for some financial loss or the death of their children; many are gentle, but towards unclean passions; many hunger and thirst, but only to seize what does not belong to them and to profit from injustice ; many are merciful, but towards their bodies and the things that serve the body; many are pure in heart, but for the sake of self-esteem; many are peace-makers, but by making the soul submit to the flesh; many are persecuted, but as wrongdoers; many are reviled, but for shameful sins. Only those are blessed who do or suffer these things for the sake of Christ and after His example. Why? Because theirs is the kingdom of heaven, and they shall see God (cf. Matt. 5.3-12). It is not because they do or suffer these things that they are blessed, for those of whom we have spoken above do the same; it is because they do them and suffer them for the sake of Christ and after His example. |

| Beatitude | Author/Text | Ref | Extract from text |
|---|---|---|---|
| vv3-12 (continued) | Peter of Damaskos Book I: *The Seven Commandments* | EGP, 3, 98 | All the Beatitudes make man a god by grace; he becomes gentle, longs for righteousness, is charitable, dispassionate, a peacemaker, and endures every pain with joy out of love for God and for his fellow men. For the Beatitudes are gifts from God and we should thank Him greatly for them and for the rewards promised: the kingdom of heaven in the age to be, spiritual refreshment in this world, the fullness of all God's blessings and mercies, His manifestation when we contemplate the hidden mysteries found in the Holy Scriptures and in all created things, and the great reward in heaven (cf. Matt. 5:12). For if we learn while on earth to imitate Christ and receive the blessedness inherent in each commandment, we shall be granted the highest good and the ultimate goal of our desire. As the apostle says, God, who dwells in unapproachable light, alone is blessed (cf. 1 Tim. 6:15-16). We, for our part, have the duty of keeping the commandments — or, rather, of being kept by them; but through them God in His compassion will give to the believer rewards both in this world and in the world to be. When through blessed inward grief all this has been realized, then the intellect finds relief from the passions; and through the many bitter tears that it sheds over its sins it is reconciled to God. |
| | Peter of Damaskos Book II: *VIII. Mortification of the Passions* | EGP, 3, 231 | From faith comes fear, and from fear comes true piety, or self-control, the endurance of grief, and the other things of which the Lord's Beatitudes speak (cf. Matt. 5:3-12) – gentleness, hunger and thirst for righteousness, that is, for all the virtues, acts of mercy – and also detachment. |
| | [Symeon the New Theologian] *Three Methods of #Prayer* | EGP, 4, 72 | Without such watchfulness you cannot become poor in spirit, or grieve, or hunger and thirst after righteousness, or be truly merciful, or pure in heart, or a peacemaker, or be persecuted for the sake of justice (cf. Matt. 5:3-10). |
| **Luke 6** | | | |
| v20 Blessed are you who are poor, for yours is the kingdom of God. | Gregory Palamas *To Xenia* | EGP, #28 (4, 304) | But if you possess a contrite, lowly and humble spirit you cannot but rejoice in outward simplicity and self-abasement, because you will regard yourself as unworthy of praise, comfort, prosperity and all such things. The poor man deemed blessed by God is he who considers himself unworthy of these things. It is he who is really poor, being poor in full measure. It was on this account that St Luke also wrote, 'Blessed are the poor' (6:20), without adding 'in spirit'. |

| Beatitude | | Philokalia | | |
|---|---|---|---|---|
| | | Author/Text | Ref | Extract from text |
| v21 | Blessed are you who are hungry now, for you will be filled. Blessed are you who weep now, for you will laugh. | | | |
| vv22–23 | Blessed are you when people hate you, and when they exclude you, revile you, and defame you on account of the Son of Man. Rejoice in that day and leap for joy, for surely your reward is great in heaven; for that is what their ancestors did to the prophets. | Gregory Palamas *To Xenia* | EGP, #57 (4, 316) | We are well aware that at this point certain people out of malice are ready to censure us, telling us, in effect, 'You are not to speak in the name of the Lord (cf. Jer. 11:21), and if you do we will repudiate your name as evil (cf. Luke 6:22), devising and spreading slanders and falsehoods about you.' But let us take no notice of these people, and let us now continue with what we were saying, believing in and affirming the teachings of the holy fathers, directing our attention to them and convincing others through them. |
| **John 20** | | | | |
| v29 | Blessed are those who have not seen and yet have come to believe. | John of Karpathos *For the Monks in India* | EGP, #71 (1, 315) | 'Blessed are those who have not seen, and yet have believed' (John 20:29). Blessed also are those who, when grace is withdrawn, find no consolation in themselves, but only continuing tribulation and thick darkness, and yet do not despair; but, strengthened by faith, they endure courageously, convinced that they do indeed see Him who is invisible. |
| **Acts 20** | | | | |
| v35 | It is more blessed to give than to receive. | John Cassian *On the Eight Vices* | EGP, 1, 80–81 | Some, impelled by their own deceit and avarice, distort the meaning of the scriptural statement, 'It is more blessed to give than to receive' (Acts 20:35). They do the same with the Lord's words when He says, 'If you want to be perfect, go and sell all you have and give to the poor, and you will have treasure in heaven; and come and follow Me' (Matt. 19:21). They judge that it is more blessed to have control over one's personal wealth, and to give from this to those in need, than to possess nothing at all. |

themes of the *Philokalia*. Thus, for example, commenting on Matthew 5:3, Peter of Damaskos sees the first stage of contemplation as being concerned with acquiring "inexpressible contrition of soul", and thus becoming poor in spirit. Symeon Metaphrastis, in his *Paraphrase of Makarios*, understands the soul that is poor in spirit as being the one that is aware of the darkness of the passions. The author of *Three Methods of Prayer*, in a similar line of thought, understands the poor in spirit to be those who are "destitute of every worldly thought". A similar understanding, concerned with the poverty that results from a humble and prayerful response to awareness of the passions within, is also found in texts from Gregory Palamas.

There are also hints in Gregory's writings on this verse of a recognition of the blessedness associated with the age to come. In *To Xenia*, he sees a choice presented – between earthly treasure (i.e. of the present age) and the treasure of the kingdom of heaven (i.e. of the age to come). For Gregory, this beatitude is both about the blessedness of addressing the passions in this present world, and about a contemplative gaze upon the blessedness of Divine glory in the age to come.

In comments made on Matthew 5:8, similar themes recur. However, the theme of purity of heart (as contrasted with poverty of heart in 5:3) attracts more comments on watchfulness, guarding of the intellect, detachment, dispassion, love, virtue, self control, and a contemplative vision of God.

The theme of deification and the blessedness of the age to come are made most explicit in Peter of Damaskos' overall comments on the beatitudes. They "make man a god by grace", and offer rewards both "in this world and in the world to be". Imitation of Christ in this world is connected with a vision of God in heaven, who "dwells in unapproachable light" and "alone is blessed". But although such themes are most explicit here, they crop up elsewhere also. Gregory Palamas, in his comments on Matthew 5:4, affirms that God makes those who grieve "partakers of his own blessedness". Symeon Metaphrastis, commenting on Matthew 5:6, urges that we should not deny the possibility of perfection. Hesychios the Priest, commenting on Matthew 5:8, sees purity of heart as the "means through which God is known to man", the "ground for the vision of God". And further examples are not hard to find.

The paradoxes that are inherent in many of the beatitudes are also inherent in the understanding of blessedness that is embedded in the *Philokalia*. Each paradox finds its parallel in the understanding of the inner life that the *Philokalia* offers. Thus, for example, the beatitudes tell us that the poor are actually rich. The *Philokalia* tells us that those who find contrition, darkness and destitution in their awareness of the passions that lay within their hearts are actually those to whom the kingdom of heaven, in all its blessedness, belongs. Again, the beatitudes tell us that the hungry and thirsty are actually those who are filled. The *Philokalia* (here, mainly Nikitas Stithatos) tells us that those who most long for virtue will find themselves the best nourished to survive the hardships that they will face.

Sometimes, the beatitudes are not paradoxical, but the *Philokalia* is. So, for example, we might not be surprised to learn that the pure in heart will see God. But the *Philokalia* tells us that those who are pure in heart are only those who first acknowledged just how impure their hearts were, and then took steps with God's help to address this. The blessed, those who gain the vision of the blessedness of God, therefore are those who have first seen the "true nature of things" – including their own impurity and shamefulness.

### g. The Beatitudes of the *Philokalia*

The general structure of the beatitudes attributed to Jesus in the New Testament is:

Blessed are.... [A]       for.... [B]

[A] describes or defines the characteristics of those who are blessed. It may be a virtue or personal characteristic, an action that is undertaken as a subject, or an action that is suffered at the hands of another.

Sometimes the "for" is replaced by a full stop and [B] is presented in a new sentence in which we are told something (usually something unexpected) about those who have (in the first sentence) been described as blessed. Sometimes (as in John 20:29 and Acts 20:35[233]) the "for... [B]" component is missing altogether.

A similar structure is encountered in a number of places in the texts of the *Philokalia* (see Table 4.2). We saw above that Evagrios introduces a set of seven beatitudes in *On Prayer*. Most other examples are of single beatitudes, although Maximos the Confessor presents a group of three in *On Love: C1*, and a group of two in *Various Texts: C3*, and Peter of Damaskos presents a group of two in

*Book I.* Most of the beatitudes of the *Philokalia* lack the "for ... [B]" component and most are in the singular rather than the plural:

> Blessed is.... [A]

Some of these beatitudes are quite lengthy, although most are only a single sentence and only two are more than three sentences.

What do these beatitudes tell us about blessedness in the *Philokalia*?

Most of them are concerned in one way or another with remedies for the passions. Thus, the person is blessed who pursues a life of virtue and ascetical discipline, who prays and engages in psalmody, and who achieves dispassion and stillness. Blessed also are the contemplative vision of Divine beauty and of Divine darkness, and the "knowledge of the celestial mysteries of the Spirit". Blessed is the soul that "enter[s] into God himself", and blessed is the man who "reposes in God".

The pattern that emerges here, then, reinforces the picture that has already been painted of blessedness in the *Philokalia* as being concerned with a life of ascetic discipline, virtue and prayer, watchfulness and stillness, overcoming the passions and advancing towards deification. Blessedness, ultimately, is to be found in God alone, but because God in Christ became human the possibility emerges for human beings, in Christ, to participate in God.

## vi. The Multifaceted Nature of Mental Well-Being in the *Philokalia*

How does the *Philokalia* understand mental well-being? To some extent, we might argue that this question has already been answered in Chapter 3. The *Philokalia* is realistic about the human condition. All human beings are afflicted by the passions, which are a dynamic process rather than a state of being, and it is in the application of the remedies that the *Philokalia* prescribes that well-being is to be found. Individuals in a state of complete apatheia or perfect hesychia are few and far between. For most of us, well-being comprises engagement with the remedial process itself. Well-being is the process of being in treatment, rather than a state of perfect health.

However, if well-being might be understood as a process of this kind, questions still arise as to what well-being might look like in the individual who had (even if only exceptionally or theoretically)

## Table 4.2: Beatitudes of the *Philokalia*

| Author/Title | Reference | Beatitude |
|---|---|---|
| Evagrios of Pontus *On Prayer* | ##117-123 (EGP 1, 68-69) | 117. I shall say again what I have said elsewhere: blessed is the intellect that is completely free from forms during prayer.<br>118. Blessed is the intellect that, undistracted in its prayer, acquires an ever greater longing for God.<br>119. Blessed is the intellect that during prayer is free from materiality and stripped of all possessions.<br>120. Blessed is the intellect that has acquired complete freedom from sensations during prayer.<br>121. Blessed is the monk who regards every man as God after God.<br>122. Blessed is the monk who looks with great joy on everyone's salvation and progress as if they were his own.<br>123. Blessed is the monk who regards himself as 'the off-scouring of all things' (1 Cor. 4:13). |
| Hesychios the Priest *Watchfulness & Holiness* | #196 (EGP 1, 197) | Truly blessed is the man whose mind and heart are as closely attached to the Jesus Prayer and to the ceaseless invocation of His name as air to the body or flame to the wax. The sun rising over the earth creates the daylight; and the venerable and holy name of the Lord Jesus, shining continually in the mind, gives birth to countless intellections radiant as the sun. |
| John of Karpathos *For the Monks in India* | #83 (EGP 1, 317-318) | Blessed is he who, with a hunger that is never satisfied, day and night throughout this present life makes prayer and the psalms his food and drink, and strengthens himself by reading of God's glory in Scripture. Such communion will lead the soul to ever-increasing joy in the age to come. |
| Maximos the Confessor *On love: C1* | ##17-19 (EGP 2, 54-55) | 17. Blessed is he who can love all men equally.<br>18. Blessed is he who is not attached to anything transitory or corruptible.<br>19. Blessed is the intellect that transcends all sensible objects and ceaselessly delights in divine beauty |
| Maximos the Confessor *For Thalassios: C2* | #31 (EGP 2, 145) | Blessed is he who like Joshua (cf. Josh. 10:12-13) keeps the Sun of righteousness from setting in himself throughout the whole day of this present life, not allowing it to be blotted out by the dusk of sin and ignorance. In this way he will truly be able to put to flight the cunning demons that rise up against him. |

| Author/Title | Reference | Beatitude |
|---|---|---|
| Maximos the Confessor *Various Texts: C3* | ##24-25 (EGP 2, 215) | 24. Truly blessed is the intellect that dies to all created beings: to sensible beings by quelling the activity of the senses, and to intelligible beings by ceasing from noetic activity. Through such a death of the intellect the will dies to all things. The intellect is then able to receive the life of divine grace and to apprehend, in a manner that transcends its noetic power, not simply created beings, but their Creator.<br>25. Blessed is he who has united his practice of the virtues to natural goodness and his contemplative life to natural truth. For all practice of the virtues is for the sake of goodness and all contemplation seeks spiritual knowledge solely for the sake of truth. When goodness and truth are attained, nothing can afflict the soul's capacity for practicing the virtues, or disturb its contemplative activity with outlandish speculations; for the soul will now transcend every created and intelligible reality, and will enter into God Himself, who alone is goodness and troth and who is beyond all being and all intellection |
| | #28 (EGP 2, 216) | Blessed is he who knows in truth that we are but tools in God's hands; that it is God who effects within us all ascetic practice and contemplation, virtue and spiritual knowledge, victory and wisdom, goodness and truth; and that to all this we contribute nothing at all except a disposition that desires what is good. |
| Thalassios *For Paul: C1* | #56 (EGP 2, 310) | Blessed is he who has attained boundless infinity, transcending all that is transitory. |
| Ilias the Presbyter *Gnomic Anthology: 2* | #86 (EGP 3, 44) | Blessed, therefore, is the man who regards spiritual work as superior to physical work: through the first he makes up for any deficiency where the second is concerned, because he lives the hidden life of prayer that is manifest to God. |
| | #106 (EGP 3, 46) | Blessed is he who in this life is granted the experience of this state[234] and who sees his body, which by nature is of clay, become incandescent through grace. |

| Author/Title | Reference | Beatitude |
|---|---|---|
| Ilias the Presbyter *Gnomic Anthology: 4* | #102 (EGP 3, 60) | Blessed is the soul that, because it expects its Lord daily, thinks nothing of the day's toil or of the night's, since He is going to appear in the morning. |
| | #103 (EGP 3, 60) | Blessed is the man who believes that he is seen by God; for his foot will not slip (cf. Ps. 73:2) unless this is God's will. |
| Peter of Damaskos *Book I: The Bodily Virtues as Tools for the Acquisition of Virtues of the Soul* | EGP 3, 103-104 | Blessed are they who are completely devoted to God, either through obedience to someone experienced in the practice of the virtues and living an ordered life in stillness, or else through themselves living in stillness and total detachment, scrupulously obedient to God's will, and seeking the advice of experienced men in everything they say or think. Blessed above all are those who seek to attain dispassion and spiritual knowledge unlaboriously through their total devotion to God: as God Himself has said through His prophet, 'Devote yourselves to stillness and know that I am God' (Ps. 46:10). |
| Symeon Metaphrastis *Paraphrase of Makarios* | #101 (EGP 3, 329) | Truly blessed and zealous for life and for surpassing joy are those who through fervent faith and virtuous conduct receive consciously and experientially the knowledge of the celestial mysteries of the Spirit and whose citizenship is in heaven (cf. Phil. 3:20). Clearly they excel all other men; for who among the powerful or the wise or the prudent could ascend to heaven while still on earth, and perform spiritual works there and have sight of the beauty of the Spirit? |
| Nikitas Stithatos *On the Inner Nature of Things* | #51 (EGP 4, 121) | Blessed in my eyes is the man who, changed through the practice of the virtues, transcends the encompassing walls of the passion-embroiled state and rises on the wings of dispassion – wings silver-toned with divine knowledge (cf. Ps. 68:13) – to the spiritual sphere in which he contemplates the essences of created things, and who from there enters the divine darkness of theology where in the life of blessedness he ceases from all outward labours and reposes in God. For he has become a terrestrial angel and a celestial man; he has glorified God in himself, and God will glorify him (cf. John 13:31-32). |

followed it through to completion. The concern also arises that settling too readily for a "process of treatment" model of well-being might engender a kind of acceptance of the status quo, or resignation to something less than perfection, which is not a sign of well-being at all. Thus, Symeon Metaphrastis warns:

> Those who deny the possibility of perfection inflict the greatest damage on the soul in three ways. First, they manifestly disbelieve the inspired Scriptures. Then, because they do not make the greatest and fullest goal of Christianity their own, and so do not aspire to attain it, they can have no longing and diligence, no hunger and thirst for righteousness (cf. Matt. 5:6).[235]

So what does mental well-being, as portrayed in the *Philokalia*, look like? Our survey has taken us through the subjects of deification, health and well-being as directly referred to, the processes of purification, illumination and perfection of the intellect, and the states of hesychia and blessedness. It has become clear that these topics are all inter-related and all tell us something about what mental well-being looks like. It has also become clear that the "well-being as treatment in process" model has much to commend it. All of these subjects have engaged with the underlying need to employ radical treatments for the disease of the passions. It has become clear that not many people attain the state of hesychia. Furthermore, the key doctrine of deification allows for degrees of progress (at least according to some authors), and is also presented as a process which may begin in the present age, but will only be completed, at least for most people, in the age to come.

However, the warning given in Symeon Metaphrastis' paraphrase of the Macarian homilies is still well made. The processes of purification, illumination and perfection of the intellect require that we be vigilant for signs of anything that sets itself against God. Much more importantly, the Christological basis for the doctrine of deification suggests that the focus should not be so much on the remedies for the passions themselves as on the therapeutic goal towards which they are orientated. And as this goal is hidden in God it will either be expressed as an ineffable, mystical and apophatic destination, to be found only in contemplative prayer, and then only in part, or it will be seen in Christ. The source of all well-being and blessedness is found in God. As only Christ is both fully human and fully divine (as eastern and western

Christians have traditionally believed) only in Christ may a visible image of human well-being be found.

## 5. Mental Well-Being – Some Reflections and Conclusions

Well-being considered only as a therapeutic goal will always simply be a question of the absence of disease. However, Classical and early Christian understandings have looked beyond this instrumental approach to ask what it is that makes a good life. When may we say that a human being is flourishing, rather than simply struggling along? This question poses further important philosophical and theological questions which are not at all irrelevant to defining the therapeutic goals of counselling, psychotherapy or the spiritual life.

In this chapter some answers to these questions have been considered. Firstly, those provided in the Classical world have been considered briefly. Rather more attention has then been given to early Christian answers, as provided in the fourth century by the Desert Fathers, and especially by Evagrios. Most attention has been focussed on the answers which may be found in the collection of writings which is the focus of this work – the *Philokalia*. Although, as one would expect of an anthology spanning the writings of more than a millennium, there is some diversity of style, expression and doctrine, some key features do emerge.

Perhaps the central feature to emerge from the Christian texts that have been considered here is the understanding that human well-being is contingent upon the only non-contingent source of well-being, which is God. This has important Christological implications for what it means to be a flourishing human being, and these hinge on traditions of interpretation of the key foundational texts of Christianity, especially the canonical gospels. Not all of these links have been followed through here, as the objective has been to assess what the *Philokalia* has to say, rather than to tease out all the textual sources or to critically assess their validity. However, it does not seem too much of a leap from what has been ascertained here to suggest that, according to this tradition, to be a flourishing human being is to participate as fully as human beings may in the life of God in Christ.

To focus exclusively on theological conclusions would be to miss the important contribution that Classical philosophy has made. Platonic, Aristotelian and Stoic ideas about human well-being have all been apparent in the tradition of scriptural interpretation that the *Philokalia* represents. This is not to say that these are not Christian ideas, and no critical attempt has been made here to affirm or reject the precise role that they have played in forming the *Philokalia*. However, it is important to be aware that they are there. Similarly, there is much wisdom about the workings of the human mind which appears to derive from the original, first hand, reflections of the Desert Fathers, the authors of the *Philokalia*, and especially Evagrios. These genuinely original insights have stood the test of time, even if in some cases they have been reinvented under different names. In a very real sense, the *Philokalia* represents a hermeneutic of the processes of human thought, as much as it represents a hermeneutic of scripture.

In this sense, we can say that the *Philokalia* is concerned primarily with flourishing or well-being of the inner life of human beings. However, this is an inner life of a different kind than we know. Although the *Philokalia* exercises a kind of reflexivity, it is not the radical reflexivity that Taylor traces back to Augustine. Although it offers an objectification of (what we would call) emotions, desires and feelings, it is not Taylor's Cartesian disengagement. Perhaps most importantly, the expressivism that gives us positive cause to articulate our own unique understanding of the voice of nature within us is completely inverted in the world of the *Philokalia*, which is much more concerned with our awareness of the negativity of the passions within and reaching out to the "measure of the stature of the fullness of Christ" beyond. But this is only to acknowledge its situation within an anthropology formed by Platonic philosophy and Christian theology in relative isolation from many of the trends that Taylor identifies. The *Philokalia* is nonetheless concerned with a radical vision of the inner life which shows as much perceptiveness of the subtleties, deceptions, intricacies and aspirations of human thoughts as anything that has come after it.

# 5

# Psychotherapy

If the *Philokalia* offers a diagnosis of the pathology of the human soul, a pharmacopoeia of remedies for the passions, and a vision of what a healthy and flourishing human-being (soul and body) can aspire to, then it begins to sound as though the *Philokalia* is really all about the health and therapy of the soul or psyche (ψυχή). Furthermore, some of the subjects tackled by the *Philokalia* sound very similar to the concerns of psychological medicine: Evagrios seems to be very aware of unconscious processes, acedia bears a marked apparent resemblance to depression, the ensnaring hostile pleasures of the passions sound very much like contemporary notions of addiction, and some of the more Stoic aspects of the theory of the *Philokalia*, especially the mastery of the passions by reason, sound very akin to some forms of cognitive behavioural therapy. But do these superficial resemblances stand up to closer scrutiny?

Unfortunately, any attempt at scrutiny of these apparent resemblances immediately encounters some very significant problems. Three issues in particular need to be addressed:

1. The *Philokalia* is first and foremost a collection of texts. Although different translations have more or less varied the boundaries of the "canon" of this collection, there exists a core assembly of texts of recognised spiritual and patristic authority that has relatively clear boundaries. This situation contrasts greatly with the world of psychotherapy, in which no assembly of texts has universally recognised authority. One might look to the complete works of Freud, perhaps, or Jung, as providing a comparable corpus of texts for psychotherapy as that provided by the *Philokalia* for the Orthodox spiritual

life. However, this comparison only works as long as one remains within a relatively confined theoretical or historical discipline of psychotherapy. The total literature on psychotherapy of all kinds is now vast, and perhaps more akin to the totality of all Christian (or even all religious) texts on spirituality rather than to a limited and defined anthology such as that of the *Philokalia*. And even if one is to remain within a single tradition of psychotherapy, it must be remembered that the collected works of Freud or Jung are defined by single authorship. No accepted multi-author canon of Freudian or Jungian texts exists to represent these schools of psychotherapy as they have been expounded or practised over the period of their history to date, a history which is in any case very short in comparison to that of the *Philokalia*.

2. The *Philokalia* and psychotherapy ostensibly address different questions, with different purposes in view. In a sense, to ask this question is to prejudge the outcome of the scrutiny and comparison that are being proposed: are both the *Philokalia* and psychotherapy talking about fundamentally the same thing? However, if any scrutiny or comparison is possible, it must at least be acknowledged at the outset that they each developed with very different applications and outcomes in mind. The former arose from the experiences of practitioners of the spiritual life, whose expressed goal was concerned with the advancement of the life of prayer and finding spiritual salvation. The latter developed in order to treat psychological disorder and improve mental well-being. The qualifications offered at the beginning of the last chapter already provide (I hope) sufficient grounds for suggesting that we can make no assumptions about the sameness of these quests, even where terminology overlaps. But, in fact, the terminology is often very different, and it is not immediately obvious that the spiritual and religious quest is at all the same as the psychological and medical one. However, this does at least draw attention to one important commonality. Both the *Philokalia* and psychotherapy are traditions supportive of the living of human life. They are not merely theoretical

bodies of theological doctrine, philosophy or science. They both exist for the purpose of improving human life, of promoting human flourishing and achieving or restoring human well-being – even if they conceive of these things in different ways, and even if they set about the task differently.¹

3. There are problems of epistemology and terminology which derive from the different times, cultures and philosophies within which the *Philokalia* was written and psychotherapy developed. The texts comprising the *Philokalia* were written between the fourth and fifteenth centuries, formed into a more or less acknowledged collection of texts over a period of almost three subsequent centuries, and the *Philokalia* itself was then compiled and edited for publication in the late eighteenth century. Since then new translations have emerged and enlarged editions have been published in Russian and Romanian, but the primary texts by definition have not changed and remarkably little secondary literature has been published. The history of psychotherapy, in contrast, is almost the inverse of this process. Although it is acknowledged that psychotherapy has drawn on classical philosophy and religious tradition, its recent history more or less starts at the point at which the *Philokalia* was published. The *Philokalia*, and the world of psychotherapy, are therefore situated in quite different historical periods. Added to this, we find that the former has developed within the culture, philosophy and theology of eastern Christendom – and especially eastern Europe – whilst the latter has a history situated primarily in western Europe and north America, and thus has engaged primarily with the concerns of western society and the western (Protestant and Catholic) Church.

It will be proposed that there are possible ways of taking forward a critical comparison which might be able to address these problems. However, before outlining a methodology for this task, it may be helpful to give further consideration to some of the relevant historical, philosophical and terminological issues.

## 1. A Brief History of Psychotherapy

A comprehensive history of psychotherapy would represent a formidable undertaking. However, a very brief and selective account, orientated towards the task at hand, is necessary at this point. In offering the following account, I have drawn especially on Brown and Pedder (1980), Bloch and Harari (2006), Allen (2006), Drummond and Kennedy (2006), and Frank (2006).

Although it is often acknowledged that psychotherapy finds its origins in the ancient world, in classical philosophy, magic, and religion, historical accounts usually begin in earnest in the late eighteenth century with the work of Anton Mesmer (1734-1815). Mesmer developed a theory of "animal magnetism" according to which magnets and (what we would now call) hypnotism were used for the treatment of a range of medical conditions. Mesmer was eventually discredited, but the apparent success of his treatments led to interest in how, if they were flawed, they might still have helped people. The work was taken up, amongst others, by the eminent French neurologist Jean Martin Charcot (1835-1893) and his pupil Pierre Janet (1859-1947). Following in this line, Josef Breuer (1842-1925) and Sigmund Freud (1856-1939) published their seminal *Studies on Hysteria* in 1895. Along with four other cases treated by Freud, this work described the treatment of Anna O, a young woman with various hysterical symptoms. *Studies on Hysteria* described the use of hypnotism, suggestion, catharsis and free association as therapeutic techniques in the course of talking with patients over a period of time about their lives. Anna O described her treatment as her "talking cure". Freud's theoretical system, and the process of treatment with which it was associated, became known as psychoanalysis. From psychoanalysis a multitude of different kinds of psychotherapy developed – all of which are now known as dynamic psychotherapies.

Dynamic therapies stress therapeutic processes of understanding (insight) and empathy, and involve talking about memories (often early) associated with the development of the condition being treated. They usually involve recognition of unconscious processes which may explain and maintain that condition. In particular, Freud noted that feelings and thoughts associated with relationships in early life may be transferred onto relationships in the present – especially the relationship with a therapist. This process, which Freud labelled "transference", came to be seen as a key opportunity for using the present therapeutic relationship to bring healing to the wounds left by past psychological trauma.

Although Freud revised his theories through the course of his lifetime, he proved unable to tolerate the dissent of his pupils and colleagues. In particular, Carl Jung (1875-1961) and Alfred Adler (1870-1937) both moved away and developed their own models of psychotherapy (analytical psychology and individual psychology respectively). Karen Horney (1885-1952), Erich Fromm (1900-1980), and "Harry" Stack Sullivan (1892-1949) established their own, neo-Freudian, schools in the United States of America. Donald Winnicott (1896-1971) and Melanie Klein (1882-1960), working in Britain, developed a focus on significant early life relationships which became known as the Object Relations School. Since then, numerous further branches and offshoots of the psychotherapeutic tree have developed. Amongst these are approaches which focus on the use of small groups, or family groups, as the basis within which to conduct therapy.

The theory and methods of dynamic psychotherapy have come under considerable scientific scrutiny since the 1950s, and are now claimed by some to be highly unscientific, but Freud never abandoned his fundamentally scientific outlook. Eventually, he hoped, all psychological disorders could potentially be explained on the basis of physical and chemical processes.

The other major approach to psychotherapy, behaviour therapy, contrasts with dynamic psychotherapy in various ways. It has an even more recent history and its foundations are in the world of experimental psychology. In the 1920s research based on the work of Ivan Pavlov (1849-1936) suggested that some neurotic disorders might be a result of classical conditioning – the process of developing an association of a stimulus and response in such a way that the stimulus reliably evokes a learned – or "conditioned" response. Most famously this was demonstrated with Pavlov's experimental dogs, which salivated on hearing the sound of a bell that had routinely been rung when they were fed. Conditioning, it was alleged, might also be the basis of some neurotic disorders. In this model, anxiety (rather than salivation) was the conditioned human response to stimuli such as the objects of a phobia. Although this simple model was subsequently significantly modified in the light of further research, it led to the development of treatments such as systematic desensitisation, which did not require a "talking cure". Thus, for example, a patient might be exposed repeatedly, in graded and increasing "doses", to the object of their phobia over a period of time. At each exposure anxiety inevitably subsides, until the patient is relatively relaxed. Over time, it becomes possible to approach the object of the phobia without fear. In keeping with its experimental scientific foundations, behaviour therapy eschews subjective experience and confines itself to observable and objective phenomena.

In the 1960s Aaron Beck (b.1921), Albert Ellis (1913-2007) and others concluded that the tenets of psychodynamic therapy could not be upheld. For example, patients engaging in dynamic therapy not infrequently seemed to gain insight and yet not improve symptomatically. From the work of Beck, Ellis and others developed a model of cognitive psychotherapy according to which feelings and behaviour are understood as causally related to underlying thoughts, or cognitions. On this basis, it is possible to pursue therapy to alter feelings and behaviour by identifying and modifying underlying faulty, irrational or erroneous cognitions. Like behaviour therapy, this model owes much to scientific psychology and does not require analysis of unconscious processes or the material and memories of early life history. Its focus is very much in the "here and now". However, it goes further than does behaviour therapy to address the complexities of human (as opposed to animal) behaviour. Cognitive psychology is now arguably the dominant paradigm within psychology, and is hugely influential in the clinical practice of psychotherapy. However, because of its common ground with behavioural psychotherapy, reference is often made to cognitive behaviour therapy (or CBT) as encapsulating both approaches.

Whilst the theoretical and practical gulf between dynamic and cognitive behaviour approaches to psychotherapy remains large, this is not to say that there are not bridges across it. Cognitive Analytic Therapy (CAT), for example, provides an evidence based approach to psychotherapy which restates psychoanalytic concepts in behavioural terms (Kerr and Ryle, 2006).

## 2. Soul and Self

The history of psychotherapy, all too briefly related here, is intimately associated with broader streams of human thought, which have both given rise to it and influenced its course, and have also been influenced by it. In particular, it is associated with the history of ideas concerned with the soul or self.[2]

Platonic understandings of the soul or psyche have had enduring influence. According to Plato, the soul – an immaterial thing – provided continuity of personal identity during life, and after death. Christianity largely adopted this model, and it is still widely popular amongst ordinary Christians, and others, today. It was largely retained by René Descartes (1596-1650), who identified the soul with the mind, albeit he no longer identified the soul with the "life force" that confers life upon the body. However, the concept of the soul began to wane as scientific thinking came into the ascendant, and the mind was increasingly understood as located in the brain. By the end of the nineteenth century it was all but entirely abandoned in scientific and philosophical circles, although more recently new understandings of the soul, such as "emergent" models, have attracted renewed interest (Warren S. Brown, 1998).

The idea of the "self" also has a long history – arguably also stretching back to classical civilisation. However, the self represents an idea rather than a substance. The self is concerned more with the persistent identity of an individual human being (and potentially also other higher animals) which has both a body and psychological states such as emotions, thoughts or feelings. According to John Locke (1632-1704) personal identity, or the self, is grounded primarily in continuing psychological links, such as memory and consciousness. For David Hume (1711-1766), however, in *A Treatise of Human Nature*, the persisting self was simply an illusion. Here, he compares the human mind to a theatre, where actors who successively appear on stage are perceptions that come and go. But he qualifies this analogy by stating that there is no such thing as a mind, and therefore no theatre. We are left only with perceptions that come and go.

In *Critique of Pure Reason*, Immanuel Kant (1724-1804) distinguished between knowledge of things as they appear to be (phenomenon) and as they are in themselves (noumenon). The soul, or self, can only be known as phenomenon – not as noumenon.[3] Despite this, philosophical speculation about the concept of a unified soul continued, but scientific speculation, from the late nineteenth century onwards, tended to divide the self into more manageable units of study. It is within this realm that both psychotherapeutic and neuro-scientific understandings of the self are largely located. Thus, for example, Martin and Barresi draw attention to the Freudian model of id, ego and superego, and neuro-physiological concepts of a "neural self" as being examples of this kind.[4] But the proliferation of models and aspects of the self has led Martin and Barresi, and others, to conclude that the self is now irretrievably fragmented – both within individual theories, and also between different theories.[5]

At this point, it might be tempting to abandon any quest for a unified self. However, Charles Taylor[6] has pointed out that the self does not fulfil the basic criteria for being an object of scientific study. It cannot be studied completely objectively, it is not independent of descriptions or interpretations it makes of itself, it is not amenable to fully explicit description, and it cannot be described independently of its surroundings, for a self is only a self in relation to other selves. Taylor's[7] thesis is that our identity, and thus our selfhood, is actually defined by our stance on moral and spiritual questions, and by our belonging to a community:

> our being selves is essentially linked to our sense of the good, and that we achieve selfhood among other selves.[8]

Taylor identifies a number of aspects of the modern identity which he considers (although by no means uncritically) to be important. These include a sense of inwardness, an affirmation of ordinary life (work, marriage and family), and an understanding of nature as source of truth or goodness. Each of these has been important in its own way to the development of psychotherapy. By way of example of this, it may be illuminating to consider briefly the relevance of one of these aspects, namely inwardness. We noted in the introduction to Chapter 4 that Taylor understands inwardness as having been formed in our society by such processes as radical reflexivity, disengagement and expressivism.

As subjective agents, human beings experience the world, have knowledge and awareness of it, and find meaning in it as an object of their attention. "Radical reflexivity" (or the "first person standpoint") is a term introduced by Taylor[9] to refer to the stance from which this subjectivity itself becomes the object of attention, a stance which he understands as originating in the work of Augustine. It is the experience of experiencing, the knowledge of having knowledge and the awareness of awareness. It is a focus on the way that the world is *for* us. It is to be distinguished from non-radical reflexivity in which human beings attend to themselves (for example to their physical or spiritual well-being) but without adopting a first-person standpoint. It is concerned with being present to ourselves, the agents of our own experience. It is thus something to which every human agent has unique and privileged access. No one else can know exactly what it is like to be *me* in the way that I can.

Taylor suggests that both Freudian and behavioural theories find their basis in the "disengagement" of human subjects from the world around them.[10] The disengaged subject is capable not only of objectifying the world around her, but also her own emotions, desires and other feelings, in such a way as to enable objective and rational judgements to be made concerning them.[11] The identity of the disengaged subject is constituted in memory of the narrative of her own, unique, life story.[12] Disengagement, a process which Taylor understands as attributable primarily to the work of Descartes, involves a kind of stepping out of the first person standpoint so as to adopt theories or ideas of how things really are.[13]

The "punctual self" is a term adopted by Taylor in reference to a stance of radical disengagement which finds its origins in the work of Locke. This radical disengagement allows the extension of rational control to the possibility of reformation. The punctual self is thus not to be identified with any of a variety of possible objects of change, but rather with "the power to objectify and remake" and this power resides in consciousness. The punctual self is defined independently of concerns about the good, and independently of relationship to a wider community or environment. Its only constitutive property is self-awareness.[14]

According to Taylor, the Freudian ego is:

> in essence a pure steering mechanism, devoid of instinctual force of its own (though it must draw power from the id to function). Its job is to manoeuvre through the all-but-unnavigable obstacle course set by id, super-ego, and external reality. Its powers are incomparably less than Locke's punctual self,[15] but like its ancestor it is fundamentally a disengaged agent of instrumental reason.[16]

Taylor contrasts this with both the Platonic view of reason as located in the cosmic order, and the Stoic view of reason as the prioritising of human goals, neither of which required introspection. The disengaged self, however, is aware both of its own activities and the processes which form it. Furthermore, it takes charge of its own construction of reality and the associations which form it, and it remakes them.[17]

Taylor[18] identifies as a central feature of Romanticism the idea of "nature as source". Whilst the idea of "nature as source" is central to Romanticism, Taylor notes that it is also encountered apart from Romanticism, and may be understood as a context within which Romanticism arose in the eighteenth century.

> [T]he Romantics affirmed the rights of the individual, of the imagination, and of feeling.[19]

The Romantics attributed importance to the "inner voice or impulse" and to feelings as a source of truth. This could be understood on an individual basis, particular to the person, where the voice is the voice of the "self", or it could be understood on a wider basis as the impulse of nature. However, in either case, it is this inner voice or impulse which becomes definitive of the good life. The good life thus becomes a "fusion of the sensual and the spiritual" and the boundaries between the ethical and the aesthetic are blurred.

"Expressivism" is a term adopted by Taylor[20] to refer to the idea that, if nature is an inner élan, voice, or principle unique to each person, then this inner nature can only be known or made manifest by articulation or expression. This process of expression is not merely a revelation of something already existing, but is a bringing into being of something inchoate and incompletely formed.

Expressivism gives rise to the idea that there are "inner depths" within each of us, which can be explored by (for example) psychotherapy. Taylor writes:

> Freud's is a magnificent attempt to regain our freedom and self-possession, the dignity of the disengaged subject, in face of the inner depths.... The very terms of Freudian science and the language of his analyses require an articulation of the depths. And Freud certainly had a sense of the great power of the human symbolic capacity, even imprisoned as it most often is in the gigantic conflict of instincts, and distorted as it is by condensations and displacements. It may turn out that Freud's project, a kind of natural science of the mind, is

> impossible in the stringent terms in which he conceived it.... But there is no doubt that as self-interpretation the Freudian theory has its power....[21]

Psychotherapy, then, must be seen within the context of the philosophical concerns, and the developing modern sense of identity, alongside which it emerged. Like Taylor, we must be careful about making assertions of causal relationships where they cannot easily be proven.[22] However, radical reflexivity would clearly appear to be conducive to therapies which seek to make the self an object of scrutiny by itself. Disengagement takes this further and sees the possibility of self expression in the process of bringing about self change. Expressivism, however, gives rise to a notion of "hidden depths" within which we do not easily know ourselves, except after much searching.

For the *Philokalia*, on the other hand, much of the above account must seem immediately foreign. Operating, as it does, with a primarily Platonic understanding of the soul, it has not engaged with any of the major strands of western philosophical discourse that have been alluded to. Descartes and Locke were both undertaking their work during the period between the writing in the fifteenth century of the last text that would be included in the *Philokalia*, and the publication of the *Philokalia*, in the eighteenth century. Hume and Kant were undertaking their work during the same century in which the *Philokalia* was first published. Andrew Louth[23] notes that in 1781, the year before the publication of the *Philokalia*, Kant published the first edition of his *Critique of Pure Reason*. Was the publication of the *Philokalia*, then, a kind of response to philosophical developments elsewhere in Europe? Even if it was only seen as a reassertion of more ancient and traditional views of the nature of the soul, or perhaps to be reasserting eastern perspectives that had been neglected by western Christianity, it might be understood as providing a response of this kind. In fact, its teachings offer a kind of reflexivity and disengagement of their own – albeit not emerging from the same currents of thought as those with which Taylor deals in his search for sources of the modern self. It offers a marked rebuttal of any kind of expressivism which is unduly optimistic about the hidden depths of human nature. But, it does share with Augustine a sense that God can be found within.

## 3. Terminology

In his book, *From Passions to Emotions*, Thomas Dixon[24] traces the way in which discourse on "passions" and "affections" was transformed during the first half of the nineteenth century (at least in psychological thought in the English language) to discourse on "emotions".

According to Descartes,[25] passions in a broad sense included all perceptions, including those arising from stimuli originating in the external world. Passions in a narrow sense, however, he understood as being internal to the human body and due to "animal spirits" in the blood. Dixon takes Augustine and Aquinas as his starting point,[26] and so he sees here a transition from a traditional Christian understanding of passions as a movement of the soul, which acted upon the body, to a new view of a change in the body which acted upon the soul. Thus, passions of the body (Augustine and Aquinas) became passions of the soul (Descartes).

The second change that Dixon understands Descartes as making is towards a more dualistic view of body and mind as separate substances ("extended" and "thinking" respectively). Dixon acknowledges that the "classical Christian view" was also dualistic, but he argues that there was "always a strong metaphorical element to such dualism". Whether Descartes was as dualistic as he is generally assumed to be, and how much of a deviation this represents from traditional Christian thought, might be debated.[27] However, it must be noted in passing that the "classical Christian view" which Dixon outlines is a western one and different in important ways from the view outlined in Chapter 2 of this book. In particular, the model of the passions found in the *Philokalia* is heterogeneous, and includes elements of understanding which reflect passions as being both "of the soul" and "of the body".

Dixon identifies Hume, in *Treatise of Human Nature*, as providing the "earliest sustained use of the term [emotions] in the English language in a way that is similar to present-day usage".[28] Hume's understanding of the passions was different again. First, perceptions of the mind were classified into "impressions" and "ideas". Then, impressions were further subdivided into primary and secondary. Primary impressions constituted (what we would refer to as) perceptions – of external and bodily stimuli. Secondary impressions, however, are those that proceed from primary impressions. These include both those that directly arise from primary sense impressions, and those that arise indirectly, with the "interposition of an idea". It is these indirect secondary impressions that Hume understood as including "the passions and other emotions resembling them". On this basis, passions were to be understood as the combination of a sensation and an idea – a model not entirely dissimilar to that proposed by Maximos the Confessor (see Chapter 2). Unfortunately, Hume's use of the term "emotions" is somewhat inconsistent, sometimes contrasting with the passions, and sometimes including them.[29]

The remainder of the history charted by Dixon will not be pursued here. However, he notes that it was not until the period of the 1850s to 1870s that physical science assumed a dominant role and emotions were understood as a physical effect of the central and peripheral nervous systems upon the body. Whilst some Christian thinkers were still using the term "passions" in the 1870s, others adopted the new language much earlier than this. The story is one of "gradual, complex and incomplete secularisation".[30] Importantly, Dixon notes that many contemporary writers continue to understand "passions" and "emotions" as historically interchangeable terms – which they clearly are not. He identifies difference both in terms of the extensions (items included as belonging to the category) and intensions (definitions) of the terms. In regard to the latter he suggests that definitions of the passions tended to be concerned with more morally and theologically relevant movements of the soul. Definitions of the emotions tend to be understood as amoral physical or mental states.[31]

Dixon provides a valuable historical account of the transition from language of the passions to a language of the emotions in the western, English speaking, world. However, it is clear that what he has to say about "classical Christian" understandings applies inexactly, or perhaps not at all, to eastern Christian understandings of the passions such as those encountered in the *Philokalia*. Interestingly, some more recent conceptions, such as those of Hume, may be closer in some ways to some of those found in the *Philokalia* than to those of traditional western Christianity. Furthermore, the *Philokalia* is still consulted, at least in Orthodox Christian communities, as a source of guidance for the spiritual life. In this arena at least, the language of the passions is a living one, not necessarily the same as either the "passions" of early and medieval western Christianity or the "emotions" of contemporary scientific discourse.

But the language of the emotions upon which psychotherapy has based its theories and practices is largely the language that Dixon identifies as having evolved, through Augustine and Aquinas, Descartes, Locke, Hume, and others, to that which is in use today. Unfortunately, this language still finds itself in search of clear definitions.

## 4. Defining Psychotherapy

In responding to the question "What is psychotherapy?" Brown and Pedder suggest that it is:

> essentially a conversation which involves listening to and talking with those in trouble with the aim of helping them understand and resolve their predicament.[32]

This seems like a very broad definition, and these authors do acknowledge that, at one level, psychotherapy includes informal conversations, friendly encouragement, and attempts to reassure those in distress. In a narrower sense, however, these authors quote Sutherland's (1968) definition:

> By *psychotherapy* I refer to a personal relationship with a professional person in which those in distress can share and explore the underlying nature of their troubles, and possibly change some of the determinants of these through experiencing unrecognized forces in themselves.[33]

Here the emphasis is on a professional relationship and on the bringing about of change through "experiencing unrecognised forces", but this still doesn't seem entirely satisfactory. A family doctor, for example, might offer a simple interpretation of a patient's problem which brings about change through the bringing to recognition of emotions that had previously been avoided. But this kind of interaction seems much closer to Brown and Pedder's more general definition than it does to a narrower sense of what psychotherapy is usually thought to be about.

Bloch and Harari offer a different definition:

> Psychotherapy – the systematic application of psychological principles to accomplish systematic or more substantial personality change[34]

This, much narrower, definition focuses on the systematic application of psychological theory and the nature and degree of change effected. However, here, the change that is expected is in the "personality" – a definition which would probably exclude much professional behaviour therapy that (for example) reduces phobic anxiety, or even brief dynamic psychotherapy with more limited therapeutic goals than personality change.

A solution to the difficulty of balancing broader and narrower definitions of psychotherapy may be found in Jerome Frank's classic paper entitled "What is psychotherapy?" Jerome Frank (1910-2005) undertook extensive study of psychotherapy, including comparison with forms of religious healing. His studies led him to formulate theories concerning the common features between different kinds of psychotherapy and healing rituals. In responding to the question "What is psychotherapy?", he therefore refers to the importance of historical/cultural perspectives, he lists the kinds of professional roles within which its practitioners are found, considers the kinds of psychotherapy available, and the kinds of people to whom it is offered, addresses the question of how effective psychotherapy is, and considers some features that all psychotherapies have in common.[35] Perhaps the question about what psychotherapy is can only adequately be answered in this kind of way and at this sort of length. However, Frank does also suggest two criteria by which broader and narrower definitions might be distinguished. Firstly, he notes the training and sanctioning by society that psychotherapists receive. Secondly, he refers to what they actually do:

> their activity is systematically guided by an articulated theory that explains the sources of the patients' distress and disability, and prescribes methods for alleviating them.[36]

This would seem to offer a good balance between unduly narrow and unhelpfully broad definitions, although it might still be argued that in practice matters of suitable training, social sanctioning and articulable theory are not always clear cut.

Frank recognises that much psychotherapy is aimed at "demoralisation":

> A common source of distress may be termed 'demoralization' – a state of mind that ensues when a

> person feels subjectively incompetent, that is, unable to cope with a problem that he and those about him expect him to be able to handle.... The individual suffers a loss of confidence in himself and in his ability to master not only external circumstances but his own feelings and thoughts. The resulting sense of failure typically engenders feelings of guilt and shame. The demoralised person frequently feels alienated or isolated, as well as resentful because others whom he expects to help him seem unable or unwilling to do so.... With the weakening of his ties often goes a loss of faith in the group's values and beliefs, which have formerly helped to give him a sense of security and significance. The psychological world of the demoralised person is constricted in space and time. He becomes self-absorbed, loses sight of his long-term goals, and is preoccupied with avoiding further failure. His dominant moods are usually anxiety, ranging from mild apprehension to panic and depression, ranging in severity from being mildly dispirited to feeling utterly hopeless."[37]

Demoralisation occurs in many degrees of severity. The milder forms are self-limiting and respond to psychotherapy of the broader kind, provided by friends and family, or perhaps to other life changes, such as a change of employment. More severe forms are self-perpetuating and may include symptoms which could lead to diagnosis of mental disorder. Frank suggests that it is usually those in the middle range who are likely to seek psychotherapy.

The features of psychotherapies which are effective against demoralisation are:[38]

1. An intense, emotionally charged, confiding *relationship* with a helping person

2. *A healing setting*

3. A *rationale* or conceptual scheme that explains the cause of the patient's symptoms and prescribes a ritual or procedure for resolving them.

4. Linked to the rationale is a *procedure* that requires active participation of both patient and therapist and which is

believed by both to be the means for restoring the patient's health.

Frank argues that the articulated theories, or rationales, of psychotherapy and the methods or procedures involved share six therapeutic functions, irrespective of differences in the actual content of these rationales and procedures:

1. They strengthen the therapeutic relationship
2. They inspire and maintain hope for help
3. They provide opportunities for cognitive and experiential learning
4. They allow or enable emotional arousal
5. They enhance a sense of mastery, self-control, competence or effectiveness through success experiences
6. They encourage a working through and practice of what has been learned amidst the activities of everyday life

Thus, Frank proposes a model in which the rationale and procedures of therapy determine effectiveness not by virtue of their specific merits or content but rather by virtue of the extent to which they fulfil these six functions. In this way, he argues, psychotherapies of widely differing rationale and method might be equally effective.

## 5. Psychotherapy and the *Philokalia*

The foregoing definitions of psychotherapy leave ample scope for understanding the rationale and methods of the *Philokalia* as providing a kind of psychotherapy.

Whilst the *Philokalia* itself is a collection of texts, the spiritual life which it promotes affirms and encourages conversations which more than fulfil the requirements of the broader definitions of what psychotherapy is. Fragments of such conversations seem to provide the bulk of the *Apophthegmata Patrum*. They are frequently related also in the pages of the *Philokalia*. The "troubles" that are referred to in these definitions might be understood here either as the particular challenges of hunger, social isolation, poverty, etc., or else the more theologically defined and universal trouble of the human predicament as understood in traditional Christian terms as the need for salvation from sin, suffering and life without God.

In terms of the narrower definitions of psychotherapy, it is also not difficult to see ways in which the criteria are fulfilled. Although perhaps "professional" (as in Sutherland's definition) would not be a good word to describe the role of spiritual instructors, elders or priests offering guidance to young monks, there are clearly ways in which the former have gained experience, have been instructed themselves, and are sanctioned and recognised by a Christian community in fulfilment of a particular role, which are not at all dissimilar to the professional training and recognition of a psychotherapist. The "articulated theory", psychological principles, conferring of understanding, and orientation towards change referred to in the definitions of Bloch and Harari, and Frank, are also all evident, and hardly need further comment.

To take in turn Frank's four features of psychotherapies that combat demoralisation, we might note that:

1.  A close confiding relationship with a spiritual instructor (an elder, or starets) has many of the characteristics of a psychotherapeutic relationship. The instructor has authority, conferred by experience and recognised by the Church, albeit not necessarily a professional training in the usual sense.

2.  The "healing setting" of spiritual instruction envisaged in the *Apophthegmata* was usually the desert. In the *Philokalia* it is most often the monastery. Today it might be a room in which spiritual direction is provided. Frank sees this setting as "heightening the therapist's prestige" and containing evidence of training.[39] The desert and the monastery must both have had this effect in a most powerful way, both providing visible evidence of the ability of the instructor to live a life of ascetic virtue and self denial.[40] Frank also notes that the setting is a place of safety, where things can be said that have not previously been vocalised.

3.  The rationale offered by the *Philokalia* is to be found in its own teachings, as expounded by a suitable instructor, and also the wider framework of Christian faith as affirmed in scripture and the creeds, and as taught by the catholic Church. Frank notes that this rationale must be shared

by patient and therapist, that it must be affirmed by the culturally dominant world view (which we may here take to be that of the Church), and that it must not be shaken by therapeutic failures. His examples are both interesting and highly relevant here:

> In the Middle Ages, the belief system underlying what we today call psychotherapy was demonology. In many primitive societies it is witchcraft. In the Western world today it is science.[41]

4. The procedures of the *Philokalia* include, but are not limited to, the remedies for the passions described in Chapter 2 of this book. Frank notes that belief in their efficacy and active participation in them by both therapist and patient are important.

Similarly, the six therapeutic functions of the rationale and procedures of the *Philokalia* can be identified:

1. The *relationship* with an abbot or other spiritual instructor is strengthened by the emphasis in the teachings of the *Philokalia* on obedience, the belief system that they share, the evidence (in his own life and that of other monks or disciples) that the instructor has practical experience of how to help, and by a sharing in the rule of life (its practices and "procedures") that the *Philokalia* provides.

2. The *hope for help*, which Frank sees as a powerful healing force, may be conveyed in a variety of ways, but not least in the vision of human well-being, and ultimately deification, outlined in Chapter 4.

3. There are clearly many opportunities for *cognitive and experiential learning*. Simply reading the *Philokalia*, especially if this task is to be undertaken meditatively and prayerfully, is a major learning exercise in itself. However, Frank emphasises that this is not a purely intellectual exercise. The remedies for human living prescribed in the *Philokalia* ensure that the true disciple will engage with its rationale ascetically, prayerfully, and in relationship with other members of a community. This is a way of life, and not simply a theoretical or dogmatic framework for faith.

4. *Emotional arousal* might be seen as a point of deviation from Frank's psychotherapeutic model. Setting a goal of dispassion could be understood as discouraging emotional expressions. However, leaving aside for the moment the important terminological distinction to be made between "passion" and "emotion", it is clear that the *Philokalia* does not anticipate that any new disciple will immediately attain dispassion. Rather, it directs attention to the challenges to the spiritual life that passion will present and it provides procedures for dealing with these. Furthermore, the establishing of the "intellect in the heart", the experience in the heart of "supracelestial fire", and prayer of the heart (see Chapter 3) all suggest that there is an important affective or emotional element to the life of prayer that the *Philokalia* describes.

5. The sense of enhancement of self-mastery, and the provision of *success experiences*, that the *Philokalia* offers may be seen in relation to instructions given for the ascetic life and the life of prayer. The Evagrian corpus also provides a good example of this, taking initiates as it does from simpler levels of learning (at which they are likely to succeed) to more complex levels of learning in a graded fashion. One would expect instructors to guide new disciples through the *Philokalia* in a similar way, in order that they may achieve success in simpler tasks before progressing to more complex or challenging ones. Frank also notes the importance of naming phenomena as a means of gaining mastery over them (cf. the naming of the animals by Adam in Genesis 2). The extensive and sophisticated vocabulary of the inner life offered by the *Philokalia* might be seen as assisting the new disciple to gain confidence in their ability to master their thoughts and passions.

6. The working through of teachings in the practice of everyday life is everywhere apparent in the *Philokalia*. Indeed, its general assumption is that its teachings will be put into practice in religious life – that the whole of life will be lived according to its rationale and devoted to adopting its procedures.

On this basis, then, there would appear to be good grounds firstly for seeing the *Philokalia* as offering a kind of psychotherapy, and secondly for seeing it as incorporating a rationale and procedures which might be highly likely to effect change in people's lives. However, this is really only the beginning of an answer to the question posed at the outset of this chapter, in that it looks back at a collection of ancient texts, in the light of current thinking, and finds evidence that their rationale and procedures are not entirely dissimilar to those identified by contemporary psychotherapists as likely to effect change in people's lives. It does not engage with the second and third issues identified above as potentially important in any critical comparison of the *Philokalia* and psychotherapy.[42] Consideration must therefore now be given to these issues – and firstly to that of the purposes for which the *Philokalia* and psychotherapy were intended, and the outcomes to which they aspire.

## 6. Purpose and Outcome

Frank observes that it is difficult to compare outcomes even between different forms of psychotherapy, as they intend different things.[43] Dynamic psychotherapies aim to bring to awareness previously unconscious thoughts and feelings. Behavioural therapists look for reduction of symptom severity. Even between dynamic therapies important differences in treatment goals may be observed. How, then, may different psychological therapies, let alone also theological or spiritual "therapies" be compared?

We have already seen that contemporary theories of the self are fragmented. If no unified view of the self can be agreed, can any comparisons be made between therapies concerned with healing of the self? Robert Innes suggests that an even more radical answer to this question might be identified in postmodern views of the self as enslaving. His review of the work of Foucault, Lacan, Deleuze, and Guattari draws attention to the ways in which notions of the self may be used to exert social control over human desires and freedoms.[44] On this basis, views of a unified self need to be deconstructed and comparisons of the kind suggested here are invalidated, or at least made worthless. However, Innes himself does not concur with this view. He suggests that postmodernism is, in this context, a self defeating protest against the order and discipline suggested by Platonic and later models which emphasise discipline and rationality.

Innes therefore proposes a way of approaching wholeness which still values those parts of the self which are not ordered or rational. So, according to Innes:

> theologies and psychologies can be evaluated in terms of their ability to supply resources for unifying the self.[45]

In his comparison:

- Augustinian spirituality aims at integration of the self through the pursuit of desire for God.

- Freudian therapy aims at extending the power of the ego over the id.

- Jungian therapy aims for individuation, which requires reorientation and integration of the Self,[46] gained through increasing insight into those parts of the self that reside in the personal unconscious

- Humanistic psychology aims at integration of the self through self-actualisation, a process that requires self-awareness and self-acceptance

Innes goes on to evaluate these resources for unifying the self in terms of their integrative power, their freedom from contradiction, and their relevance. His conclusion is that Augustine succeeds where the others fail, because of the integrative power of his reference of the self to God.[47]

We might question whether or not unification of the self is the most appropriate basis for comparison of psychologies and theologies. Had Innes included behavioural or cognitive psychotherapy amongst his comparisons, it would be difficult to imagine how they might have fared. Freedom from contradiction and relevance might not have been difficult to assess, but how would integrative power be assessed? Since behavioural and cognitive therapies seek symptom reduction rather than self-integration, assessment of the latter would appear to be relatively meaningless in relation to outcome.

Another approach to comparison might involve recent philosophical and scientific research on subjective well-being.[48] Amongst the advantages of this might be the multi-disciplinary emphasis, which is informed by both philosophy and the social and natural sciences, and the extent to which research has been undertaken on spirituality and religion as predictors of well-being. If a spiritual way of life, such as that offered by the *Philokalia*, and psychotherapy are both concerned with human well-being, then this might provide a promising way to allow comparisons to be made between what each may have to offer.

Haybron identifies five categories of well-being theory:[49]

1. Hedonistic theories
2. Desire theories
3. Authentic happiness theories
4. Eudaimonistic (or "nature-fulfilment") theories
5. List theories

Hedonistic theories more or less identify well-being with pleasure. Desire theories identify well-being with the extent to which a person's desires are actually satisfied. Authentic happiness theories assess happiness in relation to a person's own values (free of social pressure) and the actual conditions of one's life. Eudaimonistic theories usually refer to ancient theories (such as those of Aristotle), incorporating ethical values and judgements of how the good life should be lived. Finally, list theories identify well-being with more or less ad hoc lists of goods such as knowledge, pleasure, and friendship.

It might immediately be presumed that the spirituality of the *Philokalia* should be associated with Eudaimonistic theories of well-being, although desire theories might in fact distinguish well between individuals with desire for God and those whose desires actually lay elsewhere. It is a little more difficult to assess which approach might be most useful to evaluate well-being as a goal of psychotherapy.[50] However, a rather bigger problem arises insofar as this approach tends to make well-being a utilitarian good, conferred by any of a number of means, amongst which means the spiritual life (according to the *Philokalia* or any other tradition) is but one available means to the personal end. The danger here is that spirituality is made into a self-serving process aimed at achieving well-being. In fact, neither the *Philokalia* nor any other major strand of traditional Christian spirituality understands things in this way. Rather, the good is pursued out of love for God alone and (at least ideally) whether or not it leads to any measure of well-being in this world.[51]

However, the purpose here is not to design a measure for an empirical outcome study comparing spiritual instruction based on the *Philokalia* with one or more different kinds of psychotherapy. Neither is the purpose at hand Innes' somewhat different task of evaluating different discourses that all promise wholeness of the self. Rather the question is – do the *Philokalia* and psychotherapy have a purpose in common? In order to answer this, we might want to ask a number of subsidiary questions:

1. To whom might each be offered, and who might benefit?

2. What does each hope to achieve?

3. If we were evaluating their success empirically, what would we want to measure?

### i. Who might Benefit?

In one way or another, both the *Philokalia* and psychotherapy potentially have something to offer to anyone and everyone. At least, for those who wish to find benefit in them, there are insights to be gained from the *Philokalia* and from psychotherapy concerning the mental and spiritual life. Neither is it the case that the *Philokalia* only has things to say about the spiritual life, and psychotherapy only about the mental life. The *Philokalia* takes very seriously the world of thoughts and feelings and has much to say about them. Similarly, most forms of psychotherapy have had something to say about spirituality or religion. In some cases, as with Freud (who understood religion as essentially a form of neurosis), this has been very negative, but in other cases, as with Jung, religion has been perceived as a very important part of mental well-being. Mental and spiritual life are inextricably bound up with each other.

However, the *Philokalia* was clearly compiled with a view to it being read by those wishing to make progress in the spiritual life. In *The Way of the Pilgrim*, it is given to the pilgrim in response to his expressed desire to achieve unceasing prayer.[52] Psychotherapy, in contrast, is offered primarily to those suffering from various forms of mental disorder, those who are psychologically overwhelmed by life stresses, and those whose behaviour is disturbed (e.g. due to family stress in childhood, or due to addiction).[53]

## ii. What might be Achieved?

We might again identify a very general level of answer which affirms that both the *Philokalia* and psychotherapy are offered with a hope of achieving change. This might be change in (including better self awareness of) thoughts, feelings, and behaviours, or perhaps in other ways. Both have much to say about relationships. Again, the close connection between mental and spiritual life would behove us to be careful about assuming that psychotherapy would have nothing to do with relationship with God.

However, we saw in Chapter 4 that the ultimate goal of the *Philokalia* is to assist people in making progress towards deification – or union with God. It might be understood as a manual for living the Christian life, and especially for contemplative prayer. As a means to this end, the *Philokalia* is very realistic. Thoughts, feelings and behaviour must all change. Generally, the pattern seems to be one of changing behaviour (towards a more ascetic lifestyle) first. However, this lifestyle change is intimately bound up with an understanding of how patterns of thought need to be changed as a basis for changing the way that we feel about things. At this level, the objective is dispassion.

Psychotherapy, however, will be evaluated in relation to the presenting problem for which it has been offered. Indeed, for behavioural psychotherapy this might be the only therapeutic goal. However, for dynamic therapies "wholeness", or integration of the self, will usually be seen as an important means for achieving this goal and sometimes as more important than alleviation of the presenting symptoms. As we saw from our brief consideration of Innes' work on Freudian, Jungian and humanistic therapies, the form that this wholeness or integration takes will differ from one therapy to another. For cognitive therapies, wholeness and integration are not usually considered important. Rather, changing patterns of faulty, irrational or inappropriate thoughts is seen as necessary to changing feelings. None of these therapies would be likely to aim at "dispassion" as an objective, but usually rational processes will be seen as important to mental well-being.

## iii. How might Outcome be Measured?

Measurement of outcome is really a scientific question, although it might be reframed in more theological language. For example, we might ask the question as to whether and in what ways we would expect prayer or faith to change the life of a person who prays.[54] However, the theological measure of "change" is never likely to be primarily a scientific one. Although some changes which occur in the life of a person who prays might be scientifically measurable,[55] many will probably not be.

Empirical evaluation of the "success" of life lived according to the teachings of the *Philokalia* might be virtually impossible to achieve. Others may notice a change in behaviour – perhaps in regard to virtues such as humility, patience, kindness, etc. A wise and more experienced person, advanced in the spiritual life, might be able to make judgments about the degree of progress a person is making in the interior life. The person themselves could report on progress that they felt that they were making. However, ultimately, the *Philokalia* would only allow that God knows what lies in the very depths of the heart and mind of each man or woman. It would be this most interior level of orientation toward God that would be the ultimate test.

Whilst psychotherapy outcomes may be difficult to evaluate, the difficulties would be far less than this. Numerous scales for measuring symptom severity, by observation or self-rating, have been validated, as well as global measures of social, physical and psychological functioning. Measurement of integration of the self might be somewhat more difficult, but certainly not impossible for an experienced therapist to assess.

These very real differences in the measurability of outcome must not be allowed to disguise the fact that many psychological and behavioural changes might be scientifically measurable in the life of a person following the teachings of the *Philokalia*. Similarly, psychotherapy might (and sometimes does) lead to the posing of deep existential and spiritual questions which lead to a change in orientation towards the Divine. It is therefore not so much that changes brought about by reading the *Philokalia* can't be measured, whilst those brought about by psychotherapy can, but rather that the changes that the compilers of the *Philokalia* hoped to bring to people's lives are not ultimately ones that are amenable to scientific measurement.

In broad terms, then, the *Philokalia* and psychotherapy have very different purposes and goals. However, both are orientated, at some level, towards changing thoughts, feelings and behaviours. This is not the final destination towards which the *Philokalia* provides a map, but it is a necessary part of the journey, and to this extent the *Philokalia* might be said to provide a kind of psychotherapy.

## 7. Inwardness and the *Philokalia*

It will be recalled that Taylor suggests that all cultures employ a language of inwardness, but that this universal language is embedded within culturally specific notions of "inner" and "outer" which reflect something of the spiritual and moral vision of that culture. As inwardness is such an important feature of our own culture, and of that of Christianity and the *Philokalia*, and is also so important to contemporary notions of what psychotherapy is all about, we must now turn to a closer consideration of it.

Stephen Sykes has suggested that:

> It is undeniable, from even a cursory knowledge of the Christian tradition, that 'inwardness' has played an important role in the development of Christian identity.[56]

Sykes suggests that commitment is an important concern for all religions, and for society in general, because it anchors in the individual emotional life a system of meaning common to the whole society or group. This in turn, because it guides the choices that individuals make, provides the consistency of intention which is so necessary for good social order and family life. But the need for commitment places emphasis on the interior life. Because we can never know for certain what another person's intentions were, or even what our own intentions are, this in turn leads to a recognition that God alone is able to judge our intentions with unfailing accuracy.[57]

For Christianity, Sykes suggests that the extensive teaching on the heart in Judeo-Christian scripture has been a significant source of its inwardness tradition. In the Psalms, he notes that the heart is associated with a range of psychological functions, not least those concerned with the emotions, intellectual activity, and the will. But the heart is somewhat mysterious and inaccessible. A form of self-examination is therefore required which "amounts to a seeing of the heart as God himself sees it".[58] In the Pauline corpus of the New Testament, the heart is a frequently recurring term applied to the seat of thoughts, emotions, affect and will, but is also the place in which the Holy Spirit dwells. Ultimately, human intentions are known to God alone, and where they are in need of change, this may be something that God alone can bring about.[59]

Sykes recognises that this inwardness tradition has profoundly affected the use of ritual, sacrament, worship and ethical teaching, for in all of these areas what really matters is not what is visible to other people, but rather the inner intention of the individual human being in relation to God.

Sebastian Brock, writing on the prayer of the heart in the Syriac tradition, suggests that there is a different perspective on the heart in eastern and western traditions. He attributes this to the influence of Dionysius the Areopagite, drawing on Platonic and neo-Platonic thought, who virtually ignored the heart and referred to the nous as the centre of spiritual life. Dionysius having been somewhat more influential in the west than the east, Brock sees this as explaining a tendency amongst western writers to contrast heart as the seat of affective prayer with the mind (nous) as the seat of intellectual prayer.[60] Brock writes that, in the biblical account:

> the 'heart' is regarded as the focal point of *every* aspect of the 'inner person', as St Paul calls it (Rom. 7:22), the focal point of the intellect as well as of the emotions and feelings.[61]

He further contrasts this "inner heart" with the physical heart. The one is the centre of spiritual life, the other of physical life, but the wholeness of human beings is such that each requires the other.

Brock goes on to quote Isaac of Nineveh's (c700) distinction between purity of mind and purity of heart. The former is relatively easily achieved, through study of scripture, fasting, and avoidance of distraction. The latter, however, is only achieved through "great afflictions".[62] The heart is thus a place of sacrifice – a kind of altar.

The heart is also a place of revelation, or theophany. Brock quotes an eighth century mystic, Abdisho the Seer:

> True love....does not leave anything in your mind apart from the awareness of God which constitutes the spiritual key with which the inner door of the heart is opened – and inside is hidden Christ our Lord.[63]

Brock sees purity of heart, in the Syriac tradition at least, as being pure prayer. Prayer of the heart in this tradition[64] is characterised by remembrance, or total awareness, of God in "the very centre of our innermost being".[65]

It is a very similar process, in a somewhat different language, which Taylor identifies as the radical reflexivity of Augustinian thought:

> Augustine shifts the focus from the field of objects known to the activity itself of knowing; God is to be found here.[66]

And again:

> Augustine's turn to the self was a turn to radical reflexivity, and that is what made the language of inwardness irresistible. The inner light is the one which shines in our presence to ourselves; it is the one inseparable from our being creatures with a first person standpoint. What differentiates it from the outer light is just what makes the image of inwardness so compelling, that it illuminates the space where I am present to myself.[67]

This tradition of inwardness, which Sykes describes in relation to Christianity in general, which Brock identifies in the Syriac tradition, and which Augustine is credited by Taylor with having introduced to the west, finds a particularly strong and distinctive expression in the *Philokalia*.

Before turning to examples of inner and outer aspects of human experience, it is important to recall that all created things are understood in the tradition of the *Philokalia* as having an inner "essence" or "principle". These logoi, or "thoughts of God", are contained within the Logos and are manifested in the created order of the universe. They provide the focus for natural contemplation.[68] This is particularly evident in, although by no means confined to, the writings of Maximos the Confessor. For example:

> If, instead of stopping short at the outward appearance which visible things present to the senses, you seek with your intellect to contemplate their inner essences, seeing them as images of spiritual realities or as the inward principles of sensible objects, you will be taught that nothing belonging to the visible world is unclean. For

> by nature all things were created good (cf. Gen. 1:31; Acts 10:15).[69]

What is "within" any created thing is thus not so much a matter of physical location or spatial orientation as the essence or principle of the thing as created by God.

However, when we turn to human beings specifically, inwardness language is virtually ubiquitous. Table 5.1 shows a listing of inwardness language drawn from the English translation of the *Philokalia*.[70]

There are countless examples in the *Philokalia* of contrasts between inner and outer. For example, we find in the writings of Mark the Ascetic:

> When a man outwardly praises someone, while accusing and disparaging him in his heart, it is hard for the simple to detect this. Similarly a person may be outwardly humble but inwardly arrogant. For a long time such men present falsehood as truth, but later they are exposed and condemned.[71]

Or, again, Thalassios the Libyan writes:

> Prove yourself a monk, not outwardly, but inwardly, by freeing yourself from the passions.[72]

The general rule seems to be, it is not what other people see (on the outside) that matters, it is what God sees (on the inside) that is important. So, inwardness is again not so much to do with physical space as with Divine perspective.

The inner place is also spoken of as being a place of encounter with Christ as, for example, in the writings of Theoliptos:

> Copy the wisdom of the bees; when they become aware of an encircling swarm of wasps, they remain inside their hive and so escape the attacks with which they are threatened. Wasps signify commerce with the world: avoid such commerce at all costs, stay in your cell, and there try to re-enter the innermost citadel of the soul, the dwelling-place of Christ, where you will truly find the peace, joy and serenity of Christ the spiritual Sun – gifts that He irradiates and with which He rewards the soul that receives Him with faith and devotion.[73]

## Table 5.1: Inwardness language in the *Philokalia*[74]

| Inwardness language | *Philokalia* reference |
|---|---|
| **Isaiah the Solitary** | |
| Inward meditation | *Guarding the Intellect*, #26 (EGP 1, 28) |
| Inwardly, blessing (God) | *Guarding the Intellect*, #26 (EGP 1, 24) |
| **Evagrios** | |
| Inner prayer | *On Prayer, 153 Texts*, #112 (EGP 1, 68) |
| Inner watchfulness and vigilance | *Asceticism & Stillness* (EGP 1, 37) |
| Inward sorrow | *On Prayer, 153 Texts*, #43 (EGP 1, 61) |
| Inwardly divided | *Asceticism & Stillness* (EGP 1, 31) |
| **John Cassian** | |
| Inner desert | *Holy Fathers of Sketis* (EGP 1, 101) |
| Inner house (wisdom) | *Holy Fathers of Sketis* (EGP 1, 100) |
| **Mark the Ascetic** | |
| Inner dwelling place of Christ | *Righteous by Works*, #224 (EGP 1, 145) |
| Inner law | *Letter to Nicolas* (EGP 1, 154) |
| Inner man | *Letter to Nicolas* (EGP 1, 154) |
| Inner progress | *Righteous by Works*, #165 (EGP 1, 139) |
| Inner state | *Righteous by Works*, #67 (EGP 1, 131) |
| Inward action (of passion) | *Letter to Nicolas* (EGP 1, 154) |
| Inward assent | *Letter to Nicolas* (EGP 1, 147) |
| Inward enjoyment | *On the Spiritual Law*, #97 (EGP 1, 117) |
| Inward intention | *Righteous by Works*, #15 (EGP 1, 126) |
| Inward struggle | *Righteous by Works*, #161 (EGP 1, 139) |
| Inwardly arrogant | *On the Spiritual Law*, #36 (EGP 1, 113) |
| Inwardly, defiling/defiled | *Letter to Nicolas* (EGP 1, 149, 150) |
| Inwardly, grieve | *Righteous by Works*, #176 (EGP 1, 140) |
| **Hesychios the Priest** | |
| Inner ambuscades | *Watchfulness & Holiness*, #8 (EGP 1, 164) |
| Inner attention | *Watchfulness & Holiness*, #120 (EGP 1, 183) |

| Inwardness language | *Philokalia* reference |
|---|---|
| Inner eyes | *Watchfulness & Holiness*, #130 (EGP 1, 185) |
| Inner knowledge | *Watchfulness & Holiness*, #61 (EGP 1, 172) |
| Inner life | *Watchfulness & Holiness*, #68 (EGP 1, 174) |
| Inner monk | *Watchfulness & Holiness*, #71 (EGP 1, 175) |
| Inner self | *Watchfulness & Holiness*, #34, #70, #87, ##111-112, ##172-173, #178 (EGP 1, 168, 174-175, 177, 181, 193, 194) |
| Inner shrine of the soul | *Watchfulness & Holiness*, #21 (EGP 1, 165) |
| Inner stability | *Watchfulness & Holiness*, #7 (EGP 1, 163) |
| Inner struggle | *Watchfulness & Holiness*, #5 (EGP 1, 163) |
| Inner struggle | *Watchfulness & Holiness*, #32, #52 (EGP 1, 168, 171) |
| Inner vigilance | *Watchfulness & Holiness*, #10 (EGP 1, 164) |
| Inner warfare | *Watchfulness & Holiness*, #34, #105, #148 (EGP 1, 168, 180, 188) |
| Inward parts | *Watchfulness & Holiness*, ##85-86 (EGP 1, 176) |
| Inward spiritual warfare | *Watchfulness & Holiness*, #99 (EGP 1, 179) |
| Inwardly anticipates | *Watchfulness & Holiness*, #8 (EGP 1, 163-164) |
| Inwardly chastened | *Watchfulness & Holiness*, #130 (EGP 1, 185) |
| Inwardly, be a monk | *Watchfulness & Holiness*, #70 (EGP 1, 174) |
| Inwardly, purified itself | *Watchfulness & Holiness*, #122 (EGP 1, 183) |
| Inwardly, sin | *Watchfulness & Holiness*, #122 (EGP 1, 193) |
| **Neilos the Ascetic** | |
| Inner stability | *Ascetic Discourse* (EGP 1, 202) |
| Inner truth | *Ascetic Discourse* (EGP 1, 242) |
| Inner watchfulness | *Ascetic Discourse* (EGP 1, 227) |
| Inward parts | *Ascetic Discourse* (EGP 1, 220) |
| Inward state | *Ascetic Discourse* (EGP 1, 221) |
| Inwardly at peace | *Ascetic Discourse* (EGP 1, 218) |
| Inwardly restrain | Ascetic Discourse (EGP 1, 238) |

| Inwardness language | *Philokalia* reference |
|---|---|
| **Diadochos of Photiki** | |
| Inner energies | *On Spiritual Knowledge*, #9 (EGP 1, 255) |
| Inner shrine [of] the intellect | *On Spiritual Knowledge*, #69 (EGP 1, 270) |
| Inner shrine of [the] heart | *On Spiritual Knowledge*, #29 (EGP 1, 269) |
| Inner shrine of the soul | *On Spiritual Knowledge*, #28 (EGP 1, 260) |
| Inward awareness | *On Spiritual Knowledge*, #100 (EGP 1, 295) |
| Inward calm | *On Spiritual Knowledge*, #62 (EGP 1, 272) |
| Inward man | *On Spiritual Knowledge*, #82 (EGP 1, 282) |
| Inward martyrdom | *On Spiritual Knowledge*, #94 (EGP 1, 292) |
| Inward point … of sensitivity [of] the soul | *On Spiritual Knowledge*, #85 (EGP 1, 285) |
| Inward sense | *On Spiritual Knowledge*, #37 (EGP 1, 264) |
| **John of Karpathos** | |
| Inner room (the shrine of [the] heart) | *For the Monks in India*, #91 (EGP 1, 319) |
| Inner sanctuary | *For the Monks in India*, #91 (EGP 1, 320) |
| Innermost self | *For the Monks in India*, #91 (EGP 1, 320) |
| Inward heaven of the heart | *For the Monks in India*, #52 (EGP 1, 310) |
| Inward resolution | *For the Monks in India*, #19 (EGP 1, 302) |
| Inward sanctuary | *For the Monks in India*, #55 (EGP 1, 311) |
| Innermost self | *For the Monks in India*, #91 (EGP 1, 320) |
| Inward heaven of the heart | *For the Monks in India*, #52 (EGP 1, 310) |
| Inward resolution | *For the Monks in India*, #19 (EGP 1, 302) |
| Inward sanctuary | *For the Monks in India*, #55 (EGP 1, 311) |
| Inward state | *For the Monks in India*, #25, #67 (EGP 1, 304, 314) |
| Inwardly confused | *For the Monks in India*, #70 (EGP 1, 315) |
| Inwardly, full of agitation | *For the Monks in India*, #87 (EGP 1, 318) |
| Inwardly, full of turmoil | *For the Monks in India*, #87 (EGP 1, 318) |
| Inwardly, grows | *For the Monks in India*, #23 (EGP 1, 303) |

| Inwardness language | *Philokalia* reference |
|---|---|
| Inwardly, spoke (to God) | *For the Monks in India*, #56 (EGP 1, 311) |
| Inwardly, the Lord always speaks to us | *Ascetic Discourse* (EGP 1, 326) |
| **[Antony the Great]** ||
| Inner beauty | *On the Character of Men*, #20 (EGP 1, 332) |
| Inner freedom | *On the Character of Men*, #37 (EGP 1, 334) |
| Inward character | *On the Character of Men*, #21 (EGP 1, 332) |
| Inward discipline | *On the Character of Men*, #10 (EGP 1, 331) |
| **Theodoros the Great Ascetic** ||
| Inner wakefulness | *Spiritual Texts*, #99 (EGP 2, 36) |
| Inward faith | *Spiritual Texts*, #47 (EGP 2, 22) |
| Inwardly, acquiring | *Spiritual Texts*, #91 (EGP 2, 34) |
| **Maximos the Confessor** ||
| Inner attitude | *Various Texts: C3*, #20 (EGP 2, 214) |
| Inner being | *Various Texts: C5*, #49 (EGP 2, 273) |
| Inner disposition | *Various Texts: C1*, #61 (EGP 2, 177)<br>*Various Texts: C4*, ##65-66 (EGP 2, 252)<br>*Various Texts: C4*, #74 (EGP 2, 254) |
| Inner hunger | *Various Texts: C5*, #35[75] (EGP 2, 268) |
| Inner life | *On Love: C4*, #64 (EGP 2, 108) |
| Inner man | *On Love: C4*, #78 (EGP 2, 110) |
| Inner monk | *On Love: C4*, #51 (EGP 2, 106) |
| Inner practice of the virtues | *On Love: C4*, #43 (EGP 2, 105) |
| Inner quality | *Various Texts: C4*, #81 (EGP 2, 255) |
| Inner self | *On Love: C4*, #50 (EGP 2, 106) |
| Inner stability | *On the Lord's Prayer* (EGP 2, 292) |
| Inner states | *On Love: C2*, #87, #89 (EGP 2, 80)<br>*For Thalassios: C2*, ##91-92 (EGP 2, 161)<br>*Various Texts: C1*, #61 (EGP 2, 177)<br>*Various Texts: C2*, #94 (EGP 2, 207)<br>*Various Texts: C4*, #20 (EGP 2, 240)<br>*Various Texts: C5*, #10[76] (EGP 2, 263)<br>*On the Lord's Prayer* (EGP 2, 301-302 |
| Inner teaching | *Various Texts: C1*, #10 (EGP 2, 166-167) |

| Inwardness language | *Philokalia* reference |
|---|---|
| Inner vision | *For Thalassios*: *C1*, #80 (EGP 2, 131) |
| Inward disposition | *Various Texts:* *C2*, #82 (EGP 2, 205) |
| Inward law | *On the Lord's Prayer* (EGP 2, 285) |
| Inward quality or disposition | *Various Texts:* *C4*, #82 (EGP 2, 256) |
| Inward resolution | *Various Texts:* *C1*, #17 (EGP 2, 169) |
| Inward state | *Various Texts:* *C5*, #84 (EGP 2, 280)<br>*On the Lord's Prayer* (EGP 2, 301) |
| Inward unity | *On the Lord's Prayer* (EGP 2, 294) |
| Inwardly lays hold of | *Various Texts:* *C5*, #62 (EGP 2, 275) |
| Inwardly subject (to deceit) | *Various Texts:* *C4*, #18 (EGP 2, 239) |
| Inwardly sunders | *On the Lord's Prayer* (EGP 2, 301) |
| Inwardly, be a monk | *On Love*: *C4*, #50 (EGP 2, 106) |
| Inwardly, practicing the virtues | *For Thalassios*: *C2*, #24 (EGP 2, 143) |
| Inwardly, rejoice | *For Thalassios*: *C2*, #24 (EGP 2, 143) |
| **[Maximos the Confessor]** | |
| Inner states | *Various Texts:* *C3*, #61 (EGP 2, 226)<br>*Various Texts:* *C4*, #92 (EGP 2, 258)<br>*Various Texts:* *C5*, #2 (EGP 2, 261) |
| Inwardly longs | *Various Texts:* *C1*, #89 (EGP 2, 185) |
| **Thalassios the Libyan** | |
| Inner work | *For Paul*: *C1*, #18 (EGP 2, 308) |
| Inward stillness | *For Paul*: *C2*, #11 (EGP 2, 313) |
| Inwardly, cleave | *For Paul*: *C3*, #3 (EGP 2, 319) |
| Inwardly, curses | *For Paul*: *C1*, #3 (EGP 2, 307) |
| Inwardly, prove [to be] a monk | *For Paul*: *C3*, #22 (EGP 2, 320) |
| **Anonymous** | |
| Inner thoughts | *A discourse on Abba Philimon* (EGP 2, 351) |
| Inner watchfulness | *A discourse on Abba Philimon* (EGP 2, 350) |
| Inner work | *A discourse on Abba Philimon* (EGP 2, 348) |
| Inward meditation | *A discourse on Abba Philimon* (EGP 2, 347) |
| Inwardly, meditate/meditating | *A discourse on Abba Philimon* (EGP 2, 347-349, 351) |

| Inwardness language | *Philokalia* reference |
|---|---|
| **[Theognostos]** ||
| Inner beauty | *On Virtues, Contemplation & Priesthood*, #18 (EGP 2, 363) |
| Inward illumination | *On Virtues, Contemplation & Priesthood*, #23 (EGP 2, 363) |
| Inward meditation | *On Virtues, Contemplation & Priesthood*, #32 (EGP 2, 366) |
| Inward self-renunciation | *On Virtues, Contemplation & Priesthood*, #11 (EGP 2, 361) |
| Inward state | *On Virtues, Contemplation & Priesthood*, #26 (EGP 2, 265) |
| Inwardly … fill | *On Virtues, Contemplation & Priesthood*, #18 (EGP 2, 363) |
| **Philotheos of Sinai** ||
| Inner eyes | *Forty Texts on Watchfulness*, #19, #33 (EGP 3, 23, 29) |
| Inner state | *Forty Texts on Watchfulness*, #14, #35 (EGP 3, 21, 29) |
| Inner watchfulness | *Forty Texts on Watchfulness*, #3, #25 (EGP 3, 17, 26) |
| Inward man | *Forty Texts on Watchfulness*, #31 (EGP 3, 28) |
| Inwardly, fettered | *Forty Texts on Watchfulness*, #19 (EGP 3, 23) |
| Inwardly, operates | *Forty Texts on Watchfulness*, #17 (EGP 3, 22) |
| Inwardly, tell us | *Forty Texts on Watchfulness*, #28 (EGP 3, 27) |
| **Ilias the Presbyter** ||
| Inward … aspects (of the soul) | *Gnomic Anthology*: 3, #32 (EGP 3, 51) |
| Inwardly purify | *Gnomic Anthology*: 4, #109 (EGP 3, 61) |
| Inwardly, activated | *Gnomic Anthology*: 4, #133 (EGP 3, 64) |
| Inwardly, guard | *Gnomic Anthology*: 4, #59 (EGP 3, 55) |
| Inwardly, unites with | *Gnomic Anthology*: 4, #123 (EGP 3, 63) |
| **Theophanis the Monk** ||
| Inwardly experience | *Ladder of Divine Graces* (EGP 3, 68) |
| **Peter of Damaskos** ||
| Inner self | *Book II* (EGP 3, 244) |
| Inner state | *Book I* (EGP 3, 152, 243) |
| Inner wisdom | Book I (EGP 3, 204) |

| Inwardness language | *Philokalia* reference |
|---|---|
| Inward grief | *Book I* (EGP 3, 78, 88, 94, 98, 115, 119, 121, 123, 126, 183, 168, 197)<br>*Book II* (EGP 3, 217, 219, 231, 234, 245, 275) |
| Inward … virtues | *Book II* (EGP 3, 220) |
| Inwardly, grieve | *Book I* (EGP 3, 107) |
| Inwardly, master | *Book II* (EGP 3, 221) |
| Inwardly, taught | *Book I* (EGP 3, 133) |
| **Symeon Metaphrastis** | |
| Inner attitudes | *Paraphrase of Makarios*, #84 (EGP 3, 322) |
| Inner being | *Paraphrase of Makarios*, #74, #82, #137, #141 (EGP 3, 317-318, 321, 348, 349) |
| Inner bonds | *Paraphrase of Makarios*, #145 (EGP 3, 351) |
| Inner buildings | *Paraphrase of Makarios*, #115 (EGP 3, 335) |
| Inner chambers | *Paraphrase of Makarios*, #115 (EGP 3, 335) |
| Inner chambers of [the] soul | *Paraphrase of Makarios*, #83 (EGP 3, 321) |
| Inner communion | *Paraphrase of Makarios*, #112 (EGP 3, 334) |
| Inner disposition | *Paraphrase of Makarios*, #11 (EGP 3, 289) |
| Inner fetters | *Paraphrase of Makarios*, #145, #146 (EGP 3, 351, 352) |
| Inner lawlessness | *Paraphrase of Makarios*, #83 (EGP 3, 321) |
| Inner passions | *Paraphrase of Makarios*, #146 (EGP 3, 352) |
| Inner prepossessions | *Paraphrase of Makarios*, #84 (EGP 3, 322) |
| Inner struggle | *Paraphrase of Makarios*, #146 (EGP 3, 351) |
| Inner treasure house | *Paraphrase of Makarios*, #88 (EGP 3, 323) |
| Inner union (with the hidden energy of God's holiness) | *Paraphrase of Makarios*, #18 (EGP 3, 292) |
| Inner warfare | *Paraphrase of Makarios*, #49, #146 (EGP 3, 305-306, 351) |
| Inward struggle | *Paraphrase of Makarios*, #14 (EGP 3, 290) |
| Inward … light | *Paraphrase of Makarios*, #92 (EGP 3, 326) |
| Inward … travail | *Paraphrase of Makarios*, #13 (EGP 3, 290) |
| Inwardly spotless | Paraphrase of Makarios, #90 (EGP 3, 325) |

| Inwardness language | *Philokalia* reference |
|---|---|
| Inwardly, carried away | *Paraphrase of Makarios*, #91 (EGP 3, 325) |
| Inwardly, encountered | *Paraphrase of Makarios*, #37 (EGP 3, 300) |
| Inwardly, make it clear | *Paraphrase of Makarios*, #55 (EGP 3, 308) |
| Inwardly, possess | *Paraphrase of Makarios*, #62 (EGP 3, 312) |
| Inwardly, signifies | *Paraphrase of Makarios*, #31 (EGP 3, 297) |
| Inwardly, stored up | *Paraphrase of Makarios*, #141 (EGP 3, 349) |
| Inwardly, stretched | *Paraphrase of Makarios*, #55 (EGP 3, 309) |
| Inwardly … (with unveiled face) … reflect | *Paraphrase of Makarios*, #62 (EGP 3, 312) |
| Inwardly … annulled | *Paraphrase of Makarios*, #36 (EGP 3, 300) |
| Inwardly … attain | *Paraphrase of Makarios*, #73 (EGP 3, 317) |
| Inwardly … brings afflictions | *Paraphrase of Makarios*, #147 (EGP 3, 352) |
| Inwardly … regard | *Paraphrase of Makarios*, #9 (EGP 3, 288) |
| **Symeon the New Theologian** ||
| Inner disposition | *Practical & Theological Texts*, #75 (EGP 4, 40) |
| Inner state of [the] soul | *Practical & Theological Texts*, #153[77] (EGP 4, 62) |
| Inner working of the Spirit | *Practical & Theological Texts*, #73 (EGP 4, 39) |
| Inward grief | *Practical & Theological Texts*, #69, #126, #140 (EGP 4, 38, 53, 56) |
| Inward self | *Practical & Theological Texts*, #103 (EGP 4, 46) |
| Inwardly illumined | *Practical & Theological Texts*, #68 (EGP 4, 38) |
| Inwardly, are | *Practical & Theological Texts*, #70 (EGP 4, 39) |
| Inwardly … present | *On Faith* (EGP 4, 20) |
| **Nikitas Stithatos** ||
| Inner activities (of the soul) | *On Virtues: 100 Texts*, #32 (EGP 4, 87) |
| Inner activity (of the intellect) | *On Spiritual Knowledge*, #43 (EGP 4, 151) |
| Inner activity of the Spirit | *On the Inner Nature of Things*, #100 (EGP 4, 137) |
| Inner being | *On Spiritual Knowledge*, #93 (EGP 4, 170) |

| Inwardness language | *Philokalia* reference |
|---|---|
| Inner concentration | *On the Inner Nature of Things*, #74 (EGP 4, 128) |
| Inner consciousness | *On Virtues: 100 Texts*, #72 (EGP 4, 97) |
| Inner counterparts (of the activities of the outer senses) | *On Virtues: 100 Texts*, #8 (EGP 4, 80-81) |
| Inner discord | *On Spiritual Knowledge*, #16 (EGP 4, 144) |
| Inner disposition | *On the Inner Nature of Things*, #60 (EGP 4, 123) |
| Inner faith and love for God | *On Spiritual Knowledge*, #23 (EGP 4, 145) |
| Inner humility | *On the Inner Nature of Things*, ##26-28 (EGP 4, 114) |
| Inner sanctuary | *On Virtues: 100 Texts*, ##94-95 (EGP 4, 104) |
| Inner self | *On Spiritual Knowledge*, #68 (EGP 4, 161) |
| Inner stability | *On the Inner Nature of Things*, #25 (EGP 4, 114) |
| Inner state | *On Virtues: 100 Texts*, ##61-62 (EGP 4, 95) *On the Inner Nature of Things*, #60 (EGP 4, 123) |
| Inner state of the soul | *On Virtues: 100 Texts*, #31, #52 (EGP 4, 87, 92) |
| Inner stillness | *On Virtues: 100 Texts*, #89 (EGP 4, 103) |
| Inner stronghold | *On the Inner Nature of Things*, #21 (EGP 4, 113) |
| Inner turbulence (of the passions) | *On Spiritual Knowledge*, #25 (EGP 4, 146) |
| Inward humility | *On the Inner Nature of Things*, #25 (EGP 4, 114) |
| Inward peace | *On Spiritual Knowledge*, #39 (EGP 4, 150) |
| Inwardly assent | *On Virtues: 100 Texts*, #74 (EGP 4, 98) |
| Inwardly humble | *On the Inner Nature of Things*, #25, #35 (EGP 4, 113, 116) |
| Inwardly, is | *On Spiritual Knowledge*, #69 (EGP 4, 161) |
| Inwardly, psalmodising | *On Spiritual Knowledge*, #89 (EGP 4, 169) |
| Inwardly, received | *On the Inner Nature of Things*, #66 (EGP 4, 126) |
| Inwardly … pursues | On the Inner Nature of Things, #32 (EGP 4, 115) |

| Inwardness language | *Philokalia* reference |
|---|---|
| **Theoliptos** ||
| Inner distraction | *On Inner Work* (EGP 4, 179) |
| Inner self | *On Inner Work* (EGP 4, 181) |
| Inner state | *Texts*, #3 (EGP 4, 189) |
| Innermost citadel of the soul | *On Inner Work* (EGP 4, 181) |
| Innermost sanctuary of the intellect | *On Inner Work* (EGP 4, 184) |
| **Nikiphoros the Monk** ||
| Inner gate (to evil spirits) | *Watchfulness & Guarding* (EGP 4, 200) |
| Inner state | *Watchfulness & Guarding* (EGP 4, 198, 199) |
| Inner work | *Watchfulness & Guarding* (EGP 4, 200) |
| Inward heaven of the heart | *Watchfulness & Guarding* (EGP 4, 203) |
| Inwardly are adulterous | *Watchfulness & Guarding* (EGP 4, 201) |
| Inwardly derange | *Watchfulness & Guarding* (EGP 4, 203) |
| Inwardly, concentrate | *Watchfulness & Guarding* (EGP 4, 197) |
| Inwards (turning of the senses) | *Watchfulness & Guarding* (EGP 4, 197) |
| **Gregory of Sinai** ||
| Inner converse | *On Commandments & Doctrines*, #49 (EGP 4, 221) |
| Inner discrimination | *On Commandments & Doctrines*, #123 (EGP 4, 244) |
| Inner disposition | *On Commandments & Doctrines*, #40, #86, #89, #123, #125 (EGP 4, 219, 229, 230, 243, 244) |
| Inner ducts | *Further Texts*, #6 (EGP 4, 255) |
| Inner grief | *On Commandments & Doctrines*, #108 (EGP 4, 236) |
| Inner intention | *On Stillness*, #12 (EGP 4, 271-272) |
| Inner invocation | *On Prayer: 7 Texts*, #1 (EGP 4, 275) |
| Inner murkiness | *On Commandments & Doctrines*, #107 (EGP 4, 235) |
| Inner purity and saintliness | *On Commandments & Doctrines*, #90 (EGP 4, 230) |

| Inwardness language | *Philokalia* reference |
|---|---|
| Inner qualities | *On Commandments & Doctrines*, #20 (EGP 4, 216) |
| Inner stability | *On Commandments & Doctrines*, #101 (EGP 4, 234) |
| Inner stillness | *On Commandments & Doctrines*, #102, #104 (EGP 4, 234, 235) |
| Inner turbulence | *On Prayer: 7 Texts*, #5 (EGP 4, 279) |
| Inward grief | *On Prayer: 7 Texts*, #7 (EGP 4, 284) |
| Inward grief and humility | *On Stillness*, #13 (EGP 4, 272) |
| Inward jubilation | *On Prayer: 7 Texts*, #7 (EGP 4, 285) |
| Inward pressure | *On Prayer: 7 Texts*, #7 (EGP 4, 285) |
| Inwardly, grieves | *On Stillness*, #6 (EGP 4, 267) |
| Inwardly, manifested | *On Prayer: 7 Texts*, #7 (EGP 4, 285) |
| Inwardly, possess (God) | *On Prayer: 7 Texts*, #7 (EGP 4, 282) |
| **Gregory Palamas** | |
| Inner affection | *New Testament Decalogue* (EGP 4, 324) |
| Inner being | *To Xenia*, #59 (EGP 4, 316) *In Defence of Stillness*, #8 (EGP 4, 338) |
| Inner dwelling place of Christ | *To Xenia*, #65 (EGP 4, 320) |
| Inner flow (of evil thoughts) | *To Xenia*, #42 (EGP 4, 310) |
| Inner grace | *To Xenia*, #59 (EGP 4, 316) |
| Inner intelligence principle | *Topics*, #35 (EGP 4, 360) |
| Inner organ | *In Defence of Stillness*, #3 (EGP 4, 334) |
| Inner powers | *On Prayer & Purity*, #3 (EGP 4, 344) |
| Inner self | *To Xenia*, #10, #53, #54 (EGP 4, 296, 314, 315) *In Defence of Stillness*, #7 (EGP 4, 337) |
| Inner state | *To Xenia*, #15 (EGP 4, 298) |
| Innermost body (the heart) | *In Defence of Stillness*, #3 (EGP 4, 334) |
| Innermost intelligence | *Topics*, #37 (EGP 4, 362) |
| Inward grief | *On Prayer & Purity*, #1, #3 (EGP 4, 343, 345) |
| Inward monk | *To Xenia*, #1 (EGP 4, 293) |
| Inward parts | *In Defence of Stillness*, #1, #11 (EGP 4, 333, 340) |
| Inward watchfulness | *To Xenia*, #38 (*Philokalia* 4, 308) |
| Inwards, to return | *In Defence of Stillness*, #5 (EGP 4, 336) |
| Inwards, turn | *To Xenia*, #53 (*Philokalia* 4, 315) |

However, the distinction is not a simple duality between inner (good) and outer (evil). For example, we find in the writings of Philotheos of Sinai:

> The soul is walled off, fenced in and bound with chains of darkness by the demonic spirits. Because of the surrounding darkness she cannot pray as she wants to, for she is fettered inwardly, and her inner eyes are blind. Only when she begins to pray to God, and to acquire watchfulness while praying, will she be freed from this darkness through prayer. Otherwise she will remain a prisoner. For through prayer the soul discovers that there is in the heart another fight and another hidden type of opposition, and a different kind of warfare against the thoughts provoked by the evil spirits.[78]

Here we see that it is only prayer and watchfulness which redeem inner regions of the soul from the bondage to demonic spirits. Similarly, in the writings of Hesychios the Priest:

> 104. The heart which is constantly guarded, and is not allowed to receive the forms, images and fantasies of the dark and evil spirits, is conditioned by nature to give birth from within itself to thoughts filled with light. For just as coal engenders a flame, or a flame lights a candle, so will God, who from our baptism dwells in our heart, kindle our mind to contemplation when He finds it free from the winds of evil and protected by the guarding of the intellect.

> 105. The name of Jesus should be repeated over and over in the heart as flashes of lightning are repeated over and over in the sky before rain. Those who have experience of the intellect and of inner warfare know this very well. We should wage this spiritual warfare with a precise sequence: first, with attentiveness; then, when we perceive the hostile thought attacking, we should strike at it angrily in the heart, cursing it as we do so; thirdly, we should direct our prayer against it, concentrating the heart through the invocation of Jesus Christ, so that the demonic fantasy may be dispersed at once, the intellect no longer pursuing it like a child deceived by some conjuror....

> 108. Just as he who looks at the sun cannot but fill his eyes with light, so he who always gazes intently into his heart cannot fail to be illumined.[79]

Again, here, we see that guarding of the heart/intellect, and the Jesus Prayer,[80] transform the heart from a place of inner warfare against evil spirits into a place of Divine illumination.

In both of these quotations, from Philotheos and Hesychios, we see that the heart is implicitly "within". Elsewhere, Hesychios explicitly identifies the heart as the "inner self". Similarly, John of Karpathos refers to "the inward heaven of the heart where Jesus dwells".[81]

Other references to the heart in the *Philokalia* include metaphors of an "immeasurable abyss"[82] or a "tomb":

> When you hear that Christ descended into hell in order to deliver the souls dwelling there, do not think that what happens now is very different. The heart is a tomb and there our thoughts and our intellect are buried, imprisoned in heavy darkness. And so Christ comes to the souls in hell that call upon Him, descending, that is to say, into the depths of the heart; and there He commands death to release the imprisoned souls that call upon Him, for He has power to deliver us. Then, lifting up the heavy stone that oppresses the soul, and opening the tomb, He resurrects us – for we were truly dead – and releases our imprisoned soul from its lightless prison.[83]

In addition to conveying a sense of "depth" these metaphors (abyss, tomb, burial, darkness, etc) remind us that we often don't know ourselves what lays within our own hearts – let alone those of other people. Symeon Metaphrastis further leaves us in no doubt that we are unable of our own efforts to unbury what lays hidden there.

The glossary to the English translation of the *Philokalia* includes the following entry:

> HEART (καρδία – kardia): not simply the physical organ but the spiritual centre of man's being, man as made in the image of God, his deepest and truest self, or the inner shrine, to be entered only through sacrifice and death, in which the mystery of the union between the divine and the human is consummated. "'I called with my whole heart", says the psalmist – that is, with

body, soul and spirit' (John Klimakos, *The Ladder of Divine Ascent,* Step 28, translated by Archimandrite Lazarus [London, 1959], pp. 257-8). 'Heart' has thus an all-embracing significance: 'prayer of the heart' means prayer not just of the emotions and affections, but of the whole person, including the body.

On the one hand, this further expounds the tradition of the heart as being the "innermost centre", where God is encountered. However, it also affirms a tradition of the heart as the "whole person": body, soul and spirit. It is difficult to locate this idea within the *Philokalia*, and it is interesting that the English translators of the *Philokalia* choose to illustrate it from *The Ladder of Divine Ascent*, rather than from within the writings of the *Philokalia* itself. However, we do find in the writings of Gregory Palamas a quotation from Makarios the Great, which refers to the heart as ruling over the whole body and soul, and (in Gregory's own words) the reference to the heart as the "innermost body within the body". Earlier in the chapter in which these references are made, taken from *In Defence of Stillness*, Gregory also reflects on the location of the soul in the body:

> Since our soul is a single entity possessing many powers, it utilizes as an organ the body that by nature lives in conjunction with it. What organs, then, does the power of the soul that we call 'intellect' make use of when it is active? No one has ever supposed that the mind resides in the finger-nails or the eye-lashes, the nostrils or the lips. But we all agree that it resides within us, even though we may not all agree as to which of our inner organs it chiefly makes use of. For some locate it in the head, as though in a sort of acropolis; others consider that its vehicle is the centremost part of the heart, that aspect of the heart that has been purified from natural life. We know very well that our intelligence is neither within us as in a container – for it is incorporeal – nor yet outside us, for it is united to us; but it is located in the heart as in its own organ. [84]

This passage is very interesting – if not also very unusual – in that it fleetingly recognises that inward and outward imagery are merely metaphorical. Almost immediately, as though retracting the scandal of what he has said, Gregory reverts to asserting that the intelligence has its own organ – the heart.[85] However, this passage at least draws our attention to the difficulty of relying purely on spatial imagery. Inwardness and outwardness are not really any more adequate as literal terms than is "heart". That they have endured so well, and that Taylor is able to identify a universal aspect to their use which appears to be maintained across time and cultures, presumably reflects the sense that all human beings have that they (i.e. their souls or selves) are at least associated with, if not actually to be identified with, their (spatially located and boundaried) bodies. But when we – or Gregory Palamas – talk about exactly where our souls (or minds, or intelligence, or selves) are "located" the language begins to break down, and especially so in a post-Cartesian world.

What, then, might we say about the specific or characteristic aspects of inwardness language in the *Philokalia* (as opposed, that is, to universal aspects of inwardness language which may be identified in all cultures)? The brief foregoing study, and the earlier chapters of this book, would suggest that the following might be important:

1. Inwardness often seems to refer to places of encounter with, or dwelling of, the Divine.

2. Inwardness also refers to a place of encounter with demons, or passions.

3. The difference between 1. & 2. seems to be concerned with our contemplative awareness and our ability to make use of the remedies for the passions described in Chapter 3 – especially prayer. Inwardness refers to a place of prayer.

4. The more that we do make use of the remedies for the passions, the closer we come to the possibility of deification. The place of union with God is either within us, or else to be found only after death (see Chapter 4).

5. Inwardness often seems to imply hiddenness, inaccessibility and mystery. Perhaps this is a universal aspect of inwardness. (It is certainly universal within the Judeo-Christian tradition.) However, it serves here to emphasise the ensnaring, imprisoning, blinding nature of the passions. Because of this, we can have no confidence to see clearly what our own intentions are, or those of other people, except through grace.

6. Inwardness seems to imply the essence of self – what it is to be the unique individual that God created each of us to be. Again, this touches on a universal aspect of inwardness that Taylor deals with at length. However, what seems to be a specific emphasis here is the finding within of the divine essence or principle that is uniquely "me" – an essence or principle which is yet also hidden within the intentions of God.

## 8. Orthodox Psychotherapy

The term "Orthodox Psychotherapy" appears to have first been adopted by Hierotheos Vlachos, in his book of the same name.[86] In this work, Vlachos outlines the nature of the human malady and its treatment according to the Orthodox patristic texts, including the *Philokalia*. In particular he describes the relationship between soul, nous, heart and mind, the pathology of the passions, and the remedies that are to be found in the Church, in the patristic teachings, and in the practice of hesychia. However, he is careful to distinguish his use of the term "psychotherapy" from that of contemporary psychiatry and he explicitly does not engage in specific discussion about the ways in which the two uses of the term might find areas of agreement and/or disagreement.

It might be possible to leave the discussion here, and to note that there are two kinds of psychotherapy, the one concerned with spiritual teachings of the *Philokalia* and other patristic writings, and the other concerned with contemporary psychological therapies. However, we have already noted that there are important ways in which the former might still be understood as "psychotherapy" in terms of the latter, even if there are also important differences in terms of purpose and intended outcome. There are also at least three further reasons why these two kinds of psychotherapy might appear to be concerned with common themes that could profit from mutual discourse:

1. At a theoretical level these two kinds of psychotherapy often appear to be talking about the nature of the human condition in similar terms. This is not to overlook the very significant anthropological, theological and other differences that exist between them, but it does appear that there is a significant expanse of common ground which

might benefit from mutual discussion and a more integrative perspective. Thus, for example, Vasileios Thermos has explored the ways in which Donald Winnicott (the Object Relations therapist) and Gregory Palamas might both explore concepts of the "true" and "false" self.[87]

2. The *Philokalia* describes some conditions which sound very similar to contemporary diagnostic categories. Thus, for example, the sadness that Evagrios includes amongst his eight thoughts could well describe someone who is depressed. Gluttony could appear to be the kind of thought experienced by someone with bulimia. And the concept of the passions is itself in many ways similar to what today might be called addiction, especially in the way in which passions engage people in continuing behaviour which is harmful to themselves and others.

3. The kinds of remedies that are prescribed by the *Philokalia* appear to overlap significantly in places with the kinds of remedies prescribed by contemporary psychological psychotherapies, both in appearance of technique and in philosophical underpinning. For example, both draw on the insights of Stoic philosophy. Ann Hackman, a psychologist, writes:

> It is well known that the basic tenet of cognitive therapy is that 'Men are not moved by things, but by the views they take of them' (Epictetus).[88]

If, as has been argued in this chapter, there are ways in which these two kinds of psychotherapy overlap conceptually, and if they are concerned with significant common themes in terms of theory, diagnosis and therapeutic practice, does this imply that the theory and practices of the *Philokalia* might have a therapeutic function which would be of benefit in the kinds of conditions that contemporary psychological therapies are usually used to treat?

In answering this question it is first helpful to recall that the term "remedy", in relation to the passions, was considered in Chapter 3 as a helpful metaphor. The remedies for the passions are therefore metaphorical rather than literal remedies. However, it was also noted there that psychotherapy also relies heavily on metaphor.[89] Psychotherapy is itself a metaphorical "therapy" of the psyche, unless of course one adopts a very strongly medical model within which "demoralisation" (as defined by Frank) is literally understood as a disease. However, as a heavily medical model of this kind is normally not considered helpful or appropriate, it is important to remember that psychotherapy and the *Philokalia* both offer metaphorical therapies. They offer these metaphorical therapies for very different indications, with the aim of achieving different kinds of well-being, albeit with some overlapping understandings of the nature and interpretation of thoughts. But could they offer therapy for the same indications, with benefit being measured in terms of the same kind of well-being?

A full answer to this question is beyond the scope of this chapter. In particular it suggests the need to test various possible scenarios, either empirically or in some other way. For example:

- Does conventional psychotherapy produce benefit in terms of spiritual well-being?

- Do the therapeutic methods recommended in the *Philokalia* offer benefit in terms of psychological well-being?

- Does conventional psychotherapy produce any measurable benefit in terms of psychological well-being? (I.e. is it possible to demonstrate in empirical research that it is effective on its own terms?)

- Do the therapeutic methods recommended in the *Philokalia* produce benefit in terms of spiritual well-being? (I.e. does the *Philokalia* do what it says it does, and can this be tested in an empirical fashion, or is it a purely non-empirical theological question?)

The question that is of most relevance here is whether or not the methods and principles of the *Philokalia* could be used to treat demoralisation, or any other definable mental disorder, with demonstrable benefit (spiritual and/or psychological). This question raises a whole series of subsidiary questions. Which conditions might we expect this therapy to be effective for? Is it possible to measure spiritual outcomes empirically? In what ways might we expect to see benefit? What kinds of people might it be effective for? (In particular, would therapy be confined to Christians, and if so which Christian traditions might suitable subjects best be selected from?) However, leaving aside all of these questions for a moment, an even more fundamental question arises as to whether spirituality of any kind can be made to serve a utilitarian purpose of improving physical or mental health?

As more and more empirical research has shown benefits of religiosity and spirituality in healthcare,[90] this question has been raised as of general importance. Should anyone be encouraged to follow a spiritual path, purely for the benefits that it might bring to their physical or mental health? As the whole ethos of spirituality is concerned with relational and transcendent goals (as, for example, outlined by Sandra Schneiders' definition, discussed in chapter 6) can it ethically, practicably or theologically be pressed to the purpose of a very practical, non-transcendent, goal of improving health?[91] These are very serious questions, which cannot adequately be addressed here. However, in passing, it is interesting to note that mindfulness, a state of mental awareness deriving from Buddhism, which has various features in common with hesychia, has been of growing interest to mental health professionals over recent years and has been subjected to empirical research with very positive results.[92]

The central problem in respect of our specific instance of the general questions that are posed here is that the understanding of well-being offered by the *Philokalia* is so radically different to, and so much more transcendent than, the kind of well-being that most people receiving psychotherapy are currently seeking.[93] However, with all of these qualifications in mind, it is well not to completely evade the question of whether the *Philokalia* offers therapy for the Christian struggling with demoralisation or mental disorder, over and above the therapy that it offers to any and every Christian soul.

Firstly, the *Philokalia* has much to say about suffering, adversity, afflictions and trials[94] that are involuntarily experienced, and how they may be managed. Amongst such experiences we might include demoralisation and mental or physical ill health. However, much of what the *Philokalia* has to say on these subjects would be difficult to introduce to someone experiencing mental suffering who was not already well advanced in Christian spirituality. Indeed, it could even seem very pastorally insensitive. For example, Peter of Damaskos writes:

> Just as sick people need surgery and cautery to recover the health they have lost, so we need trials, and toils of repentance, and fear of death and punishment, so that we may regain our former health of soul and shake off

> the sickness which our folly has induced. The more the Physician of our souls bestows upon us voluntary and involuntary suffering, the more we should thank Him for His compassion and accept the suffering joyfully; For it is to help us that He increases our tribulation, both through the sufferings we willingly embrace in our repentance and through the trials and punishments not subject to our will. In this way, if we voluntarily accept affliction, we will be freed from our sickness and from the punishments to come, and perhaps even from present punishments as well. Even if we are not grateful, our Physician in His grace will still heal us, although by means of chastisement and manifold trials. But if we cling to our disease and persist in it, we will deservedly bring upon ourselves agelong punishment.[95]

Note that the imagery presented here completely reverses the usual idea of what constitutes sickness. Here, sickness is subjection to the passions. A mental disorder, or a form of demoralisation, which brings unwanted suffering could constitute the kind of trial or suffering which "the Physician of souls bestows upon us" as a means of healing. The therapy that is advised here is therefore one of acceptance and thanksgiving, but it is aimed at the condition of the soul rather than the relief of suffering. All of this might well be helpful to someone who has embarked upon the spiritual path that the *Philokalia* prescribes, and who then encounters mental trials or sufferings of some kind. But it would be a difficult, if not highly insensitive, place with which to start pastoral care for someone who came asking for help with such trials and sufferings who was either not a Christian, or else was beginning from a very different tradition or starting point of Christian spirituality.

Do the remedies offered by the *Philokalia* therefore offer a therapy appropriate to these contemporary disorders?

It would seem that the answer to this question should probably be a cautious "yes", but this answer immediately invites qualification. For example, Archbishop Chrysostomos provides a clear example of an insensitive and inappropriate application of such a model to the case of depressive disorder.[96] The Archbishop, who is himself a qualified and experienced psychologist as well as an Orthodox priest, argues that spiritual depression and clinical depression should be distinguished.[97] Whilst I have much sympathy with this view, and would agree that clinical depression needs to be distinguished from the more everyday (in a medical sense, non-pathological) depression that Evagrios seems to have been talking about, I am not sure that this means that the *Philokalia* has nothing to offer the person who is clinically depressed. Rather, it might be argued, all kinds of depression are spiritual concerns – to which the teachings of the *Philokalia* (or John of the Cross) do have great relevance. The danger is in imagining that no other kind of therapy will ever be needed, and thus that antidepressants or cognitive therapy (or other appropriate medical and psychological treatments) will not be employed when necessary.

There is, of course, the possibility of combining the kind of therapy that the *Philokalia* espouses with more psychologically and medically informed therapies. This may either take the form of spiritual direction offered in parallel to psychotherapy (for example) or else of some kind of integration of the two. Examples of the latter kind are provided in publications arising from conferences of the Orthodox Christian Association of Medicine, Psychology and Religion.[98] Much more empirical and theological research on such approaches is required.

The kinds of issues that are presented in terms of the tension between different theoretical and therapeutic models are well illustrated in the case of addiction. The concept of addiction has important similarities with the concept of the passions. Both concepts are concerned with the way in which human beings find themselves "enslaved" to inner forces (and outer objects), from which they struggle to be free. This applicability of similar metaphors reflects an underlying phenomenological similarity between traditional Christian concerns and the concerns of contemporary scientific and medical endeavour.[99] Both recognise social, psychological, physical and spiritual elements, and neither are adequate when applied in a completely reductive fashion.

The spiritual approach to addictive disorders has been made popular particularly by the 12 Step programme of Alcoholics Anonymous. So influential has this been that it has made the spiritual component of treatment an important focus for contemporary medical and scientific research on addiction, as well as an important consideration in clinical care.[100] The 12 Step programme drew historically upon Christian and psychological/psychotherapeutic thinking, but has become a mutual help programme which adopts a secular spirituality that is open to people from all faith traditions, as well as agnostics and atheists.[101] Regardless of this process of secularisation, a process which was engaged with in order to ensure that the programme was open to people from any/every spiritual background, it still shows a deep consonance with a broad range of Christian spiritual traditions, from the Desert Fathers to Ignatian spirituality and Julian of Norwich.[102]

Victor Mihailoff, in *Breaking the Chains of Addiction*, has produced a book which is explicitly targeted at "members of the Orthodox Church who want to conquer addictions such as smoking, alcohol abuse and any drug/substance abuse or addictive behaviour, such as gambling, eating disorders, exhibiting a bad temper, obsessive compulsive disorder, some psychological behavioural problems and any bad habits".[103] In keeping with this intention, Mihailoff argues that "atheists and agnostics will have to become believers during the course of reading in order to gain benefit".[104] Whilst Mihailoff has narrowed the target audience in this way, so as to restrict the potential therapeutic benefits of his approach to those who are willing to accept Christian faith, he has widened the scope of what constitutes "addiction" beyond the usual boundaries of internationally accepted diagnostic criteria, so as to include a wide range of behavioural problems and habits, as well as obsessive compulsive disorder. This is in keeping with his definition of passions as "the object of any strong desire or fondness",[105] and his practice of more or less identifying passion and addiction as the same phenomenon. Amongst the remedies for addiction/passion that Mihailoff recommends are the examination of thoughts, reading of scripture, confession, holy communion and prayer. Overall, although Mihailoff includes reference to the 12 Steps of Alcoholics Anonymous, and to scientific accounts of addiction, his approach is strongly formed by the traditions of the *Philokalia* (which he quotes throughout) and other patristic writings. It is therefore only partially integrative.

Meletios Webber, in *Steps of Transformation*, takes a somewhat different approach. The two express purposes of his book are to explore and explain the 12 Step programme for those who are unfamiliar with it, and to present that programme in such a way "that members of the Orthodox Church might find [it] a valuable resource for their own personal spiritual development, should they choose to use [it]".[106] Webber also has a broad approach to addiction:

> It is possible that everyone alive, particularly anyone who lives in relative affluence, is affected by addiction in one form or another.[107]

However, his approach to treatment is much more centred on the 12 Step programme than is Mihailoff's. It is this programme that provides the structure for the second half of his book, and he achieves his second expressed purpose of writing (above) on the basis of the premise that "the Twelve Steps can be shown to share some element in the thought and experience, the Scripture and prayer life, of the Orthodox Church".[108] The spirituality of the 12 Step programme and of Orthodoxy thus find a more equal balance in the book and its therapeutic approach is more dominated by the former than the latter.

A third approach might be found in a very different kind of book, the *Handbook of Psychotherapy and Religious Diversity*.[109] Although this book is not about the treatment of addiction specifically, it provides a handbook for psychotherapists and other mental health professionals to support better awareness of religious and spiritual traditions, and to enable more effective working with clients/patients from particular faith traditions. The chapter on working with Eastern Orthodox Christians[110] provides helpful information on the beliefs, spirituality and practices of Orthodoxy and their implications for counselling or psychotherapy. Close working with clergy is encouraged. Here, the model is one of secular psychotherapy which endeavours to be sensitive to, and compatible with, the spirituality and faith of the Orthodox person.

This brief series of examples simply illustrates that there are various ways of integrating Orthodox psychotherapy with contemporary psychological therapies in the clinical context. These vary from a hegemony of one approach or the other to a more integrative assimilation of both approaches, but the possible variations in practice are doubtless innumerable.

### 9. Therapy of the Soul: Inwardness, Prayer and the Talking Cure

Based upon what has been said thus far, a simple answer to our question of whether or not the *Philokalia* offers a kind of psychotherapy would seem to be that it does, but that this needs to be qualified. It needs to be qualified not so much because it is possible to identify ways in which it does not go far enough with the inner world of thoughts and feelings to qualify as psychotherapy, for it is difficult to identify any such shortcomings. Neither is the qualification simply a concern about it having ventured beyond those domains that contemporary realms of psychology and psychotherapy might usually address, for all psychotherapy has its spiritual and religious implications, even if these are left unspoken of in therapy or in the psychology classroom (and increasingly such things are not left unspoken at all). Rather, the qualification is that the *Philokalia* insists on discussing everything in primarily theological terms. The effect of this is not simply to broaden the discussion in such a way that God must be included, but rather to make the inner world of thoughts and feelings something that must be discussed when a conversation about prayer is begun.

If the question that we began this chapter with might be reframed as a question as to whether or not the *Philokalia* is inviting us to discuss psychotherapy, the answer might well be no. The *Philokalia* invites us to discuss prayer, and then advises that in order to have that conversation we will need to talk about things which are usually considered the domain of psychotherapy. Whereas Anna O saw the treatment that she was offered as a "talking cure", the *Philokalia* might be said to offer a "praying cure". But, just as talking about the psyche might lead eventually to existential or spiritual questions, so praying (in the language of the *Philokalia*, at least) will necessarily start with questions of our inner thoughts and feelings.

It would appear, then, that the *Philokalia* is deeply concerned with matters which are usually considered the province of psychotherapy. Herein lies a challenge, for the world of psychotherapy exists in a post-Cartesian, post-Kantian philosophical age where dualism is frowned upon and the nature of the subjective self is no longer universally agreed upon. How may the *Philokalia* be interpreted for this age?

The deep modern (or even postmodern) concern with inwardness would seem to offer a promising way forward. The language of inwardness is common to psychotherapy and the *Philokalia*, even if they have different emphases and interpretations to offer. Both worlds of discourse recognise that the psyche is in need of a cure, even if they have different diagnoses and prescriptions to offer. At least here there is scope for a conversation – even if the starting point will have to be exactly what the conversation is going to be about.

# 6

# On Thoughts and Prayer

If the *Philokalia* is concerned with mental well-being, or with the proper ordering of the inner life of thoughts, then its only understanding of this is in the context of prayer. It is concerned primarily with prayer, yet it insists that prayer may only be properly understood and practised if attention is given first to the world of thoughts. This understanding of an inextricable relationship between thoughts and prayer runs all the way through the *Philokalia*.

Whilst the *Philokalia* has come down to us through the Eastern Church, and though its origins are in Classical and early Christian thought, it seems remarkably relevant to contemporary western concerns about mental well-being and the inner life. Even if its understanding of inwardness is somewhat different than that inherited in the west through Augustine, Descartes and Hume, inwardness is nonetheless a matter of common concern. Its points of contact with western psychotherapy, in particular its common inheritance of the cognitive emphases of Stoic philosophy, are remarkable, even if there are also equally remarkable points of divergence. The *Philokalia* also shares with western mental healthcare a concern for a holistic approach to human life. Physical, psychological, social and spiritual dimensions of being human all receive attention and are engaged with one another. All in all, the authors and editors of the *Philokalia* show a keen psychological awareness, which is highly relevant to contemporary western concerns about mental well-being.

The *Philokalia* also offers important insights into the life of prayer which would be of interest to many western Christians, and perhaps also members of other faith traditions, if only it was better known to them. It does not allow prayer to be sidelined as a separate matter than the practical matters of virtuous daily living. It is realistic about the psychological challenges of prayer. It recognises the challenge presented by distractions of memory, perception, emotions, biological and cognitive processes. It is also realistic about the seemingly impossible task of relating to a God who is always above and beyond any words that we may bring to our prayers or any concepts that we may try and employ to understand him.

This psychological and spiritual relevance does, however, cut across the Enlightenment legacy of a separation between matters secular and religious. Whilst there is evidence that this is breaking down, and that spirituality is again being considered highly important in mental healthcare and in psychotherapy,[1] the theological rationale of the *Philokalia* will clearly be seen by some as exclusive. However, in practice, many Christians and others find that they cannot and do not separate prayer from their inner psychological experiences. Perhaps the *Philokalia* has some lessons to teach about its central concern with the relationship between thoughts and prayers which may transcend the gulf that history and culture have placed between them?

On the one hand, the relationship between thoughts and prayers is so obvious as to hardly need any comment. Just as any worthwhile human act or intention requires some level of thought, so does prayer. We are grateful to people who show thoughtfulness in acts of kindness or compassion which reveal that they had thought about the needs of others. We appreciate the careful choice of words that reveals the thoughts of a writer or speaker. Sometimes the silence of a friend or lover reveals their concern for us, and we take this as thoughtful on their part. Or, again, simple and routine things can be said in a thoughtful way that marks them out from the thoughtless repetition of social custom, and we are good at recognising this. So, in our prayers, we know the difference between thoughts that are engaged with our intentions and thoughts that are careless or occupied elsewhere. We can tell when intercessions are led by someone who has given thought to the real needs of a congregation or community. We know when our personal devotions have been thoughtful and when they have been careless or hurried.

Yet, despite the obviousness of the connection, the relationship between thoughts and prayers is profoundly complex, mysterious and even paradoxical. Sometimes, as Evagrios so perceptively noticed, our apparent thoughts of hospitality, chastity or humility might conceal thoughts which are much less respectable, such as restlessness, pride, or vainglory. Or else, we may know very well what we should pray, even what we would like to pray, and yet our feelings betray completely the opposite. We want to forgive, but we feel angry. We want to care, but we feel careless. Sometimes, apparently holy and devoted thoughts so crowd our minds that God is squeezed out. Or else, we are left so bereft of words that we are simply left in God's presence not knowing what to say.

The relationship between thoughts and prayers is therefore not at all straightforward. But it goes also very much to the heart of our sense of inwardness, our sense of who we are (and who God is). It is a very real indicator of our state of mental and spiritual well-being, in relationship to ourselves, and others and God. It is therefore very deserving of the considerable attention that the *Philokalia* devotes to it.

In this chapter, a number of aspects of the relationship between thoughts and prayer will be explored further, and some of the themes of the *Philokalia* will be engaged with some strands of western thinking about thoughts and prayer. But, first, it may be helpful to give a little more attention to the question: why are thoughts so important?

## 1. On Thoughts

Thoughts are important to human beings in a general sense, because they are the means by which we know ourselves. Although there are philosophical arguments about the possibility (or impossibility) of self-knowledge, and whether self awareness is more a function of perception or of thought,[2] thoughts are nonetheless integrally involved in the sense of inwardness, and the processes of reflexivity, disengagement and expressivism which characterise the contemporary sense of inwardness, which is so important to us. Even though philosophical arguments against the very existence of the self, or against any unified sense of self, perhaps have to be taken seriously, in a practical day to day sense, it is difficult or impossible to imagine how human beings would manage their lives, in any recognisably human sense, without thoughts.[3] Thoughts are important because they are the means by which we manage our relationships with ourselves, other human beings, and the wider world.

Thoughts are also important to human beings because of the way in which they enable a sense of self transcendence or spirituality. The word "spirituality" has only become popular during the last few decades, and there is still much debate about how exactly it should be defined,[4] but arguably it is a very fundamental aspect of what it is to be human. Sandra Schneiders has suggested that spirituality, as a lived human experience, may be defined as:

> conscious involvement in the project of life integration through self-transcendence toward the ultimate value one perceives.[5]

It is in the world of thoughts that human beings consciously involve themselves in their lives, seek to find a sense of integration (whatever that may be), and are able to identify transcendent value.

Thoughts are important to Christians, however, in a further and more specific sense. In the western tradition, this has perhaps been most importantly promoted by Augustine, Anselm and Aquinas, in their affirmation of the importance of human reason (understood as an aspect of the *imago Dei*) in understanding and exploring faith.[6] However, in the eastern tradition, as exemplified by the *Philokalia*, the link between thought and Christian faith is arguably even more intrinsic to the language, philosophy, anthropology and theology that are employed. As discussed in Chapter 1, the intellect (νοῦς), or spirit, is understood as the highest faculty of the soul, and is to be distinguished from "reason" (διάνοια), or mind. The ruling aspect of the intellect is the intelligence (λογιστικόν), which is etymologically connected to Logos (Λόγος), and therefore theologically closely connected with the concept of the divine Intellect. Thoughts, where they are understood as products of the pure intellect rather than being impassioned thoughts, or else mere reason, are thus more or less direct spiritual perceptions of God or of the inner essences of things (λόγοι). On the other hand, thoughts which are impassioned, or else mere products of the mind, potentially lead the soul away from God. Thoughts are thus intimately related to prayer.[7]

Paradoxically, the *Philokalia* also teaches that thoughts are closely related to passions. However, thoughts may or may not be passions. At this point, some further clarification of the distinctions made in the *Philokalia* between various kinds of thoughts might be helpful.

**Logismoi** (λογισμοί), as in Evagrios' *Eight Thoughts*, and as understood by Maximos and other authors of the *Philokalia*, are more like trains of thought than simple thoughts. For Evagrios, there is a somewhat complex causal relationship between thoughts and

## Chapter 6: On Thoughts and Prayer

passions (as discussed in Chapter 2) in which thoughts may lead to passions, or passions may lead to thoughts. Logismoi are usually set in motion by demons, and generally have a negative connotation for Evagrios, but may exceptionally be benign or good.[8] "Simple thoughts" (ψιλοὶ Λογισμοί) are neutral thoughts, which are neither associated with passion nor provoked by demons.[9]

**Noemata** (νοήματα) are conceptual images, somewhere between fantasies and abstract concepts, which are usually understood by Evagrios as arising from neutral sense perception, or else as being inspired by angels.[10] Noemata are likened by Evagrios to sheep, which require nurture and care.[11] However, there are again exceptions in Evagrian usage of this term, and noemata may sometimes be hostile.[12] A subcategory of noemata are homoiomata (ὁμοιώματα) or "likenesses", which are specifically representations of material objects.[13] The source of Evagrios' understanding of the relationships between images and knowledge appears to be from Aristotle, via Clement of Alexandria.[14]

The term noemata is frequently used by Maximos, and is understood as a "simple" thought (ψιλὰ νοήματα) in contrast to composite thoughts (or logismoi) which are combined with passions. For example, in *On Love: C2*, he writes:

> Some thoughts are simple, others are composite. Thoughts which are not impassioned are simple. Passion-charged thoughts are composite, consisting as they do of a conceptual image combined with passion. This being so, when composite thoughts begin to provoke a sinful idea in the mind, many simple thoughts may be seen to follow them. For instance, an impassioned thought about gold rises in someone's mind. He has the urge mentally to steal the gold and commits the sin in his intellect. Then thoughts of the purse, the chest, the room and so on follow hard on the thought of the gold. The thought of the gold was composite – for it was combined with passion – but those of the purse, the chest and so on were simple; for the intellect had no passion in relation to these things.[15]

For Evagrios, simple thoughts and noemata are a positive feature of natural contemplation, indicating as they do that impassioned thoughts are being left behind. However, as they are also essentially plural, their multiplicity also provides a distraction from the unity that is inherent in God. Eventually, therefore, all such thoughts must be left behind in pursuit of theological contemplation. For Maximos, as Andrew Louth argues,[16] exactly the opposite appears to be true. Noemata are associated with the highest state of dispassion, and thus the presence of such thoughts in the heart is a good sign.[17] It is indicative of an outlook on the world which is passion-free. However, for Maximos also, there appears to be a higher state of contemplation in which all images and thoughts are eventually discarded:

> Through fulfilling the commandments the intellect strips itself of the passions. Through spiritual contemplation of things visible it casts off impassioned conceptions of such things. Through knowledge of things invisible it discards the contemplation of things visible. Finally it denudes itself even of this through knowledge of the Holy Trinity.[18]

For Evagrios and Maximos, in different ways, an understanding of the nature of thoughts, and an ability to manage thoughts effectively, is therefore essential to prayer. We shall return to this connection with prayer, below, but it may be helpful at this stage to note in passing that for both Evagrios and Maximos the relationship between thoughts and prayer appears to be governed by Christology.

For Evagrios, natural contemplation is concerned with the "manifold wisdom" (πολυποίκιλος σοφία) of Christ (or God), a phrase which is found as a recurring reference in *Kephalaia Gnostica*[19] to Ephesians 3:10. Konstantinovsky argues that these references are best understood as revealing an Evagrian distinction between God as the source of all wisdom, and Christ as the source of the "manifold" wisdom associated with creation (but not the unified wisdom which finds its origin in God alone).[20] Christ (who is distinguished by Evagrios from the eternal Logos) thus mediates natural contemplation, but theological contemplation is direct and unmediated (albeit Christ may play some kind of instructional role in it).[21] For Maximos, in contrast, Christ (undistinguished from the eternal Logos) appears to be integrally involved in both cataphatic and apophatic prayer,[22] and in direct contemplation of God.[23] Louth argues that Maximos develops the notion of a Christological convergence of cataphatic and apophatic theology in the incarnation.[24]

We have seen that, although shorter and longer lists abound, the basic thoughts with which the *Philokalia* is most concerned are those eight originally identified by Evagrios:

| | |
|---|---|
| Gluttony | γαστριμαργία |
| Fornication | πορνεία |
| Avarice | φιλαργυρία |
| Anger | ὀργή |
| Sadness | λύπη |
| Acedia | ἀκηδία |
| Vainglory | κενοδοξία |
| Pride | ὑπερηφανία |

Whilst Evagrios claims that these categories include "every sort of thought",[25] it might at first appear that he cannot really mean this in a completely literal way. For example the list, at least as found in *Eight Thoughts,* does not include thoughts associated with the corresponding opposing virtues: abstinence, chastity, freedom from possessions, joy, patience, perseverance, freedom from vainglory, and humility. Neither does it include guilt, gratitude, fear or love. It does not include thoughts associated with natural contemplation, thoughts which prayerfully seek out the logoi, or inner essences of things. However, this first impression is somewhat dispelled by a recognition that Evagrios is talking about logismoi, not noemata, and that he usually reserves the former term for thoughts that are harmful, pernicious and demonic. His list therefore does not include thoughts that are neutral, or helpful to prayer.

In *On the Vices Opposed to the Virtues*, Evagrios does describe virtues in terms opposite and complementary to those used to describe the vices (or logismoi). Interestingly, he also includes here a ninth vice (or logismos) of jealousy, which might suggest that he did not necessarily see his list of eight logismoi as completely comprehensive and exhaustive. However, it is also clear in this work that he understands jealousy as closely related to pride.[26] We might conclude, therefore, that the list of eight logismoi is to be understood as a list of categories of thought with particular hostile and seductive qualities, qualities which Evagrios distinguishes from the qualities of noemata, "simple thoughts", forms of natural contemplation, or other benign kinds of thought.

This recognition still leaves some arguable anomalies. What about guilt or fear, for example? Whilst each of these thoughts can be good (in encouraging or preserving a life of virtue, bringing about restoration of relationship with God or others, and encouraging the avoidance of harm, for example) each can also be preoccupying as a train of thought that distracts from prayer in the way that logismoi do. It is also possible to experience false guilt (over peccadilloes, or as a form of self indulgence, or even over a course of action that was morally correct) or false fear (as in phobias or obsessional ruminations). Perhaps Evagrios considered these to be forms of sadness, vainglory or pride,[27] or else in someway more basic than logismoi?[28] Or perhaps he recognised that guilt and fear more often encourage prayer, rather than distract from it?

Evagrios selected the thoughts for his list on the basis of his concern to lay the foundation for a life of prayer. The eight thoughts are therefore presumably the ones that Evagrios considers likely to cause trouble to the person who wants to pray. As we have seen (in Chapter 1) these thoughts do in fact have adverse consequences for prayer. Their train like quality confers the potential to lead to bad outcomes – either in terms of more bad thoughts, or in terms of sinful actions, or simply in terms of occupying enough mental space to exclude good thoughts. Hence, in *On the Vices Opposed to the Virtues* and elsewhere the thoughts are also referred to as vices.

Given the purpose of instruction on prayer, it is still not entirely obvious why Evagrios has limited his list in the way that he has. Why not list good thoughts, alongside the bad ones, so that all kinds of thoughts are comprehensively classified? Why not give the good thoughts more attention rather than less? To some extent, it might be argued that this is exactly what he has done in some of his other works – in *On the Vices Opposed to the Virtues*, and in *Antirrhetikos*, for example.[29] And even in *Eight Thoughts*, there is reference to abstinence in the sayings dealing with gluttony, chastity in the sayings about fornication, freedom from possessions in the sayings dealing with avarice, etc. Or again, it might be that he is simply drawing attention to thoughts that are problematic – in the way that modern psychotherapists will focus on troublesome thoughts (anxiety, depression, etc) and may not speak much about peace, joy, or other thoughts that do not represent any kind of problem or barrier to well-being. However, it is also clearly the case that Evagrios is aware that thoughts can be deceptive. A thought of chastity, for example, may actually be hiding a thought of pride or vainglory. Given that the works in which the eight thoughts are primarily addressed are intended for beginners, it may well be that he deliberately intends to encourage a vigilant search for problematic thoughts rather than risk complacency about apparently good thoughts which are actually hiding insidiously bad ones.

If Evagrios has limited his list, so as to exclude some thoughts that we might have considered important topics for discussion, he has a very broad understanding of what thoughts are. His list includes items that we might consider as appetites or emotions or even simply physical tiredness rather than thoughts in the sense of cognitions. His descriptions also include perceptions and behaviours. Thus, for example, his account of fornication in *Eight Thoughts* notes that the mere sight of a woman can wound the soul[30] and that guarding against fornication will therefore involve staying away from places where women might be encountered.[31] But fornication (like the other thoughts) is also concerned with an inner disposition of virtue (or lack of it), and with memory and fantasy.[32] Avoiding encounters with women does not provide immunity against it, and neither does an encounter with a woman necessarily interfere with prayer or lead to sin.[33]

As discussed in Chapter 2, the authors of the *Philokalia* expand on Evagrios' list of thoughts, and various shorter lists are proposed, but the basic principles of Evagrios' approach are retained throughout. Thoughts are understood as being of fundamental importance to the life of prayer and thus, ultimately, to human well-being. The basic distinction amongst thoughts is seen to be between those which open up a theocentric view of reality that facilitates prayer, and those which induce a seductive and self-referential illusion or fantasy that impedes prayer.

## 2. The Interpretation of Thoughts

To what extent is it valid to speak of the "interpretation" of thoughts? To suggest that thoughts may be interpreted presupposes that they have meaning, and that this meaning is not necessarily immediately and superficially obvious. In the context of spoken language, it is usually unnecessary to provide an interpreter for someone speaking in the same language as their listener(s), because the meaning of the speech will immediately be understood. That thoughts might need interpretation therefore suggests that their real meaning may not readily be understood, either by the thinker of the thoughts, or by those to whom these thoughts are relayed by means of speech or writing.

It might be supposed that the thinker herself must always understand the meaning of what she has thought and that interpretation will only be needed (if at all) when she wishes to describe and explain her thoughts to another person. However, it has long been recognised that this is not so. Thoughts in dreams have been recognised as a subject for interpretation since ancient times (including some notable biblical examples, such as the dreams of Joseph in the Genesis narratives) for the obvious reason that their meaning is not always clear to the person who has had the dream. Most people recognise, at least in the context of complex, important or emotionally charged decisions, such as vocation or marriage that they do not always know themselves what they really want. Only after careful thought and discussion are they able to interpret their own thoughts and feelings in such a way as to be able to make a decision. This is not (necessarily) a question of finding out more facts, or understanding new arguments for or against a particular course of action. It is, rather, a matter of interpreting one's own thoughts and feelings so as to judge what they really mean. Sometimes, having made a decision for a particular course of action, a person realises that she feels disappointed, or guilty, or anxious. Only having made the decision does she realise what she really wanted or (to put it another way) what her own thoughts and feelings really meant. And many other examples could be added, such as feelings of anxiety or sadness that arise for no reason of which we are consciously aware, slips of the tongue that betray things that we did not consciously intend to mean or say, artistic inspirations which surprise even the artists who have them, the psychogenic causation of physical symptoms, and the experimental evidence for subliminal perception, amongst others.[34]

If interpreting our own thoughts is not straightforward, then interpreting other people's thoughts must assume another order of difficulty altogether, for we can never have as full access to another person's thoughts as we may have to our own. However, this does not prevent human beings from interpreting one another's thoughts as a frequent occurrence in daily life. In political debate, or in personal disputes, we readily accuse the other person (but less readily accuse ourselves) of untoward motives, such as self interest or prejudice. Or, perhaps, when someone is choosing their words carefully, so as not to cause offence, we say "Yes.... But what you really mean is...." and then disclose our understanding of what we think they really meant.

Of course, awareness of all of this has become commonplace since the advent of Freudian psychoanalysis and the assimilation of concepts of the unconscious into everyday life and conversation. Psychotherapy, as a means of interpreting thoughts with a view to bringing about mental or behavioural change, has become an accepted treatment in mental healthcare and is even pursued by some simply for the purpose of deepening self awareness. The Evagrian corpus is but one reminder from the ancient world that suspicions about the need to interpret the real meaning of our own and other people's thoughts have a much longer history than all of this. But to what extent is interpretation of thoughts a valid enterprise?

One possible approach to answering this question derives from the work of Paul Ricoeur (b.1913). Ricoeur has suggested that, although the paradigm for hermeneutics has been the interpretation of written texts, human actions and even the human psyche may be considered as a kind of text that is amenable to interpretation.[35] For Ricoeur, the criteria for textuality comprise:[36]

1. The realisation of language as discourse
2. The realisation of discourse as a structured work
3. The relation of speaking to writing in discourse
4. Discourse as "projection of a world"
5. Discourse as the mediation of self-understanding

Whilst thoughts may readily be understood to employ language in support of a kind of structured discourse which projects an account of its world (the world of thoughts) as a way of mediating self-understanding, there is an obvious problem in that thoughts are not normally written down. They are transient and ephemeral and, even if spoken, have a very different relationship to the spoken word than does the written word. However, Ricoeur circumvents this problem by drawing attention to what he refers to as the criteria for "facts" in psychoanalysis. These criteria are:[37]

1. Only that part of the experience that is capable of being spoken is brought into the field of treatment/investigation.

2. The analytic situation singles out from that which is capable of being spoken only that which is actually said to another person.

3. The analytic situation is concerned with psychical reality, not material reality. One of the important features of psychical reality is the substitutability of objects (e.g. the transferential object for the parental object, or the symbol in a dream for the reality in daily life).

4. The analytic situation is selective from the entire experience of the subject so as to include only that which may be incorporated into a story or narrative. Thus, case histories are the "primary texts" of psychoanalysis.

Ricoeur further draws attention to the way in which psychoanalysis is at once a method for the investigation of mental processes, a method of treatment for mental disorder, and a body of theoretical knowledge. It is the first of these, that is the investigatory procedure, which is obviously akin to hermeneutics. However, Ricoeur sees a tension between this and the therapeutic procedure such that, at one and the same time, it is necessary for the psyche to be metaphorically understood "both as a text to be interpreted and as a system of forces to be manipulated".[38] Ricoeur does not see Freud's theoretical understanding as having adequately accommodated these different understandings, even though he does accept the status of psychoanalysis as one of the social sciences, and even though he does see the Freudian system as being an indispensible starting point for future work. However, even more importantly, he argues that psychoanalysis cannot simply be a hermeneutical procedure, for it must always incorporate alongside the process of self-interpretation those "economic" procedures which aim to change the system that is being interpreted.

Doubtless there are other hermeneutical approaches which could be taken to exploring the basis for attempting to construct a means of interpreting thoughts. However, the work of Ricoeur draws attention to a number of important considerations relevant to the present purpose:

1. The process of interpreting thoughts might in theory be accomplished for its own sake alone, but in practice is inevitably linked to a therapeutic, or transformative, element. The challenge for any theoretical model is to adequately incorporate both of these processes.

2. The use of metaphor to enable both the processes of interpretation and transformation of the psyche would seem to be important, if not inevitable.

3. Whilst the psyche might be considered a kind of "text", our access to its contents is humanly limited in various significant ways; in respect of other people most importantly by what they tell us and in respect of ourselves by what we are willing and able to bring to the process of reflection and interpretation.

## 3. The Interpretation of Thoughts in the *Philokalia*

Evagrios does not merely classify and describe thoughts, he is committed to the interpretation of thoughts. This hermeneutic process is extremely complicated, for it is not always clear exactly what is being interpreted. Is Evagrios interpreting his own experience? For example, is he retrospectively interpreting his own flight from Constantinople and the sexual feelings that he encountered in the affair that he escaped from there? Is he interpreting the teaching and experience handed down to him by Makarios in the Egyptian desert, or is he interpreting the experiences of the monks who sought his own counsel and instruction there? Is he interpreting thoughts in the light of scripture and Christian tradition, or are scripture and tradition being interpreted in the light of his own thoughts? Probably all of these hermeneutical processes are at play, and it is not supposed that it will be possible to disentangle all of them here. Usually he reflects upon them only in general terms and he does not separate questions of investigation from those of therapy and theory. A few general observations may, however, be made about the ways in which Evagrios, and subsequently other authors of the *Philokalia*, appear to go about the interpretation of thoughts:

1. The facility with which authors of the *Philokalia* move between talking of thoughts, passions, vices and demons suggests an ambiguous, unsystematised, but sophisticated,

recognition of the complexity of the hermeneutic task that is being undertaken. Each of the terms, passion, vice and demon, is itself an interpretation of thoughts. For example, when the term "demon" is employed, it implies external agency. In this case, the response to such thoughts (although not the origin of them) is therefore the responsibility of the subject concerned.

2. Discourse in the *Philokalia* about thoughts, and their interpretation, employs heavily metaphorical language. This is an interesting and significant parallel to Ricoeur's observations concerning the use of metaphor in psychoanalytic language. In the prologue, having encountered the metaphor of thoughts as sheep, or else as rocks scattered on a shore line, the question arose as to whether such metaphors assist discourse on the subject at hand. It would appear that Ricoeur would argue that they do and, indeed, that in such an area of discourse as this their use may even be inevitable.

3. We have already seen that the interpretative processes employed in the *Philokalia* were informed initially both by Classical (especially Stoic) philosophy, and also by the traditions of the Desert Fathers and the early Church. The former is evident primarily in the extent to which beliefs are intrinsically implicated in the passions, and the latter is evident, for example, in the way in which they are interpreted as being concerned with a struggle with temptation and with demons. Subsequently, the early Patristic texts have themselves become sources of authority which have informed the on-going interpretative process. In particular, the influence of Evagrios on other authors of the *Philokalia* (whether directly or indirectly) has been enduring.

4. The authors of the *Philokalia* recognise an inner tension concerned with thoughts which are both hostile but pleasurable. This is interpreted as being contrary to nature, since it is presumed that the natural order, in accordance with Divine purpose, should be that hostile thoughts would not be pleasurable. That they are pleasurable is attributed

ultimately to the sinfulness of human beings. An implicit theology of creation and the fall is therefore evident. In passing, it might be observed that a not dissimilar theology, but differently emphasised, might lead many Christians today to affirm the natural goodness of (for example) sexual desire. However, the fundamental problem of how to respond to such thoughts and the validity of the method provided by the *Philokalia* for dealing with them arguably remain the same.

5. The authors of the *Philokalia* recognise a tension between the inwardness of thoughts and their apparent origin in the outer world. On the one hand, the passions arise in response to a perception (or memory of a perception) of an object located in the external world. Or, elsewhere, they arise as the result of the assault of demons upon the soul. On the other hand, the pathology underlying the passions is understood as being located within the soul, or even as being an impulse of the soul. Passions are thus both impulses to which the soul is passively subjected from without, and also internal matters of choice insofar as they invite varying response (according to, or contrary to, nature).

6. The *Philokalia* incorporates a rich, albeit poorly systematised, body of theoretical knowledge concerning the proper interpretation and therapy of thoughts. For example, as discussed in Chapter 2, there are a series of analyses of the thought processes by which temptation is experienced and by which passions are generated.

7. The interpretation of thoughts requires both spiritual instruction and engagement with remedial measures which include ascetic discipline, watchfulness, psalmody and prayer.

8. The authors of the *Philokalia* understand thoughts as being significant by virtue of the way in which they influence relationships between human beings and, more importantly, between human beings and God in prayer. However, prayer has not merely been the end-point. Rather, the interpretative process is an aspect of prayer, and is

undertaken in a context of prayer, as are the remedies to be applied. Thoughts – all thoughts – therefore become understood in the context of the apostolic injunction to continual prayer.[39]

To return for a moment to Ricoeur's model of psychoanalysis as being at once an investigatory process, a therapeutic process and a body of theory, we may see that the above eight observations on the interpretation of thoughts in the *Philokalia* reflect this same interplay. The first five are all concerned with the investigatory process. Points 7 & 8 are primarily concerned with the therapeutic process. Points 2 to 6 are concerned with the *Philokalia* as a body of theoretical knowledge.

We have also seen (in Chapter 2) that metaphor plays an important part in the *Philokalia*, to enable both the processes of interpretation of thoughts, and also to assist in the transformation or therapy of the psyche (as discussed in Chapter 3). The diversity and richness of this metaphorical reference enables a dialectical tension to be maintained in various aspects of interpretation, for example as to inwardness/outwardness. Whilst the psyche might be considered a kind of "text" in psychotherapy, the dominant image in the *Philokalia* is imposed by the "word" (λόγος). This is both because of the significance of the divine Λόγος in theological contemplation, but also because natural contemplation is concerned with the λόγοι of all things. It is the interpretation of these words which leads the psyche ever more deeply into prayer.

As in Ricoeur's understanding of psychoanalysis, access to the contents of the psyche in the *Philokalia* is humanly limited in various significant ways. In particular, in the *Philokalia*, emphasis is placed upon inner watchfulness in respect of thoughts and on openness and honesty with a spiritual director. Thoughts which escape the inner process of watchfulness cannot be interpreted and subjected to rebuttal or other specific remedies. Only those thoughts which are disclosed in speech to a spiritual director are open to the process of reflection and interpretation with the benefit of their greater objectivity and wisdom.

What is the meaning of thoughts, as understood by Evagrios and by the other authors of the *Philokalia*? Clearly, different meanings are attributable to different thoughts, but different meanings may also be ascribed to the same thought. Thus, a thought of offering

Chapter 6: On Thoughts and Prayer                                    273

hospitality may be an indication of vainglory or of desire to serve God and others.[40] Similarly, if evil thoughts are easily overcome, this may either be because of recognition of the impossibility of attaining their object, or else because of apatheia.[41] In general terms then, where discrimination is exercised, thoughts may provide an indication of spiritual progress. Specifically, thoughts are understood to arise from different sources, according to which a different human response is required. Evagrios suggests that thoughts may have angelic, human or demonic origin, and that with experience these can be distinguished.[42] The meaning of thoughts is thus extended beyond the boundaries of inwardness to a cosmic realm in which spiritual powers are engaged. And through all of this is extended the possibility of eventual union with God through deification.[43]

## 4. The Interpretation of Thoughts in Psychotherapy

What might a contemporary psychological listing of "thoughts" look like? Just as Evagrios' list was selective, based upon his particular reasons for interest in the inner life, so the precise nature of any contemporary categorisation or lexicon of thoughts would doubtless depend upon the purpose for which it was being compiled. It is likely that for most psychological or therapeutic purposes the list would look very different than Evagrios' although, as seen in Chapter 5, this is not to say that direct applications of the Evagrian list are not possible.

Psychiatrists usually classify thought disorder according to stream, possession, form and content.[44] Disorders of emotion are generally classified separately, although this is not to suggest that the two are unrelated. The purpose of this is to identify signs of mental disorder which might enable a diagnosis to be made – for example of an underlying depressive illness. On this basis, Evagrios' list would comprise largely examples of content of thought, or of emotional reaction, and mostly non-pathological ones at that. Thoughts of sadness, for example, might be considered completely appropriate if concerned with living in the Egyptian desert without adequate shelter, food or clothing, but would be considered pathological (delusional) if concerned with demonstrably false beliefs about personal guilt or worthlessness. This model therefore almost inverts the Evagrian system. The kind of sadness (or anger, lust, etc) against which Evagrios warns is normalised and some concerns which Evagrios might have considered healthy (albeit, perhaps, not in delusional intensity) are pathologised.

In contrast to psychiatrists, cognitive therapists seek to identify automatic thoughts, cognitive distortions (or thinking errors), and the maladaptive cognitive schemata that underlie these automatic and erroneous thoughts.[45] Here, the psychopathology is understood as being located in the thoughts themselves – with cognitive therapy offering a variety of strategies for modifying, or treating, such thoughts. On this basis, thoughts of sadness at the loss of a job would usually be considered normal, whereas thoughts that this job loss will inevitably now make one unlovable as a husband or wife would normally be considered erroneous (and therefore an appropriate target for therapy). It is unlikely that any contemporary cognitive therapist would consider Evagrios' list a satisfactory catalogue of either automatic or erroneous thoughts. Rather, it is likely that thoughts such as those associated with sexual attraction, anger or sadness would be normalised, unless excessive, intrusive, or maladaptive in some way. However, in some ways, Evagrios proves to be a very perceptive cognitive therapist. Thus, for example, he recognises that underneath the thoughts that he calls "avarice", there are valuations (which the cognitive therapist might call schemata) concerned with the relative importance of money, goods and material things as compared with prayer, knowledge and heavenly reward.[46]

The kind of list of thoughts that a dynamic psychotherapist might wish to compile would undoubtedly depend specifically upon the particular school of dynamic psychotherapy that they belong to. However, amongst other thoughts, those indicative of unconscious processes, emotional pain, ego defence mechanisms and motivational drives might be considered important.[47] In some ways this list has a close resonance with some of Evagrios' descriptions of the eight thoughts. For example, Evagrios notes the way in which unconscious material emerges in dreams and fantasy,[48] the dangers associated with the pain of resentful or troubled thoughts,[49] and the power that lies behind sexual drives.[50] However, it is also a very different kind of list insofar as it is informed by a very different model of human well-being and very different normative values. Evagrios is concerned with the potential for sexual drives to impede prayer and prevent a deepening relationship with God. The dynamic therapist is aware of the way in which sexual drives, especially where they are not consciously acknowledged, may cause distress and emotional pain.

The interpretation of thoughts in contemporary psychiatry, psychology and psychotherapy is likely to take place in one of three ways. Firstly (as in psychiatry) thoughts might be understood as signs or symptoms of pathology. Secondly (as in cognitive therapy) they might be understood as themselves representing a kind of pathology. Or, thirdly (as in dynamic psychotherapies), they might be understood as both causes and signs of psychopathology. In each case, the significance of the interpretation will primarily be in terms of the possibility that it provides for directing an intervention directed towards the relief of distress. However, it may also have the benefit of increasing self-understanding.

Traditionally, organic psychiatry and behaviour therapy have not acknowledged the importance of meaning. According to the deterministic rationale underlying these disciplines, meaning does not have causal power. However, as cognitive therapy began to address the treatment of conditions such as depression and anxiety, a cognitive understanding of the importance of meaning began to gain acceptance. In particular, misinterpretation of meaning has been seen as important, as in circumstances where physical symptoms of anxiety are interpreted as indicating onset of serious physical illness, or where negative interpersonal cues are interpreted as indicating rejection. Although this model is clearly far removed from the meanings identified in relation to thoughts by authors of the *Philokalia*, yet the Evagrian instruction not to misinterpret the origins of thoughts does suggest a parallel of a certain kind.

The meanings that emerge from dynamic psychotherapy include feelings and impulses which may be excluded from consciousness due to their social and/or personal unacceptability.[51] Although the ultimate spiritual or theological meaning that is understood by the authors of the *Philokalia* is clearly different to this, the Evagrian awareness that apparently good motives may hide less respectable ones is clearly of a very similar kind.

Overall, then, Evagrios' process of identifying problematic thoughts might be considered not dissimilar to that of the modern day psychiatrist or therapist, except that it is orientated towards the radically different goal of identifying potential problems with prayer, rather than towards making a psychiatric diagnosis or identifying thoughts which might cause distress. Whereas the psychiatrist or psychotherapist maintains a non-judgmental stance, Evagrios easily lapses from talk of thoughts into talk about vices. Where necessary, however, Evagrios' recognises that thoughts are influenced by drives, judgments and values in a complex and not always consciously determined fashion. To this extent, he proves to be a perceptive psychotherapist, as well as a devoted theologian.

## 5. The Interpretation of Dreams

Dreams are arguably only thoughts that we have whilst we are asleep. According to Freud:

> At bottom, dreams are nothing other than a particular *form* of thinking, made possible by the conditions of the state of sleep.[52]

And yet, dreams have assumed great importance, both in the ancient world and in the much more recent history of psychotherapy. The Hebrew and Christian scriptures include accounts of a variety of dreams, the meanings of which variously communicate warning, prophecy and revelation.[53] The interpretation of dreams was famously referred to by Freud as being the "royal road to a knowledge of the unconscious"[54] and analysis of dreams formed an important part of his therapeutic method of psychoanalysis, used in the treatment of neurotic disorders. Dreams continue to play a significant part in the work of psychoanalytic psychotherapy today.[55] If dreams are simply thoughts occurring during sleep, then they are still often perceived as a special kind of thought, because of the belief that they potentially give access to significant religious, spiritual or psychological meanings which are normally inaccessible during waking life.

### i. Dream Interpretation in the Ancient World

In the ancient world, ordinary dreams might be ascribed particular significance according to natural phenomena which were considered portentous. Such dreams may be understood as akin to deductive divinatory practices actively employed by individuals seeking to understand divine purpose in their lives. In a different category altogether were dreams thought to be divinely inspired, and passively received, within which there might be symbolic significance or manifest theophanic content. Incubation of dreams, through ritual preparation and the spending of a night in a temple or holy site, drew on both deductive and inspired approaches, often with a therapeutic aim, such as seeking healing from illness (as, for example, in the Aesclepian cult).⁵⁶

Artemidorus of Daldis (mid/late second century C.E.), a Stoic, distinguished between dreams with and without divinatory value. In the latter category a further distinction was made between those with manifest significance and those which require interpretation, labelled theorematic and allegorical respectively. Interestingly, Artemidorus believed that all dreams originated within the human soul and so a third category, of dreams understood to be of divine origin, is sometimes added to this taxonomy. However, the theorematic and allegorical categories correspond more or less with the basic classification into message dreams and symbolic dreams used in contemporary historical-critical approaches.⁵⁷

Message dreams take the form of direct communication of a message by a divinity or other personal being. They are immediately intelligible, they do not require interpretation, and any detailed scenario is usually limited or absent. Message dreams tend to emphasise auditory over visual content. Symbolic dreams, however, although they also bring a message of some kind, take the form of images, pictures and events with a hidden significance which is not immediately intelligible and which therefore requires interpretation after waking. Symbolic dreams tend to emphasise visual over auditory content.

This binary classification is not entirely adequate to every situation. Husser notes, for example, that it does not really accommodate dreams of mixed type (especially with significant auditory and visual content), dreams in which the message is intended for another person (which might be termed "prophetic" dreams), or nightmares.⁵⁸

## ii. Dream Interpretation in Psychotherapy

A full account of the place of dream analysis in contemporary psychotherapy is beyond the scope of this book. However, as illustrative material for comparison with the account of dreams found in the *Philokalia*, a few comments and reflections on dream interpretation in the works of Freud and Jung are offered here.

*The Interpretation of Dreams* was first published by Freud in 1900.⁵⁹ In it, he distinguished between the manifest and latent content of dreams. The former represents the content of the dream as reported by the dreamer, the latter the repressed underlying wishes and concerns of the dreamer. These are represented symbolically in the manifest content. The latent content is often concerned with emotional responses of the dreamer in early life, and the system of symbols employed in dreams is therefore understood in a primarily individual way, and is often (but not exclusively) concerned with sexual themes. The conversion of the latent content into the manifest content he referred to as "dream work".

Jung was also concerned with symbolic interpretation of dreams as a therapeutic tool.[60] However, for Jung the symbols that appeared in dreams were potentially representative of a wide range of possible psychic contents, including both subjective material (about the dreamer, or about material from the unconscious) and objects (places, people or things). Included amongst the subjective material might be archetypes that are drawn from the collective unconscious of all human beings. Whereas for Freud religion was to be understood as a form of neurosis, Jung drew positively from religion and mythology in his understanding of the symbols that are encountered in dreams. Whereas for Freud the meaning of dreams was hidden, for Jung dreams were a natural phenomenon without deception. For Freud symbols in dreams related to real objects in the external world; for Jung the dream led to knowledge of the inner world. For Jung, dreams therefore served a self-regulating function of seeking to find meaning in life's struggles.

Freud and Jung therefore shared with ancient dream interpreters a belief that symbolic content within dreams may have significance. This is not necessarily to be encountered in every dream, and some contemporary psychiatrists would argue that it is not present in any dream.[61] However, it is clearly an ancient tradition. Freud, like Artemidorus, did not believe that dreams had their origin in anything external to the human soul and its memories. Their significance was therefore largely an individual matter, of significance more or less exclusively to the dreamer. Jung, on the other hand, shared an equally ancient view that dreams might have religious significance and drew from resources beyond those of the individual.

Two brief examples may be helpful here. First, an example given by Freud of a dream "of an uneducated woman whose husband was a policeman" is interpreted as symbolising sexual themes:

> Then someone broke into the house and she was frightened and called out for a policeman. But he had quietly gone into a church, to which a number

of steps led up, accompanied by two tramps. Behind the church there was a hill and above it a thick wood. The policeman was dressed in a helmet, brass collar and cloak. He had a brown beard. The two tramps, who went along peaceably with the policeman, had sack-like aprons tied round their middles. In front of the church a path led up to the hill; on both sides of it there grew grass and brushwood, which became thicker and thicker and, at the top of the hill, turned into a regular wood.[62]

Here, male genitalia are interpreted as symbolically represented by persons in the dream, and female genitalia by features of the landscape. The church is therefore representative of the vagina. The steps are said to be a symbol of sexual intercourse.

A second example, a dream which Jung had himself, also involves a church:

> I was walking along a little road through a hilly landscape; the sun was shining and I had a wide view in all directions. Then I came to a small wayside chapel. The door was ajar, and I went in. To my surprise there was no image of the Virgin on the altar, and no crucifix either, but only a wonderful flower arrangement. But then I saw that on the floor in front of the altar, facing me, sat a yogi – in lotus posture, in deep meditation. When I looked at him more closely, I realised that he had my face. I started in profound fright, and awoke with a thought: "Aha, so he is the one who is meditating me. He has a dream, and I am it." I knew that when he awakened, I would no longer be.[63]

Jung interprets this as a dream about the self. His analysis reverses the usual sense of egocentricity, with images in the unconscious as products of that ego, and invites us to see the unconscious world as somehow more real, with our conscious world a mere illusion or projection of that reality, "like a dream".

For Jung, the chapel here symbolises the religious posture adopted by the self in its meditation on its own earthly form (a process which we might identify, using the language of Charles Taylor, as reflexivity).

### iii. Dream Interpretation in the *Philokalia*

The treatment afforded to dreams in the *Philokalia* is both circumscribed and cautious. The number of references is few, and rather more than half the authors have virtually nothing to say on the subject at all. This is at first surprising, given the interest in dreams in the ancient world, the accounts of dreams in Christian scripture, the concerns of the *Philokalia* with the inner world of thoughts, and the apparent relevance of dreams to the interpretation of thoughts. However, a closer examination of the treatment given to dreams in the *Philokalia* is illuminating.

Evagrios deals with the matter of dreams in *Praktikos* and in *On Thoughts*.[64] Both works appear to identify dreams as a kind of diagnostic test of the state of the soul. Demons are described as presenting images to the soul which give strength to the passions and affect the state of the soul during the following day. Where sleep is free of images, this is taken as a sign of relative health; where the images show the monk resisting temptation or else behaving in response to it without passion, this is taken as a sign of impassibility.[65]

The only Evagrian chapter on dreams to be included in the *Philokalia* is taken from *On Thoughts* 4. In this chapter, Evagrios reflects on the way in which the demons work through images ("shapes and forms") taken in through the senses. As the bodily senses are inactive during sleep, he concludes that it must be the memory of these images that is aroused by the demons and which then "imprints" the intellect. But they are only able to arouse these memories because of the passions. Thus, those who are dispassionate are not troubled in this way.

Evagrios gives examples of the kinds of images that may cause problems in dreams. Thus, in *On Thoughts* 27, he writes of dreams which affect the concupiscible and irascible parts of the soul:

> This is how the anchorites are tempted by the demons in the daytime and fall victim to various thoughts, but in the night time during sleep they fight with winged asps, are encircled by carnivorous wild beasts, entwined by serpents, and cast down from high mountains. It sometimes happens that even after awakening they are again encircled by the same wild beasts and see their cell afire and filled with smoke. And when they do not

give in to these fantasies nor fall into cowardice, they in turn see the demons immediately transform into women who conduct themselves with wanton indecency and wish to play shameful games.[66]

In *Praktikos 28* we find an account of dreams which attack the intellect through temptations to pride or sadness:

> Frequently one sees oneself rebuking demons, healing certain bodily conditions, or wearing the clothing of a shepherd and pasturing a little flock. And immediately upon waking one gets a fantasy of the priesthood and then spends the entire day thinking through the things that that involves, or as if the charism of healings were about to be granted, one sees in advance the miracles that happen and fantasies about the people who will be healed, the honours coming from the brothers, and the gifts brought by outsiders, and those that come from Egypt and also from abroad, drawn by our renown. Often they cast anchorites into an inconsolable sadness by showing them members of their families in sickness or in danger on land or at sea. Sometimes they predict to the brothers themselves in dreams the shipwrecks of the monastic life, throwing down from high ladders those who have climbed up upon them and in turn leaving them blind and feeling their way along the walls.[67]

Evagrios does not see the soul as influenced only by the demons in sleep. In contrast:

> Angelic dreams are not like this, but possess a great peace of soul, an ineffable joy, suppression of impassioned thoughts by day, pure prayer, and even certain reasons of beings, which slowly emerge under the Lord's influence and reveal the wisdom of the Lord.[68]

Neither demonic nor angelic dreams are subjected to symbolic interpretation. The closest that Evagrios approaches to such a process of decoding is in the dream of the shepherd and the flock, as symbolic of priest and congregation. Apart from the fact that such imagery is likely to have been sufficiently familiar to his Christian readers (for example from Psalm 23 or John 10) that it would hardly be expected to need any interpretation, the dreamer described by

Evagrios has completely literal, conscious and unsymbolic fantasies related to priesthood "immediately upon waking". What the monk needs here, according to Evagrios, is not decoding of hidden symbols in the dream but awareness of the tactics of the demons and methods for combating them.[69] If there is any interpretation to be conducted, it is interpretation of cause rather than meaning and is affective rather than symbolic. Peace and joy may be interpreted as evidence of dreams with angelic origin and such dreams lead to dispassion, and pure prayer. Fear or craving are evidence of demonic origin.

Not dissimilar themes are found in Cassian,[70] Diadochus,[71] Maximos,[72] Thalassios,[73] and Theognostos.[74] Abba Philimon is attributed with suggesting as a remedy for "vain fantasies" in sleep that the monk should go to sleep whilst praying.[75] For Symeon Metaphrastis, elation by dreams is a sign of inattention to inner warfare consequent upon acedia.[76] For Gregory of Sinai, fantasies in sleep are due to too much food.[77] In general, then, the Evagrian tradition of dream interpretation seems to be accepted in the *Philokalia*, with only occasional and minor variation or addition. However, two significant strands of addition to, or variation from, this tradition are evident.

Diadochus adds a word of caution to the tradition that he acknowledges he has received. Having indicated that dreams are an indicator of the soul's health, and that God given dreams are associated with joy (but sometimes, in those advanced in humility, sadness and tears), whereas demonic dreams are menacing, he goes on to advise that, because of the danger of discerning wrongly:

> the safest rule is never to trust to anything that appears to us in our dreams. For dreams are generally nothing more than images reflecting our wandering thoughts, or else they are the mockery of demons. And if ever God in His goodness were to send us some vision and we were to refuse it, our beloved Lord Jesus would not be angry with us, for He would know we were acting in this way because of the tricks of the demons.[78]

Peter of Damaskos offers similar advice as a safeguard against demonic delusion, but now indicating that this is what "the fathers, in their discrimination, wrote", suggesting that the note of caution about the possibility of deception has by this stage become widely accepted.[79] This note of caution is also later apparent in the *Philokalia* in the writings of Gregory of Sinai.[80] The general sense that creeps in, in this strand of thinking, is therefore that dreams offer nothing that we can do without but that they are easily misinterpreted and they offer potentially great dangers of being deceived and led away from God. As a general rule, they are therefore best disregarded.

Symeon the New Theologian, with characteristic interest in the theme of light, brings a positive perspective which appears to dispense with this note of caution, and is radically different than almost anything in the *Philokalia* that has preceded it:

> If the eyes of a person who can see sensible light are closed for an instant or covered by someone else, he suffers and is distressed and cannot bear it, especially if he was looking at something important or unusual. But if someone is illumined by the Holy Spirit and, whether asleep or awake, sees spiritually those blessings that 'the eye has not seen, and the ear has not heard, and man's heart has not grasped' (1 Cor. 2:9), and 'that angels long to glimpse' (1 Pet. 1:12), how much more will he suffer and be tormented if he is torn away from the vision of these things? For this will seem to him like death, a veritable exclusion from eternal life.[81]

Perhaps Symeon distinguishes between ordinary dreams (about which he might conceivably retain an unmentioned sense of caution) and illumination by the Holy Spirit during sleep? Or perhaps he has in mind dreams of divine illumination akin to his waking visions, the overwhelmingly positive nature of which has eliminated for him any possibility that he could be deceived? Whatever the explanation, his enthusiasm for vision of the divine light, whether in a dream or otherwise, clearly eliminates any fear that he may have about being deceived.[82]

It is Nikitas Stithatos, in *On the Inner Nature of Things*, who provides the most detailed account of dreams that we find in the *Philokalia*,[83] and it is here that we may identify the second strand of development upon the Evagrian tradition of dream interpretation. This begins with a fairly typical Evagrian account of the diagnostic value of dreams, at least for the spiritually mature. He goes on to give examples (not dissimilar to the Evagrian examples) of dreams that reflect inner disposition towards, or preoccupation with, concerns of each of the three parts of the soul. Rather than distinguishing between demonic and angelic dreams, he then contrasts the examples he has just given with the visions in sleep of those who are "devoted to God, diligent in the practice of the virtues, scrupulous in the struggle for holiness and with a soul purged of material preoccupations".[84] In contrast to those whose souls continue to be afflicted by disposition towards the passions, these souls will awake from sleep peacefully, in prayer, with tears on their cheeks.

This initial account is discernibly similar to the Evagrian tradition, although without reference to demons and with more emphasis on dreams as diagnostic of particular "inner disposition and preoccupations". The tradition is developed, however, in the following paragraphs,[85] where Nikitas distinguishes between images occurring in sleep that are dreams, visions and revelations.

Dreams are concerned with "everything in the image-forming faculty of the intellect that is mutable"; they are confusing, constantly changing, and usually disappear on waking. They are associated with the "passion-polluted" life. Nikitas recommends that they should be ignored. Visions are constant and do not change, they are awe inspiring; they "remain imprinted upon the intellect unforgettably for many years". They are experienced by those "well advanced on the spiritual path". They should be treated with great seriousness. Revelations are associated with the contemplations of the "purified and illumined soul":

> They have the force of things and thoughts miraculous and divine, initiating us into the hidden mysteries of God, showing us the outcome of our most important problems and the universal transformation of things worldly and human.

Revelations are experienced only by the perfect, "whose soul through mystical prayer is united to God".

In summary,[86] Nikitas concludes that the veracity of things seen in sleep, and whether or not they leave an enduring imprint on the intellect, is a function of the purity of intellect of the one who has the dream and their advancement in hesychia and in natural contemplation.[87] It is not so much that those who are pure have dreams (or rather, visions and revelations) given by angels, but rather that "Their life is the life of angels and is hidden in God (cf. Col. 5:3)". It is not so much that their dreams (i.e. visions and revelations) require interpretation as that their visions and revelations are an interpretation, for them, of all things that really matter.

This approach to dreams clearly draws on the Evagrian tradition of dreams as offering diagnostic utility. However, whereas Evagrios was concerned that in dreams passions "imprinted" the soul, here they are ephemeral. It is visions and revelations (as distinguished by Stithatos from dreams) that are enduringly imprinted on the soul.

Nikitas' approach to visions and revelations in sleep has something of the same quality as Jung's dream of his meditation upon himself as a yogi in a chapel. It reverses the attribution of reality held in sleeping and waking consciousness. The true, unchanging, reality is to be perceived only by the purified soul in union with God and, whether this is from a state of sleep or wakefulness, and whether it be termed a dream, vision or revelation, it is only from this stance that conscious waking life can be properly interpreted. Dreams, visions and revelations do not require interpretation, but they themselves interpret the progress of the human soul towards dispassion.

### iv. Dreams, Psychotherapy and the *Philokalia*

Like Jung, and unlike Artemidorus and Freud, the *Philokalia* understands dreams as influenced by sources external to the human soul. These external sources may be demonic, or angelic, or they may be theophanic, as in dreams or visions of the divine light. However, we have already noted that the demonology and psychology of Evagrios and much of the *Philokalia* preserves a degree of ambiguity about what is internal and what is external. Evagrian thoughts cannot be blamed entirely on the demons; thoughts also belong to the human being who thinks them. Thus, Evagrian dreams are diagnostic of the progress of or, to use terminology employed by Nikitas Stithatos, the disposition or preoccupations of the human soul. In this sense, they reveal as much or more about what is within the human soul as they do anything about anything external to it. However, one strand of tradition subsequent to Evagrios seems to have been increasingly sceptical that dreams could be relied upon to provide any useful information at all.

The *Philokalia* seems to find little or no need for symbolic or allegorical interpretation of dream elements, and complex scenarios are almost entirely absent. To this extent the dreams that it describes are closer to the theorematic type of Artemidorus, or the message dream of modern literary form criticism. However, this is a very unsatisfactory classificatory choice where Philokalic dreams are concerned. The dreams described in the *Philokalia* are much more often visual than auditory and they do not often carry a "message", except insofar as they are perceived to be of diagnostic utitility, in the Evagrian schema, or else provide a more mystical and therefore ineffable vision or revelation, as in the dreams described by Symeon the New Theologian or Nikitas Stithatos. Some of the Evagrian dreams might well be described as nightmares.

The infrequency with which dreams are discussed in the *Philokalia* is perhaps not surprising. The strand of caution that is found here is evident in different forms elsewhere in Christianity, and in other religious traditions. Where dreams are too easily taken as revelatory, history suggests that heterodoxy, superstition and schism follow.[88] Symeon the New Theologian, and Nikitas Stithatos, do see dreams as potentially a place of revelatory encounter, but this is set firmly within a wider, discriminatory, and much more challenging understanding of a life of prayer.

## 6. On Prayer

The importance of thoughts in the *Philokalia* is attributable to their relationship with prayer. They are impediments to prayer, but they are also a means of prayer. Since prayer, especially contemplative prayer, is the means of attaining union with God, or divinisation, and as this is of ultimate importance in the Christian life, an understanding of thoughts is crucial to the central discourses of the *Philokalia*.

Firstly, and at the simplest level, thoughts are potential distractions from prayer.[89] For example, Isaiah the Solitary, in a passage which also draws attention to guarding of the heart as a measure which enables prayer, writes:

> Stand guard, then, over your heart and keep a watch on your senses; and if the remembrance of God dwells peaceably within you, you will catch the thieves when they try to deprive you of it. When a man has an exact knowledge about the nature of thoughts, he recognizes those which are about to enter and defile him, troubling the intellect with distractions and making it lazy. Those who recognize these evil thoughts for what they are remain undisturbed and continue in prayer to God.[90]

## Chapter 6: On Thoughts and Prayer

Gregory of Sinai provides a vivid description of the mind that is distracted from stillness (hesychia):

> Unless your life and actions are accompanied by a sense of inner grief you cannot endure the incandescence of stillness. If with this sense of grief you meditate – before they come to pass – on the many terrors that await us prior to and after death you will achieve both patience and humility, the twin foundations of stillness. Without them your efforts to attain stillness will always be accompanied by apathy and self-conceit. From these will arise a host of distractions and day-dreams, all inducing sluggishness. In their wake comes dissipation, daughter of indolence, making the body sluggish and slack and the intellect benighted and callous. Then Jesus is hidden, concealed by the throng of thoughts and images that crowd the mind (cf. John 5:13).[91]

Thoughts, then, can provide a barrier to prayer – they immobilise, distract, hide, crowd out – albeit they also provide a means[92] of achieving stillness (and thus prayer).

Secondly, as discussed in Chapters 1 to 3, thoughts are intimately related to the passions. Not that all thoughts are passions, but thoughts that are passionate pose an especial problem to prayer. Ilias the Presbyter contrasts three states of prayer – one in which the passions are unrestrained, one in which they are restrained, and passionless prayer:

> Those who indulge their passions, being materially-minded, are distracted during prayer by their thoughts as by frogs. Those who restrain their passions are gladdened during prayer by the changing forms of contemplation, which are like nightingales moving from one branch to another. But in the dispassionate there is silence and great quiescence of both thought and intellection during prayer.[93]

Like Evagrios, Maximos understands the passions as a fundamental barrier to contemplative prayer:

> Only a soul which has been delivered from the passions can without error contemplate created beings. Because its virtue is perfect, and because its knowledge is

spiritual and free from materiality, such a soul is called 'Jerusalem'. This state is attained through exclusion not only of the passions but also of sensible images.[94]

The soul that is not dispassionate, and which yet attempts to engage in contemplative prayer, is in danger of making the passions worse, and thus simply regressing rather than advancing in prayer:

> Until you have been completely purified from the passions you should not engage in natural contemplation through the images of sensible things; for until then such images are able to mould your intellect so that it conforms to passion. An intellect which, fed by the senses, dwells in imagination on the visible aspects of sensible things becomes the creator of impure passions, for it is not able to advance through contemplation to those intelligible realities cognate with it.[95]

Thoughts, then, may be a hindrance in prayer. However, as we have also already seen (in Chapter 3) the remedies for the passions employ a variety of strategies designed to identify the origins of thoughts and to conform thoughts to the process of prayer. These include behavioural measures (of ascetic discipline), cognitive measures (as in watchfulness), scripture (e.g. in psalmody), and prayer itself (e.g. the Jesus Prayer). Each of these remedies for the passions, in its own way, involves thoughts. Thoughts are thus a part of the solution, as well as the problem, for the passion bound human being who is separated from God. To take these remedies in turn:

1. The emphasis on ascetic discipline, at least in places, appears to operate on thoughts on a very behavioural basis. Thus, for example, avoiding women is likely to avoid provocation by thoughts of fornication, and will avoid laying down further memories of women which might in their turn present further such thoughts.[96] Evagrios, Maximos and others also appear to have believed that diet exerted some kind of physical influence upon thoughts – such that a frugal diet would render one less subject to thoughts of fornication.[97]

2. The process of watchfulness is concerned with cognitive vigilance, in order that evil thoughts may be rebutted, and helpful thoughts (e.g. meditation on death, or the words of the Jesus Prayer) invoked.

Chapter 6: On Thoughts and Prayer

3. The use of scripture, especially in psalmody, clearly provides a means of focussing on good thoughts and thus opening the mind to a good influence. To some extent, it might be seen as the reverse of the effect of evil thoughts which provide a distraction in prayer. Here, the intention is to distract the mind from evil thoughts, so as to engage in prayer. However, as discussed in Chapter 3, Evagrios' understanding of psalmody is more sophisticated that this alone might suggest. Psalmody is understood as preparing the whole person for prayer, exerting a calming effect upon the body and soul, focussing the mind upon God, imprinting the meaning of the psalm upon the mind, and refuting evil thoughts.

4. Prayer itself might be understood as a bringing of thoughts to the purpose of communion with God (cf. Evagrios),[98] as a bringing of thoughts to the purpose of petitioning God for his blessing (cf. Maximos),[99] or simply of a purification of thoughts (cf. Gregory Palamas).[100]

However, there is also a strong theme in the *Philokalia* of the need to eventually eliminate thoughts altogether. How can this be possible? Nikiphoros suggests banishing thoughts from the heart by replacing them with the Jesus Prayer, which suggests that a distinction may be made between "thoughts" of the Jesus Prayer and "thoughts" of other kinds.[101] Maximos writes that "contemplation is illumined by divine conceptual images",[102] again suggesting that thoughts (here conceptual images, νοήματα) can be a part of prayer, whereas Gregory of Sinai speaks of the need for hesychasts to eschew "all conceptual images".[103] Is the intention, then, to banish thoughts completely, or only to banish thoughts of a certain kind?

Ultimately, "pure prayer" or contemplative prayer (especially of the kind that Evagrios would refer to as theological contemplation) is wordless and imageless. Theophanis, for example, describes pure prayer as being associated with "peace from thoughts of every kind",[104] Peter of Damaskos describes spiritual prayer as being "offered by the intellect and free from all thoughts"[105] and pure prayer as being "beyond all conceptual thought".[106] Gregory of Sinai understands stillness (hesychia) as freedom from all thoughts – even those which are divine.[107] However, in the final chapters of

*Kephalaia Gnostica*, where contemplative prayer is more generally associated with knowledge than thoughts, Evagrios writes:

> It is said that the *nous* sees things that it knows and that it does not see things that it does not know; and because of this it is not all thoughts that the knowledge of God forbids it, but those which assail it from *thumos* and *epithumia* and those which are against nature.[108]

This would suggest that "natural thoughts" will endure, whereas those contrary to nature will be eliminated by those who reach the more advanced stages of contemplative prayer. On the other hand, we have already seen (in Chapter 4) that Maximos understands contemplation as leading to an end to natural thoughts immediately prior to deification. Similarly, Ilias the Presbyter writes of natural thoughts being at rest in the state of contemplative prayer associated with vision of the Divine light:

> He who is distracted during prayer stands outside the first veil. He who undistractedly offers the single-phrased Jesus Prayer is within the veil. But he alone has glimpsed the holy of holies who, with his natural thoughts at rest, contemplates that which transcends every intellect, and... has in this way been granted to some extent a vision of the divine light...[109]

It may be that there are subtle differences in the thinking of Evagrios, Maximos and Ilias as to whether "natural thoughts" continue in contemplative prayer. Or, it may be that there is a distinction to be made between states of contemplative prayer and other states of mind (non-contemplative prayer, or not being at prayer) amongst those of an advanced spiritual state. Perhaps, amongst such people, the texts of Evagrios and Ilias, if not also of Maximos, may be understood as suggesting that only natural thoughts remain and that even these are laid aside (or are "at rest") during contemplative prayer.[110]

Regardless of any such distinctions that may be made, the general trend towards a more apophatic, imageless and wordless, approach to contemplative prayer would seem most in keeping with the accounts of contemplative prayer and divinisation generally provided in the *Philokalia*. As was seen in Chapter 4, this imageless and wordless state of prayer is referred to in various places in terms of light, or illumination of the intellect. According to Konstantinovsky,

Evagrios was the first Christian writer, apart from Luke's account of the conversion of Saul, to provide an account of theophanic visions of light.[111] Konstantinovksy argues that Evagrios understood these visions as entirely immaterial, and therefore graspable only by the immaterial intellect, or nous, and even then only by grace.[112] Other contributors to the *Philokalia*, as we have seen, have taken up the same theme in various ways in an attempt to convey an account of a form of prayer, and vision of the Divine energies, which is essentially beyond ordinary (physical) sense experience, and also beyond words and thoughts.

A related theme, which has been important in the Christian tradition generally, but which receives relatively little attention in the *Philokalia*, is that of the Divine essence as darkness. Darkness mysticism is arguably understood as originating with Gregory of Nyssa, who brought together Platonic imagery with the Exodus account of the encounter of Moses with God on Mount Sinai.[113] Gregory proved to be a significant influence on Pseudo-Denys the Areopagite,[114] who in turn influenced Maximos the Confessor.[115] In essence, the argument is that in Plato's allegory of the cave, and also in the Exodus narrative, there is an ascent towards a light which proves to be so bright as to be perceived as darkness. This darkness is a "luminous darkness", for it is caused not by lack of light but by an overwhelming excess of light. Within this darkness, the darkness of God, all that is known becomes insignificant in the context of the knowledge of God, who is far greater than all that can humanly be known. It is therefore a darkness of unknowing.

Although Divine light receives much more attention, the theme of Divine darkness is not completely absent from the *Philokalia*. In the *Theoretikon* (attributed to Theodoros) Adam is said to have been judged unworthy by God "of what he had rejected – the contemplation of God and of created beings" and so God makes "darkness His secret place".[116] [Theognostos] similarly makes reference to darkness as the "secret place" of God.[117] Maximos, making allegorical reference to the Exodus account of Moses' encounter with God on Mount Sinai, understands the darkness as the "immaterial realm of spiritual knowledge".[118] Gregory of Sinai refers to the "the divine darkness of theological wisdom".[119] However, it is Nikitas Stithatos who gives most attention to this theme.

In a series of references,[120] all explicitly or implicitly in the context of a discussion of contemplative prayer, he speaks of the "divine darkness of theology" or the "darkness of mystical theology". This darkness theology appears to be understood by Stithatos as a state conferred by God on those who have achieved dispassion and have engaged in natural contemplation. It is a place of revelation of divine knowledge, a place of closeness to God or union with God or of resting with God, a place of joy or ecstasy, and a place of unspeakable silence. It is a place of contemplation of God:

> surpassing its own limitations, rebelling against the fetters of the senses and transcending all creatureliness, [the soul] penetrates the divine darkness of theology in unutterable silence and – to the degree that grace permits – it perceives in the intellective light of inexpressible wisdom the beauty of Him who truly is. Reverentially entering ever more deeply into intellective contemplation of that beauty, it savours, in loving awe, the fruits of immortality – the visionary intellections of the Divine. Never withdrawing from these back into itself, it is able to express perfectly their magnificence and glory. Activated, as it were, in a strange way by the Spirit, it experiences this admirable passion in unspeakable joy and silence; yet how it is activated, or what it is that impels it, and is seen by it, and secretly communicates to it unutterable mysteries, it cannot explain.[121]

Although Maximos makes only one reference to the divine darkness, he makes a series of reference to "unknowing" as the supreme way of knowing God.[122] Maximos, Thalassios and Gregory Palamas also make explicit reference to apophatic theology,[123] and Theoliptos and Gregory of Sinai are discernibly apophatic in their approach.[124] The unknowability of God's essence was a central point of contention in the fourteenth century hesychast controversy, in which Gregory Palamas played such a significant part, and against which a defence is included as one of the texts of the *Philokalia*.[125] It is therefore reasonable to say that there is a strong apophatic element to the *Philokalia*. This is illustrated well in a passage from Maximos:

> If you theologize in an affirmative or cataphatic manner, starting from positive statements about God, you make the Logos flesh, for you have no other means of knowing

> God as cause except from what is visible and tangible. If you theologize in a negative or apophatic manner, through the stripping away of positive attributes, you make the Logos spirit or God as He was in His principial state with God: starting from absolutely none of the things that can be known, you come in an admirable way to know Him who transcends unknowing.[126]

In *The Darkness of God*, Denys Turner[127] argues that, originating in the work of Pseudo-Denys the Areopagite, there is a negating of the negation that is built into apophatic theology in the western tradition. For example, he points out that in Chapter 68 of the *Cloud of Unknowing*[128] there is a warning against inwardness language such that the distinction between inner and outer is subverted. This means that distinctions between inner and outer are a feature of an outer view on things. True inwardness, of an apophatic kind, loses any sense of such distinctions. This, he argues, is a feature of negation within this tradition, that it first creates a dialectic between what can be said and what cannot be said, or known and unknown, and then negates its own negation so as to remove the very difference between them.

Unfortunately, apart from his consideration of the work of Pseudo-Denys the Areopagite, Turner does not consider examples from the eastern tradition. However, it has to be said that it is difficult to find this kind of dynamic within the texts of the *Philokalia*. It might be argued that the reference of Maximos (above) to "Him who transcends unknowing" might be understood as a reference of this kind, but it is not elaborated upon. Similarly, the above quotation from Nikitas Stithatos refers both to the "divine darkness" and to the "intellective light" of God, thus setting up the kind of dialectic that Turner refers to, but still it lacks the negation of this dialectic. And again, Gregory Palamas comes close to the same kind of thing in *Topics*,[129] in a passage where he is arguing that God's attributes are to be distinguished from his essence. Here he argues that neither all of the things that can be said of God apophatically, nor all of the things that can be said cataphatically, can be said to disclose God's essence. Thus, a kind of dialectic between apophatic and cataphatic is established, although it is here more a categorisation of things that can be said (negatively and positively) about the attributes of God than it is a dialectic as such. But still the negation of the dialectic is either only very weakly implicit or else completely absent. In fact, Gregory goes on to try to resolve the dialectic, rather than to negate it, and to "embrace both modes of theology" (i.e. cataphatic and apophatic) on the grounds that neither excludes the other.[130]

If I am correct that the negation of the negation (what Turner refers to as the "second level" of negativity of the apophatic dialectic)[131] is missing in the *Philokalia*, it might still be argued that this is simply evidence of the different historical course that eastern and western apophatic theologies have taken. In other words, it might be of little practical importance. However, it is this second level of apophaticism that Turner argues has a capacity to transform our understanding of the goal of Christian spirituality – that of union with God. Specifically, it challenges the dialectic between union with God and the distinctiveness of human identity from God, between inner and outer worlds. Although in the case of Meister Eckhart this process has been perceived to progress beyond the bounds of doctrinal orthodoxy, it more positively appears to provide a check against a self-indulgent and excessively introverted focus on relationship with God. Turner also argues that it is this second level of negativity that subverts any tendency towards experientialism – a seeking of negative spiritual experiences for their own sake.[132] If this second level of negativity is absent from the *Philokalia*, then what impact does this have upon its understanding of theosis, and what checks does it have against experientialism?

Significantly, Turner draws attention to the way in which the darkness metaphor works at both levels of negativity:

> the imagery of 'divine darkness' is employed *both* to describe the product of ascending scales of affirmations and denials as the soul, like Moses, climbs the mountain to God; *and* also to describe the *excessus* by which the soul transcends and surpasses the contradiction between affirmation and denial, and so transcends the distinction between 'similarity and difference' itself, passing beyond all language into oneness with God.[133]

However, as we have seen, the darkness metaphor is used less frequently in the *Philokalia* than the light metaphor (and references to divine light in the *Philokalia* are not necessarily metaphorical). It is the latter – light not darkness – which is used to describe the final process of theosis. This difference is reflected in the focus of

## Chapter 6: On Thoughts and Prayer

the hesychasts on the transfiguration in light of Christ on Mount Tabor as the paradigm for their theology, rather than the focus of Pseudo-Denys on the encounter of Moses with God in Darkness on Mount Sinai. However, it clearly has its origins long before the fourteenth century, being found in early form in the light visions of Evagrios and subsequently in various forms by numerous authors of the *Philokalia*.[134] This suggests that we might expect that, if there is one, the second level of negation in the *Philokalia* (if not also the first level) or its equivalent, will be associated with metaphors of light rather than darkness. Is there any evidence that this is in fact the case?

As discussed in Chapter 4,[135] the Divine light associated with theosis is understood in the *Philokalia* as arising in the context of contemplative prayer in those who have achieved apatheia. Apatheia, which might be considered here as a renunciation of the passions associated with human experience, is the result of a process of ascetic discipline and prayer which has challenged at root the tendency towards attachment to things or experiences. Because contemplation of God is generally seen as following experience of natural contemplation, when it is eventually achieved boundaries between things in the "outer" world – creation and God – are already blurred, for God is found in all things. Furthermore, theosis is understood as the fruit of an ascetic life and a process of self emptying modelled on the kenosis of Christ. The light metaphor in the *Philokalia* is therefore embedded in a process – we might even wish to call it a psychotherapeutic process – which fundamentally challenges questions of relationship between inner and outer, self and other.

Various authors of the *Philokalia* take care to distinguish the divine light associated with theosis from sensory perceptual experience. Although in some way it appears to be a perceptual "experience" of the intellect, it is clearly not a sensory experience in the usual sense. Evagrios warns against pride and the "deceit of demons", which might be associated with false experiences of this light. Diadochos, although perhaps atypical in seeing experiences of light as occurring at an early stage of spiritual progress, even expects that genuine experiences may be followed by a sense of the absence of God which will prevent such pride.

In those who perceive the divine light, the boundaries between the individual human being and God, between inner and outer worlds, are blurred. Nikitas Stithatos suggests that the pure intellect assents only to divine thoughts and writes of being "united and interfused with the primordial light".[136] Gregory of Sinai speaks of the light drawing the soul towards an ineffable spiritual union with God[137] and Gregory Palamas of a state in which "both intellect and God work together".[138]

In none of this are second order negations of the kind identified by Turner readily identifiable. However, the breaking down of barriers between the inner and outer worlds, the blurring of the boundaries between self and God in theosis, and the negation of experientialism are all strongly evident. Indeed, the process of theosis looks more like a losing of the self in God, a going outwards to God, than it does a self indulgent inwardness, and the remedies for the passions described in Chapter 3 might be considered equally as effective remedies for experientialism.

It is interesting that the fourteenth century saw the hesychasts embroiled in controversy in the east, and Eckhart accused of heresy in the west. There must be a warning here about the dangers that arise when apophatic theology blurs boundaries between inner and outer, self and God, to the point where they are too easily misunderstood. However, unlike Eckhart, the hesychasts were vindicated and it might be argued that Turner's second level of negation allows a potentially more serious vulnerability to doctrinal misunderstanding than does the theology of the hesychasts.

## 7. On Thoughts and Prayer

> If you are a theologian, you will pray truly; and if you pray truly, you will be a theologian.[139]

Is it possible to be a theologian without understanding how to interpret thoughts? Evagrios clearly thought not. To "pray truly" requires that prayers be purified of thoughts that are not true, and it is not possible to identify which thoughts these are without some kind of hermeneutical process by means of which to interpret their true meaning. Equally, to pray truly requires that a true interpretation of thoughts be made, in order that these thoughts may be offered to God in prayer. Eventually, however, thoughts in any ordinary human sense become inadequate for prayer, just as all human language is inadequate to express the superabundant excess of meaning that is God.

The *Philokalia* demonstrates that thoughts are powerful. They have the capacity to enslave and control, to deceive, to blind, to make sick and to kill. But they also have the capacity to set free, to empower, to illuminate, to heal and to bring life. Thoughts have the power to deny prayer, and to enable prayer, to obscure God and to reveal God.

The *Philokalia* offers a therapeutic programme aimed at finding God in prayer. In order to implement this programme, it is necessary to undergo a kind of psychotherapy. This psychotherapy of the *Philokalia* overlaps in places with psychological therapies that aim at other kinds of psychological well-being, but it is distinctive by virtue of its therapeutic focus on well-being understood in terms of prayer and union with God. As we saw in Chapter 4, this well-being depends ultimately on grace. The therapy that the *Philokalia* offers, through grace, leads to a breakdown in boundaries between inwardness and the outer world, between knowledge and unknowing, and between God and self. And then it has served its purpose.

# Epilogue

> Let us pasture our sheep below Mount Sinai, so that the God of our fathers may speak to us, too, out of the bush (cf. Exod. 3) and show us the inner essence of signs and wonders.
>
> Evagrios
> *Texts on Discrimination*, #16 (EGP 1, 48-49)

Being a shepherd, I am told, is not as romantic as it may sound. It is hard work. It requires perseverance in all weathers. It requires patience. Similarly, the process of "shepherding thoughts" that is described in the *Philokalia* is not for the faint hearted. It requires a self emptying that imitates that of Christ, it requires discipline, it requires watchfulness and patience. Above all, it requires perseverance in prayer. Just as sheep require pasture and protection every day, so do thoughts. [Theognostos] employs an image of the intellect as a sheep dog that has to keep watch lest the "cunning wolves" of the passions ravage the flock.[1] This is the kind of task that is tiring and relentless. The *Philokalia* does not offer an easy way into the spiritual life, but it is very realistic and very practical in the measures that it prescribes.

Just as the task is demanding, the rewards that the *Philokalia* offers are great. The above quotation from Evagrios associates the successful outcome as being a pasturing of sheep below Mount Sinai, the place in which Moses first encountered God in the burning bush and later "drew near to the thick darkness where God was".[2] The reference to the "inner essence" of signs and wonders provides an allusion to the facility of contemplative prayer to penetrate to the inner essences of things. Through purification, illumination and perfection of the intellect, the *Philokalia* promises to bring the faithful shepherd of thoughts to the place of theosis, to participation in the divinity of Christ.

Sheep have a tendency to go astray. Thoughts may lead us away from God, just as they may lead us to God. They can obscure God, just as much as they can be a place of divine revelation. The shepherding of thoughts is thus at once a matter of a kind of psychotherapy and of prayer. The *Philokalia* provides a kind of manual for this psychotherapy that leads to, and enables, prayer. Not that this therapy shares in common with contemporary psychological therapies many of its underlying assumptions, or indeed its intended outcomes. However, one of its fundamental premises seems to be that it is not possible to talk about prayer without talking first about thoughts, and some of its insights into the world of thoughts are remarkably akin to those of the contemporary psychological therapies. It thus brings together the domain of spirituality and the sciences concerned with mental well-being in a way that is highly pertinent to contemporary concerns about the relationship of spirituality to mental and physical health.

The *Philokalia* challenges us to look afresh at the ways in which we interpret thoughts – our own and those of other people. It presents a radical approach to psychotherapy which, like psychoanalysis, provides at once an investigative tool, a therapeutic method, and a theoretical understanding of the human psyche to inform these procedures. Unlike psychoanalysis and other contemporary psychological therapies, however, it pursues its method of therapy beyond any pathology that may be located within or behind our thoughts to a point where language and words begin to fail. It stretches knowing to the point of requiring unknowing, it blurs the boundaries between inner and outer worlds, and it enters a world of luminous darkness, within which God dwells.

**Appendix 1: Constituent works of the Greek *Philokalia***

| No. of Work | No. in DS | Author(s) | Volume Number | Pages | English Translation (1979-1995) Title | Abbreviated Title |
|---|---|---|---|---|---|---|
| 1 | 1 | [Antony the Great] | 1 | 329-356 | *On the character of men and on the virtuous life: 170 Texts* | *On the Character of Men* |
| 2 | 2 | Isaiah the Solitary | 1 | 22-28 | *On guarding the intellect: 27 Texts* | *Guarding the Intellect* |
| 3 | 3a | Evagrios the Solitary | 1 | 31-37 | *Outline teaching on asceticism and stillness in the solitary life* | *Asceticism & Stillness* |
| 4 | 3b | Evagrios the Solitary | 1 | 38-52 | *Texts on discrimination in respect of passions and thoughts* | *Texts on Discrimination* |
| 5 | 3c | Evagrios the Solitary (See also under Neilos the Ascetic) | 1 | 53-54 | *Extracts from the texts on watchfulness* | *Watchfulness – Extracts* |
| 6 | 4a | John Cassian | 1 | 73-93 | *On the eight vices* | *Eight Vices* |
| 7 | 4b | John Cassian | 1 | 94-108 | *On the Holy Fathers of Sketis and on discrimination* | *Holy Fathers of Sketis* |
| 8 | 5a | Mark the Ascetic | 1 | 110-124 | *On the spiritual law: 200 Texts* | *On the Spiritual Law* |
| 9 | 5b | Mark the Ascetic | 1 | 125-146 | *On those who think that they are made righteous by works: 226 Texts* | *Righteous by Works* |
| 10 | 5c | Mark the Ascetic | 1 | 147-160 | *Letter to Nicolas the Solitary* | *Letter to Nicolas* |
| 11 | 6 | Hesychios the Priest | 1 | 162-198 | *On watchfulness and holiness* | *Watchfulness & Holiness* |
| 12 | 7a | [Neilos the Ascetic] (actually by Evagrios) | 1 | 55-71 | *On prayer: 153 Texts* | *On Prayer: 153 Texts* |
| 13 | 7b | Neilos the Ascetic | 1 | 200-250 | *Ascetic discourse* | *Ascetic Discourse* |
| 14 | 8 | Diadochos of Photiki | 1 | 253-296 | *On spiritual knowledge and discrimination: 100 Texts* | *On Spiritual Knowledge* |

| No. of Work | No. in DS | Author(s) | Volume Number | English Translation (1979-1995) Title | | Abbreviated Title |
|---|---|---|---|---|---|---|
| | | | | Pages | Title | |
| 15 | 9a | John of Karpathos | 1 | 298-321 | *For the encouragement of the monks in India who had written to him: 100 Texts* | *For the Monks in India* |
| 16 | 9b | John of Karpathos | 1 | 322-326 | *Ascetic discourse sent at the request of the same monks in India* | *Ascetic Discourse* |
| 17 | 10a | Theodoros the Great Ascetic | 2 | 14-37 | *A century of spiritual texts* | *Spiritual Texts* |
| 18 | 10b | [Theodoros the Great Ascetic] | 2 | 38-47 | *Theoretikon* | *Theoretikon* |
| 19 | 11a | Maximos the Confessor | 2 | 52-113 | *Four hundred texts on love* | |
| | | | | 52 | *Foreword to Elpidios the Presbyter* | *On Love: Foreword* |
| | | | | 53-64 | *First Century* | *On Love: C1* |
| | | | | 65-82 | *Second Century* | *On Love: C2* |
| | | | | 83-99 | *Third Century* | *On Love: C3* |
| | | | | 100-113 | *Fourth Century* | *On Love: C4* |
| 20 | 11b | Maximos the Confessor | 2 | 114-163 | *Two hundred texts on theology and the incarnate dispensation of the Son of God. Written for Thalassios* | |
| | | | | 114-136 | *First Century* | *For Thalassios: C1* |
| | | | | 137-163 | *Second Century* | *For Thalassios: C2* |
| 21 | 11c | Maximos the Confessor (actual and attributed)[1] | 2 | 164-305 | *Various texts on theology, the divine economy, and virtue and vice* | |
| | | | | 164-187 | *First Century* | *Various Texts: C1* |
| | | | | 188-209 | *Second Century* | *Various Texts: C2* |
| | | | | 210-234 | *Third Century* | *Various Texts: C3* |
| | | | | 235-260 | *Fourth Century* | *Various Texts: C4* |
| | | | | 261-284 | *Fifth Century* | *Various Texts: C5* |
| 22 | 11d | Maximos the Confessor | 2 | 285-305 | *On the Lord's Prayer* | *On the Lord's Prayer* |

| No. of Work | No. in DS | Author(s) | Volume Number | Pages | Title | Abbreviated Title |
|---|---|---|---|---|---|---|
| 23 | 12 | Thalassios the Libyan | 2 | 307-342 | On love, self-control, and life in accordance with the intellect. Written for Paul the Presbyter (4 centuries) | |
| | | | | 307-312 | First Century | For Paul: C1 |
| | | | | 313-318 | Second Century | For Paul: C2 |
| | | | | 319-324 | Third Century | For Paul: C3 |
| | | | | 325-332 | Fourth Century | For Paul: C4 |
| 24 | 13 | [John of Damaskos] | 2 | 334-342 | On the virtues and the vices | On Virtues & Vices |
| 25 | 14 | Anonymous | 2 | 344-357 | A discourse on Abba Philimon | Abba Philimon |
| 26 | 15 | [Theognostos] | 2 | 359-378 | On the practice of the virtues, contemplation and the priesthood | On Virtues, Contemplation & Priesthood |
| 27 | 16 | Philotheos of Sinai | 3 | 16-31 | Forty texts on watchfulness | Forty Texts on Watchfulness |
| 28 | 17 | Ilias the Presbyter | 3 | 34-65 | A gnomic anthology | |
| | | | | 34-42 | Part I | Gnomic Anthology: 1 |
| | | | | 43-46 | Part II | Gnomic Anthology: 2 |
| | | | | 47-51 | Part III | Gnomic Anthology: 3 |
| | | | | 52-65 | Part IV | Gnomic Anthology: 4 |
| 29 | 18 | Theophanis the Monk | 3 | 67-69 | The ladder of divine graces | Ladder of Divine Graces |
| 30 | 19a | Peter of Damaskos | 3 | 74-210 | Book I. A treasury of divine knowledge | Book I |
| 31 | 19b | Peter of Damaskos | 3 | 211-281 | Book II. Twenty-four discourses | Book II |
| 32 | 20 | Symeon Metaphrastis | 3 | 285-354 | Paraphrase of the homilies of St Makarios of Egypt | Paraphrase of Makarios |

| No. of Work | No. in DS | Author(s) | Volume Number | Pages | English Translation (1979-1995) Title | Abbreviated Title |
|---|---|---|---|---|---|---|
| 33 | 21 | Symeon the New Theologian | 4 | 25-50 | One hundred and fifty-three practical and theological texts (Texts 1-118) | Practical & Theological Texts |
|  |  | [Symeon the New Theologian] (Texts 127-152 by Symeon the Studite; 153 by Nikitas Stithatos) | 4 | 50-63 | One hundred and fifty-three practical and theological texts (Texts 119-153) | Practical & Theological Texts |
| 34 | 22 | Nikitas Stithatos | 4 | 79-106 | On the practice of the virtues: One hundred texts | On Virtues: 100 Texts |
|  |  |  |  | 107-138 | On the inner nature of things and on the purification of the intellect: One hundred texts | On the Inner Nature of Things |
|  |  |  |  | 139-174 | On spiritual knowledge, love and the perfection of living: One hundred texts | On Spiritual Knowledge |
| 35 | 23a | Theoliptos, Metropolitan of Philadelphia | 4 | 177-187 | On inner work in Christ and the monastic profession | On Inner Work |
| 36 | 23b | Theoliptos, Metropolitan of Philadelphia | 4 | 188-191 | Texts | Texts |
| 37 | 24 | Nikiphoros the Monk | 4 | 194-206 | On watchfulness and the guarding of the heart | Watchfulness & Guarding |
| 38 | 25a | Gregory of Sinai | 4 | 212-252 | On commandments and doctrines, warnings and promises; on thoughts, passions and virtues, and also on stillness and prayer: One hundred and thirty-seven texts | On Commandments & Doctrines |
| 39 | 25b | Gregory of Sinai | 4 | 253-256 | Further texts | Further Texts |
| 40 | 25c | Gregory of Sinai | 4 | 257-262 | On the signs of grace and delusion, written for the Confessor Longinos: Ten texts | For Longinos |
| 41 | 25d | Gregory of Sinai | 4 | 263-274 | On stillness: Fifteen texts | On Stillness |
| 42 | 25e | Gregory of Sinai | 4 | 275-286 | On prayer: Seven texts | On Prayer: 7 Texts |
| 43 | 26a | Gregory Palamas | 4 | 293-322 | To the Most Reverend Nun Xenia | To Xenia |

| No. of Work | No. in DS | Author(s) | Volume Number | Pages | English Translation (1979-1995) Title | Abbreviated Title |
|---|---|---|---|---|---|---|
| 44 | 26b | Gregory Palamas | 4 | 323-330 | *A New Testament decalogue* | *New Testament Decalogue* |
| 45 | 26c | Gregory Palamas | 4 | 331-342 | *In defence of those who devoutly practise a life of stillness* | *In Defence of Stillness* |
| 46 | 26d | Gregory Palamas | 4 | 343-345 | *Three texts on prayer and purity of heart* | *On Prayer & Purity* |
| 47 | 26e | Gregory Palamas | 4 | 346-417 | *Topics of natural and theological science and on the moral and ascetic life: One hundred and fifty texts* | *Topics* |
| 48 | 26f | Gregory Palamas | 4 | 418-426 | *The declaration of the Holy Mountain in defence of those who devoutly practise a life of stillness ("The Hagiorite Tome")* | *Declaration of the Holy Mountain* |
| 49 | 27 | Kallistos & Ignatios of Xanthopoulos | 5 | | *Directions to Hesychasts in a Hundred Chapters*[2] | *Directions to Hesychasts* |
| 50 | 28 | Kallistos, Patriarch | 5 | | *Fourteen Texts on Prayer*[3] | *On Prayer – 14 Texts* |
| 51 | 28 | [Kallistos, Patriarch] (actually by Kallistos Telecudes) | 5 | | (*Supplementary Chapters*) [Not yet published] | |
| 52 | 29 | Kallistos Telecudes | 5 | | (*On the Practice of Hesychasm*) [Not yet published] | |
| 53 | 30 | Anonymous (? Kallistos Telecudes) | 5 | | (*Selected Writings of the Fathers on Prayer*) [Not yet published] | |
| 54 | 31 | Kallistos Cataphygiotes | 5 | | (*On Union with God and the Contemplative Life*) [Not yet published] | |
| 55 | 32 | Symeon, Archbishop of Thessalonica | 5 | | (*On Prayer & Deification*) [Not yet published] | |

| No. of Work | No. in DS | Author(s) | English Translation (1979-1995) | | | Abbreviated Title |
|---|---|---|---|---|---|---|
| | | | Volume Number | Pages | Title | |
| 56 | 33 | Anonymous (actually by Mark Eugenikos) | 5 | | (Treatise on the Jesus Prayer) [Not yet published] | |
| 57 | 34 | Anonymous | 5 | | (Interpretation of the words 'Lord Have Mercy') [Not yet published] | |
| 58 | 35a | Symeon the New Theologian | 4 | 16-24 | On faith | On Faith |
| 59 | 35b | [Symeon the New Theologian] | 4 | 64-75 | The three methods of prayer | Three Methods of Prayer |
| 60 | 36 | Gregory of Sinai | 5 | | Instructions to Hesychasts[4] | Instructions to Hesychasts |
| 61 | 37 | Anonymous (actually by Theophanis of Batopedi) | 5 | | (On the Life of Maximos Kapsokalivitos) [Not yet published] | |
| 62 | 38 | Anonymous (actually by Philotheos Kokkinos) | 5 | | (On the Life of Gregory of Thessalonica) [Not yet published] | |

| No. | C&C No. | Author | Date | Biographical details | Source of biographical information |
|---|---|---|---|---|---|
| 1 | 1a | Author(s) of *On the Character of Men* | 1st to 4th cc. | This work is attributed to Antony the Great – but is actually thought to be by various unknown Stoic and Platonic authors whose views apparently reflect those of Seneca, Epictetus, Marcus Aurelius and Sallustius. The compiler is also unknown, but has edited out some non-Christian terminology. | EGP |
| 2 | 2 | Isaiah the Solitary | ?d.489/491 | There is some uncertainty concerning the identity of this author, but he is thought to be a monk who lived at Sketis and then moved to Palestine at a date after 431. He died in old age as a recluse at Gaza on 11 August 491 (or possibly 489). | EGP |
| 3 | 3 | Evagrios the Solitary (Evagrius of Pontus) | b. 345/346 d. 399 | See Chapter 1 | |
| 4 | 4 | John Cassian | b. *c.*360 d. *c.*435 | See Chapter 1 | |
| 5 | 5 | Mark the Ascetic | early 5th c. | Also known as Mark the Monk, or Mark the Hermit. May have been a disciple of John Chrysostom. May have been superior of a community near Ancyra in Asia Minor. Lived at one stage after this as a hermit in the desert, but it is not known whether this was in Egypt or Palestine. Possibly also a priest and superior of a monastery at Tarsus. In addition to the 3 works by him included in the *Philokalia*, he wrote at least 6 other works. His teaching is against Messalianism and also lays emphasis on baptismal grace. | EGP ODCC |
| 6 | 6 | Hesychios (Hesychius) the Priest | ?8th or 9th c. | Abbot of the monastery of the Mother of God of the Burning Bush (Vatos) at Sinai. | EGP |

| No. | C&C No. | Author | Date | Biographical details | Source of biographical information |
|---|---|---|---|---|---|
| 7 | 7 | Neilos (Nilus) the Ascetic | d. c.430 | Founder and abbot of a monastery near Ancyra in the early 5th c. Disciple of John Chrysostom. According to legend (now rejected) was a high officer in the court at Constantinople and then became a hermit on Mt Sinai. He is the earliest writer to refer explicitly to the Jesus Prayer. Was influential and prolific correspondent. | EGP ODCC |
| 8 | 8 | Diadochos of Photiki | b. c.400 d. before 486 | Bishop of Photiki in Epirus (N. Greece). Wrote against Monophysitism and Messalianism and supported the Council of Chalcedon (451). Emphasised the fundamental unity of the human body and soul. Also wrote a homily on the ascension, and *Vision*, a dialogue with John the Baptist. | EGP ODCC |
| 9 | 9 | John of Karpathos | 5th-7th c. | Presumably came from the island of Karpathos, between Crete and Rhodes. Thought to have been a monk there, and later became bishop. May be the same John from "Karpathion" who signed the acts of the 6th Ecumenical Council (680-681). | EGP |
| 10 | 10a | Theodoros the Great Ascetic | ?9th c. | A monk at the monastery of St Sabas, near Jerusalem, and later Bishop of Edessa in Syria. According to Nikodimos, he lived in the 7th c., but probably should be considered 9th c. *Spiritual Texts*, which is largely a paraphrase of Evagrios, was written not earlier than the 7th c. (since it draws on Maximos the Confessor) and not later than early 11th c. (since it is found in a manuscript of 1023). | EGP |
| 11 | 10b | Author of *Theoretikon* | ?14th to 17th c. | This work is attributed in the Greek *Philokalia* to Theodoros the Great Ascetic, but actual authorship is unknown. Style and perspective indicate possibly 14th c. authorship, but it might be as recent as 17th c. | EGP |

| No. | C&C No. | Author | Date | Biographical details | Source of biographical information |
|---|---|---|---|---|---|
| 12 | 11 | Maximos the Confessor | 580-662 | The largest single contributor to the *Philokalia*, according to the generally accepted account, Maximos was born to an aristocratic family in Byzantium and became Imperial Secretary under Emperor Heraclius in 610. In c.614, he became a monk at the monastery of Philippikos in Chrysopolis, near Constantinople, and in 624/5 moved to the monastery of St George at Cyzikos. In 626, at the Persian invasion, he fled to Crete and then to Africa by 630. From 633-634 he played a major role in opposing the heresies of Monoergism and Monotheletism. He was arrested for this in 654, tried in Constantinople, and then exiled. Eventually, following a series of further trials, he was condemned in 662 and subjected to flogging, cutting out of his tongue, and cutting off his right hand. He died soon after as an exile in Caucasus. His teaching was subsequently affirmed at the 6th Ecumenical Council in Constantinople in 680-681. He was a prolific and highly influential writer. | EGP ODCC AL1 |
| 13 | | Other authors of *Various Texts*: Scholiast Dionysius the Areopagite | c.500 (Dionysius) 10th c. (Scholiast) | *Various Texts* is considered by the English translators of the *Philokalia* to be more a "Maximian anthology" than an authentic work of Maximos himself. Authentic Maximian sources incorporated here include *Letters*, *To Thalassios: On Various Questions relating to Holy Scripture*, and *Ambigua*. However, also included are various *scholia* (commentaries on *To Thalassios*) which are not by Maximos, and also extracts from Dionysius the Pseudo-Areopagite (*c*.500). | EGP ODCC |
| 14 | 12 | Thalassios the Libyan | 7th c. | Thalassios was a priest and Abbot at a monastery in Libya. He was a friend of Maximos the Confessor, and various works by Maximos are addressed to him, dedicated to him, or written in response to questions that he raised. Maximos may have been a disciple of Thalassios, or else possibly Thalassios was a disciple of Maximos. *For Paul*, the work of Thalassios included in the *Philokalia*, is his only known work. | EGP |
| 15 | 13 | Author of *On Virtues and Vices* | d. 750 | *On Virtues and Vices* is attributed in the Greek *Philokalia* to John of Damaskos (c.675-c.749), but is also attributed elsewhere to Athanasios of Alexandria (c296-373) and Ephrem the Syrian (c.306-373). Actual authorship is hard to determine, but draws on Mark the Ascetic, Evagrios, Maximos the Confessor, and possibly also John Climacus, and John the Solitary (*c*.500). | EGP |

| No. | C&C No. | Author | Date | Biographical details | Source of biographical information |
|---|---|---|---|---|---|
| 16 | 14 | Author of *Abba Philimon* | 6th-7th c. | This work is anonymous. Nothing is known about Abba Philimon other than what is included in this text. It is the earliest text to include the precise formula of the Jesus Prayer: "Lord Jesus Christ, Son of God, have mercy upon me". | EGP |
| 17 | 15 | Author of *On Virtues, Contemplation & Priesthood* | ?14th c. | This text is attributed by Nikodimos to Theognostos of Alexandria (3rd c.) but it cannot be by him as it quotes John of Damaskos. It includes a long passage (#26) by John of Karpathos, which is a later insertion. | EGP |
| 18 | 16 | Philotheos of Sinai | ?9th/10th c. | Philotheos is thought to have been a monk at the monastery on Mount Sinai. He quotes John Climacus and his work shows common concerns with Hesychios the Priest, notably that of "watchfulness" (or inner attentiveness, or guarding of the intellect). | EGP |
| 19 | 17 | Ilias the Presbyter | Late 11th/early 12th c. | Ilias is thought to have been a lawyer, probably a judge in an ecclesiastical court, before becoming a monk and being ordained. It is possible that he is one and the same as Ilias, Metropolitan of Crete, who wrote commentaries on Gregory of Nazianzus and John Climacus. | EGP |
| 20 | 18 | Theophanis the Monk | ? | In the Greek *Philokalia* the poem *Ladder of Divine Graces* is included without introduction, and nothing at all is known concerning its author. | EGP |
| 21 | 19 | Peter of Damaskos | 11th/12th c. | Peter of Damaskos makes the second largest contribution to the *Philokalia* after Maximos the Confessor, and yet little is known about him. Nikodimos understood him to be Bishop Peter the Hieromartyr (8th c.), who died in exile in southern Arabia, but it is now known that he must be a later figure, as he refers to Symeon Metaphrastis. He was clearly a monk and his name suggests some family (although not necessarily personal) connection with Damaskos. He refers to a wide range of sources but probably drew upon existing anthologies and may not have had access to all the original works. | EGP |

| No. | C&C No. | Author | Date | Biographical details | Source of biographical information |
|---|---|---|---|---|---|
| 22 | 20a | Symeon Metaphrastis | fl. c.960 | Symeon appears to have been a high ranking civil servant who became a monk late in life. He is probably to be identified with a chronicler, Symeon Magistros. His most famous work is *Menologian* (or *Lives of the Saints*), an edited but uncritical compilation of hagiography. | EGP ODCC |
| 23 | 20b | Pseudo-Makarios | c380/390-430 | The Macarian homilies were the work of an unknown 4th, or early 5th c. author writing in Syria or Mesopotamia. They show evidence of Messalianism, but are fundamentally orthodox in content, being concerned with the inner work of the Holy Spirit in the human heart, and have had enduring influence. Nikodimos and Makarios did not include the original homilies in the *Philokalia*, but rather a paraphrased selection attributed to Symeon Metaphrastis. | |
| 24 | 21a 35a | Symeon the New Theologian | 949-1022 | Born in Asia Minor to lesser nobility in the provinces, Symeon was placed in the care of an uncle in Constantinople at the age of 11 years, and subsequently entered imperial service. At the age of 14 years he met, and came under the influence of, Symeon the Studite (c.917-986/7). Aged 20 years he had the first of a series of visions of the "divine and uncreated light". In 977 he became a novice in the same monastery (Studios) as his mentor, Symeon, but was forced to leave within a year because of jealousies surrounding his relationship with Symeon. After moving to another monastery (St Mamas) he was quickly professed as a monk, ordained priest (c980) and then elected abbot. Under his leadership the monastery was transformed from a state of decline to revival and Symeon was much sought after as a spiritual advisor. He was a compassionate but exacting abbot, demanding that no monk should receive communion with shedding tears. His teaching on lay confession, amongst other things, attracted criticism and in 1005 he consequently resigned his position as abbot. In 1009 he was tried and condemned to exile. Although the sentence was revoked, he continued to live there until his death in 1022. Symeon left extensive writings. His title "theologian" reflects his concern with the inner life and experience of prayer. | EGP ODCC |
| 25 | | Symeon the Studite | c.917-986/7 | ##119-152 of *Practical & Theological Texts*, attributed in the Greek *Philokalia* to Symeon the New Theologian, is actually by his mentor, Symeon the Studite. This Symeon was a lay monk at the monastery of Studios, and was also known as Symeon the Pious, or Symeon the Devout. | EGP |

| No. | Author | C&C No. | Date | Biographical details | Source of biographical information |
|---|---|---|---|---|---|
| 26 | Nikitas Stithatos | 22 | 11th c. | Nikitas Stithatos was born in the early 11th c., and entered the monastery at Studios at an early age (c1020). He was subsequently ordained priest, but remained at Studios for the rest of his life. He was, briefly, a disciple of Symeon the New Theologian and after the death of the latter Nikitas experienced a vision in which the saint appeared to him. He subsequently compiled an edition of Symeon's works and also became his biographer. He was known as "stithatos" (meaning brave) because of his outspokenness against the Emperor in regard to his affair with his mistress, Skliraina. He may have been abbot at Studios prior to his death. In addition to the above mentioned writings, and the works included in the *Philokalia*, he also wrote a defence of Orthodoxy, and a number of theological treatises. Like Symeon the New Theologian, he is concerned with divine light, inner prayer and with the place of tears in the spiritual life. His work shows the influence of Evagrios, Maximos the Confessor, Dionysius the Pseudo-Areopagite, Isaac the Syrian, and John Climacus. The first part of #153 of *Practical & Theological Texts*, attributed in the *Philokalia* to Symeon the New Theologian, is actually taken from the *Life of Symeon the New Theologian* by Nikitas Stithatos. | EGP |
| 27 | Theoliptos, Metropolitan of Philadelphia | 23 | b. c.1250 d. 1322 | Theoliptos was married prior to becoming a monk. He was imprisoned because of his opposition to re-union between the eastern and western churches. He became bishop of Philadelphia in 1284, a position which he retained for almost 40 years and which included his defence of Philadelphia against the Turks in 1310. He was a widely respected spiritual director and teacher of hesychasm. | EGP |
| 28 | Nikiphoros the Monk | 24 | 13th c. – 2nd half | Nikiphoros the Monk, also known as Nikiphoros the Hesychast, or Nikiphoros the Athonite, was born in Italy, and started life as a Roman Catholic. He subsequently traveled to the Byzantine Empire, embraced the Orthodox tradition, and became a monk at Athos, where he withdrew into isolation. He was imprisoned and exiled (1276-1277) for his opposition to reunion with the western church. He is thought to have died before 1300. | EGP |

| No. | C&C No. | Author | Date | Biographical details | Source of biographical information |
|---|---|---|---|---|---|
| 29 | 25 | Gregory of Sinai | b. c.1265 d. 1346 | Gregory of Sinai was born perhaps c1265 near Klazomenai, in Asia Minor. As a young man he was taken prisoner in a Turkish raid but released after payment of a ransom. He entered a monastery in Cyprus, but was professed at a monastery in Sinai. From there he went to Crete where he was pupil of a monk called Arsenios, from whom he learned about the practice of inner prayer, and then (c1300) he moved to Mount Athos, where he remained for a quarter of a century. Like Nikiphoros, he chose to live in seclusion. He left Athos, c1325-8, and returned only briefly in the 1330s. He spent the last years of his life in the wilderness of the Strandzha mountains, on the border with Bulgaria, where he gathered a large band of disciples. He died there on 27 November 1346. | EGP |

| No. | C&C No. | Author | Date | Biographical details | Source of biographical information |
|---|---|---|---|---|---|
| 30 | 26 | Gregory Palamas | c.1296-1359 | Gregory Palamas was born and raised in Constantinople. His father was a personal friend of the Emperor. In his youth, Gregory was influenced by Theoliptus of Philadelphia. Rejecting a promising career in secular life, he entered monastic life on Mount Athos in about 1318. Simultaneously, his mother, brothers and sisters also entered religious life in response to his encouragement. Gregory, like Nikiphoros and Gregory of Sinai, lived on Athos as a hesychast in relative seclusion. The advance of the Turkish armies forced him to flee to Thessalonica, where he was ordained priest in 1326. He retired again as a hermit on a mountain near Beroea, but returned to Athos in 1331. From 1335-1351 he was deeply involved in the hesychast controversy, and although his position in this controversy was upheld at the Councils of Constantinople in 1341, 1347 and 1351, he briefly suffered condemnation and excommunication in 1344. His teaching was also upheld by his fellow monks on Mount Athos, who, at their synod of 1340-1341 agreed and signed a supportive statement known as the *Hagiorite Tome*, written by Gregory himself, which was subsequently included in the *Philokalia*. Gregory was made Archbishop of Thessolonica in 1347, but owing to political turmoil could not take possession of his see until 1350. He was sacramental in his preaching and deeply concerned for the poor and oppressed. In 1354 he was taken prisoner by the Turks and remained in captivity for a year. During this time he was engaged in doctrinal discussion with local Muslims. He died in 1359 and was made a saint only 9 years later. He left numerous writings. His teaching on hesychasm was based on his belief in the fundamental unity of human beings as body and soul together. He distinguished between God's unknowable essence and his uncreated energies. Whilst the former is beyond human experience, the latter, he argued, is not. Like Symeon the New Theologian, he emphasized the importance of vision of the Divine Light. | EGP ODCC |

| No. | C&C No. | Author | Date | Biographical details | Source of biographical information |
|---|---|---|---|---|---|
| 31 | 27 | Kallistos & Ignatius Xanthopoulos | d. 1397 & late 14th c. respectively | Kallistos Xanthopoulos became Patriarch Kallistos II of Constantinople for only 3 months before his death in 1397. Ignatius Xanthopoulos was a close friend (and possibly brother) of Kallistos. Ignatius and Kallistos were hesychast monks together at the Monastery of the Xanthopouloi in Constantinople. Ignatius survived Kallistos and became head of the community. | DB MEC |
| 32 | 28a | Kallistos, Patriarch | 14th c. – 2nd half | *Texts on prayer* is attributed to "Patriarch Kallistos", but it is not entirely clear whether this is Kallistos of Xanthopoulos (Kallistos II, Patriarch 1397) or Kallistos I (Patriarch 1350-1353, 1355-1363). Kallistos I presided at the synod of 1351, which found in favour of the heyschasts. | AL2 |
| 33 | 29 | Kallistos Telecudes | 14th c. – 2nd half | Kallistos Telecudes (Telicudes) is probably the same person as Angelicudes Melenikeates (aka Kallistos Angelicudes, Kallistos Meliteniates). This Kallistos was a Palamite monk and mystical writer who wrote a handbook of hesychastic doctrine. | DS NCE |
| 34 | 30 | Author of *Selected Texts of the Holy Fathers on Prayer and Watchfulness* | 14th c. – 2nd half | *Selected Texts of the Holy Fathers on Prayer and Watchfulness* is included in the Greek *Philokalia* as an anonymous text, but it is now thought that it may be by Kallistos Telecudes (above). | DS |
| 35 | 31 | Kallistos Cataphygiotes | Late 14th/ early 15th c. | Nothing known. Could be named after the Church of the Theotokos, called Kataphygi (refuge). Could be Kallistos Xanthopoulos, but Nikodimos doesn't seem convinced. | DS, NGP |

| No. | C&C No. | Author | Date | Biographical details | Source of biographical information |
|---|---|---|---|---|---|
| 36 | 32 | Symeon, Archbishop of Thessalonica | d. 1429 | Symeon, Archbishop of Thessalonica from around 1416 or 1417 until his death in 1429, was one of the most significant writers of his time. His principal work, *Dialogue against all Heresies and on the One Faith*, includes work on doctrine, liturgy and sacraments, as well as polemical passages concerning other faiths and the western Christian tradition. Symeon was born in Constantinople, and probably became a monk in his early youth. He appears to have been a disciple of Kallistos and Ignatios Xanthopoulos and to have spent his early years in monastic seclusion as a hesychast. In contrast his years as Archbishop were in the context of a complex political situation in which he displayed both deep humility and a controversial outspokenness which was at times widely unpopular. He was canonized in 1981. | ODCC DB |
| 37 | 33 | Mark Eugenikos of Ephesus | d. 1445 | Although *On the words of the holy prayer "Lord Jesus Christ, Son of God, have mercy on me"* is included in the Greek *Philokalia* as an anonymous work, it is now known to be by Mark Eugenikos. | DS |
| 38 | 34 | Author of the *Interpretation of the Kyrie Eleison* | ?12th c. | The *Interpretation of the Kyrie Eleison* is included in the Greek *Philokalia* as an anonymous work. Irénée Hausherr (p.297) argues that it is a 12th c. work by Eustathius of Thessalonica. | IH |
| 39 | 35b | Author of *The Three Methods of Prayer* | 13th c. 2nd half | Although attributed to Symeon the New Theologian since at least the 14th c. *The Three Methods of Prayer* is now thought to be by another author, possibly from amongst Symeon's disciples, or possibly the monk Nikiphoros (see above). | EGP IH MEA |
| 40 | 37 | Theophanis of Batopedi | 14th c. | Extract of the *Life of Maximos of Kapsokalyvia* is included in the Greek *Philokalia* as an anonymous work, but is now known to be by Theophanis of Batopedi. | DS |
| 41 | 38 | Philotheos Kokkinos | d. 1379 | Although the *Extract of the Life of Gregory of Thessalonica* is included in the Greek *Philokalia* as an anonymous work, it is now known to be by Ecumenical Patriarch Philotheos Kokkinos. Philotheos also wrote a biography of Nikodimos of Ematha (fourteenth century) and an office for Gregory Palamas. | BDEC |

# Notes

## Prologue

1. John 10
2. Thus, in 358-359 C.E., Basil the Great and Gregory of Nazianzus compiled an anthology of the works of Origen which was also known as the *Philokalia* (Cross and Livingstone, 1997, p.1280)
3. A second edition was printed in Athens in 1893, in two volumes, and then a third edition was published between 1957 and 1963 in five volumes (see Chapter 1).
4. In *On Love: C2*, #55 (EGP, 2, 75)
5. Ilias the Presbyter, in *Gnomic Anthology: 4*, ##136-137 (EGP 3, 65)

## Chapter 1:

## Influences and Foundations

1. Louth, 1996, p.19
2. EGP 1, 15
3. EGP, 4, 433
4. EGP, 4, 435-6
5. Cross and Livingstone, 1997, pp.763-764
6. Sheldrake, 2005, pp.335-336; EGP 1, 14-15
7. Cross and Livingstone, 1997, p.1152; Nikodimos wrote in one of his later works "We must hate and detest the misbeliefs and unlawful customs of the Latins and others who are Heterodox; but if they have anything sound and confirmed by the Canons of the Holy Synods, this we must not hate." (quoted in Cavarnos, 1994, p.31). Two of his works, *The Unseen Warfare* and *Spiritual Exercises*, were adaptations of writings by Roman Catholic authors (ibid. pp.31-35).
8. Cavarnos, 1972, p.31
9. *Evergetinos* and *Concerning Continual Communion*. The former was an eleventh century work on the lives and teachings of the Desert

Fathers. The latter is a text attributed to Makarios himself (Cavarnos, 1994).
10. See Ibid. and Chamberas, Bebis and Harakas, 1989, pp.5-65, from where these biographical details are drawn.
11. Cavarnos, 1994, p.60
12. Cavarnos, 1972, pp.23-24. Cavarnos does not appear to have any firm evidence for this view.
13. Ware, 1991, p.10
14. Ibid. p.11, Ware, 2005, pp.96-97
15. Cavarnos, 1972, pp.24, 100
16. Sheldrake, 2005, pp.488-490; EGP 1, 14
17. Cavarnos, 1972, p.101
18. Smith, Palmer, Sherrard and Ware, 2006, p.viii
19. EGP 1, 13
20. EGP 1, 14
21. Ware, 1991; see also Ware, 2005
22. Abbreviated titles that will be used here to refer to these texts are also given in Appendix 1
23. Cavarnos, 1972, pp.24-25, 100
24. EGP 1, 11. It is this third edition which was used as the basis for the English translation.
25. Cross and Livingstone, 1997, p.1685, Schema-monk Metrophanes, 1976, Featherstone and Tachiaos, 1989
26. Schema-monk Metrophanes, 1976, pp.232-238. Metropolitan Gabriel, having received the translation from Velichkovsky, then assigned a team of scholars to the process of checking it for accuracy before publication.
27. Parry, Melling, Brady, Griffith and Healey, 1999, p.460
28. Schema-monk Metrophanes, 1976, pp.64-67
29. For more detailed analysis of the constituent works included in the Greek, Slavonic, Russian and Romanian versions of the *Philokalia* discussed here, as well as some more recent translations, see Conticello and Citterio, 2002, Ware, 1984
30. Kallistos Ware – personal communication
31. Schema-monk Metrophanes, 1976, pp.180, 183
32. Ibid. p.93
33. See, for example: Chamberas, Bebis and Harakas, 1989, p.21; and EGP 1, 12.
34. Ware, 1984
35. Biographical details here are drawn primarily from Schema-monk Metrophanes, 1976. See also Parry, Melling, Brady, Griffith and Healey, 1999, p.488, Cross and Livingstone, 1997, p.1606
36. Schema-monk Metrophanes, 1976, p.73.
37. For example, Athanasius' *Life of Anthony*, various texts attributed to Antony, a fuller version of Cassian's *Conferences*, and extracts from works of Dorotheos of Gaza, John Climacus and Isaac the Syrian were all included. On the other hand, Maximos' *On the Lord's Prayer*, all of Peter of Damaskos' works (*Book I & Book II*), and

Palamas' *Declaration of the Holy Mountain*, as well as other works and portions of works, were omitted. See Ware, 1984, Conticello and Citterio, 2002

38. Additions include Gregory Palamas' *Triads*, as well as works by Dorotheos of Gaza, John Climacus, and Isaac the Syrian, and an exposition by various authors of the history of hesychasm in Romania. Omissions include (amongst others) the *Various Texts* by Maximos (actual and attributed) and various works of Gregory Palamas. See Conticello and Citterio, 2002, Ware, 1984, Bielawski, 1997
39. Bielawski, 1997, p.9
40. Stăniloae's translation of the Greek *Philokalia* includes additional material by various authors (notably Maximos the Confessor, Symeon the New Theologian, and Gregory Palamas) but also omits some texts and portions of texts.
41. Including John Climacus, Dorotheos of Gaza, Isaac of Nineveh, Barsanuphios and John of Gaza, and Isaiah the Hermit (Bielawski, 1997, p.39).
42. Conticello and Citterio, 2002, Ware, 1984. The English translation by Palmer et al (Palmer, Sherrard and Ware, 1979, Palmer, Sherrard and Ware, 1981, Palmer, Sherrard and Ware, 1984, Palmer, Sherrard and Ware, 1995) will provide the primary source of reference for this book (see Appendix 1) but with reference to the original Greek text where appropriate. This translation is currently published in four volumes, with a fifth volume still awaiting publication.
43. Theophan the Recluse, in an introduction to *Dobrotolubiye*, states that "it was necessary to amplify the '*Philokalia*' as compared with the Greek edition, because, although the Greek '*Philokalia*' was fuller than the existing Slavonic translation, it did not contain all the guidance left to us by the holy fathers concerning the spiritual life." (Kadloubovsky and Palmer, 1979, p.16). Having justified his additions in this way, he goes on to say "This then is the method adopted in compiling the new '*Dobrotolubiye*'. It will conform to the old one, with additions. We have only one end in view: not to deprive the reader of anything we find which may be of value in guiding his life in God." (ibid, p.17).
44. Lee, 2003, pp.139-149
45. *On the Character of Men*, #93 (EGP 1, 344)
46. *On Prayer: 153 Texts*, #132 (EGP 1, 69)
47. See, for example, Peter of Damaskos, in *Book I* in the *Sixth Stage of Contemplation* (EGP 3, 135), or Theodoros the Great Ascetic in *Theoretikon* (EGP 2, 39). In the latter, "intellect" and "soul" appear to be used almost interchangeably.
48. *On the Character of Men*, #117 (EGP 1, 347)
49. EGP 2, 43-44
50. *On Virtues, Contemplation & Priesthood*, #11 (EGP 2, 361)
51. In *Book I* on the *Sixth Stage of Contemplation* (EGP 3, 135-6)
52. See also, for example, Gregory of Sinai, in *On Commandments & Doctrines*, #81 (EGP 4, 228)

53. Gregory Palamas, in *Topics*, #24 (EGP 4, 356)
54. Gregory of Sinai, in *On Commandments & Doctrines*, #82 (EGP 4, 228)
55. See, for example: Isaiah the Solitary in *Guarding the Intellect*, #26 (EGP 1, 28); Hesychios the Priest in *Watchfulness & Holiness*, #34 (EGP 1, 168); Philotheos of Sinai in *Forty Texts on Watchfulness*, #16 (EGP 3, 21-22); Peter of Damaskos in *Book I* in *The Four Virtues of the Soul* (EGP 3, 100) and in *Book II* in *XV. Love* (EGP 3, 253); and Nikitas Stithatos in *On Virtues: 100 Texts*, #15 (EGP 4, 82). (See also the entry on "Appetitive Aspect of the Soul", in the Glossary to the English Translation.) There are occasional apparently alternative models offered, as for example where Maximos the Confessor in *On Love: C3*, #32 (EGP 2: 88) refers to the three powers of the soul as being "first the power of nourishment and growth; second, that of imagination and instinct; third, that of intelligence and intellect". This is clearly the rare exception rather than the rule, but here appears to reflect the influence of an Aristotelian model. In *Nichomachean Ethics* (Thomson, Treddenick and Barnes, 1983, pp.88-90) Aristotle offers a division of the soul into rational and irrational parts, the latter being further subdivided into that which is receptive of reason, and that which is not (the latter being the "vegetative" aspect). These divisions would appear to approximate to Maximos's division into the power of nourishment and growth (i.e. the vegetative part), the imagination and instinct (i.e. the irrational which is receptive of reason), and the intelligence and intellect (i.e. the rational part). This model was further elaborated by Nemesius of Emesa (fl c390) whose work was clearly known to Maximos (Telfer, 1955, pp.203, 345-347).
56. As, for example, in Isaiah the Solitary in *Guarding the Intellect*, #26 (EGP 1, 28), where "intellect" is used, or in Peter of Damaskos where, in *Book I* in *The Four Virtues of the Soul* (EGP 3, 100), "intelligence, or intellect" is referred to as though the terms are in this context completely interchangeable.
57. Although "reason" is used in discussion about the soul – for example, it is referred to in *On Virtues & Vices*, a text attributed to John of Damaskos (EGP 2, 334) and by Nikitas Stithatos in *On Virtues: 100 Texts*, #10 (EGP 4, 81) as one of the "senses" or "faculties" of the soul.
58. EGP 4, 434
59. In *Gnomic Anthology: 3*, #3 (EGP 3, 47); see also #26 (p.50), where reason is seen as a kind of intermediary between sense-perception and intellect. What Palmer et al translate here as "fantasy" might better be understood as "imagination".
60. EGP 4, 432
61. Ibid.
62. EGP 2, 202-203, #73
63. In the previous paragraph the intelligence, desire and the incensive power are actually referred to as the three powers of the soul.
64. e.g. in *On the Character of Men*, #94 (attributed to St Antony; EGP

1, 344), where it is explicitly stated that the "Intellect is not the soul"; and in *For Paul: C1*, #81, by Thalassios (EGP 2, 311).
65. Diadochos of Photiki, in *On Spiritual Knowledge* (EGP 1, 280)
66. In *On Virtues & Vices* (attributed to John of Damaskos; EGP 2, 335)
67. Nikitas Stithatos, in *On Virtues: 100 Texts*, #85 (EGP 4, 102)
68. Nikitas Stithatos, in *On the Inner Nature of Things*, #37 (EGP 4, 116)
69. Nikitas Stithatos, in *On the Inner Nature of Things*, #67 (EGP 4, 126)
70. Nikiphoros the Monk, in *Watchfulness & Guarding* (EGP 4, 205)
71. Hesychios the Priest, in *Watchfulness & Holiness*, #145 EGP 1, 187)
72. Theodoros the Great Ascetic, EGP 2, 18, #23
73. Peter of Damaskos, in *Book II* in *XXIV. Conscious Awareness in the Heart* (EGP 3, 277)
74. From Nikitas Stithatos, *On the Inner Nature of Things*, #93 (EGP 4, 134-135)
75. Ferguson, McHugh and Norris, 1999, pp.895-899
76. e.g. Luke 9:23
77. Ward, 2003, pp.viii-ix
78. Ibid. p.ix
79. Ibid. p.viii
80. Gregg, 1980
81. Monasticism, of course, predates Christianity. See Ferguson, McHugh and Norris, 1999, pp.769-774. Furthermore, it would now appear that asceticism in Europe was widespread prior to the fourth century C.E. and that Christian monasticism should not be seen as arising solely, or perhaps even primarily, as a result of the tradition that has its origins in the Egyptian desert. (See Louth, 2004).
82. As, for example, in a saying attributed to Serapion, given in response to a brother whose window ledge was (rather unusually) lined with books: "What can I say to you? You have taken what belongs to widows and orphans and put it on your window-ledge." (Ward, 2003, p.56)
83. See, in particular, Louth, 2004, upon which the following account is based.
84. Ward, 1984, Ward, 2003
85. Ward, 2003, pp.x-xi
86. This is illustrated, for example, by the anonymous story of the pilgrim who relied almost exclusively upon the Bible and the *Philokalia* in the course of his travels on foot through nineteenth century Russia (Savin and Hopko, 2001).
87. Ward, 1984, p.80
88. #146 (EGP 1, 187)
89. EGP 1, 21
90. EGP 1, 29; Casiday, 2006, pp.9-13
91. *Eight Vices* is taken from *Institutes*, and *Holy Fathers of Sketis* is taken from *Conferences* (EGP 1, 72). See also Cross and Livingstone, 1997, p.205, Ferguson, McHugh and Norris, 1999, p.219

92. EGP 1, 109
93. EGP 3, 282-3. They are now generally thought to be of fourth century Syrian origin (Maloney and Ware, 1992, p.7)
94. EGP 3, 71
95. EGP 4, 192-206
96. Louth, 1996, pp.23-24, 34
97. There is also evidence that the *Apophthegmata Patrum* were put together from an Evagrian perspective (Andrew Louth – Personal Communication).
98. Sinkewicz, 2003, p.199, #60. All translations and quotations from Evagrios in this section are from Sinkewicz, 2003, even where the texts are also to be found in the *Philokalia*, unless otherwise stated.
99. I am grateful to my colleague Augustine Casiday, on whose excellent book *Evagrius Ponticus* the following account is largely based (Casiday, 2006). See especially Chapter 2 (pp.5-22).
100. Sinkewicz, 2003, pp.xix-xx. One might well ask what sexual temptations could possibly present themselves to a man secluded in a remote region of the Sahara desert. Quite apart from the possibilities of temptations presented by women who occasionally visited, homoerotic encounters, masturbation, or a return to urban areas with a view to engaging in sexual encounters there, it would appear that the temptations which most concerned Evagrios and others in the desert were in fact those which took place entirely within their own thoughts. The temptations were thus to lust and sinful fantasy in the mind as much as to sexual immorality in actual behaviour. Not only did the isolation of the desert not provide any protection from such temptations, but it would seem that it actually provided a place of immediate and direct encounter with them.
101. Ibid. pp.1-11. Included in the *Philokalia* as *Outline teaching on asceticism and stillness in the solitary life*. From hereon this work will be referred to simply as *Foundations*
102. Ibid. pp.91-114. From hereon this work will be referred to simply as *Praktikos*
103. Ibid. pp.183-209. From hereon this work will be referred to simply as *On Prayer*
104. Ibid. pp.66-90. From hereon this work will be referred to simply as *Eight Thoughts*
105. Ibid. pp.136-182
106. *Antirrhetikos*, *Gnostikos*, and the *Kephalaia Gnostika*. A complete English translation of *Antirrhetikos* has recently been published (Brakke, 2009). Where English translations of *Gnostikos* or *Kephalaia Gnostica* are quoted here, they are taken from Luke Dysinger's translations of the Syriac texts (http://www.ldysinger.com/Evagrius/02_Gno-Keph/00a_start.htm).
107. Although Evagrios was not condemned in name at the Council, the anti-Origenist anathemas arguably did condemn elements of his Christology (his distinction between Christ and the Logos), protology (pre-existence of souls) and eschatology (the so-called "apokatastasis"). In any event, the Council was perceived at the time

as condemning him and his more speculative Greek texts began to be destroyed thereafter. (See Konstantinovsky, 2009, pp.19-22, Casiday, 2006, pp.14-22, Sinkewicz, 2003, p.xl)
108. Sinkewicz, 2003, pp.xxi-xxiv
109. Evagrios does not define ἡσυχία (at least not in the Greek ascetic corpus, Ibid.). Its meaning is taken as understood. Furthermore, he does not use the term much, preferring usually to talk of ἀπάθεια ("apatheia", impassibility or imperturbability).
110. *Praktikos*, 6; It is interesting to note, however, that in *On the Vices opposed to the Virtues* he unusually includes a ninth vice – that of jealousy. He more generally seems to consider that this should be subsumed under the headings of vainglory or pride (ibid. pp.61-65).
111. As far as I have been able to establish within the ascetic Evagrian corpus, this is nowhere specifically stated. Where distinctions are made, the thoughts afflicting the concupiscible and irascible aspects of the soul are treated together (e.g. *Thoughts* 18, *Reflections* 40). However, it would seem obvious that this is the case, and it is implicit in the separate treatment of these three thoughts in *Thoughts* 1).
112. *Praktikos* 11
113. Sinkewicz, 2003, *Reflections*, p.214, #40
114. *Eight Thoughts* 5.10 & 5.1 respectively; see also *Thoughts* 10
115. Depression, in contemporary usage, denotes both a symptom (of low mood) and also a diagnosis. The latter is thought to be heterogeneous in aetiology and presentation. Perhaps, it might be argued, Evagrios has something in mind rather more like "reactive" than "endogenous" depression (Gelder, Gath, Mayou and Cowen, 1996, p.204), although presumably anything resembling the latter concept would have been completely alien to him.
116. *Eight Thoughts* 6.1
117. *Eight Thoughts* 6.6
118. In the next paragraph (6.7), Evagrios refers to the monk's "own satisfaction" as being the guiding precept, but again, he leaves a degree of ambiguity as to whether the monk has conscious awareness of the extent to which he is motivated merely by self-satisfaction.
119. Sinkewicz, 2003, p.75, #26
120. Ibid. p.86, #12
121. Glossary to the English translation of the *Philokalia*
122. Glossary to the English translation of the *Philokalia*
123. *Praktikos* 60; Sinkewicz, 2003, p.257
124. *Praktikos* 81
125. Sinkewicz, 2003, p.xxxiv
126. *On Thoughts* 43
127. *On Thoughts* 1
128. Luke 4:1-13
129. *On Thoughts* 2
130. Ibid.
131. *On Thoughts* 3
132. *On Thoughts* 8

133. *On Thoughts* 17
134. *On Thoughts* 9 & 11 respectively
135. *On Thoughts* 34 & 35 respectively
136. *On Thoughts* 9
137. *On Thoughts* 19
138. *On Thoughts* 20 & 29
139. *On Thoughts* 40-42
140. *On Prayer* 3
141. *On Prayer* 35
142. *On Prayer* Prologue
143. e.g. *Praktikos* 87; See also *To Eulogius* 15.15
144. *Praktikos* 60, 81; *Thoughts* 29
145. *Eulogius* 29.31; *Praktikos* 32
146. *On Prayer* Prologue
147. *On Prayer* 56
148. Sinkewicz, 2003, pp.279-280, note 39.
149. See, for example, *On Prayer* 36 & 57
150. *On Prayer* 1-4
151. *On Prayer* 5-8
152. *On Prayer* 9-11
153. *On Prayer* 12-27
154. *On Prayer* 46-50; Evagrios sees this as a continuing problem – even in the later stages of prayer (for which, see 67-68 and 72-73)
155. The implied reader of Evagrios is clearly male, but this is not intended by the present author to imply that the texts have nothing to say to women who read them today.
156. *On Prayer* 31
157. *On Prayer* 54, 77
158. *On Prayer* 55-56, 65, 78
159. *On Prayer* 57; See also *Reflections* 20, 23 & 25
160. *On Prayer* 61
161. *On Prayer* 65
162. *On Prayer* 58, 63, 65, 69
163. *On Prayer* 51
164. *On Prayer* 53-57, 61-65
165. *On Prayer* 66-73
166. *On Prayer* 74-81
167. *On Prayer* 87-88
168. *On Prayer* 82-87
169. *On Prayer* 83
170. *On Prayer* 85-86
171. *On Prayer* 82 & 87 respectively
172. *On Prayer* 153
173. *Praktikos* Prologue, 9; Sinkewicz, 2003, p.249, Dysinger, 2005, p.21
174. *Gnostikos* 4, 5, 31
175. *Gnostikos* 10, 22
176. *Gnostikos* 24, 30
177. *Gnostikos* 24, 29

178. *Gnostikos* 31, 37, 38
179. *Gnostikos* 5, 6, 17, 45
180. *Gnostikos* 25
181. *Gnostikos* 4, 45
182. *Gnostikos* 12-16, 21, 23-27, 31, 34-36
183. *Gnostikos* 16-23, 32, 44; what is dealt with here is not that knowledge which is the object of contemplation, but rather that knowledge which is necessary or good as a basis for contemplation and/or the teaching of others: that one should know what one is talking about (16, 17, 25), that one should understand how to interpret scripture (18-20, 34), and that speech about such things should be free from passion (22, 24, 25).
184. *Gnostikos* 27. See also 41
185. *Gnostikos* 28; Dysinger, 2005, pp.188-192; see also *On Thoughts* 10, and comments on this by Sinkewicz, 2003, p.269. It is argued that Evagrios may have drawn these ideas from Abba Paphnutius, but Sinkewicz also draws attention to their presence in the writings of Abba Ammonas.
186. *Gnostikos* 40, 42, 43
187. *Gnostikos* 44-48. He also quotes "Gregory" (but is this Gregory of Nyssa or Gregory of Nazianzus?), and Serapion.
188. *Gnostikos* 49-50
189. Bundy, 1990, p.176
190. *Kephalaia Gnostika* 1.34; See also 2.83, 3.61, 4.47, 5.40, 5.57, 6.63; Similarly, contemplation is referred to as a form of illumination: 3.84, 5.15
191. *Kephalaia Gnostika* 1.74; See also 2.3, 2.5, 2.16, 2.23, 3.6, 3.24, 3.26, 3.41, 3.42, 4.6, 4.11, 4.43, 4.47, 5.57
192. *Kephalaia Gnostika* 5.12
193. *Kephalaia Gnostika* 2.47, 4.77, 4.87, 5.51, 5.55, 5.61
194. *Kephalaia Gnostika* 6.65
195. e.g. *Kephalaia Gnostika* 1.71, 2.3, 2.11, 3.1, 3.13, 4.18
196. Taking just the sixth century of *Kephalaia Gnostika*, see, for example chapters 4, 10-14, 29, 75.
197. e.g. *Kephalaia Gnostika* 3.1-3.3, 3.72, 4.8, 4.89, 6.39, 6.79
198. *Kephalaia Gnostika* 2.83; Dysinger: Syriac has "through the contemplations"
199. *Kephalaia Gnostika* 2.15
200. *Kephalaia Gnostika* 2.13, 3.26
201. *Kephalaia Gnostika* 2.32, 4.11
202. *Kephalaia Gnostika* 3.42
203. *Kephalaia Gnostika* 4.51
204. Dysinger, 2005, pp.171-195; reference to the logoi of judgement and providence is not lacking in *Kephalaia Gnostika* (see, for example, 1.27, 5.4, 5.7, 5.16, 5.23, 6.43, 6.75), but is perhaps less evident here than one might expect from the prominent place that Dysinger sees it as taking in Evagrian thought. Could it be that this is because Evagrios ascribes it a low place in the hierarchy of contemplation

(1.27), whereas *Kephalaia Gnostika* is written for the monk who is at an advanced stage of progress in contemplative life?
205. *Kephalaia Gnostika* 3.42; elsewhere, Dysinger translates "former rank", rather than "first rank" (ibid. p.38)
206. *Kephalaia Gnostika* 6.19
207. *Kephalaia Gnostika* 3.61; see also 2.4, which presents a four stage progression.
208. Dysinger, 2005, pp.41-42 identifies ten instances of this (2.2, 2.4, 2.20, 3.61, 3.67, 3.84, 3.86, 3.87, 4.19 & 4.51), amongst which first natural contemplation is only explicitly named in three (3.61, 3.67 & 3.87) but is alluded to in three more (2.2, 2.4 & 2.61). However, in his translation, first natural contemplation (or first contemplation of nature) is also apparently clearly referred to in 2.13, 3.27, 3.33, 4.10, and second contemplation of nature in 4.10. First and second natural contemplation are not unambiguously defined, and Dysinger discusses various possible interpretations (p.42).
209. *Kephalaia Gnostika* 1.27; See also reference to a "third" contemplation in 3.21
210. *Kephalaia Gnostika* 1.70; See also a three-fold classification in 1.74
211. *Kephalaia Gnostika* 3.19, 4.27, 6.2
212. Dysinger, 2005, p.44
213. *Kephalaia Gnostika* 3.24, 3.26. See also 2.3, where "spiritual knowledge" is referred to in a similar way.
214. The only obvious exception being the work attributed to Antony the Great in the first volume of the original Greek *Philokalia*, now known not to be of Christian authorship.
215. #23 (EGP 1, 26-27)
216. In *Watchfulness & Holiness*, #60 (EGP 1, 172); see also John Cassian in *Eight Vices* (EGP 1, 75), Mark the Ascetic in *On the Spiritual Law*, #85 (EGP 1, 116), John of Karpathos in *For the Monks in India*, #20 (EGP 1, 302), and Peter of Damaskos in *Book I* in *The Bodily Virtues as Tools for the Acquisition of Virtues of the Soul* (EGP 3, 103) and in *Spurious Knowledge* (ibid. p.191)
217. #20 (EGP 1, 302); see also Peter of Damaskos in *Book II* in *VI. Hope* (EGP 3, 227), the teaching attributed to Abba Philimon in *Abba Philimon* (EGP 2, 346), and Nikitas Stithatos in *On the Inner Nature of Things*, #70 (EGP 4 127). For Nikitas Stithatos, scripture has a different part to play at different stages of the spiritual life, assisting first in the struggle for virtue, then in turning the intellect towards God in prayer, and finally in bestowing divine illumination (Ibid, #90; EGP 4, 133-134)
218. For Thalassios: C2, #73 (EGP 2, 155); Maximos appears to be concerned that the reader will become focussed on the literal sense of the text, rather than upon God revealed in and through the text.
219. *Various Texts:* C4, #82 (EGP 2, 255-256), and *Various Texts:* C5, #31 (p.267)
220. See, for example, Peter of Damaskos in *Book I* in *The Seven Commandments* (EGP 3, 99) and in *Book II* in *XXIV. Conscious*

*Awareness in the Heart* (ibid, p.275)
221. For a more detailed account, to which I am indebted here, see Louth, 1989, pp.96-131.
222. In *Eight Vices* (EGP 1, 76-77)
223. In *Ascetic Discourse* (EGP 1, 210)
224. In *Various Texts: C3*, #29 (EGP 2, 193-194)
225. In *On the Inner Nature of Things*, #90 (EGP 4, 133-134)
226. From: *XII. Contemplation of the Sensible World* (EGP 3, 248)
227. cf. Peter of Damaskos again in *Book I* in *That There are no Contradictions in Holy Scripture* (EGP 3, 144-145)
228. cf. Peter of Damaskos elsewhere, such as in *Book I* in *That the Frequent Repetition found in Divine Scripture is not Verbosity* (EGP 3, 189-190), Maximos the Confessor in *Various Texts: C5*, #31 (EGP 2, 267), and Nikitas Stithatos in *On Spiritual Knowledge*, #78 (EGP 4, 165). Note that this model does not appear to deny the place for study and learning, but rather places it in the context of holiness of life and reliance upon divine grace (see Peter of Damaskos, again, in *Book II* in *XXIII. Holy Scripture* [EGP 3, 267-268]).
229. In *On Spiritual Knowledge*, #9 (EGP 1, 255)
230. #53 (EGP 2, 273); Peter of Damaskos also frequently refers to contemplation of scripture, which he appears to understand as a specific form of the contemplation of created beings. (See, for example, EGP 3, 99, 144, 227, 255, 264, 266, 275). Whilst God is revealed to the Christian in such prayer (see, for example, in *Book II* in *VI. Hope* [EGP 3, 227]) this is still to be distinguished from the contemplation of God himself (see, for example, *Book II, XVI. Knowledge of God* [EGP 3, 255])
231. See, for example, Peter of Damaskos in *Book II* in *XXIII. Holy Scripture* (EGP 3, 264-265)
232. In *Eight Vices* (EGP 1, 86)
233. See, for example, Peter of Damaskos again in *Book I* in *The Sixth Stage of Contemplation* (EGP 3, 138)

Chapter 2:

# The Passions

1. cf. Stapakis and Coniaris, 2004, p.xiii
2. Thomson, Treddenick and Barnes, 1983, p.369
3. Sorabji, 2002, pp.7, 17; whilst Sorabji's concern about this possibility is undoubtedly well founded, the use of the word "emotion" is also not without its shortcomings. In particular, in contemporary usage, it has a rather narrower field of meaning than τα πάθη had in classical thought. Reference here will therefore be to "the passions", except where particular reference is made to emotion or appetite or other particular aspects.

4. Rowe, 2005, pp.26-39
5. Lawson-Tancred, 1991, p.141. Note that πάθη is here translated by Lawson-Tancred as "Emotions".
6. Thomson, Treddenick and Barnes, 1983, p.98. Note that πάθη is here translated by Thomson as "feelings".
7. Leighton, 1982, especially see p.169 (note 2); Thomson, Treddenick and Barnes, 1983, p.187.
8. Lawson-Tancred, 1986, p.128, Leighton, 1982, p.173, note 35
9. Leighton, 1982
10. Nussbaum, 1994, pp.81-91
11. Ibid. pp.91-96
12. Sorabji, 2002, pp.54-65
13. Ibid. p.33
14. Ibid. pp.29-54
15. Ibid. pp.169-193
16. Ibid. pp.94-98
17. Ibid. pp.253-260
18. Ibid. pp.261-272
19. Nussbaum, 1994, pp.91-93
20. Ibid. pp.371-372
21. Ibid. pp.396-398
22. Ware, 1989b
23. Ward, 1984, p.20, #1; however, see also p.238, #3, where Hyperechius appears to distinguish between an uncontrolled tongue and the passions themselves.
24. Ibid. pp.33-34, #1; p.143, #4
25. Ibid. pp.33-34
26. Ibid.
27. Ibid. p.131, #17; p.200, #1; p.233, #13
28. Ibid. p.143, #4
29. Ibid. p.188, #149
30. Ibid. p.33
31. Ibid. p.34
32. Ibid. p.10, #9; in another saying, attributed to Abba Poemen (Ward, 1984, p.172, #34), the passions are said to work in four stages: in the heart, in facial expression, in speech and in action. According to this model the passions are therefore neither wholly an interior nor an exterior affair, but rather begin within the heart and thus affect successively external demeanour, speech and behaviour.
33. Ward, 1984, p.220, #44
34. Ibid. pp.88-89, #16
35. cf. Abba Joseph, who talks about whether or not to "let [the passions] enter" (ibid. p.102, #3)
36. See also a saying attributed to Abba Pityrion, where the passions are distinguished from the demons ibid. p.200
37. e.g. *On Eight Thoughts* 1.3, 2.12, 3.1
38. e.g. *To Eulogius* 13.12, 15.15; *Praktikos* 6
39. e.g. *Praktikos* 4

40. e.g. *Praktikos* 34-39; *On Thoughts* 19
41. *Praktikos* 34, 36, 39, 51, 54, *On Thoughts* 3, 4, 8, 13, 25, 34, *On Prayer* 46, 50, 72-73, *Reflections* 59. Evagrios further seems to have believed that the demons primarily exerted their influence on human beings through physical influence, primarily a cooling effect (Dysinger, 2005, pp.120-121)
42. *To Eulogius* 3.3, 13.12, 14.14, *On the Vices Opposed to the Virtues* 7, *Praktikos* 83, *On Thoughts* 21
43. *Eight Thoughts* 1.34, *On Thoughts* 13, *On Prayer* 71, *Maxims* 1.10, 3.6
44. *Eight Thoughts* 5.8-5.10
45. *Eight Thoughts* 2.15
46. *Praktikos* 54, *On Prayer* Prologue
47. *Foundations* 3, 7
48. *On Thoughts* 19, *On Prayer* 30, 46, 50, 53, 71-73, 146, *Reflections* 23
49. *Eight Thoughts* 5.8-5.15
50. *To Eulogius.* 16.17
51. *To Eulogius.* 20.21
52. *On the Vices Opposed to the Virtues* 7, *Eight Thoughts* 7.1, 8.31, *On Prayer* 72, 73
53. *On the Vices Opposed to the Virtues* 7, *Eight Thoughts* 8.31, *Praktikos* 24
54. *On the Vices Opposed to the Virtues* 7
55. *Eight Thoughts* 1.3; *On Prayer* 50
56. *Eight Thoughts* 1.34, 2.12; *On Prayer* 50
57. *Eight Thoughts* 2.10, 2.15
58. *Eight Thoughts* 3.1, 3.14, *Praktikos* 19; *On Prayer* 50
59. *Eight Thoughts* 4.1, *Praktikos* 11, 23; *On Prayer* 50
60. *Eight Thoughts* 8.26
61. *On Thoughts* 8
62. *Praktikos* 23, *Eight Thoughts* 5.9
63. *On Prayer* 50
64. The notable exception would appear to be acedia, which is never explicitly referred to as a passion in the ascetic corpus of Evagrios' works. However, it is listed along with the other seven thoughts as being capable of stirring up the passions (*Praktikos* 6), and it is referred to as a "kinsman" of sadness which is named as a passion (*On the Vices Opposed to the Virtues* 4.3) – albeit infrequently. Acedia is usually named as a spirit or demon (e.g. *To Eulogius* 8.8-9.9, *Praktikos* 27-28) and it is clear that demonic activity is closely related to the passions in Evagrian thought (see, for example, *Praktikos* 34-39).
65. *Praktikos* 3, 18. In para 3 it is actually the "concupiscible part [of the soul]" that is referred to as a passion.
66. *Praktikos* 3, 13, 18. In para 3 it is actually the "irascible part [of the soul]" that is referred to as a passion.
67. *Praktikos* 35-36, *To Eulogius* 21.23
68. *On Thoughts* 19
69. See *Eight Thoughts* 5.10

70. e.g. *Eight Thoughts* 1.34
71. *Praktikos* 36
72. *On Thoughts* 34
73. *On Prayer* 50
74. *Reflections* 59
75. *On Thoughts* 8
76. Ware, 1989b
77. #35 (EGP 3, 29)
78. #35 (EGP 2, 56)
79. #16 (EGP 2, 67)
80. #42 (EGP 2, 89) The examples of "things" which Maximos gives here are "a man, a woman, gold and so forth".
81. #58 (EGP 2, 176) See also in *Various Texts: C3*, #33 (EGP 2, 217): "He who makes his intelligence the master of his innate passions – that is to say, of his incensive and desiring powers – receives spiritual knowledge." Note, however, that the editors of the English translation do not consider this to be an authentic Maximian text (EGP 2, 393).
82. #60 (EGP 2, 177)
83. #42 (EGP 2, 89)
84. In *Book I*, in *A List of the Passions* (EGP 3, 205-206)
85. cf. *Praktikos*. In *On the Vices Opposed to the Virtues* he unusually inserts jealousy as an additional vice, after vainglory and before pride. The English translations of terms in this row are taken from Sinkewicz, 2003. Note that (in comparison with the English translators of the *Philokalia*) this author prefers "fornication" rather than "unchastity", "sadness" rather than "dejection", "acedia" rather than "listlessness", and "vainglory" rather than "self-esteem".
86. Peter identifies a causal sequence here: gluttony leading to unchastity, which in turn leads to avarice, which in turn leads to anger, etc. However, in *Book II*, in *VIII. Mortification of the Passions* (EGP 3, 233) Peter refers instead to "the six passions that surround [a person] – those, that is, above him and below, to his right and to his left, within him and without."
87. This work appears to be a shortened version of *On Thoughts*
88. Referred to also as "three giants" or "vices" (p.159)
89. Referred to also as the "three most general passions" (p.89)
90. These lists were compiled by searching for references to the passions in the *Philokalia Concordance* on CD-ROM, compiled by Basileios S. Stapakis. Searches were made for "passion" and "passions" and all relevant adjectives, nouns and verbs encountered in reference to these terms were catalogued. Metaphors were included in the lists, but similes were generally not. Most references are to "the passions" generically, but some are made specifically to a particular passion or group of passions. Every effort was made to ensure reasonable comprehensiveness, but, in such a large collection of texts, it is likely that some terms have been overlooked.
91. Words have only been allocated to one thematic heading. It is recognised that in fact the boundaries of the themes overlap and

that some terms could easily be classified under multiple headings. Equally, the boundaries could be redrawn and different themes identified. The aim here has not been to eliminate all subjectivity, but rather to engage in a preliminary qualitative exploration of the kind of language employed by the authors of the *Philokalia* in relation to the passions.
92. See Helman, 1985, pp.12-15, Lloyd, Chadwick, Mann, Lonie and Withington, 1983, p.70, Nutton, 2006, pp.202-215
93. See, for example, his dissertation on the demon "vagabond" in *On Thoughts* 9.
94. EGP 1, 119-120, ##140-141
95. EGP 1, 145, #224
96. EGP 1, 119, ##138-139
97. See the Glossary to any of the four currently published volumes: e.g. EGP 1, 364-366. What Mark refers to as "entertainment" is here referred to as communion, or coupling, which, as we shall see, is the terminology more consistently applied by other authors of the *Philokalia*.
98. As has already been stated, Mark's distinction between entertainment and assent appears to rest primarily either on the linking of the thought with images, or on the acceptance of the thought with pleasure. His understanding of the movement from assent to prepossession is not explicitly considered at all, and his emphasis in defining prepossession appears to rest more with the presence of sins in the memory than with considerations of repetition or habit.
99. EGP 1, 153
100. Again, this may be found in the glossary to any of the volumes of the English translation: e.g. EGP 1, 365
101. Luibheid, Russell and Ware, 1982, pp.10-16
102. Ibid. pp.181-182
103. The English translators of *The Ladder* also do not hesitate to include a footnote giving reference to the work of Mark the Ascetic, albeit also to Maximos the Confessor (about which, see below).
104. Indeed, his only reference here to images is at the stage of provocation, where it seems that the image itself may be a provocation.
105. In Step 15 (Luibheid, Russell and Ware, 1982, p.183)
106. It is also referred to as "wrestl[ing]" rather than "struggle".
107. See *Book I: The Difference Between Thoughts and Provocations* (EGP 3, 207)
108. *On Love: C1*, #83 (EGP 2, 62)
109. *On Love: C1*, ##83-84 (EGP 2, 62-63)
110. *On Love: C2*, #31 (EGP 2, 70-71)
111. "Put to death therefore whatever is earthly in you: unchastity, uncleanness, passion, evil desire and greed" (Colossians 3:5; translation from the English translation of the *Philokalia*)
112. However, the process is somewhat confused – not least because Maximos chooses to interpret Paul's reference to "passion" as actually meaning "impassioned thoughts" in his first account, but then not referring further to impassioned thoughts (as opposed to passion) in

this account, and subsequently apparently distinguishing passions and impassioned thoughts in his second account.
113. "Wrestling" is also moved to an earlier stage in the sequence than that described by John Climacus.
114. The first account in *Watchfulness & Holiness*, #46, does not make reference to the passions. The second account, in ##143-144 of the same work, makes reference only to "impassioned fantasy" and thoughts "passionately" conformed to fantasy.
115. *Spiritual Texts*, #19 (EGP 2, 17-18)
116. *Paraphrase of Makarios*, #55 (EGP 3, 308-309)
117. *Gnomic Anthology: 4*, #123 (EGP 3, 63)
118. ##62-75 (EGP 4, 223-225)
119. And, of course, by John Climacus, not to mention the English translators of the *Philokalia*, whose Glossary of terms has been referred to here on several occasions.
120. *Ladder of Divine Ascent*. All other rows in the table represent material drawn from the *Philokalia* (see references in Tables 2.4a to 2.4e).
121. The process and terminology presented in this row is a summary/composite of three models which may be found in Maximos's writings in the *Philokalia* (see Table 2.4c)
122. Nutton, 2006, pp.115-116, Lloyd, Chadwick, Mann, Lonie and Withington, 1983, pp.260-271. The Hippocratic corpus consists of about sixty dissertations, mostly written between 430 and 330 B.C.E. (Lloyd, Chadwick, Mann, Lonie and Withington, 1983, p.9). Many, perhaps most, of these writings are now known not to have been written by Hippocrates himself.
123. Helman, 1985, pp.12-15
124. *Letter to Nicolas* (EGP 1, 153-154)
125. *Watchfulness & Holiness*, #31 (EGP 1, 167)
126. *For Longinos*, ##7-8 (EGP 4, 261) The desiring power appears here to be associated with "excess" blood, although the reference is a little obscure.
127. *Forty Texts on Watchfulness*, #12 (EGP 3, 19)
128. *Gnomic Anthology: 4*, #134 (EGP 3, 64-65)
129. *On Spiritual Knowledge*, #10 (EGP 4, 142)
130. In *On the Lord's Prayer* (EGP 2, 293-294)
131. Simon, 1978, p.224. These anatomical associations of particular organs with Platonic divisions of the soul were also known to Clement of Alexandria (Osborn, 2005, pp.237-238).
132. The only other possible instance of this sort which I have been able to find concerns the Evagrian reference to demonic influence upon a "certain area" of the brain as a means of affecting "the light surrounding the intellect" (*On Prayer: 153 Texts*, ##73-75 [EGP 1, 64]).
133. The Glossary to the English translation of the *Philokalia* defines temperament as follows:

> TEMPERAMENT (κράσις – *krasis):* primarily the well-balanced blending of elements, humours or qualities in animal bodies, but sometimes extended to denote the whole soul-body structure

of man. In this sense it is the opposite to a state of psychic or physical disequilibrium.

134. On Prayer: 153 Texts, #62 (EGP 1, 62-63) Sinkewicz sees here three degrees of withdrawal that precede pure prayer, in which withdrawal from thoughts arising from temperament appears to be the stage closest to the frontier of pure prayer (Sinkewicz, 2003, p.280, note 45). See also Thalassios the Libyan in *For Paul: C1*, #46 (EGP 2, 309) and in *For Paul: C3*, ##32-33 (EGP 2, 320-321)
135. *On Prayer: 153 Texts*, #69 (EGP 1, 63)
136. *On Spiritual Knowledge*, #76 (EGP 1, 279)
137. *On Spiritual Knowledge*, #82 (EGP 1, 283)
138. *On Love: C2*, #92 (EGP 2, 81)
139. *For Paul: C3*, #36 (EGP 2, 321)
140. *On Commandments & Doctrines*, #81 (EGP 4, 227-228)
141. *On Commandments & Doctrines*, #8 (EGP 4, 213) and ##45-46 (p.221)
142. [Maximos], the anonymous scholiast, for example, refers to the passions in this way in *Various Texts: C2*, #20 (EGP 2, 192).
143. *Various Texts: C2*, #90 (EGP 2, 206)
144. *Various Texts: C2*, #90 (EGP 2, 206-207)
145. See also: *Various Texts: C3*, #21 (EGP 2, 214), a text thought to have been written partly by Maximos and partly by an unknown scholiast.
146. *To Xenia*, #42 (EGP 3, 310)
147. #1 (EGP 1, 22)

Chapter 3:
# Remedies for the Passions

1. Thus, in *Collins English Dictionary*, the main two meanings of the noun *remedy* are given as: 1. "any drug or agent that cures a disease or controls its symptoms" and 2. "anything that serves to put a fault to rights, cure defects, improve conditions, etc." (Anderson, Butterfield, Daintith, Holmes, Isaacs, Law, Lilly, Martin, McKeown, Stibbs and Summers, 2004). A third meaning, which need not be considered further here, is concerned with the legally permitted variation in weight or quality of coins.
2. e.g. by Evagrios in *On Prayer: 153 Texts*, #7 (EGP 1, 58); by Maximos the Confessor in *On Love: C1*, ##66-67 (EGP 2, 60) and in *On Love: C2*, #44 (p.73); and by Gregory of Sinai in *On Commandments & Doctrines*, #107 (EGP 4, 236)
3. e.g. "solutions", "responses", "answers" and a variety of other non-medical terms
4. Nussbaum, 1994
5. Ibid. pp.28-29

6. Not all of these are discussed here. In particular, value relativity, and the instrumental use of reason and the virtues of argument, are also discussed by Nussbaum, as well as various other questions (see pp.13-47).
7. Matthew 9:12, Mark 2:17, Luke 5:31
8. Dysinger, 2005, p.104
9. *On Thoughts* 3 & 10 (these passages are also both included in the *Philokalia*), *Praktikos* 38. An English translation of *Thirty-Three Ordered Chapters* is provided by Sinkewicz, 2003, pp.224-227. See also Dysinger, 2005, pp.115-123
10. Ward, 1984, p.180, #93
11. Ibid. p.233, #13
12. Ibid. p.231, #3
13. Dysinger, 2005, pp.104-114. Larchet also draws attention to the references to sickness, illness or disease of the soul, and other medical language, employed by the Desert Fathers, John Cassian, John Chrysostom, and others (Larchet, 2005, pp.89-125).
14. John of Karpathos in *Ascetic Discourse* ("great Physician"; EGP 1, 325)
15. By John Cassian in *Eight Vices* in the section on *The Demon of Unchastity and The Desire of the Flesh* ("Doctor of our souls"; EGP 1, 76), cf. "Doctor of souls" in the section of the same work entitled *On Anger* (EGP 1, 84), by Diadochos of Photiki in *On Spiritual Knowledge*, #53 (EGP 1, 268), and by Symeon Metaphrastis in *Paraphrase of Makarios*, #100 ("good doctor" [EGP 3, 329] This could be taken as reference to God as doctor, but the gospel reference indirectly implies that it is Jesus).
16. By Maximos the Confessor in *On Love: C2*, #39 ("good and loving physician": EGP 2, 72) and #44 ("Physician of souls": EGP 2, 73); see also the more general reference to God as physician in *Various Texts: C1*, #20 (EGP 2, 169), although Maximian authorship of this text is uncertain (EGP 2, 391); and by Peter of Damaskos in his *Introduction to Book I* ("Physician of our souls": EGP 3, 77 and "our Physician": EGP 3, 78), in *Book I* in *The Great Benefit of True Repentence* ("your Physician": EGP 3, 170), in *Book II* in *VIII. Mortification of the Passions* ("your Physician": EGP 3, 233), and in *Book I* in *The Sixth Stage of Contemplation* ("the Physician": EGP 3, 140)
17. By John Cassian in *Eight Vices*, in the section entitled *On Dejection* ("Doctor of men's souls": EGP 1, 87) and by Nikitas Stithatos in *On the Inner Nature of Things*, #23 ("doctor of our souls": EGP 4, 113)
18. *Various Texts: C1*, #66 (EGP 2, 179)
19. *For Paul: C4*, #44 (EGP 2, 328)
20. *On the Inner Nature of Things*, #22 (EGP 4, 113)
21. *To Xenia*, #29 (EGP 4, 304)
22. Nussbaum, 1994, p.26
23. Jackson, 1969, p.380, Harkins and Riese, 1963
24. It must also be noted, however that many reservations have been expressed about the medical model in this context, and perhaps especially so where the less biological and more psychological

disturbances of mental well-being are concerned.
25. Cook, Powell and Sims, 2009
26. *Republic* 603e – 604d
27. Nussbaum, 1994, pp.96-101
28. Sorabji, 2002, pp.194-195
29. *Nichomachean Ethics* 2.6, 1106
30. *Nichomachean Ethics* 2.6, 1107
31. Nussbaum, 1994, p.82
32. Ibid. p.97
33. *Nichomachean Ethics* 2.1-2.4
34. Sorabji, 2002, pp.288-300
35. Nussbaum, 1994, pp.390, 395
36. Quoted by ibid. p.390
37. Sorabji, 2002, pp.187-189
38. Nussbaum, 1994, pp.389-398; Nussbaum points out that there is a degree of circularity in some of these arguments. It is only because passions are defined as false judgements that they must be eliminated, but the argument for elimination rests upon their evaluation as false. Similarly, passions are not necessary to motivate virtuous action, according to the Stoic position, because external things are held to be of no value. But if some external things are held to be of value then that evaluation does provide the proper motivation for virtue. See also Sorabji, 2002, pp.181-193
39. Nussbaum, 1994, p.399, Sorabji, 2002, pp.47-51
40. Sorabji, 2002, pp.213-220, 222-224, 235-238, 241-242
41. Anaxagoras, on hearing that his son was dead, is quoted as saying "I know I had begotten a mortal" (ibid. p.235)
42. It seems that, in certain circumstances, the Stoics were willing to accept the imagining of, or even belief in, that which is not actually true.
43. Sorabji, 2002, p.222, Nussbaum, 1994, pp.179-181
44. Ward, 1984, pp.33-34, #1
45. Ibid. pp.42-43, #12
46. Perhaps the closest we get to this is in a somewhat enigmatic saying of Abba Sisoes. In response to a disciple who asks why the passions do not leave him, he says "Their tools are inside you; give them their pay and they will go." (ibid. p.213, #6)
47. Ibid. p.185, #127
48. Ibid. p.10, #9
49. Ibid. p.104, #10
50. Ibid. p.200, #1
51. Ibid. p.172, #34
52. Ibid. p.217, #22
53. Ibid. p.220, #44
54. Ibid. p.20, #1
55. Ibid. p.238, #3
56. Ibid. p.86, #3
57. Ibid. p.115, #2

58. Ibid. p.131, #17
59. Ibid. #20
60. Ward, 2003, p.40, #22
61. Ibid. pp.46-47, #37
62. *Praktikos* 38. Cf. *Praktikos* 35, where he identifies abstinence as the remedy for passions of the body, and spiritual love as the remedy for passions of the soul.
63. *Kephalaia Gnostika* 3.35
64. *Praktikos* 15
65. Genesis 32; *Praktikos* 26
66. *Praktikos* 43, 50-51; *On Thoughts* 9; see also comments by Dysinger, 2005, pp.119-120
67. *Praktikos* 38, 52; *On Thoughts* 3
68. *On Thoughts* 19
69. *On Thoughts* 19
70. *On Thoughts* 24
71. Dysinger, 2005, pp.135-136
72. Ibid. pp.137-139
73. *On Prayer* 83 (see also *On Prayer* 82, 85 & 87, and *Praktikos* 15 & 71); see ibid.
74. *Praktikos* 49; See also *On Prayer* 135
75. Evagrios in *On Prayer: 153 Texts*, #7 (EGP 1:58)
76. Diadochus of Photiki in *On Spiritual Knowledge*, #99 (EGP 1:295)
77. Maximos the Confessor in *On Love: C2*, #66 (EGP 2:60)
78. Maximos the Confessor in *On Love: C2*, #67 (EGP 2:60)
79. Maximos the Confessor in *On Love: C2*, ##45-46 (EGP 2:73)
80. Gregory of Sinai in *On Commandments & Doctrines*, #107 (EGP 4:236)
81. *On Prayer: 153 Texts*, #7 (EGP 1:58)
82. *Various Texts: C1*, #66 (EGP 2:179)
83. *On Love: C2*, #44 (EGP 2:73)
84. *On Love: C2*, #47 (EGP 2:73)
85. *For Paul: C4*, ##35-36 (EGP 2:327)
86. We now know that the first of these was not, in fact, by Antony the Great. However, that does not change the fact that its inclusion as the opening work would clearly have originally conveyed the authority of this great Desert Father upon the *Philokalia*, by association.
87. Retitled in the *Philokalia* as: *Outline Teaching on Asceticism and Stillness in the Solitary Life*.
88. *Various Texts: C2*, #14 (EGP 2, 190-191)
89. *Various Texts: C1*, ##73-74 (EGP 2, 180-181) and ##86-88 (EGP 2, 184)
90. *On Love: C4*, #63 (EGP 2, 108)
91. *On Love: C2*, #19 (EGP 2, 68)
92. *On the Lord's Prayer* (EGP 2, 287). See also Louth, 1996, p.34
93. *On Love: C2*, #57 (EGP 2, 75)
94. Louth, 1996, pp.38-42
95. *On Love: C3*, #67 (EGP 2, 93)

96. EGP 3, 89-93
97. EGP 3, 151
98. EGP 3, 103-104
99. EGP 3, 162-164
100. EGP 3, 231-234
101. p.231
102. p.232
103. p.233
104. EGP 4, 212-252
105. ##99-102 (EGP 4, 233-234)
106. #102 (EGP 4, 234)
107. ##106-107 (EGP 4, 235-236)
108. #127 (EGP 4, 246)
109. #131 (EGP 4, 246)
110. This volume of the Greek *Philokalia* has not yet been translated into English. A translation of this text into English from the Russian *Dobrotolubiye* is provided by Kadloubovsky & Palmer (Kadloubovsky and Palmer, 1979)
111. Ibid. p.169
112. *On Love: C2*, #39 (EGP 2, 72)
113. EGP 3, 76
114. *On Commandments & Doctrines*, #86 (EGP 4, 229-230)
115. See the entry on "Watchfulness" in the glossary to the English translation of the *Philokalia*
116. Glossary to the English translation of the *Philokalia*.
117. *The Three Methods of Prayer*. See the section on the *Third Method of Prayer* (EGP 4:71).
118. In *Watchfulness & Guarding* (EGP 4, 204)
119. EGP 3, 15
120. *Watchfulness & Holiness*, #3 (EGP 1, 162-163). He appears here to understand stillness of the heart as identical with watchfulness. Elsewhere, he indicates that guarding of the intellect is necessary in order to achieve watchfulness (#157, p.90), or else that watchfulness is necessary in order to achieve guarding of the heart (#168, p.191). Nikiphoros the Monk, quoting in *Watchfulness & Guarding* from John Climacus, also appears to distinguish between guarding (of the intellect?) and watchfulness, but is more at pains to emphasise that there is a difference than to clarify exactly what the difference is (EGP 4, 200). Reference back to the full text of *The Ladder of Divine Ascent* (Luibheid, Russell and Ware, 1982, pp.239-240) does not make things much clearer. Although John goes on to make a distinction between praying for rescue from bad thoughts, resisting them, and despising them, it is not clear how (or even whether) these three categories relate to the two categories of guarding and watchfulness. As John emphasises that watching is more "significant and laborious" than guarding, and as the despising of bad thoughts is the more advanced of the three categories of dealing with bad thoughts, we might imagine that watchfulness is equivalent to the latter.

121. *Watchfulness & Holiness*, #153 (EGP 1:189)
122. See the entry on "Rebuttal" in the glossary to the English translation of the *Philokalia*
123. Specifically, paragraphs appear to correspond as follows: 1. cf. *Praktikos* 29; 2. cf. *Praktikos* 32; 3. cf. *Praktikos* 91; 4. cf. *Praktikos* 94; 5. cf. *Praktikos* 15. In addition to the reordering of paragraphs, there appears to have been some abbreviation and other editing.
124. Whether or not the speculations offered here as to the significance of this are correct, one imagines that it nonetheless offers a potential key to understanding some of the principles that Nikodimos and Makarios applied in their selection of texts for the *Philokalia* as a whole.
125. #1 (EGP 1, 162)
126. See the entry on "Watchfulness" in the glossary to the English translation of the *Philokalia*
127. *Watchfulness & Holiness*, #3 (EGP 1, 162-163)
128. *Watchfulness & Holiness*, #159 (EGP 1, 190)
129. *Watchfulness & Holiness*, #165 (EGP 1, 191)
130. *Watchfulness & Holiness*, #171 (EGP 1, 192)
131. *Watchfulness & Holiness*, #6 (EGP 1, 163)
132. See, for example, Isaiah the Solitary in *Guarding the Intellect*, #23 (EGP 1, 26-27)
133. *Watchfulness & Holiness*, #12 (EGP 1, 164)
134. *Watchfulness & Holiness*, ##13-17 (EGP 1, 164-165)
135. *Watchfulness & Holiness*, #143 (EGP 1, 186-187)
136. This is my analysis of the process. However, see *Watchfulness & Holiness*, #105 (EGP 1, 180), where Hesychios describes things in not dissimilar terms.
137. *Watchfulness & Holiness*, ##152-153 (EGP 1, 189)
138. *Forty Texts on Watchfulness*, #3 (EGP 3, 17)
139. *Forty Texts on Watchfulness*, #1 (EGP 3, 16)
140. *Forty Texts on Watchfulness*, #6 (EGP 3, 17)
141. *Forty Texts on Watchfulness*, #5 (EGP 3, 17)
142. *Forty Texts on Watchfulness*, #13 (EGP 3, 20)
143. *Forty Texts on Watchfulness*, #26 (EGP 3, 26)
144. EGP 3, 15
145. EGP 4, 67-75
146. EGP 4, 70
147. EGP 4, 70-71
148. EGP 4, 71
149. As we have already seen, this author considers attentiveness, watchfulness, guarding of the heart, etc, as synonymous.
150. EGP 4, 73-74
151. EGP 4, 72-73
152. EGP 4, 195-204
153. EGP 4, 204-206
154. He first clarifies that this is synonymous with watchfulness, guarding of the intellect, etc.
155. EGP 4, 204-205

156. EGP 4, 205
157. EGP 4, 206
158. Interestingly, if the pupil finds difficulty with the technique of establishing the intellect in the heart, Nikiphoros recommends use of the Jesus Prayer as a means to achieve this. The process can thus, apparently, be reversed.
159. EGP 4, 193
160. EGP 4, 194
161. EGP 4, 194
162. *Watchfulness – Extracts*, #5 (EGP 1, 53-54). As discussed above, this is a redaction of *Praktikos* 15
163. Dysinger, 2005, pp.70-71; The fifth text, *Praktikos* 69, concerned with a comparison of psalmody and prayer, will be considered below.
164. *On Prayer: 153 Texts* (EGP 1, 65)
165. Dysinger, 2005, pp.71-72, Sinkewicz, 2003, pp.199-204
166. Dysinger, 2005, pp.62-103
167. Ibid. pp.84-85
168. Ibid. pp.88-89
169. Ibid. pp.93-96
170. *Praktikos* 11
171. Dysinger, 2005, pp.124-125
172. *Praktikos* 15 (*Watchfulness – Extracts*, #5 [EGP 1, 53-54]), *Praktikos* 71, and *Institutio ad Monachos* (see ibid. p.127)
173. *Antirrhetikos* 4.22 (Brakke, 2009, p.104)
174. *On Thoughts* 10. See Dysinger, 2005, p.130
175. Ibid. pp.97-102
176. I am indebted to Dysinger for his comments on these chapters, upon which the following reflections are largely based (ibid. pp.98-100)
177. *Praktikos* 69-71. Translation: Sinkewicz, 2003, p.109
178. *Scholia on Psalms* 137:1. Translation from Dysinger, 2005, pp.100-101
179. Ibid. pp.100-102
180. We might imagine that psalmody, as understood thus far, is a separate affair from antirrhesis, or at least that the two activities might take place in different times and places. However, the complex interplay of mental processes entailed within the description of undistracted psalmody in *Praktikos* 69-71 leaves plenty of scope to image that, at least at times, antirrhesis might be the kind of mental activity that contributed to the overall complex of psychological and spiritual processes that Evagrios understood psalmody to imply.
181. Dysinger, 2005, pp.131-149
182. Ibid. p.132
183. Ibid. pp.136-137
184. Ibid. pp.142-149
185. Stapakis and Coniaris, 2004
186. Dysinger, 2005, pp.48-61
187. *On Commandments & Doctrines*, #99 (EGP 4, 233)
188. *On Stillness*, #5 (EGP 4, 266)
189. *On Love: C1*, #45 (EGP 2, 57); *On Love: C2*, #54 (EGP 2, 74); *On*

Love: C3, #50 (EGP 2, 91)
190. For Paul: C3, #35 (EGP 2, 321)
191. Gnomic Anthology: 1, #4 (EGP 3, 34); Gnomic Anthology:4, #61 (EGP 3, 55)
192. On the Inner Nature of Things, #72 (EGP 4, 127-128)
193. For the Monks in India, #87 (EGP 1, 318-319)
194. On Love: C4, #48 (EGP 2, 106)
195. EGP 3, 91, cf. 3, 119
196. Attributed to Symeon the New Theologian, but not actually written by him – see above.
197. EGP 4, 73-74
198. This assertion raises the interesting question as to when watchfulness (or guarding of the heart, etc.) was first described. However, it would seem reasonable to assert that the practice was already implicit in the writings of Evagrios, even if the technical terminology did not arise until later.
199. Stapakis and Coniaris, 2004
200. On Prayer: 153 Texts, #3 (EGP 1, 57)
201. On the Lord's Prayer (EGP 2, 290)
202. To Xenia, #61 (EGP 4, 318)
203. Book II, XXIV. Conscious Awareness in the Heart (EGP 3, 277)
204. The progression proposed by Peter therefore does not quite work, for pure prayer is equivalent to theological contemplation in the Evagrian schema, and (as understood by Evagrios) a move from imageless prayer to natural contemplation would not be a progression to a higher level of prayer.
205. See also the different stages of the spiritual life proposed by the author of *Three Methods of Prayer* (see above).
206. *Book I*: In *The Seven Forms of Bodily Discipline* (EGP 3, 91) and in *The Third Stage of Contemplation* (EGP 3, 119)
207. See also *Book II: XXIV. Conscious Awareness in the Heart* (EGP 3, 272), where Peter appears to be describing the kind of life required of the beginner. In particular, he emphasises humility, self-control, and endurance in affliction. Psalmody is not mentioned here, but we might imagine that, along with psalmody, such things constitute what Peter has in mind as "prayer of the body".
208. Sheldrake, 2005, pp.382-383, Ware, 1989a, pp.33-38
209. EGP 1, 251-296. See especially, ##31-33, 59, 61, 85, 88, 97. Irénée Hausherr sees this as an intermediate stage in the evolution of the Jesus Prayer from short prayers of variable nature to the Jesus Prayer in its developed form. He notes that within the thinking of Diadochos this form of prayer assumes an importance for reintegrating, or healing, a divided intellect (Hausherr, 1978, pp.220-229).
210. EGP 1, 199-250
211. Hausherr, 1978, pp.268-269, Wheeler, 1977, p.42
212. EGP 2, 343, 347-348. See also Hausherr, 1978, pp.274-277
213. p.347
214. A Monk of the Eastern Church, 1987, p.40; EGP 1, 161-198, see ##7, 42, 94, 102, 116, 122, 137, 143, 168, 174, 182, 183, 188, 189

215. 1 Thessalonians 5:17; Irénée Hausherr suggests that it was from a desire to achieve continual prayer that the Jesus Prayer took its origins (Hausherr, 1978, pp.119-189).
216. cf. Evagrios in *On Prayer*, 70
217. Ware, 1989a
218. Pentkovsky and Smith, 1999
219. EGP 1, 15
220. In the first four volumes, these are: Hesychios the Priest, Diadochos of Photiki, John of Karpathos, Maximos the Confessor, the author of *Abba Philimon*, Philotheos of Sinai, Ilias the Presbyter, Peter of Damaskos, the author of *Three Methods of Prayer*, Nikitas Stithatos, Nikiphoros the Monk, Gregory of Sinai, and Gregory Palamas. In Volume 5, the work entitled *Directions to Hesychasts, in a Hundred Chapters*, by Kallistos & Ignatius of Xanthopoulos, also makes significant reference to the Jesus Prayer. Reference to "constant memory of Jesus" is also made in the brief work *Texts on Prayer*, also by a Kallistos (although not necessarily the same Kallistos). As yet, I have not been able to search the other works belonging to Volume 5. It is thus possible to assert that 13 out of 29 authors contributing to the first four volumes do refer to the Jesus Prayer (or invocation of the name of Jesus, etc) in some way or another. At least 15 of the total 39 authors contributing to the five volumes make such reference (but I have not yet checked the works of 8 of these).
221. *Ascetic Discourse*, #94 (EGP 1, 178)
222. *Ascetic Discourse*, #102 (EGP 1, 180)
223. *Watchfulness & Holiness*, #28 (EGP 1, 166). Elsewhere he refers to the impossibility of "repuls[ing] the provocation of an evil thought without invoking Jesus Christ" (#142: EGP 1, 186), and to invocation of Jesus Christ as driving evil thoughts from the heart (#143: EGP 1, 186) and cleansing the heart of the stain of destructive thoughts (#170: EGP 1, 192)
224. *Watchfulness & Holiness*, #122 (EGP 1, 183). Elsewhere he refers to the Jesus Prayer as able to erase from our hearts "even those thoughts rooted there against our will" (EGP 1, 186, #137)
225. *Watchfulness & Holiness*, #8 (EGP 1, 164); cf. #42 (EGP 1, 169); #62 (EGP 1, 173); #97 (EGP 1, 178)
226. *Watchfulness & Holiness*, #24 (EGP 1, 166)
227. *Watchfulness & Holiness*, #20 (EGP 1, 165); cf. #39 (EGP 1, 169)
228. *Watchfulness & Holiness*, #26 (EGP 1, 166). He also refers to the Jesus Prayer as destroying and consuming "the deceits of the demons" (#174: EGP 1, 193)
229. *Watchfulness & Holiness*, #32 (EGP 1, 168); cf. #102 (EGP 1, 179-180)
230. *Watchfulness & Holiness*, #98 (EGP 1, 179); cf. #188 (EGP 1, 196)
231. #2 (EGP 3, 16)
232. #8 (EGP 3, 18)
233. #25 (EGP 3, 26). See also #26 – quoted above.
234. *Forty Texts on Watchfulness*, #2 (EGP 3, 16). See also #26 (EGP 3, 26)

235. *Forty Texts on Watchfulness*, #27 (EGP 3, 27)
236. *Forty Texts on Watchfulness*, #22 (EGP 3, 25). See also #25 (EGP 3, 26)
237. EGP 4, 72-73
238. The description is a little confusing, and appears to locate this description in the second stage. However, in order to be congruent with the previous description of the four stages, and in order to make sense of the progression described, it would appear that the invocation of Jesus Christ must be located in the third stage. This is still somewhat confusing, as the method of prayer described appeared to be offered for use from the first stage onwards. All that can be said with any degree of certainty is that, both in the description of the method itself, and in the description of the four stages of the spiritual life (as offered on p.74) invocation of the name of Jesus appears to be something that comes into play after guarding of the heart has been established, rather than as being integral to it.
239. EGP 4, 206
240. EGP 4, 206

# Chapter 4:
# Mental Well-Being

1. Taylor, 1989, p.7
2. Ibid. p.113
3. Anderson, Butterfield, Daintith, Holmes, Isaacs, Law, Lilly, Martin, McKeown, Stibbs and Summers, 2004
4. Ibid.
5. "Health is a state of complete physical, mental and social well-being and not merely the absence of disease or infirmity". (Preamble to the Constitution of the World Health Organization as adopted by the International Health Conference, New York, 19-22 June, 1946; signed on 22 July 1946 by the representatives of 61 States (Official Records of the World Health Organization, no. 2, p. 100) and entered into force on 7 April 1948.)
6. Eid and Larsen, 2008, Searle, 2008
7. MacMahon, 2006
8. Nutton, 2006, p.47
9. Ibid. p.50
10. Nussbaum, 1994, p.15. As Nussbaum notes, translation of eudaimonia as "happiness" is misleading. Her preferred translation is "human flourishing".
11. The account here is based on MacMahon, 2006, pp.1-9
12. Ibid. p.2
13. Ibid. p.7
14. Ibid. pp.2-4

# Notes: Chapter Three

15. Lee, 2003, pp.40, 149-150
16. Taylor, 1989, pp.115-126
17. Thomson, Treddenick and Barnes, 1983, p.84, Taylor, 1989, p.125
18. Sorabji, 2002, pp.182, 208, Nussbaum, 1994, pp.300-306, 500
19. Taylor, 1989, p.126
20. Nussbaum, 1994, pp.344, 366
21. Taylor, 1989, p.126
22. Ward, 1984, p.154, #8
23. Ibid. p.3, #10
24. Ibid. p.55
25. Ibid. p.103, #8
26. Ibid. p.210, #1
27. Ibid. p.171, #29
28. By keeping him in mind, following the example of scripture, and not being in a hurry to move on from any place (Ward, 2003, p.3, #1)
29. Self control and contentment with what is minimally necessary (ibid. pp.3-4, #6)
30. Ibid. p.4, #8
31. By being despised and avoiding self-will and worldly concern (ibid. p.6, #17)
32. Ibid. p.7, #23
33. cf. Matthew 10:39, 16:25; Mark 8:35; Luke 9:24; John 12:25
34. #25
35. For reference to sickness, see: *Eight Thoughts* 5.15, 7.20, and *On Thoughts* 15; for reference to disease see *On the Vices Opposed to the Virtues* 1; for reference to illness see *On Thoughts* 15; for reference to being wounded see *On Thoughts* 36; for reference to infirmity and injury see *Kephalaia Gnostika* 3.46
36. Sinkewicz, 2003, p.62 and p.103, #29
37. Ibid. pp.82 (#5.15), 86 (#7.20), 163 (#15), 178 (#36); *Antirrhetikos* 7.9, 7.39, 7.41. *Kephalaia Gnostika* 6.63. I have not been able to find a specific reference contrasting avarice to health. However, Evagrios refers to avarice as "an abundance of illnesses.... insatiable madness" (*On the Vices Opposed to the Virtues* 3) and also to wounds inflicted by the demon of avarice (*On Thoughts* 1).
38. *Eight Thoughts* 5:15; *Praktikos* 56. However, note that it is possible to experience degrees of impassibility, and that a small degree of impassibility does therefore not imply that a person can no longer be afflicted by the passions (see *On Thoughts* 15).
39. See *On Thoughts* 2
40. *Praktikos* 55
41. Sinkewicz, 2003, p.83, #6.1
42. *Scholia on Ecclesiastes* 3:21
43. e.g. *Praktikos* 29
44. Sinkewicz, 2003, p.5
45. Ibid. pp.128, #98
46. Ibid. p.40
47. Ibid. p.84

48. *Asceticism & Stillness* (EGP 1, 31). However, notice the somewhat different wording of the translation by Sinkewicz, in which the adjectives are slightly different (ibid. p.5).
49. *Asceticism & Stillness* (EGP 1, 33)
50. Sinkewicz, 2003, p.33
51. Ibid. p.193, #7
52. Ibid. p.80, #8 (and see note 33 on p.245); p.173, #28; p.213, #25 (and see note 19 on p.286)
53. *Texts on Discrimination*, #10 (EGP 1, 45) and #21 EGP 1, 51)
54. *On Prayer: 153 Texts*, #70 (EGP 1, 63) and #152 (EGP 1, 71) respectively
55. Sinkewicz, 2003, p.33
56. *On Prayer: 153 Texts*, ##117-123 (EGP 1, 68-69). Note that the order of ##121-123 is reversed in comparison with the translation provided by ibid. p.206
57. The last mentioned being a reference to 1 Corinthians 4:13, which is rendered in the NRSV as "the dregs of all things".
58. See *Kephalaia Gnostika* 1.41, 2.8
59. See *Kephalaia Gnostika* 2.15, 3.46
60. See Chapter 1
61. See Parry, Melling, Brady, Griffith and Healey, 1999, p.159, Parry, 2007, p.81, Cross and Livingstone, 1997, p.465, Sheldrake, 2005, pp.229-230, on which the following account is based.
62. Andrew Louth, in Sheldrake, 2005, p.229
63. Anatolios, 2004, p.191
64. Meyendorff, 1996, p.471
65. EGP 4, 393, #105
66. Louth, 1996, p.34. See also Russell, 2004, pp.262-295
67. Elsewhere, perhaps in order to emphasise that this grace is something which human beings passively receive, one of the *Various Texts* attributed to Maximos (but not actually written by him, see EGP 2, p.391) even refers to "the passion of deification… actualised by grace" (*Various Texts: C1*, #63 [EGP 2, 178]).
68. *On the Lord's Prayer* (EGP 2, 287)
69. *On the Lord's Prayer* (EGP 2, 288)
70. *On the Lord's Prayer* (EGP 2, 297)
71. *On the Lord's Prayer* (EGP 2, 304)
72. See also, for example, *Various Texts: C1*, #62 (EGP 2, 177-178, a text partly by Maximos and partly by an unknown Scholiast) & *Various Texts: C4*, #25 (EGP 2, 241)
73. *On the Lord's Prayer* (EGP 2, 297)
74. *Various Texts: C4*, #19 (EGP 2, 239)
75. *Various Texts: C4*, #19 (EGP 2, 239)
76. EGP 2, 391
77. *Various Texts: C1*, #63 (EGP 2, 178). The Christological context is made clear in the previous paragraph (#62) which is thought to be at least partly by Maximos himself.
78. *For Thalassios: C2*, #88 (EGP 2, 160)

79. See *Various Texts: C3*, #36 (EGP 2, 218), another paragraph which is thought not to be by Maximos himself (EGP 2, 393), and *Various Texts: C4*, #79 (EGP 2, 255), a paragraph which is thought to be at least partly by Maximos (EGP 2, 394).
80. *On Spiritual Knowledge*, #31 (EGP 4, 148)
81. *On Spiritual Knowledge*, #33 (EGP 4, 148)
82. *On Commandments & Doctrines* (EGP 4, 222)
83. *On Commandments & Doctrines*, #44 (EGP 4, 220)
84. By Cassian in *Eight Vices*, in the section entitled *On Dejection* (EGP 1, 87-88) and by Ilias in *Gnomic Anthology: 1*, #32 (EGP 3, 37). Cf. Philotheos of Sinai, in *Forty Texts on Watchfulness*, #16 (EGP 3, 21), and Peter of Damaskos, in *Book I* in *The Seven Forms of Bodily Discipline* (EGP 3, 92-93) and *The Seven Commandments* (EGP 3, 96), and in *Book II* in *VIII. Mortification of the Passions* (EGP 3, 231).
85. For Paul: *C2*, #2 (EGP 2, 313). Cf. [John of Damaskos] in *On Virtues & Vices* (EGP 2, 339)
86. *Gnomic Anthology: 1*, ##30-33 (EGP 3, 37-38). Cf. Symeon Metaphrastis, in *Paraphrase of Makarios*, #100 & #146 (EGP 3, 329, & 351-351)
87. *Gnomic Anthology: 1*, #94 (EGP 3, 44). These are signs of health of the intellect, intelligence and sense perception respectively.
88. *Book I*, in *The Seven Forms of Bodily Discipline* (EGP 3, 92-93)
89. *To Xenia*, #29 (EGP 4, 304)
90. *Ascetic Discourse* (EGP 1, 206, 247, 248 respectively)
91. *On Spiritual Knowledge*, #73 (EGP 1, 277-278)
92. *On Spiritual Knowledge*, #90 (EGP 4, 170)
93. *Various Texts: C4*, ##51-55 (EGP 2, 249-250; ##53-55 are thought not to be by Maximos himself [EGP 2, 394]); *Various Texts: C5*, #80 (EGP 2, 279)
94. *On Love: C3*, ##23-24 (EGP 2, 86)
95. *For Thalassios: C1*, ##55-56 (EGP 2, 125)
96. This latter equivalence, between eternal well-being and deification, is one that appears elsewhere in writings of Maximos included in the *Philokalia*. E.g: *For Thalassios: C2*, #88 (EGP 2, 160), #88; *Various Texts: C4*, #32 (EGP 2, 243), *Various Texts: C5*, #13 (EGP 2, 263-264). Cf. *For Thalassios: C2*, #67 (EGP 2, 153-154)
97. Peter of Damaskos, in *Book I*, in *The Third Stage of Contemplation* (EGP 3, 119)
98. Peter of Damaskos, in *Book I*, in *The Third Stage of Contemplation* (EGP 3, 119) and in *The Sixth Stage of Contemplation* (EGP 3, 138)
99. *Abba Philimon* (EGP 2, 347)
100. Peter of Damaskos, in *Book I*, in *The Third Stage of Contemplation* (EGP 3, 119)
101. Peter of Damaskos, in *Book I*, in *The Sixth Stage of Contemplation* (EGP 3, 138) and in *Book II* in *XXIV. Conscious Awareness in the Heart* (EGP 3, 273)
102. See, for example, John Cassian in *Holy Fathers of Sketis* (EGP 1, 95-96), Hesychios the Priest in *Watchfulness & Holiness*, ##1-2 & 193

(EGP 1, 162, 196); Theodorus the Great Ascetic in *Spiritual Texts*, #86 (EGP 2, 33), Maximos the Confessor in *On Love: C4*, ##71-73 (EGP 2, 109), *For Thalassios: C2*, #79 (EGP 2, 157-158); Philotheos of Sinai in *Forty Texts on Watchfulness*, #37 (EGP 3, 30), Symeon Metaphrastis in *Paraphrase of Makarios*, #31 (EGP 3, 297); [Symeon the New Theologian] in *Three Methods of Prayer* (EGP 4, 70, 72). John Cassian considered purity of intellect to be the equivalent of purity of heart (see *Philokalia* Glossary, under "dispassion"), and it may be this that the compilers of the *Philokalia* had in mind when making reference to purification of the intellect.
103. See, for example, Philotheos of Sinai in *Forty Texts on Watchfulness*, #24 (EGP 3, 25-26) and Peter of Damaskos in *Book I* in *True Discrimination* (EGP 3, 159)
104. See, for example, Evagrios in *On Prayer: 153 Texts*, ##53-57 (EGP 1, 62); Mark the Ascetic in *Righteous by Works*, ##174-175 (EGP 1, 140); Peter of Damaskos in *Book I* in *The Seven Forms of Bodily Discipline* (EGP 3, 91), *The Seven Commandments* (EGP 3, 99) and *The Eighth Stage of Contemplation* (EGP 3, 142)
105. These are discussed in detail by Konstantinovsky, who concludes that these light visions were understood by Evagrios as a fusion of the light of the purified intellect with the uncreated light of God's essence (Konstantinovsky, 2009, pp.77-107).
106. *On Prayer: 153 Texts*, ##73-74 (EGP 1, 64)
107. *On Spiritual Knowledge*, #40, #59 (EGP 1, 265, 270-271)
108. *On Spiritual Knowledge*, #69 (EGP 1, 276)
109. *For the Monks in India*, #82 (EGP 1, 317)
110. *On Love: C2*, #48 (EGP 2, 73). Cf. *On Love: C3*, #97 (EGP 2, 98)
111. *On Love: C4*, ##79-80 (EGP 2, 110)
112. EGP 2, 355
113. *For Paul: C1*, #50 (EGP 2, 310) is clearly an analogy, with an apparently clear metaphorical usage in the following paragraph (#51). *For Paul: C3*, #29 (EGP 2, 320) is similar to the more mysterious mode of reference illustrated above in the writings of Diadochos, John of Karpathos, and Maximos. In the following paragraph the word "light" is again used metaphorically.
114. *Gnomic Anthology: 2*, ##80-82 (EGP 3, 43). Here it is prayer that appears to confer luminosity, but "an intellect subject to passion" is also said to be unable to "penetrate the narrow gate of prayer". Hence it would again appear to be passion that darkens the intellect.
115. ##8-11 (EGP 4, 80-81)
116. #67 (EGP 4, 126-127)
117. *On Commandments & Doctrines*, #116 (EGP 4, 239)
118. ##59-62 (EGP 4, 316-319)
119. *To Xenia*, #62 (EGP 4, 319)
120. Ware, 1996, pp.410-411, deCatanzaro, Maloney and Krivocheine, 1980, pp.1-36, EGP 4, 11-24
121. EGP 4, 18. The "angelic elder" to whom he refers in the vision is Symeon the Studite.

122. Maximos the Confessor in *For Thalassios: C2*, #88 (EGP 2, 160); Symeon Metaphrastis in *Paraphrase of Makarios*, #90 (EGP 3, 325); Nikitas Stithatos in *On the Inner Nature of Things*, #50 (EGP 4, 121), and *On Spiritual Knowledge*, #20 (EGP 4, 145)
123. Symeon Metaphrastis in *Paraphrase of Makarios*, #90 (EGP 3, 325)
124. Nikitas Stithatos in *On Spiritual Knowledge*, #52 (EGP 4, 155)
125. Maximos the Confessor in *For Thalassios: C2*, #88 (EGP 2, 160)
126. Maximos the Confessor in *Various Texts: C4*, #79 (EGP 2, 255) and *On the Lord's Prayer* (EGP 2, 297); Symeon Metaphrastis in *Paraphrase of Makarios*, #93 (EGP 3, 326); Gregory of Sinai in *On Commandments & Doctrines*, #55 (EGP 4, 222)
127. Maximos the Confessor in *For Thalassios: C2*, #88 (EGP 2, 160); Symeon Metaphrastis in *Paraphrase of Makarios*, #38 (EGP 3, 301); Gregory of Sinai in *On Commandments & Doctrines*, #85 (EGP 4, 229)
128. John Cassian in *Holy Fathers of Sketis* (EGP 1, 94-96); Theophanis the Monk in *Ladder of Divine Graces* (EGP 3, 67), Peter of Damaskos in *Book I* in the section entitled *Dispassion* (EGP 3, 149), Symeon Metaphrastis in *Paraphrase of Makarios*, #30 (EGP 3, 296); Gregory of Sinai in *On Commandments & Doctrines*, #120 (EGP 4, 241)
129. John Cassian in *Holy Fathers of Sketis* (EGP 1, 96)
130. #88 (EGP 2, 160)
131. *Various Texts: C4*, #79 (EGP 2, 255). This text is thought to be partly by Maximos and partly by an unknown scholiast (EGP 3, 394)
132. EGP 2, 297
133. #50 (EGP 4, 121)
134. #52 (EGP 4, 155)
135. See the entry on "Intellections" in the glossary to the English translation of the *Philokalia*.
136. #3 (EGP 4, 189)
137. #60 (EGP 4, 318)
138. EGP 2, 355
139. *On Virtues, Contemplation & Priesthood*, #22 (EGP 2, 363)
140. *Ladder of Divine Graces* (EGP 3, 67)
141. *Paraphrase of Makarios*, #82 (EGP 3, 321)
142. #3 (EGP 4, 345)
143. Glossary to the English translation of the *Philokalia*.
144. EGP 1, 14-16
145. EGP 3, 89: see translators' footnote.
146. That is, every author of the first four volumes of the English translation.
147. See the entry on "Theology" in the glossary of the English translation of the *Philokalia*. See also EGP 3, 17
148. See entries on "Theology" and "Watchfulness" in the glossary of the English translation of the *Philokalia*. See also Hesychios the Priest in *Watchfulness & Holiness*, #11 (EGP 1, 181), and Philotheos of Sinai in *Forty Texts on Watchfulness*, #3 (EGP 3, 17)
149. Hesychios the Priest, in *Watchfulness & Holiness*, #10 (EGP 1, 164)
150. Gregory of Sinai, in On Stillness, #4 (EGP 4, 266)

151. Gregory of Sinai, in *On Commandments & Doctrines*, #107 (EGP 4, 236)
152. Gregory of Sinai, in *On Stillness*, #13 (EGP 4, 272)
153. Gregory of Sinai, in *On Commandments & Doctrines*, #108 (EGP 4, 236)
154. Gregory of Sinai, in *On Commandments & Doctrines*, #111 (EGP 4, 237)
155. Hesychios the Priest in *Watchfulness & Holiness*, #10 (EGP 1, 164); Gregory of Sinai, in *On Commandments & Doctrines*, #113 (EGP 4, 238), in *Further Texts*, #5 (EGP 4, 254); and in *On Stillness*, #4 (EGP 4, 266)
156. Gregory of Sinai in *On Stillness*, #4 (EGP 4, 266)
157. Neilos the Ascetic in *Ascetic Discourse* (EGP 1, 230). Cf. Peter of Damaskos in *Book I*, in the section entitled *The Third Stage of Contemplation* (EGP 3, 119)
158. Thalassios the Libyan in *For Paul: C3*, #8 (EGP 2, 319)
159. Ilias the Presbyter in *Gnomic Anthology: 1*, #74 (EGP 3, 42)
160. Hesychios the Priest in *Watchfulness & Holiness*, #32 (EGP 1, 185); Peter of Damaskos in *Book I* in the sections entitled *Obedience and Stillness* (EGP 3, 107) and *Spurious Knowledge* (EGP 3, 194); Nikitas Stithatos in *On Virtues: 100 Texts*, #89 (EGP 4, 103) and in *On the Inner Nature of Things*, #64 (EGP 4, 125); Gregory of Sinai, in *Further Texts*, #5 (EGP 4, 254)
161. Nikitas Stithatos in *On Spiritual Knowledge*, #25 (EGP 4, 146)
162. Diadochus of Photiki in *On Spiritual Knowledge*, #16 (EGP 1, 257)
163. In *Abba Philimon* (EGP 2, 349)
164. Peter of Damaskos in *Book I*, in the section entitled *Obedience and Stillness* (EGP 3, 106)
165. Nikitas Stithatos in *On Virtues: 100 Texts*, #89 (EGP 4, 103)
166. Nikitas Stithatos in *On Spiritual Knowledge*, #25 (EGP 4, 146). Symeon Metaphrastis also includes hesychia amongst the characteristics of those who are "close to perfection" in *Paraphrase of Makarios*, #89 (EGP 3, 324-325).
167. Nikitas Stithatos in *On Spiritual Knowledge*, ##33-35 (EGP 4, 148-149)
168. Gregory of Sinai, in *Further Texts*, #5 (EGP 4, 254)
169. Gregory of Sinai, in *On Stillness*, #13 (EGP 4, 272)
170. In *Book I*, in the section entitled *The Seven Forms of Bodily Discipline* (EGP 3, 89)
171. *On the Inner Nature of Things*, #64 (EGP 4, 125)
172. *On Spiritual Knowledge*, #29 (EGP 4, 147)
173. #111 (EGP 4, 237)
174. #9 (EGP 4, 270). Cf. also: *On Prayer: 7 Texts*, #5 (EGP 4, 278) and *Instructions to Hesychasts*, #5 (Kadloubovsky and Palmer, 1979, p.76)
175. EGP 2, 345
176. EGP 2, 43
177. EGP 2, 47

178. Diadochus of Photiki in *On Spiritual Knowledge*, #95 (EGP 1, 292); Maximos the Confessor in *Various Texts: C2*, #96 (EGP 2, 208)
179. *For Thalassios: C1*, #50 (EGP 2, 124)
180. EGP 1, 96-97
181. #89 (EGP 1, 177)
182. *On Love: C3*, #22 (EGP 2, 86)
183. *For Thalassios: C1*, #54 (EGP 2, 125). Cf. *Various Texts: C3*, #38 (EGP 2, 219), a text which is thought to be partly by Maximos and partly by an unknown scholiast (EGP 2, 392)
184. *On Spiritual Knowledge*, ##1-3 (EGP 4, 139)
185. *To Xenia*, #47 (EGP 4, 312)
186. Maximos the Confessor in *Various Texts: C3*, #28 (EGP 2, 216)
187. Gregory Palamas in *To Xenia*, #44 (EGP 4, 311)
188. Hesychios the Priest in *Watchfulness & Holiness*, #90 & #115 (EGP 1, 171 & 182); cf. #120 (EGP 1, 183), where it is the delight that arises from the practice of attentiveness that is described as blessed.
189. Maximos the Confessor in *Various Texts: C3*, #28 (EGP 2, 216)
190. John of Karpathos in *For the Monks in India*, #15 (EGP 1, 301); Theodoros the Great Ascetic in *Spiritual Texts*, #25 (EGP 2, 19); Nikitas Stithatos in *On Virtues: 100 Texts*, #30 (EGP 4, 87) and in *On the Inner Nature of Things*, #80 (EGP 4, 129); Gregory of Sinai in *On Commandments & Doctrines*, #110 (EGP 4, 237)
191. Symeon Metaphrastis in *Paraphrase of Makarios*, #30 (EGP 3, 296)
192. Maximos the Confessor in *Various Texts: C3*, #28 (EGP 2, 216) and in *Various Texts: C4*, #90 (EGP 2, 257). The latter text is thought to be partly by Maximos and partly by an unknown scholiast (EGP 2, 394)
193. Peter of Damaskos in *Book I* in the section entitled *The Seven Commandments* (EGP 3, 94, 98); Gregory Palamas in *To Xenia*, #48, #49, #57 (EGP 4, 312, 313, 316)
194. Gregory of Sinai in *On Commandments & Doctrines*, #99 (EGP 4, 233)
195. Hesychios the Priest in *Watchfulness & Holiness*, #64, #164 (EGP 1, 173, 191); Theodoros the Great Ascetic in *Spiritual Texts*, #27, #45 (EGP 2, 19, 22)
196. Gregory Palamas in *To Xenia*, #50, #53 (EGP 4, 313, 314)
197. Maximos the Confessor in *On Love: C1*, #97 (EGP 2, 63); Dionysios the Areopagite (attributed to Maximos) in *Various Texts: C5*, #83 (EGP 2, 280); Thalassios the Libyan in *For Paul: C2*, ##82-83 (EGP 2, 317)
198. [Maximos the Confessor] in *Various Texts: C2*, #24 (EGP 2, 193)
199. Gregory Palamas in *To Xenia*, #27, #33, #49 (EGP 4, 303, 306, 313)
200. Thalassios the Libyan in *For Paul: C2*, ##82-83 (EGP 2, 317); Gregory of Sinai in *On Commandments & Doctrines*, #99 (EGP 4, 233)
201. Gregory of Sinai in *On Commandments & Doctrines*, #99 (EGP 4, 233)
202. Theodoros the Great Ascetic in *Spiritual Texts*, #25 (EGP 2, 19)
203. Philotheos of Sinai in *Forty Texts on Watchfulness*, #22 (EGP 3, 25)

204. Thalassios the Libyan in *For Paul: C2*, ##82-83 (EGP 2, 317)
205. Maximos the Confessor in *Various Texts: C3*, #28 (EGP 2, 216)
206. Maximos the Confessor in *On Love: C2*, #19 (EGP 2, 68); Thalassios the Libyan in *For Paul: C2*, ##82-83 (EGP 2, 317); *Abba Philimon* (EGP 2, 346)
207. Nikitas Stithatos in *On Spiritual Knowledge*, #2 (EGP 4, 139)
208. Maximos the Confessor in *Various Texts: C3*, #28 (EGP 2, 216)
209. Maximos the Confessor in *Various Texts: C3*, #28 (EGP 2, 216)
210. Nikitas Stithatos in *On Spiritual Knowledge*, #2 (EGP 4, 139)
211. *Watchfulness & Holiness*, #27 (EGP 1, 166). Cf. *Forty Texts on Watchfulness*, #27 (EGP 3, 26), where Philotheos of Sinai describes as blessed the "heart of one who has reached a state of watchfulness".
212. *Watchfulness & Holiness*, #110 (EGP 1, 181). Other examples include patient endurance of afflictions (Peter of Damaskos in *Book I* in the section entitled *God's Universal and Particular Gifts* [EGP 3, 172]) or purification of the senses and heart from all evil desires (Symeon the New Theologian in *Practical and Theological Texts*, #92 [EGP 4, 44]).
213. *Ascetic Discourse* (EGP 1, 214)
214. *Practical and Theological Texts*, #88 (EGP 4, 43). Cf. Gregory of Sinai in *On Commandments & Doctrines*, #99 (EGP 4, 233), where a rule for the hesychastic life is summarised.
215. John of Karpathos in *For the Monks in India*, #89 (EGP 1, 319); Theodoros the Great Ascetic in *Spiritual Texts*, #29, #49 (EGP 2, 19-20, 23); Maximos the Confessor in *For Thalassios: C2*, #26 (EGP 2, 143); Peter of Damaskos in *Book I*, in the section entitled *The Fourth Stage of Contemplation* (EGP 3, 125); Theoliptos in *Texts*, #8 (EGP 4, 190)
216. Maximos the Confessor in *For Thalassios: C1*, #54 (EGP 2, 125). Cf. Nikitas Stithatos in *On the Inner Nature of Things*, #43 (EGP 4, 118), which shows some of the features of deification, but is not called deification, and seems to refer to the indwelling of God rather than union with God.
217. [John of Damaskos] in *On Virtues & Vices* (EGP 2, 338). Cf. Symeon Metaphrastis in *Paraphrase of Makarios*, #100 (EGP 3, 329)
218. See the entry for "Age" in the glossary of the English translation of the *Philokalia*.
219. *Watchfulness & Holiness*, #1 (EGP 1, 162)
220. #130 (EGP 1, 349)
221. #28 (EGP 2, 19). Note also the Platonic influence in this passage – where an immaterial soul is liberated from a physical body after death.
222. #46 (EGP 2, 22)
223. *On Virtues, Contemplation & Priesthood*, #8 & #75 respectively (EGP 2, 360-361 & 377)
224. *On Inner Work* (EGP 4, 187)
225. *On Spiritual Knowledge*, #41 (EGP 1, 265)
226. *On Virtues & Vices* (EGP 2, 339)
227. *Gnomic Anthology: 4*, #104 (EGP 3, 60)

228. *For Thalassios: C2*, #25 (EGP 2, 143)
229. *On the Inner Nature of Things*, #100 (EGP 4, 137)
230. These references are compiled from the English translation of Volumes 1 to 4, and hence do not include the authors or texts of Volume 5.
231. Counting the authors of *Three Methods of Prayer* and *Practical & Theological Texts* as two individuals and not the same persons as each other or Symeon the New Theologian
232. This is clearly an error in the English translation and must refer to verse 8, not verse 18
233. In Acts 20:35 the "Blessed are.... " form is also missing, and is replaced by "It is more blessed to.... ".
234. "This state" refers to the previous paragraph, where Ilias describes a state of concentrated prayer in which a flame surrounds the soul, "as fire surrounds iron", making it "wholly incandescent".
235. *Paraphrase of Makarios*, #30 (EGP 3, 296)

## Chapter 5:
# Psychotherapy

1. Were it not for this common ground, it is acknowledged that the comparison would be invalidated altogether. Although reference will be made repeatedly here to comparisons "between the *Philokalia* and psychotherapy", this is really shorthand for what might be more adequately described as a comparison between therapeutic relationships based upon the rationale and procedures of the *Philokalia* and those based upon the rationale and procedures of contemporary psychotherapy. However, even this wording would need more careful analysis. What is meant by "therapeutic", "rationale" and "procedures"? Do any of these terms borrow too much more from the philosophy and culture of the world of psychotherapy than that of the *Philokalia* (or vice-versa) to invalidate comparison? If so, can more value neutral terms be found?
2. I am indebted to Martin and Barresi, 2006 and Sorabji, 2006, on whose works in this field I have drawn extensively here.
3. Mackey, 2000, pp.21-30
4. Martin and Barresi, 2006, pp.279-281, 296-297
5. Ibid. pp.295-305
6. Taylor, 1989, pp.33-35
7. Ibid. p.50
8. Ibid. p.51
9. Ibid. pp.130-131
10. Ibid. p.174
11. Ibid. p.21
12. Ibid. pp.288-289
13. Paradoxically, this requires that we be able to adopt the first person standpoint in the first place, in order that we can step out of it (ibid. pp.162-163).

14. Ibid. pp.49-50, 171-172
15. Taylor sees the Freudian ego as "imprisoned... in the gigantic conflict of instincts, and distorted... by condensations and displacements" (ibid. p.446)
16. Ibid. p.174
17. Ibid. pp.174-175
18. Ibid. pp.368-374
19. Ibid. p.368
20. Ibid. pp.374-375
21. Ibid. pp.446-447
22. Ibid. pp.199-207
23. Louth, 2003
24. Dixon, 2003
25. Ibid. pp.76-81
26. Ibid. pp.26-61
27. See, for example, Mackey, 2000, pp.11-15
28. Dixon, 2003, p.104
29. Ibid. pp.104-109
30. Ibid. p.21
31. Ibid. p.18
32. Brown and Pedder, 1980, p.ix
33. Ibid. p.5
34. Bloch and Harari, 2006, p.3
35. Frank, 2006
36. Ibid. p.60
37. Ibid. p.66
38. Ibid. pp.67-68. The text quoted here is abbreviated from the original, but the words used, and emphases, are exactly as in the published text.
39. Ibid. p.67
40. This is not to deny that humility is frequently emphasised as an important virtue for those who would offer spiritual instruction. However, the humility of the instructor seems to have only increased their "prestige" in the eyes of others. An example of this might be found in a story of John the Dwarf (Ward, 1984, p.93, #38). There is therefore also a strand of teaching which emphasises living life in such a way that one does not stand out, and thus gain prestige through acts of extreme humility (e.g. Ward, 1984, p.148/#1). Paradoxically, this would have meant that some of the best potential instructors (on grounds of humility) would not in fact have prestige in the eyes of the community.
41. Frank, 2006, p.68
42. Insofar as it deals with the first, it does this merely by selecting a text by one author (albeit a very distinguished one) who has reflected on what might be unifying features amongst diverse approaches to psychotherapy and using this as a basis for reflecting on ways in which the *Philokalia* might be understood as describing a form of psychotherapy. The asymmetry remains, in that there is no corpus of texts in psychotherapy which might be seen as comparable to the *Philokalia*. However, there are seminal psychotherapeutic texts which

are applied to practice in a not dissimilar way to the *Philokalia*. It is possible to envisage an empirical programme of research in which spiritual direction based on the *Philokalia* might be compared with psychotherapy based on (for example) the works of Freud.
43. Frank, 2006, p.65
44. Innes, 1999, pp.35-75
45. Ibid. p.35
46. Self is a technical term in Jungian analytical psychology, and therefore given here with an initial capital.
47. Innes, 1999, pp.202-205
48. Eid and Larsen, 2008
49. Haybron, 2008
50. Emmy van Deurzen (Deurzen, 2009), having argued that psychotherapy cannot be about trying to make people "happy", concludes her work on *Psychotherapy and the Quest for Happiness*, with the proposal that psychotherapy is about helping people to be more realistic about life, finding meaning in life, and finding resolution amidst adversity. This perhaps approximates most closely to Haybron's authentic happiness theory but, although van Deurzen writes from a non-theistic perspective, it gets closer to a view of well-being that could perhaps be common ground between the *Philokalia* and psychotherapy.
51. Joel Shuman and Keith Meador explore the problem of utilitarianism in relation to spirituality and health in their book *Heal Thyself* (Shuman and Meador, 2003).
52. Pentkovsky and Smith, 1999, pp.60-61
53. Frank, 2006, p.64
54. Note that this is a rather different question than that addressed by controlled scientific trials of whether or not prayer "works". These trials (e.g. Harris, Gowda, Kolb, Strychacz, Vacek, Jones, Forker, O'Keefe and McCallister, 1999) usually measure scientific outcomes in those being prayed *for*. The question here is more about whether the lives of those who pray might be discernibly different in any way from those who don't.
55. We might note, for example, scientific scales of "spirituality" or spiritual well-being which are used as outcome measures in treatment research programmes (see Culliford and Eagger, 2009).
56. Sykes, 1984, p.35
57. Ibid. pp.37-38
58. Ibid. p.39
59. Ibid. pp.39-40
60. We might note that there was no evidence of such a "western" tendency in Sykes' account, discussed above.
61. Brock, 1982, p.133
62. Ibid. pp.136-137
63. Ibid. p.138
64. Brock distinguishes the prayer of the heart in the Syriac tradition from that in the Greek tradition, chiefly on the basis of absence of a formula sufficiently resembling the Jesus Prayer.

65. Brock, 1982, p.141
66. Taylor, 1989, p.130
67. Ibid. p.131
68. See entry under "Logos" in the glossary to the English translation of the *Philokalia*.
69. [Maximos the Confessor] in *Various Texts: C1*, #92 (EGP 2, 185)
70. A search was made using the *The Philokalia Concordance* CD-ROM, compiled by Basileios S. Stapakis. This is based on the first four volumes of the English translation. The search included "inner" and "inward" and their derivatives.
71. *On the Spiritual Law*, #36 (EGP 1, 113)
72. *For Paul: C3*, #22 (EGP 2, 320)
73. *On Inner Work* (EGP 4, 180-181)
74. This list was compiled by searching for references to inwardness language in the *Philokalia* Concordance on CD-ROM, compiled by Basileios S. Stapakis. See note 70, above.
75. This chapter is partly by Maximos and partly by an anonymous scholiast.
76. This chapter is partly by Maximos and partly by an anonymous scholiast.
77. Attributed in the *Philokalia* to Symeon; actually by Nikitas Stithatos
78. *Forty Texts on Watchfulness*, #19 (EGP 3, 23-24)
79. *Watchfulness & Holiness* (EGP 1, 180)
80. It is also interesting to note here reference to use of the incensive power of the soul (in the form of anger) as a means of inner warfare against the evil spirits (or passions).
81. *For the Monks in India*, #52 (EGP 1, 310)
82. Symeon Metaphrastis in *Paraphrase of Makarios*, #83 (EGP 3, 321)
83. Symeon Metaphrastis in *Paraphrase of Makarios*, #116 (EGP 3, 337)
84. #3 (EGP 4, 334)
85. The the location of cognitive processes was a matter of some debate in antiquity, and was not settled until perhaps the nineteenth century. See, for example, Simon, 1978, pp.220-225, Eijk, 2005, pp.119-135
86. Vlachos, 1994
87. Thermos, 2002
88. Hackmann, 1997, p.125
89. See also the comments on the place of metaphor in psychotherapy in the work of Ricoeur, in Chapter 6.
90. Koenig, McCullough and Larson, 2001
91. This question is explored helpfully by Shuman and Meador, 2003
92. Mace, 2008. It should be noted that mindfulness also differs from hesychia in some very important ways. In particular, it is based in the non-theistic context of Buddhist psychology rather than Christian theology, and it is devoid of the element of judgment that is introduced into hesychia by the practice of watchfulness.
93. Archbishop Chrysostomos provides a helpful analysis of the limitations and dangers that arise in relation to the clinical applications of Orthodox Psychotherapy (Chrysostomos, 2007, pp.99-111).

94. See, for example, Mark the Ascetic in *On the Spiritual Law*, #65 (EGP 1, 114) and in *Righteous by Works*, ##45-46 (EGP 1, 129); Maximos the Confessor in *Various Texts: C1*, #91 (EGP 2, 185) and in *Various Texts: C3*, ##87-90 (EGP 2, 232); [Symeon the New Theologian] in *Practical and Theological Texts*, #133 (EGP 4, 54)
95. *Book I, Introduction* (EGP 3, 77-78)
96. Chrysostomos, 2007, pp.104-105
97. It is interesting to note in passing that similar distinctions have been made in respect of the teaching of John of the Cross on the dark night of the soul, and that similar considerations apply there also (Turner, 1999, pp.226-251).
98. Chirban, 2001, Muse, 2004
99. Cook, 2006
100. Cook, 2007a, Cook, 2004, Cook, 2007b, Jackson and Cook, 2005
101. Kurtz, 1996
102. Thyer, 2004
103. Mihailoff, 2005, p.2
104. Ibid.
105. Ibid. p.12
106. Webber, 2003, p.11
107. Ibid. p.12
108. Ibid. p.13
109. Richards and Bergin, 2000
110. Young, 2001

Chapter 6:
# On Thoughts and Prayer

1. Cook, Powell and Sims, 2009
2. Sorabji, 2006, pp.201-261 gives a helpful review of these arguments.
3. I do not wish to engage here with debates about whether animals have thoughts, or about the serious ethical issues raised by severe brain damage, developmental disorder, or degenerative brain diseases which might impair or even completely prevent normal human thought processes. I hope that it is sufficient simply to argue that the very way in which these ethical debates challenge our understanding of what it is to be human, and what constitutes a life worth living, are sufficient to demonstrate that thoughts are very important to our sense of self identity. There are however obviously many other and complex issues to be taken into account when making ethical and philosophical decisions about what it is to be human, and what constitutes human life.
4. Cook, 2004
5. Schneiders, 2005, p.1
6. Hastings, Mason and Pyper, 2000, pp.596-597, Cross and Livingstone, 1997, p.820
7. See entries in the Glossary of the English translation of the *Philokalia*

under "Intellect", "Intellection", "Intelligent", "Logos", "Reason", and "Thought"
8. Konstantinovsky, 2009, p.35, Dysinger, 2005, p.35; See, for example, *On Thoughts* 8, for an example of logismoi inspired by angels.
9. Konstantinovsky, 2009, p.35
10. Dysinger, 2005, p.35, Konstantinovsky, 2009, p.35
11. *On Thoughts* 17
12. See, for example, *Praktikos* 42
13. Konstantinovsky, 2009, p.35
14. Ibid.
15. #84 (EGP 2, 79). See also *On Love: C3*, #43 (EGP 2, 89)
16. Louth, 1996, p.42
17. *On Love: C1*, #93 (EGP 2, 64)
18. *On Love: C1*, #94 (EGP 2, 64); Maximos goes on to state that the "pure intellect" may be occupied with "passion-free conceptual images" or natural contemplation, or "the light of the Holy Trinity" (#97). He concludes this century of texts with a very apophatic affirmation that "knowing nothing is knowledge surpassing the intellect" (#100).
19. *Kephalaia Gnostika* 1.43, 2.2, 2.21, 3.11, 4.7, 5.84
20. Konstantinovsky, 2009, p.59
21. Ibid. pp.65-66
22. *For Thalassios: C2*, #39 (EGP 2, 147). This is quoted in full, below.
23. *On the Lord's Prayer* (EGP 2, 293)
24. Louth, 1996, pp.52-54
25. *Praktikos* 6
26. *On the Vices Opposed to the Virtues* 8
27. For example, Evagrios notes fear of fantasies as an example of pride (*Eight Thoughts* 8.10)
28. Evagrios appears to associate the potentially harmful kind of fear with different logismoi, and to understand the solution as being found in the measures to combat the logismoi or demons with which it is associated (e.g. *Eight Thoughts* 1.30, *To Eulogius* 22.23, *On Prayer* 97)
29. The "interaction of good and bad thoughts" is discussed in *Praktikos*, 7
30. *Eight Thoughts* 2.6
31. *Eight Thoughts* 2.7-2.10
32. *Eight Thoughts* 2.17-2.20
33. *Eight Thoughts* 2.17
34. Brown and Pedder, 1980, pp.15-21
35. Ricoeur, 1981, pp.197-221, 247-273
36. Ibid. pp.131-144
37. Ibid. pp.247-254
38. Ibid. p.258
39. 1 Thessalonians 5:17
40. *On Thoughts* 7
41. *On Thoughts* 20
42. *On Thoughts* 8. This is taken up by Peter of Damaskos in *Book I*, in the section entitled *The Sixth Stage of Contemplation* (EGP 3, 134). Gregory of Sinai, in *On Commandments & Doctrines*, #69 (EGP 4, 224)

identifies four categories: material, demonic, natural and supernatural.
43. It is recognised that Evagrios did not ascribe to an understanding of deification that would later be considered orthodox. His heavily gnostic approach to contemplation of God leading to eventual assimilation to Christ through shedding of the material body was condemned at the Fifth Ecumenical Council. (Russell, 2004, pp.238-241)
44. Hamilton, 1981, pp.34-51.
45. Allen, 2006, pp.147-148
46. *Eight Thoughts* 3.6-3.14
47. Brown and Pedder, 1980
48. *Eight Thoughts* 4.20-4.21
49. *Eight Thoughts* 4.13
50. *Eight Thoughts* 2.11
51. Brewin and Power, 1997, pp.2-3
52. Strachey, Tyson and Richards, 1982, p.650
53. Husser, 1999
54. Strachey, Tyson and Richards, 1982, p.769
55. Mizen and Holmes, 2006, p.99
56. Husser, 1999, pp.19-22
57. Ibid. pp.22-26
58. Ibid. p.24
59. Strachey, Tyson and Richards, 1982
60. See, for example, Jaffé, Winston and Winston, 1963, McLynn, 1997, pp.368-383, Mattoon, 2006
61. Hobson, 2005
62. Strachey, Tyson and Richards, 1982, p.485
63. Jaffé, Winston and Winston, 1963, p.355
64. *Praktikos* 54-56, and *On Thoughts* 4, 27-29. *On Thoughts* 4 is included in the *Philokalia* as *Texts on Discrimination*, #4 (EGP 1, 40). See also *The Monk* 52, and *Antirhettikos* 7.26.
65. *Praktikos* 56 and *On Thoughts* 29 respectively.
66. Sinkewicz, 2003, p.172
67. Ibid. p.173
68. Ibid.
69. In fact, in a similar dream in *Antirrhetikos* 7.26, it is the demon that interprets the dream the following day.
70. *Eight Vices*: *On the demon of unchastity and the desire of the flesh* (EGP 1, 76); *Holy Fathers of Sketis* (EGP 1, 102)
71. *On Spiritual Knowledge*, ##37-39 (EGP 1, 264-265)
72. *On Love: C1*, #89 (EGP 2, 63); *On Love: C2*, ##68-69 (EGP 2, 76-77); *On Love: C2*, #85 (EGP 2, 79-80)
73. *For Paul: C1*, #54 (EGP 2, 310)
74. *On Virtues, Contemplation & Priesthood*, #68 (EGP 2, 375)
75. *Abba Philimon* (EGP 2, 348)
76. *Paraphrase of Makarios* (EGP 3, 305-306)
77. *On Prayer: 7 Texts*, #6 (EGP 4, 280-281). Gregory also engages in an extended discussion about nocturnal emissions of semen, their association in some cases with demonic fantasy, and the various

causes of this phenomenon. *Further Texts* (EGP 4, 254-256)
78. *On Spiritual Knowledge*, #38 (EGP 1, 264)
79. *Book I: Introduction* (EGP 3 81). See also: *Book I: The Seven Commandments* (3, 99) and *Book I: Dispassion* (3, 148)
80. *On Commandments & Doctrines, #131* (EGP 4, 248-250)
81. *Practical & Theological Texts*, #87 (EGP 4 42-43)
82. A later text in *Practical & Theological Texts*, #119 (EGP 4 50-51), not written by Symeon, draws attention to other problems due to the passions that may arise in sleep, notably nocturnal emissions of semen.
83. *On the Inner Nature of Things*, 60-63 (EGP 4, 123-125)
84. #60 (EGP 4, 123-124)
85. ##61-63 (EGP 4, 124-125)
86. #63 (EGP 4, 125)
87. "contemplation of the inner essences of created things"
88. Hastings, Mason and Pyper, 2000, p.182, Sheldrake, 2005, pp.253-254
89. Passion free conceptual images may also form distractions in prayer (see Maximos the Confessor in *On Love: C3*, #49 [EGP 2, 90])
90. *Guarding the Intellect*, #12 (EGP 1, 24)
91. *On Commandments & Doctrines*, #108 (EGP 4, 236)
92. Here, in the quoted text from Gregory of Sinai, this is through meditation on death. However, as will be considered below, thoughts are involved in all of the remedies for the passions discussed in Chapter 3.
93. *Gnomic Anthology: 4*, #76 (EGP 3, 57)
94. *Various Texts: C2*, #67 (EGP 2, 201)
95. *Various Texts: C2*, #75 (EGP 2, 203). This text is thought not to be by Maximos, but to have been written by an anonymous scholiast. However, see also *Various Texts: C3*, #58 (EGP 2, 225)
96. Maximos the Confessor in *On Love: C2*, #19 (EGP 2, 68)
97. e.g. Maximos the Confessor in *On Love: C2*, #19 (EGP 2, 68)
98. *On Prayer: 153 Texts*, #3 (EGP 1, 57)
99. *On the Lord's Prayer* (EGP 2, 290)
100. *To Xenia*, #61 (EGP 4, 318)
101. EGP 4, 206
102. *For Thalassios: C2*, #51 (EGP 2, 150). Cf. #59 (EGP 2, 151)
103. *On Prayer: 7 Texts*, #5 (EGP 4, 278)
104. *Ladder of Divine Graces* (EGP 3, 67)
105. *Book I, The Seven Forms of Bodily Discipline* (EGP 3, 91)
106. *Book I, The Third Stage of Contemplation* (EGP 3, 119). Gregory Palamas also writes, in *On Prayer & Purity*, #1 (EGP 4, 343) of prayer which "transcends...conceptual thoughts".
107. *On Stillness*, #9 (EGP 4, 270); cf. *On Prayer: 7 Texts*, #5 (EGP 4, 278)
108. 6.83
109. *Gnomic Anthology: 2*, #104 (EGP 3, 45)
110. This understanding receives support in *On Love: C4*, #97 (EGP 2, 64) where Maximos writes: "The pure intellect is occupied either with passion-free conceptual images of human affairs, or with the natural contemplation of things visible or invisible, or with the light of the

Holy Trinity." This would seem to imply that the light of the Holy Trinity is not a thought (logismos or noema) in the normal sense. (See also Thalassios the Libyan in *For Paul: C3*, #29 (EGP 2, 320)

111. Konstantinovsky, 2009, p.77
112. Ibid. pp.85-86
113. Turner, 1999, pp.11-18; Laird, 2007, pp.175-177; Sheldrake, 2005, pp.227-228; Ware, 1996, p.410 See also Exodus 20:21. This field is clearly controversial. Philo appears to have been the first to identify God with darkness, but Christian claims to precedence are more contested, with Origen and Clement arguably playing an important part.
114. Denys (also known as Dionysios) the Areopagite, was thought to be a member of the Council of the Areopagus, to whom the apostle Paul preached (Acts 17:34). It is now known that this name was assumed by an unknown author (referred to here as Pseudo-Denys the Areopagite), probably of Syrian origin, in the fifth or sixth century. The corpus of texts that he left are strongly influenced by Platonic thought. *Mystical Theology* provides an account of apophatic theology, and of deification, which was subsequently highly influential – especially in western Christianity. (Parry, Melling, Brady, Griffith and Healey, 1999, pp.162-163)
115. Louth, 1996, pp.28-32. Some texts by Pseudo-Denys were included in the *Philokalia* within documents by Maximos (see Appendix 1). Pseudo-Denys is quoted within the *Philokalia* by Maximos, Peter of Damaskos, and (most frequently by) Gregory Palamas. The influence of Pseudo-Denys on Nikitas Stithatos is also evident (see EGP 4, 77)
116. EGP 2, 44
117. *On Virtues, Contemplation & Priesthood*, #5 (EGP 2, 360)
118. *For Thalassios: C1*, #84 (EGP 2, 133)
119. *On Commandments & Doctrines*, #43 (EGP 4, 220)
120. *On Virtues: 100 Texts*, #1, #42 (EGP 4, 79, 90); *On the Inner Nature of Things*, ##50-51 (EGP 4, 121); *On Spiritual Knowledge*, #39, #53 (EGP 4, 150, 155)
121. *On Spiritual Knowledge*, #53 (EGP 4, 155)
122. *On Love: C1*, #100 (EGP 2, 64); *On Love: C3*, #45, #99 (EGP 2, 90, 99); *For Thalassios: C2*, #8, #39 (EGP 2, 139, 147); *Various Texts C3*, #39 (EGP 2, 219). See also *Various Texts: C5*, #4, #43 (EGP 2, 261-262, 271), both of which are partly from Maximos, and *Various Texts: C1*, #93 (EGP 2, 186), which are attributed to Maximos in the *Philokalia*, but are actually by an unknown scholiast (EGP 2, 391-395).
123. e.g. Maximos in *For Thalassios: C2*, #39 (EGP 2, 147); Thalassios in *For Paul: C4*, #83 (EGP 2, 330); Gregory Palamas in *Topics*, #118 (EGP 4, 401)
124. EGP 4, 176, 210. See also Peter of Damaskos in *Book I, The Eighth Stage of Contemplation* (EGP 3, 143)
125. *Declaration of the Holy Mountain* (EGP 4, 418-426)
126. For *Thalassios: C2*, #39 (EGP 2, 147)
127. Turner, 1999
128. Wolters, 1978, pp.142-143, Turner, 1999, pp.186-210

129. #118 (EGP 4, 402)
130. *Topics*, #123 (EGP 4, 404). Turner explicitly denies that the negation of the negation is a synthesis of this kind. It is, rather, he says: "the collapse of our affirmation and denials into disorder" (Turner, 1999, p.22).
131. Ibid. p.252
132. Ibid. p.259
133. Ibid. p.253
134. Including Diadochos, John of Karpathos, Maximos, the author of the *Discourse on Abba Philimon*, Thalassios, Ilias the Presbyter, Nikitas Stithatos, Gregory of Sinai, and Gregory Palamas: see Chapter 4.
135. For source references to the assertions in this paragraph and the next two paragraphs, and for further detail, see Chapter 4.
136. *On Spiritual Knowledge*, #31 (EGP 4, 148)
137. *On Commandments & Doctrines*, #116 (EGP 4, 239)
138. *To Xenia*, #62 (EGP 4, 319)
139. Sinkewicz, 2003, p.199, #60

# Epilogue

1. *On Virtues, Contemplation & Priesthood*, #68 (*Philokalia* 2, 375)
2. Exodus 3, and Exodus 20:21, respectively.

Appendix 1:
# Constituent works of the Greek *Philokalia*

1. The English translators of the *Philokalia* helpfully provide a detailed account, on a paragraph by paragraph basis, of which parts of these texts are known to be by Maximos and which are wholly or partly by another author (either an unknown scholiast, or Dionysios the Areopagite; see Palmer, Sherrard and Ware, 1984, pp.49-50, 391-395)
2. Published in English translation from the Russian *Dobrotolubiye* by Kadloubovsky and Palmer, 1979, pp.162-270
3. Published in English translation from the Russian *Dobrotolubiye* by ibid. pp.271-273
4. Published in English translation from the Russian *Dobrotolubiye* by ibid. pp.74-94

# Bibliography

A Monk of the Eastern Church (1987) *The Jesus Prayer,* Crestwood, St Vladimir's Seminary.

Allen, N.B. (2006) Cognitive Psychotherapy. In Bloch, S. (Ed.) *An Introduction to the Psychotherapies.* 4th ed. Oxford, Oxford. 141-166.

Anatolios, K. (2004) *Athanasius,* London, Routledge.

Anderson, S., Butterfield, J., Daintith, J., Holmes, A., Isaacs, A., Law, J., Lilly, C., Martin, E., Mckeown, C., Stibbs, A. & Summers, E. (2004) *Collins English Dictionary,* Glasgow, Collins.

Balfour, D. (1982) St Symeon of Thessalonica: A Polemical Hesychast. *Sobornost,* 4, 6-21.

Bielawski, M. (1997) *The Philocalical Vision of the World in the Theology of Dumitru Stăniloae,* Bydgoszcz, Homini.

Bloch, S. & Harari, E. (2006) An Historical Context. In Bloch, S. (Ed.) *An Introduction to the Psycotherapies.* 4th ed. Oxford, Oxford. 3-17.

Brakke, D. (Ed.) (2009) *Evagrius of Pontus: Talking Back. A Monastic Handbook for Combating Demons,* Trappist, Cistercian Publications.

Brewin, C.R. & Power, M.J. (1997) Meaning and Psychological Therapy: Overview and Introduction. In Power, M. & Brewin, C.R. (Eds.) *The Transformation of Meaning in Psychological Therapies.* John Wiley, Chichester. 1-14.

Brock, S. (1982) The Prayer of the Heart in Syrian Tradition. *Sobornost,* 4, 131-142.

Brown, D. & Pedder, J. (1980) *Introduction to Psychotherapy,* London, Tavistock.

Brown, W.S. (1998) Cognitive Contributions to Soul. In Brown, W.S., Murphy, N. & Malony, H.N. (Eds.) *Whatever Happened to the Soul? Scientific and Theological Portraits of Human Nature.* Minneapolis, Fortress. 99-125.

Bundy, D. (1990) Evagrius Ponticus, the Kephalaia Gnostica. In Wimbush, V.L. (Ed.) *Ascetic Behavior in Greco-Roman Antiquity. A Sourcebook.* Minneapolis, Fortress. 175-186.

Casiday, A.M. (2006) *Evagrius Ponticus,* London, Routledge.

Cavarnos, C. (1972) *St Macarios of Corinth,* Belmont, Institute for Byzantine and Modern Greek Studies.

Cavarnos, C. (1994) *St Nicodemos the Hagiorite,* Belmont, Institute for Byzantine and Modern Greek Studies.

Chamberas, P.A., Bebis, G.S. & Harakas, S.S. (1989) *Nicodemos of the Holy Mountain: A Handbook of Spiritual Counsel,* New York, Paulist Press.

Chirban, J.T. (Ed.) (2001) *Sickness or Sin? Spiritual Discernment and Differential Diagnosis,* Brookline, Holy Cross Orthodox Press.

Chrysostomos, A. (2007) *A Guide to Orthodox Psychotherapy,* Lanham, University Press of America.

Conticello, V. & Citterio, E. (2002) La Philocalie Et Ses Versions. In Conticello, C.G. & Conticello, V. (Eds.) *La Théologie Byzantine Et Sa Tradition.* Turnhout, Brepols. 999-1021.

Cook, C. (2007a) Considering the Link between Spirituality and Addiction. *SCANbites,* 4, 10-11.

Cook, C., Powell, A. & Sims, A. (Eds.) (2009) *Spirituality and Psychiatry,* London, Royal College of Psychiatrists Press.

Cook, C.C.H. (2004) Addiction and Spirituality. *Addiction,* 99, 539-551.

Cook, C.C.H. (2006) *Alcohol, Addiction and Christian Ethics,* Cambridge, Cambridge.

Cook, C.C.H. (2007b) AA's First European Experience and the Spiritual Experience of AA. *Addiction,* 102, 846-847.

Cross, F.L. & Livingstone, E.A. (1997) *The Oxford Dictionary of the Christian Church,* Oxford, Oxford.

Culliford, L. & Eagger, S. (2009) Assessing Spiritual Needs. In Cook, C., Powell, A. & Sims, A. (Eds.) *Spirituality and Psychiatry.* London, Royal College of Psychiatrists Press. 16-38.

Decatanzaro, C.J., Maloney, G. & Krivocheine, B. (1980) *Simeon the New Theologian: The Discourses,* London, SPCK.

Deurzen, E.V. (2009) *Psychotherapy and the Quest for Happiness,* Los Angeles, Sage.

Dixon, T. (2003) *From Passions to Emotions,* Cambridge, Cambridge.

Drummond, L.M. & Kennedy, B. (2006) Behavioural Psychotherapy. *An Introduction to the Psychotherapies.* 4th ed. Oxford, Oxford. 167-196.

Dysinger, L. (2005) *Psalmody and Prayer in the Writings of Evagrius Ponticus,* Oxford, Oxford.

Eid, M. & Larsen, R.J. (Eds.) (2008) *The Science of Subjective Well-Being,* New York, Guilford.

Eijk, P.J.V.D. (2005) *Medicine and Philosophy in Classical Antiquity,* Cambridge, Cambridge.

Featherstone, J.M.E. & Tachiaos, A.E.N. (1989) *The Life of Paisij Velyčkovs'kyj,* Cambridge, MA, Harvard.

Ferguson, E., Mchugh, M.P. & Norris, F.W. (1999) *Encyclopedia of Early Christianity,* New York, Garland.

Frank, J.D. (2006) What Is Psychotherapy? In Bloch, S. (Ed.) *An Introduction to the Psychotherapies.* 4th ed. Oxford, Oxford. 59-76.

Gelder, M., Gath, D., Mayou, R. & Cowen, P. (1996) *Oxford Textbook of Psychiatry,* Oxford, Oxford.

Gregg, R.C. (1980) *Athanasius: The Life of Antony and the Letter to Marcellinus,* Mahwah, Paulist Press.

Hackmann, A. (1997) The Transformation of Meaning in Cognitive Therapy. In Power, M. & Brewin, C.R. (Eds.) *The Transformation of*

*Meaning in Psychological Therapies: Integrating Theory and Practice.* Chichester, Wiley. 125-140.
Hamilton, M. (1981) *Fish's Clinical Psychopathology,* Bristol, Wright.
Harkins, P.W. & Riese, W. (1963) *Galen on the Passions and Errors of the Soul,* Ohio State University.
Harris, W.S., Gowda, M., Kolb, J.W., Strychacz, C.P., Vacek, J.L., Jones, P.G., Forker, A., O'keefe, J.H. & Mccallister, B.D. (1999) A Randomized, Controlled Trial of the Effects of Remote, Intercessory Prayer on Outcomes in Patients Admitted to the Coronary Care Unit. *Archives of Internal Medicine,* 159, 2273-2278.
Hastings, A., Mason, A. & Pyper, H. (2000) *The Oxford Companion to Christian Thought,* Oxford, Oxford.
Hausherr, I. (1978) *The Name of Jesus,* Kalamazoo, Cistercian Publications.
Haybron, D.M. (2008) Philosophy and the Science of Subjective Well-Being. In Eid, M. & Larsen, R.J. (Eds.) *The Science of Subjective Well-Being.* New York, Guilford Press. 17-43.
Helman, C. (1985) *Culture, Health and Illness,* Bristol, Wright.
Hobson, J.A. (2005) *13 Dreams Freud Never Had,* New York, Pi Press.
Husser, J.M. (1999) *Dreams and Dream Narratives in the Biblical World,* Sheffield, Sheffield Academic Press.
Innes, R. (1999) *Discourses of the Self: Seeking Wholeness in Theology and Psychology,* Bern, Peter Lang.
Jackson, P. & Cook, C.C.H. (2005) Introduction of a Spirituality Group in a Community Service for People with Drinking Problems. *Journal of Substance Use,* 10, 375-383.
Jackson, S.W. (1969) Galen – on Mental Disorders. *Journal of the History of the Behavioral Sciences,* 5, 365-384.
Jaffé, A., Winston, R. & Winston, C. (Eds.) (1963) *C.G. Jung: Memories, Dreams, Reflections,* London, Collins.
Kadloubovsky, E. & Palmer, G.E.H. (1979) *Writings from the Philokalia on Prayer of the Heart,* London, Faber & Faber.
Kerr, I.B. & Ryle, A. (2006) Cognitive Analytic Therapy. In Bloch, S. (Ed.) *An Introduction to the Psychotherapies.* Oxford, Oxford. 267-286.
Koenig, H.G., Mccullough, M.E. & Larson, D.B. (2001) *Handbook of Religion and Health,* New York, Oxford.
Konstantinovsky, J. (2009) *Evagrius Ponticus: The Making of a Gnostic,* Farnham, Ashgate.
Kurtz, E. (1996) Twelve Step Programs. In Van Ness, P.H. (Ed.) *Spirituality and the Secular Quest.* London, SCM. 277-302.
Laird, M. (2007) *Gregory of Nyssa and the Grasp of Faith,* Oxford, Oxford.
Larchet, J.C. (2005) *Mental Disorders and Spiritual Healing: Teachings from the Early Christian East,* Hillsdale, Sophia Perennis.
Lawson-Tancred, H. (1986) *Aristotle: De Anima (on the Soul),* London, Penguin.
Lawson-Tancred, H.C. (1991) *Aristotle: The Art of Rhetoric,* London, Penguin.
Lee, D. (2003) *Plato: The Republic,* London, Penguin.
Leighton, S.R. (1982) Aristotle and the Emotions. *Phronesis,* 27, 144-174.

Lloyd, G.E.R., Chadwick, J., Mann, W.N., Lonie, I.M. & Withington, E.T. (1983) *Hippocratic Writings,* London, Penguin.

Louth, A. (1989) *Discerning the Mystery: An Essay on the Nature of Theology,* Oxford, Clarendon.

Louth, A. (1996) *Maximus the Confessor,* London, Routledge.

Louth, A. (2003) The Theology of the *Philokalia.* In Behr, J., Louth, A. & Conomos, D. (Eds.) *Abba: The Tradition of Orthodoxy in the West. Festschrift for Bishop Kallistos (Ware) of Diokleia.* Crestwood, St Vladimir's Seminary Press. 351-361.

Louth, A. (2004) The Literature of the Monastic Movement. In Young, F., Ayres, L. & Louth, A. (Eds.) *The Cambridge History of Early Christian Literature.* Cambridge, Cambridge. 373-381.

Luibheid, C., Russell, N. & Ware, K. (1982) *John Climacus: The Ladder of Divine Ascent,* Mahwah, Paulist.

Mace, C. (2008) *Mindfulness and Mental Health,* London, Routledge.

Mackey, J.P. (2000) *The Critique of Theological Reason,* Cambridge, Cambridge.

Maloney, G.A. & Ware, K. (1992) *Pseudo-Macarius: The Fifty Spiritual Homilies and the Great Letter,* New York, Paulist.

Martin, R. & Barresi, J. (2006) *The Rise and Fall of Soul and Self,* New York, Columbia University Press.

Mattoon, M.A. (2006) Dreams. In Papadopoulos, R. (Ed.) *The Handbook of Jungian Psychology.* London, Routledge. 244-259.

McDonald, W.J., Magner, J.A., Mcguire, M.R.P. & Whelan, J.P. (Eds.) (1981) *New Catholic Encyclopedia,* Washington DC, Catholic University of America.

McLynn, F. (1997) *Carl Gustav Jung,* New York, St Martin's.

McMahon, D. (2006) *The Pursuit of Happiness: A History from the Greeks to the Present,* London, Allen Lane.

Meyendorff, J. (1996) Theosis in the Eastern Christian Tradition. In Dupré, L. & Saliers, D.E. (Eds.) *Christian Spirituality Iii: Post-Reformation and Modern.* London, SCM. 470-476.

Mihailoff, V. (2005) *Breaking the Chains of Addiction,* Salisbury, MA, Regina Orthodox Press Inc.

Mizen, S. & Holmes, J. (2006) Individual Long-Term Psychotherapy. In Bloch, S. (Ed.) *An Introduction to the Psychotherapies.* 4th ed. Oxford, Oxford. 79-110.

Muse, S. (Ed.) (2004) *Raising Lazarus: Integral Healing in Orthodox Christianity,* Brookline, Holy Cross Orthodox Press.

Nussbaum, M.C. (1994) *The Therapy of Desire: Theory and Practice in Hellenistic Ethics,* Princeton, Princeton.

Nutton, V. (2006) *Ancient Medicine,* London, Routledge.

Osborn, E. (2005) *Clement of Alexandria,* Cambridge, Cambridge.

Palmer, G.E.H., Sherrard, P. & Ware, K. (1979) *The Philokalia: The Complete Text Compiled by St Nikodimos of the Holy Mountain and St Makarios of Corinth,* Volume 1, London, Faber & Faber.

Palmer, G.E.H., Sherrard, P. & Ware, K. (1981) *The Philokalia: The Complete Text Compiled by St Nikodimos of the Holy Mountain and St*

*Makarios of Corinth,* Volume 2, London, Faber & Faber.

Palmer, G.E.H., Sherrard, P. & Ware, K. (1984) *The Philokalia: The Complete Text Compiled by St Nikodimos of the Holy Mountain and St Makarios of Corinth,* Volume 3, London, Faber and Faber.

Palmer, G.E.H., Sherrard, P. & Ware, K. (1995) *The Philokalia. The Complete Text Compiled by St Nikodimos of the Holy Mountain and St Makarios of Corinth,* Volume 4, London, Faber & Faber.

Parry, K. (2007) *The Blackwell Companion to Eastern Christianity,* Oxford, Blackwell.

Parry, K., Melling, D.J., Brady, D., Griffith, S.H. & Healey, J.F. (1999) *The Blackwell Dictionary of Eastern Christianity,* Oxford, Blackwell.

Pentkovsky, A. & Smith, T.A. (1999) *The Pilgrim's Tale,* New York, Paulist Press.

Richards, P.S. & Bergin, A.E. (Eds.) (2000) *Handbook of Psychotherapy and Religious Diversity,* Washington DC, American Psychological Association.

Ricoeur, P. (1981) *Hermeneutics and the Human Sciences,* Cambridge, Cambridge.

Rowe, C. (2005) *Plato: Phaedrus,* London, Penguin.

Russell, N. (2004) *The Doctrine of Deification in the Greek Patristic Tradition,* Oxford, Oxford.

Savin, O. & Hopko, T. (2001) *The Way of a Pilgrim and the Pilgrim Continues His Way,* Boston, Shambhala.

Schema-Monk Metrophanes (1976) *Blessed Paisius Velichkovsky: The Life and Ascetic Labours of Our Father, Elder Paisius, Archimandrite of the Holy Moldavian Monasteries of Niamets and Sekoul. Optina Version,* Platina, Saint Herman of Alaska Brotherhood.

Schneiders, S.M. (2005) Christian Spirituality: Definition, Methods and Types. In Sheldrake, P. (Ed.) *The New SCM Dictionary of Christian Spirituality.* London, SCM. 1-6.

Searle, B.A. (2008) *Well-Being: In Search of a Good Life?,* Bristol, Policy Press.

Sheldrake, P. (2005) *The New SCM Dictionary of Christian Spirituality,* London, SCM.

Shuman, J.J. & Meador, K.G. (2003) *Heal Thyself: Spirituality, Medicine, and the Distortion of Christianity,* Oxford, Oxford.

Simon, B. (1978) *Mind and Madness in Ancient Greece,* Ithaca, Cornell University Press.

Sinkewicz, R.E. (2003) *Evagrius of Pontus: The Greek Ascetic Corpus,* Oxford, Oxford.

Smith, A., Palmer, G.E.H., Sherrard, P. & Ware, K. (2006) *Philokalia: The Eastern Christian Spiritual Texts – Selections Annotated & Explained,* Woodstock, Skylight Paths.

Sorabji, R. (2002) *Emotion and Peace of Mind: From Stoic Agitation to Christian Temptation,* Oxford, Oxford.

Sorabji, R. (2006) *Self: Ancient and Modern Insights About Individuality, Life, and Death,* Chicago, University of Chicago Press.

Stapakis, B.S. & Coniaris, A.M. (2004) *The Philokalia: Master Reference Guide,* Minneapolis, Light & Life.

Strachey, J., Tyson, A. & Richards, A. (1982) *The Interpretation of Dreams*, Harmondsworth, Penguin.
Sykes, S. (1984) *The Identity of Christianity*, London, SPCK.
Taylor, C. (1989) *Sources of the Self: The Making of the Modern Identity*, Cambridge, Cambridge.
Telfer, W. (1955) *Cyril of Jerusalem and Nemesius of Emesa*, London, SCM.
Thermos, V. (2002) *In Search of the Person: "True" And False Self" According to Donald Winnicott and St. Gregory Palamas*, Montreal, Alexander Press.
Thomson, J.A.K., Treddenick, H. & Barnes, J. (1983) *Aristotle: Ethics*, Harmondsworth, Penguin.
Thyer, J. (2004) *Steps to Life: A Spiritual Journey with Christian Mysticism and the Twelve Steps*, Sydney, ABC.
Turner, D. (1999) *The Darkness of God: Negativity in Christian Mysticism*, Cambridge, Cambridge.
Vlachos, H. (1994) *Orthodox Psychotherapy*, Levadia, Birth of the Theotokos Monastery.
Ward, B. (1984) *The Sayings of the Desert Fathers: The Alphabetical Collection*, Kalamazoo, Cistercian Publications.
Ward, B. (2003) *The Desert Fathers: Sayings of the Early Christian Monks*, London, Penguin.
Ware, K. (1984) Philocalie. In Viller, M., Cavallera, F., De Guibert, J., Rayez, A., Derville, A. & Solignac, A. (Eds.) *Dictionnaire De Spiritualité*. Paris, Beauchesne. 1335-1352.
Ware, K. (1989a) *The Power of the Name: The Jesus Prayer in Orthodox Spirituality*, London, Marshall Pickering.
Ware, K. (1991) The Spirituality of the *Philokalia*. *Sobornost*, 13, 6-24.
Ware, K. (1996) Ways of Prayer and Contemplation. I. Easter. In McGinn, B., Meyendorff, J. & Leclercq, J. (Eds.) *Christian Spirituality: Origins to the Twelfth Century*. London, SCM. 395-414.
Ware, K. (2005) St Nikodimos and the *Philokalia*. In Conomos, D. & Speake, G. (Eds.) *Mount Athos the Sacred Bridge: The Spirituality of the Holy Mountain*. Oxford, Peter Lang. 69-121.
Ware, K.T. (1989b) The Meaning Of "Pathos" In Abba Isaias and Theodoret of Cyrus. *Studia Patristica*, XX, 315-322.
Webber, M. (2003) *Steps of Transformation: An Orthodox Priest Explores the Twelve Steps*, Ben Lomond, Conciliar Press.
Wheeler, E.P. (1977) *Dorotheos of Gaza: Discourses and Sayings*, Kalamazoo, Cistercian Publications.
Wolters, C. (1978) *The Cloud of Unknowing and Other Works*, London, Penguin.
Young, T.R. (2001) Psychotherapy with Eastern Orthodox Christians. In Richards, P.S. & Bergin, A.E. (Eds.) *Handbook of Psychotherapy and Religious Diversity*. Washington D.C., American Psychological Association. 89-104.

# Index

## People

Abdisho the Seer, 230
Abraham, Abba, 53, 106
Adler, Alfred, 207
Agathon, Abba, 108
Ammonas, Abba, 19, 325-326 (note 185)
Antony the Great (Antony of Egypt), 18, 156, 319 (note 37)
  *Life of Antony* by Athanasius, 19, 130, 319 (note 37)
  *On the Character of Men* (attributed to Antony), 11-12, 21, 161, 174, 182, 307, 338 (note 86)
Anselm, 260
Aquinas, Thomas, 214, 216, 260
Aristotle
  anger, 134
  eudaimonia, 155
  images (noemata), 261
  passions, on the, 48-49, 51-52; remedy for, 102-104
  soul, 320 (note 55)
Arsenius, Abba, 53, 106
Artemidorus of Daldis, 277-278, 285
Athanasius
  *Gnostikos*, quotation in, 36
  medical language, 101
  *see also under* Antony the Great
Augustine of Hippo
  inwardness, 152, 213, 231, 257
  passions, 214, 216
  reason, 260
  reflexivity, 202, 210, 231
  spirituality, 224

Basil of Caesarea, 36, 134
Basil the Great, 317 (note 2)
Bessarion, Abba, 106
Brianchaninov, Ignatii, 9
Brock Sebastian, 230

Cassian, John, 7, 170, 184, 193, 301, 307
  dreams, 282
  inwardness, 233
  medical language, 335 (note 13)
  purity of heart, 170, 348 (note 102)
  soul, health of, 164-165
Charcot, Jean Martin, 206
Chrysippus of Soli, 50, 52
Clement of Alexandria, 101, 160, 261, 334 (note 131), 362 (note 113)
Cronius, Abba, 108

Democritus of Abdera, 154
Descartes, René, 152, 209, 211, 213, 214, 216, 257
Diadochos of Photiki, 301, 308
  blessedness, 182
  humours, 94
  illumination of, 167
  inwardness, 235
  Jesus Prayer, 143
  light, divine, 167, 295
  stillness, 44, 165
  well-being, 165

Didymus the Blind, 36
Dionysios (Denys) the Areopagite, 45, 57, 291, 293, 295, 363 (notes 114 & 115), 364 (note 1)
Dixon, Thomas, 214-215
Doulas, Abba, 156
Dysinger, Luke, 38, 101, 113, 133-135, 137

Eckhart, Meister, 294, 296
Ellis, Albert, 208
Epictetus, 249
Evagrios the Solitary (Evagrius of Pontus), 22-40, 301
  anthropology, 11
  beatitudes of, 158-159, 197
  beatitudes, on the, 158
  contemplation, 33-40, 113, 141, 159, 261-262, 287, 289-290, 360 (note 43)
  deification, 360 (note 43)
  depression, 249, 253
  dreams, 280-282, 285-286
  hesychia, 23, 115, 158
  impassibility, 31, 33, 157
  inwardness, 233
  medical language, 55, 101
  passions, 23-33, 54-57, 60, 62, 64, 157; remedies for, 109-114, 142
  practical life, the, 31, 33-34, 115-116, 142
  prayer, 22, 33-39, 114, 140-141, 289, 296
  psalmody, 35, 110, 113, 132-139, 142, 158, 289
  stillness, 55
  thoughts, xiii, 23-33, 54-55, 60, 258, 260-265, 289: influence of diet on, 288; interpretation of, 269-273, 296; unconscious processes, 203
  visions of light, 166-167, 291, 295
  well-being, 157-159

Frank, Jerome, 206, 217-223, 250
Freud, Sigmund, xv-xvi, xviii, 44, 101, 211-213, 227, 268
  dreams, 276-279, 285
  ego, 211, 224

  medical language, 101
  psychoanalysis, 206-207
  religion, 226
  works of, 203-204

Galen, 51, 101, 134
Gregory Nazianzen, 21, 310, 317 (note 2)
Gregory of Nyssa, 134, 291
Gregory of Sinai, 304, 306, 313, 361
  darkness, divine, 291-292
  deification, 161, 164
  dreams, 282-283, 361 (note 77)
  hesychast tradition, 4
  hesychia, 176-177, 287, 289
  illumination of the intellect, 168, 176-177
  inwardness, 242-243
  light, divine, 296
  passions, 63, 66, 83, 88, 91, 93-94
  practical life, the, 118-119, 121
  psalmody, 138
  stillness, 119
  thoughts, origin of, 360 (note 42)
Gregory of Thessalonica, 306, 316
Gregory Palamas, 7, 57, 249, 304-305, 314, 316, 319 (notes 38 & 40)
  anthropology, 13
  apophatic theology, 292-294
  beatitudes, on the, 184-187, 190, 192-194
  blessedness, 181
  deification, 160-162
  hesychast controversy, 160, 292, 314
  hesychast tradition, 4
  illumination of the intellect, 168-170, 172-174, 296
  inwardness, 243, 246-247
  medical language, 101
  passions, 96
  prayer, 141, 289
  soul, health of, 165

Herodotus, 154
Hesychios (Hesychius) the Priest, 301, 307, 310

beatitudes of, 197
beatitudes, on the, 188, 194
blessedness, 180-182
contemplation, 20
humours, 93
inwardness, 233-234, 244-245
Jesus Prayer, 143-145
scripture, 41
temptation, 83, 85, 90
watchfulness, 123-128
Hippocrates, 93, 333 (note 122)
Hume, David, 209, 213-216, 257
Hyperechius, Abba, 108

Ignatius of Antioch, 101
Ignatius Xanthopoulos, 119-120, 305, 315, 316, 343 (note 220)
Ilias the Presbyter, 303, 310
anthropology, 15
beatitudes of, 198-199
blessedness, 183
deification, 161
humours, 93
illumination of the intellect, 167
inwardness, 238
light, divine, 290
passions, 65, 83, 86-87, 91
prayer, 139, 167, 287, 290, 354 (note 234)
soul, health of, 165
thoughts, xix, 290
Innes, Robert, 223-224, 227
Isaac of Nineveh (Isaac the Syrian), 141, 168, 230, 312, 319 (notes 37, 38, 41)
Isaiah the Solitary (Abba Isaias), 20, 301, 307
guarding of the heart, 40, 286
inwardness, 233
passions (affirmative view), 57, 96

John Climacus, 76, 309-310, 312, 319 (notes 37, 38, 41)
temptation (process of), 3, 76-78, 81, 83, 90
John of Karpathos, 302, 308, 310
beatitudes of, 197
beatitudes, on the, 184, 193
intellect, illumination of, 167
inwardness, 235-236, 245

psalmody, 139
soul, renewal of, 41
John the Dwarf, Abba, 108
Joseph, Abba, 106-107, 156, 329 (note 35)
Jung, Carl, 101, 227
analytical psychology, 207
dreams, 277-279, 285
religion, 226
works of, 203-204

Kallistos Cataphygiotes, 305, 315
Kallistos Telecudes, 305, 315
Kallistos Xanthopoulos, 119-120, 305, 315, 316, 343 (note 220)
Kallistos, Patriarch, 7-8, 305, 315
Kant, Immanuel, 209, 213, 256
Konstantinovsky, Julia, 262, 290-291, 348-349 (note 105)

Locke, John, 209, 211, 213, 216
Louth, Andrew, 213, 262

Makarios, Abba (Makarios the Great, Makarios of Egypt), 20-23, 108, 246, 269, 303
Makarios of Alexandria, 21
Makarios of Corinth, xv, 4-5, 7-9, 123, 311, 340 (note 124)
Mark Eugenikos of Ephesus, 306, 316
Mark the Ascetic, 21, 301, 307, 309
humours, 93
inwardness, 232, 233
passions, 64; process of, 73-77, 81, 83, 87, 90, 332 (notes 97, 98, 103)
Mavrogordatos, John, 7
Maximos Kapsokalivitos, 306
Maximos the Confessor, 2, 7, 302, 308-310, 312, 319 (note 40)
anthropology, 16, 320 (note 55)
apophatic theology, 292-293, 359 (note 18)
beatitudes of, 195, 197-198
beatitudes, on the, 184, 187-189, 191
blessedness, 180, 183
Christology, 161, 262

contemplation, 165, 231, 290,
  359 (note 18)
darkness, divine, 291-292
deification, 161-165, 170-171,
  290, 348 (note 96)
humours, 93-94
inwardness, 236-237
light, divine, 167, 359 (note 18)
medical language, 101
passions, 57-60, 65, 72, 81-83,
  87, 90, 93-96, 116-117, 163,
  215, 287-288, 333 (note 112);
  remedies for, 114, 116-117
practical life, the, 116-117, 120
prayer, 140, 262, 287-289
psalmody, 138-139
scripture, 41-44
thoughts, xvi, 260-262, 288-290
well-being, 165, 348 (note 96)
Mesmer, Anton, 206
Mihailoff, Victor, 254
Moses, Abba, 170

Neilos (Nilus) the Ascetic, 1, 33,
  42, 143, 165, 168, 181, 234,
  301, 308
Nietzsche, Friedrich, 44
Nikiphoros the Monk, 21, 304,
  312-314, 316
  inwardness, 242
  Jesus Prayer, 148-149, 289
  watchfulness, 122-123, 130-132
Nikitas Stithatos, 304, 312
  beatitudes of, 199
  beatitudes, on the, 187, 195
  blessedness, 180-181, 183-184
  contemplation, 139
  darkness, divine, 291-293
  deification, 161, 163-164
  dreams, 283-286
  hesychia, 175-176
  humours, 93
  illumination of the intellect, 168,
    171-172
  inwardness, 240-241
  light, divine, 180, 296
  medical language, 101
  passions, 66
  psalmody, 139

scripture, 42, 327 (note 217)
well-being, 165
Nikodimos of the Holy Mountain,
  xv, 4-8, 20, 123, 159, 317 (note
  7), 340 (note 124)
Nilus, Abba, 156
Nussbaum, Martha, 52, 100-101,
  336 (note 38), 345 (note 10)

Origen, 2, 23, 101, 317 (note 2),
  323 (note 107), 362 (note 113)

Paphnutius, Abba, 325-326 (note
  185)
Pavlov, Ivan, 207
Peter of Damaskos, 7, 21, 303, 310
  anthropology, 13
  beatitudes of, 195, 199
  beatitudes, on the, 184-192, 194
  contemplation, 328 (note 230)
  dreams, 282
  hesychia, 175
  inwardness, 238-239
  passions, 60, 62, 66, 77, 80-81,
    90, 331 (note 86); remedies
    for, 117-118, 139, 142
  practical life, the, 117-118, 120-
    121, 139
  prayer, 141-142, 289, 342 (notes
    204 & 207)
  psalmody, 139, 142
  scripture, 40, 42-44
  soul, health of, 165
  stillness, 117, 199
  suffering, 251-252
  thoughts, 289
Philimon, Abba, 143, 167, 172,
  177, 282, 310, 327 (note 217)
Philotheos Kokkinos, 306, 316
Philotheos of Sinai, 303, 310
  humours, 93
  inwardness, 238, 244-245
  Jesus Prayer, 145-147
  passions, 57-58, 77, 79, 90
  watchfulness, 123, 126-128
Pityrion, Abba, 106, 329 (note 36)
Plato, 160, 211, 213
  anthropology, 10-12, 14, 209
  darkness mysticism, 291
  eudaimonia, 155

humours, 93
inwardness, 152
passions, 48, 51-52, 94, 134; remedies for, 102
Poemen, Abba, 106-107, 156, 329 (note 32)
Posidonius, 50-51
Pseudo-Makarios, 311

Ricoeur, Paul, xix, 44, 267-270, 272, 358 (note 89)
Rufus, Abba, 156

Sisoes, Abba, 53, 107-108, 337 (note 46)
Sorabji, Richard, 47-48, 328 (note 3)
Stăniloae, Dumitru, 9-10
Sykes, Stephen, 229, 231
Symeon Metaphrastis, 21, 303, 311
  beatitudes of, 199
  beatitudes, on the, 185, 187, 189, 194
  dreams, 282
  intellect, perfection of, 173
  inwardness, 239-240, 245
  passions, 83, 86-87, 90
Symeon the New Theologian, 304, 306, 311-312
  beatitudes, on the, 189
  blessedness, 181
  inwardness, 240
  light, divine, 169-170, 283
Symeon the Studite, 304, 311
Symeon, Archbishop of Thessalonica, 305, 316

Taylor, Charles, 155
  disengagement, 202, 211, 213
  expressivism, 212-213
  inwardness, 151-152, 210, 229, 231, 247-248
  reflexivity, 202, 210-211, 213, 279

Romanticism, 212
Thalassios the Libyan, 303, 309
  apophatic theology, 292
  deification, 161
  intellect, illumination of, 167
  inwardness, 232, 237
  medical language, 101
  passions, 65, 94; remedies for, 114
  psalmody, 138-139
  soul, health of, 165
Theodoros the Great Ascetic, 302, 308
  beatitudes, on the, 188
  blessedness, 182
  deification, 161
  inwardness, 236
  passions, 64, 83, 85, 90
Theoliptos, Metropolitan of Philadelphia, 304, 312
  apophatic theology, 292
  blessedness, 182
  deification, 161
  intellect, illumination of, 171
  intellect, perfection of, 171
  inwardness, 232, 242
  prayer, 171
Theonas, Abba, 20
Theophan the Recluse, 9, 319 (note 43)
Theophanis of Batopedi, 306, 316
Theophanis the Monk, 173, 174, 238, 289, 303, 310
Turner, Denys, xix, 293-294, 296

Velichkovsky, Paisius, 8-9, 318 (note 26)
Vlachos, Hierotheos, 248

Ware, Kallistos, 6, 9, 57
Webber, Meletios, 254-255

Zeno of Citium, 49, 52

## Subjects

addiction, 102, 226
  Orthodox spiritual therapy, 253-255
  passions, similarity to, 98, 203, 249, 253
  Twelve Step treatment programmes, 253-255
allegory, xvi, 102
  cave, Plato's, 291
  dreams, 277, 285
  medical, 101
  passions, for, 24, 26-29, 54
  scripture, interpretation of, 42-43, 125, 158, 165, 171, 291
angels
  bodily temperament, effect on, 94
  dreams inspired by, 281-285
  noemata inspired by, 261
  prayer, 35, 133, 170
  psalmody, 136
  terrestrial, 199
  see also thoughts (angelic)
apatheia, see dispassion
appetite(s)
  nature, in accordance with, 95
  passions and, 50, 88
  soul, of the, 11
  see also desire(s)
*Apophthegmata Patrum*, 19-21
  passions, 52-54, 97-98; remedies for, 101, 105-109
  well-being, 156-157
ascetic discipline
  classical tradition, 105
  excess as a form of gluttony, 33
  moderation, need for, 116-117
  remedy for the passions, 101, 113, 115-121

beatitudes
  Jesus, of, 184-195
  *Philokalia*, of the, 195-199
blessedness, 158, 177-196
  definition, 177-180

  God, of, 180-181, 186, 194
  life, eternal, 181-184
  life of, 199
  virtues, 181
  see also under Christology (blessedness), hesychia, virtue, well-being
  see also beatitudes
body
  disorderly impulses, 134, 172
  dissolution, 183
  heart, relationship to, 243, 246-247
  humoural theories, 92-95
  mortification of, 118
  passions of, 14, 55, 65, 106, 116, 188, 337 (note 62)
  physiology, see humours
  prayer of the, 141-142, 342 (note 207)
  soul, relationship with, 11-14, 121, 155, 157-158, 209, 214, 246
  virtues of, 11, 116
  see also under angels, darkness, desire(s)

Christology
  blessedness, 183
  contemplation, 38, 159, 262
  controversies over, 1-2
  deification, 160-162, 200
  guarding of the intellect, 127, 132
  well-being, 201
  see also under deification, Logos
conscious(ness), 165, 241, 285
  fantasies, 282
  motivation, of, xvii, 30, 324 (note 118)
  passion(s), and, 83, 86, 91
  self identity, and, 209, 211
  spirituality, and, 260
  thoughts, and, 105, 260, 266, 275-276
  virtue, and, 30, 121
  watchfulness, and, 131
  wisdom, of, 175

contemplation, 34, 198
  classical tradition, 104, 155-156
  darkness mysticism and, 292
  definition, 38
  deification, second stage to attaining, 163
  hesychia and, 175-177
  intellect: illumination of, associated with, 167; perfection of, and, 172-173; power of, 15-16, 173-174
  *Kephalaia Gnostika* on, 37-39
  natural, 113, 231, 261-264, 284, 288, 292
  noetic, 119
  *Philokalia* as guide to, 6
  poverty of spirit as first stage of, 185, 194
  psalmody as, 35, 139
  rejected by Adam, 291
  revelations associated with, 284
  spiritual, 117
  theological, 262, 272, 289
  thoughts in, 135, 289-290, 359 (note 18), 362 (note 110)

darkness, 193
  bodily, 11-12
  demonic, 244
  divine, 196, 199, 291-295, 299-300, 362 (note 113)
  heart, of the, 147, 245
  intellect, of the, 167
  passions, of the, 67, 69, 73, 74, 185, 195
deification, 159-164
  Christology, 116, 160-161
  definition, 159
  passion of, 163
  *Philokalia*, aim of the, 6
  stages to attaining, 163-164
demons
  banishing of, 106, 113, 145-146, 244
  dreams, action in, 280-282, 284-285
  humours, action on, 94
  passions, close relationship with, 54-56, 94
  prayer as struggle against, 33-35
  qualities of acquired by the human soul, 14
  tactics of, 32-33
  *see also under* darkness, fear, light, thoughts, warfare
desert fathers, 17-21
  passions, 52-54; remedies for, 105-109
  well-being, on, 156-157
  *see also Apophthegmata Patrum*
desire(s)
  body, of the, 12-14
  control of, 223
  elimination of, 117-118, 136
  God, for, 12, 148, 158, 163, 179, 224, 273
  hostile, 33
  humoural theories, 93-94
  inwardness of, 151
  objectification of, 202, 211
  passion, 47-49, 53-54, 59, 65, 71, 103, 107-109, 118, 254; process of, 77-78, 81-83, 85-88, 90-91, 97
  sadness as frustration of, 25, 28
  sexual, 25-26, 49, 271
  soul, of the, 10, 11-12, 14, 16-17, 24
  unsatisfied, 165
  well-being and, 225
  *see also* appetite(s)
dispassion (apatheia, impassibility), 14, 31, 94, 104, 107, 127, 346 (note 38)
  blessing of, 158, 181
  divine darkness and, 292
  dreams and, 280, 282, 285
  hesychia and, 175, 177, 323 (note 109)
  interpretation of scripture and, 43
  love, state of, 116-117
  noemata and, 262
  prayer and, 31, 159, 287-288, 295
  psychotherapy, as outcome of, 222, 227
  soul, health of, 157-159, 165
  watchfulness and, 131

distress
  passions and, 50, 65
  psychotherapy directed to relief of, 216-218, 274-275
dreams, 268, 276-286

eldership (starchestvo), 8, 220
emotion
  catharsis, 103
  disorders of, 273
  distraction from prayer, 258
  human identity and, 209
  inwardness, 229, 230, 246
  objectification of, 202, 211
  passion, distinction from, 47-49, 55, 214-216, 328 (note 3)
  psychotherapy, in, 216, 218, 219, 222
fear, xix-xx, 263-264
  death, of, 251
  demonic, 282, 360 (note 28)
  God, of, 29, 32, 41, 141, 156, 175, 185
  moderation of, 103
  passion and, 48-52, 65, 104, 360 (notes 27 & 28)
  psychotherapy directed to relief of, 208
guilt, 67, 74, 89, 218, 263, 264, 266, 273

health
  definition, 153
heart
  Judeo-Christian tradition, 229
  *Philokalia* on the, 244-247
  purity of, 31, 107, 124, 170, 174, 188-190, 194, 230, 348 (note 102)
  Syriac tradition, 230
  *see also under* body, darkness, humours, prayer, watchfulness
heresy
  Meister Eckhart, 296
  Origenist, 2, 23
hermeneutics, 44-45, 152
  humility, of, 44-45
  psyche as text, 267-269
  scripture, of, 40-45, 202

suspicion, of, 44
thoughts, of, 202, 269-270, 296
*see also* interpretation
hesychasm, 2, 174
hesychast controversy, 2, 160, 164, 292, 296, 314
hesychastic tradition, xv, 3-4, 8
  divine light, vision of, 164, 295
  guarding of the heart in, 40
  Jesus Prayer in, 2
  practical life in, 119-120
  rule of life, 353 (note 214)
hesychia (stillness), xv, 4, 145, 200, 248, 289
  beatitudes of the *Philokalia*, 196, 199
  blessedness, 181
  definition, 174-175
  desert fathers on, 156
  distraction from, 287
  inwardness, 237, 241, 243
  mindfulness, comparison with, 251, 358 (note 92)
  *Philokalia*, in the, 6, 174-177
  watchfulness, 122, 125, 145, 339 (note 120)
humours, 92-95
  balance, 94, 134-136, 139, 334 (note 133)
  heart and, 93-94, 131
  medicine, 93, 110
  passions and, 72, 93-94
  theory of, 93

image (noemata), *see under* thoughts
impassibility, *see* dispassion
intellect (nous), 6, 11-12, 14-17, 152
  beatitudes of the *Philokalia*, 197-198
  hesychia, 175-177
  illumination, 166-170
  imprinting in sleep, 280, 284
  momentary disturbance of, 74, 76
  passions, 26-27, 79-80, 82, 85
  perfection, 170-174
  prayer, 32, 133, 140-142, 147-148, 286-296
  primal, 17

Index 375

psalmody, 139
purification, 166
  thoughts, and, 260-262
  watchfulness (guarding of the intellect), 121-132
interpretation
  dreams, 276-286
  scripture, 41-44, 81, 165, 171, 201-202, 269
  self, 210, 213
  thoughts, 202, 250, 265-276
  *see also* hermeneutics
inwardness, 210
  *Philokalia* and, 229-248
  *see also under* desire(s), emotion, metaphor, scripture, soul

jealousy, 47-48, 55, 110, 263, 323 (note 110), 331 (note 85)

knowledge, 36, 209-210
  body of, 268, 271-272
  contemplative, 36, 38-39, 166, 325 (note 183)
  divine, 133, 168, 171, 175, 190-191, 292
  God, of, 32, 37-39, 124, 133, 156, 159, 175, 180, 290-292
  inner, 234
  intellectual, 262
  noemata and, 261
  nous, healing by, 109
  passion-free, 117
  principial, 11
  pseudo-, 43
  self, 259
  soul, of the, 209
  spiritual, 15-16, 20, 38, 44, 59-60, 118, 133, 163, 165, 173, 181, 198-199, 291, 331 (note 81)
Kollyvades, 4-5

light
  contemplation of, 175
  demonic, 334 (note 132)
  divine, visions of, 4, 125, 164, 166-173, 180, 194, 245, 283, 290-296
  dreams of, 283
  eternal, 184
  inwardness, 231, 239, 244-245

noetic, 37, 127
primordial, 163
logoi (inner essences of things), 37-39, 135, 157, 169, 231, 263, 326 (note 204)
Logos, 34, 45, 140, 171
  Christology, 183, 262, 323 (note 107)
  creator, 17, 231
  deification and the, 161, 164, 183
  divine Intellect, 17, 260
  incarnation, 17, 161, 183
  kenosis of, 116, 161
  theology: apophatic, 293; cataphatic, 292-293

medical language, *see under* allegory, metaphor, passions, vice
memory
  dreams, 280
  Jesus, of, 343 (note 220)
  passion, as part of the process of, 74-75, 77, 81-82, 94, 332 (note 98)
  scripture committed to, 19
  self identity, and, 209, 211
  simple, 77
  sins, of former, 74-75, 332 (note 98)
metaphor(s), xiii, 18, 99, 145, 147, 249-250, 253
  darkness, 294-295
  dualism as, 214
  inwardness, 245-246
  light, 167, 294-295, 349 (note 113)
  medical, 99, 101-102, 134, 137, 157
  passions, for, 24, 26-29, 61, 67-73, 110
  psyche as text, 268-270, 272
  vision, 37
  watchfulness, for, 130
  *see also under* thoughts

passions
  affirmative tradition, 95-96
  classical tradition, 47-52
  definition, 47, 48, 53, 55-60, 215,

254
  desert fathers on the, 52-54
  lists, 60-66
  medical language, 99-102
  Philokalic vocabulary of the, 61-73
  remedies, 114-115, 149-150:
    classical, 102-105; desert
    fathers, 105-109; moderation,
    103, 155; practical life,
    the, 115-121; prayer, 140-149; psalmody, 132-140;
    scripture, 113, 254, 288-289;
    watchfulness, 121-132
  see also thoughts, vice
perception, 214
  God, of, 260
  inner essences, of, 15, 169, 260
  intellectual, 15
  noetic, 178-179
  self identity, and, 209
  sense: noemata arising from, 261;
    passion arising from, 31, 54, 56,
    60, 271; sin arising from, 77;
    thoughts arising from, 94, 98,
    265; transcendence of, 168
  spiritual, 166, 173
  subliminal, 266
pleasure(s)
  deification and, 161-162
  Epicureans, 155
  mindless, 94
  moderation, 103, 117
  nature, in accordance with, 95
  passions, 26, 29, 48-50, 55-56, 58,
    64-65: hostile pleasures, 55-57,
    98-99, 149, 203; process, 74, 83,
    85-86, 91, 332 (note 98)
  renunciation, 112, 115
  sensual, 20
  soul, of the, 11
  spiritual, 28, 179
  well-being and, 225
power(s)
  Christ, of, 245
  divine, 120
  ego, of the, 211, 224
  noetic, 133, 171, 198
  passions, 66, 70, 72, 99

punctual self, of the, 211
soul, of the, 12, 14, 16, 55, 59-60, 93-94, 129, 133, 146-147,
  165, 169, 171, 173, 246, 320
  (note 55)
Spirit, of, 176-177
spiritual, 273
thoughts, of, 297
prayer, 22, 286-297
  allegoical interpretation of
    scripture as, 42, 44
  angelic, 35, 168
  definition, 33, 140-141
  heart, prayer of the, 4, 229-230,
    246, 357 (note 64)
  Jesus Prayer, 2, 142-149, 165
  pure, 31, 33-35, 118-119, 135,
    141-142, 158-159, 168, 174,
    182, 231, 281-282, 289, 334
    (note 134)
  remedy for the passions, 114,
    140-149
  stages, 141-142
  see also contemplation
psalmody, see under angels,
  contemplation, passion(s)
psychotherapy
  behavioural, 207-208
  cognitive, 208
  definition, 216-219
  dynamic, 206-207
  history, 205-208
  Orthodox, 248-255
  outcome, 223-229
  Philokalia as a kind of, 219-223
reason
  Aristotle, 103, 155, 320 (note 55)
  dianoia, 15, 152, 260
  disengaged, 211
  intellect and, 15, 42
  Plato, 10, 155
  Stoics, 49, 150, 155, 203
scripture
  beatitudes of Jesus, 184-195
  inwardness, 229
  Philokalia, influence on, 40-45
self, 209-213
  fragmentation, 210, 223

Index 377

integration, 224, 227-228
postmodern views as enslaving, 223
punctual self, 211
sin
  actions, sinful, 75, 81-82, 85, 88-90
  Adam, of, 14
  attentiveness as rejection of, 130
  confusion of, 95
  energies, sinful, 179
  idea, sinful, 261
  inward, 234
  passions, sinful, 69
  voluntary, 74
  *see also* temptation
soul, 152, 260
  disease of the, 101, 335 (note 13)
  dreams, 277-278, 280-285
  dwelling place of Christ, 232
  harmony of the, 155
  health of the, 157-158, 164-165, 177
  inwardness, 54, 234, 235, 238-242
  location, 246
  marriage of the, 161
  passions, 14-15, 47-51, 54-55, 58-60, 77-78, 81-83, 85-86, 271
  perfection of the, 170-172
  physician of the, 100-101, 252, 336 (note 16)
  powers of the: appetitive (desiring, concupiscible, epithumia), 14, 17, 24, 32, 94, 176, 182; incensive (thumos), 11, 16, 32, 59, 93-94, 134-135, 165, 176, 190, 357 (note 80); intelligence (logistikon),14-16, 59, 60, 93, 163, 165, 176, 182, 260; *see also* intellect
  pre-existence of the 323 (note 107)
  self identity, and, 208-213
  tripartite model, 10-17, 48, 136, 176, 320 (note 55), 331 (note 81)
  virtues of the, 11, 116
  wounded, 26, 265
spirituality, xix, 98, 258-260, 294
  Augustinian, 224
  definition, 260

Orthodox, 4, 255
*Philokalia*, of the, 2, 7, 40, 225, 300
psychotherapy and, 226
Twelve Step, 253-255
utilitarianism and, 250-252
well-being and, 225
stillness, *see* hesychia
Stoicism, 211, 249
  eudaimonia, 155-156
  passions, 49-52, 336-337 (note 38); remedies for, 104-105
  *Philokalia* influenced by, 11-12, 57, 97

temperament
  definition, 334 (note 133)
  humoural balance and, 94
  passions and, 94
  prayer and, 334 (note 134)
  psalmody, effect on, 134-135, 138-139
temptation, 73-92
  actualisation, 84
  assent, 73-75, 77-85 84, 87-91
  captivity, 77-80, 84, 87, 90
  coupling, 77-81, 83-85, 87, 89-95, 332 (note 97)
  entertainment, 73-75, 77, 87, 90, 332 (notes 97 & 98)
  momentary disturbance, 74, 76, 78, 89, 90
  prepossession, 74-77, 89, 90, 332 (note 98)
  provocation, 73-80, 84-85, 87, 89-91, 332 (note 104)
  struggle, 77-79, 90
  wrestling, 80, 84, 90
thoughts
  angelic, 32, 273
  demonic, 31-33, 81-83, 123, 145, 261, 263, 269-271
  eight, the, 23-30, 55, 60-63, 110-112, 157, 249, 263-265, 274: acedia, 25, 28-30, 112, 282, 330 (note 64); anger, 27, 51, 94, 96, 111-112, 134-135, 357 (note 80); avarice, 27, 55-56, 111, 274, 345-346 (note

37); fornication, 25-27, 111, 265, 288; gluttony, 26, 33, 111, 157, 249; pride, 29, 112, 281; sadness, 25, 28, 112, 249, 273-274, 281; vainglory, 29-30, 112
fantasy, 15, 85, 88, 126, 145, 244, 265, 274, 321 (note 59)
ideas, 88, 211, 215, 261
logismoi, 54, 260-261, 263-264
noemata, 261-264
sheep, likeness to, xiii-xx, 32, 43, 261, 270, 299-300

unconscious, xv, 267
collective, 278
dreams as means of access to, xv, 274, 276, 278-279
personal, 224
processes, 203, 206, 208, 274
thoughts, xvii, 223
unknowing, 292, 297
*Cloud of Unknowing*, 293
darkness of, 291, 300
transcendence of, 293

vice, 24, 263-264, 270
akrasia (imbalance) as, 134
intellect, effect on, 173
lists, 62-66
medical language, 101
virtues, opposed to, 110
virtue, 24, 129, 263-265
beatitudes, 186-190, 192, 198-199
blessedness, 179-181
classical understandings of, 49-51, 155-156
desert fathers, 156-157

passions, 29, 59; remedy for, 110, 114-121, 137

warfare
demons, against the, 146
inner, 234, 239, 244-245, 282
passions, against the, 55, 74-75
spiritual, 125, 234, 244
watchfulness, 121-132
attentiveness, 41, 122, 125, 128, 130, 144, 146, 181, 244
cognitive process, 288
custody of the heart, 122
definition, 124
guarding of the heart, 40, 122, 123, 129, 139, 148, 245, 286
guarding of the intellect, 122, 123, 126, 194, 244
investigation of thoughts, 122
noetic stillness, 122
*Philokalia*, scope defined by, 6
rebuttal, 122, 123, 126, 272
stillness of the heart, 122
well-being, 164-166
blessedness as, 177-196
classical understandings of, 154-156
definition, 153
deification as, 159-164
desert fathers, 156-157
eudaimonia, 154-155, 345 (note 10)
hesychia as, 174-177
intellect (purification, illumination and perfection of), 166-174
mental, 152-153, 196, 200-202

## Quotations from the English translation of the Greek *Philokalia*

All references in brackets are to the EGP.
Page numbers in **bold** refer to tables in this book.

Anonymous, *Abba Philimon*, (2:345) 177; (2:355) 172-173
[Antony the Great], *On the Character of Men*, (1:344, #93) 11; (1:347, #117) 11-12
Diadochos of Photiki, *On Spiritual Knowledge*, (1:264, #38) 282
Evagrios the Solitary, *On Prayer: 153 Texts*, (1:65, ##82-87) 133
*Texts on Discrimination*, (1:48, #16) xiii; (1:48-49, #16) 299
*Watchfulness - Extracts*, (1:68-69, ##117-123) **197**
Gregory of Sinai, *On Commandments & Doctrines*, (4:222, ##55-56) 164; (4:223-225, ##62-75) **88**; (4:228, #82) 14; (4:229-230, #86) 121; (4:234, #102) 119; (4:236, #108) 287; (4:237, #111) 176-177; (4:239, #116) 168
*On Stillness*, (4:266, #5) 138; (4:270, #9) 177
Gregory Palamas, *In Defence of Stillness*, (4:333, #2) **190**; (4:334, #3) 246
*On Prayer & Purity*, (4:345, #3) 173-174
*Topics*, (4:356, #24) 13
*To Xenia*, (4:316, #57) **193**; (4:318, #60) 172; (4:303, #27) **185**; (4:304, #28) **192**; (4:306, #34) **186**; (4:310, #42) **186**; (4:311, ##43-44) **186**; (4:312, ##47-48) **186**; (4:314, #53) **187**, (4:319, #62) 169
Hesychios the Priest, *Watchfulness & Holiness*, (1:162, #1) 124, **188**; (1:163, #6) 125; (1:170, #46) **85**; (1:171, #52) **188**; (1:175, #75) **188**; (1:180, ##104, 105, 108) 244; (1:186-187, #143) 126-127; (1:186-187, ##143-144) **85**; (1:188, #150) **188**; (1:189, #153) 122-123; (1:191, #165) 125; (1:197, #196) **197**
Ilias the Presbyter, *Gnomic Anthology: 2*, (3:44, #86) **198**; (3:45, #104) **290**; (3:46, #106) **198**
*Gnomic Anthology: 4*, (3:57, #76) 287; (3:60, #102) **199**; (3:60, #103) **199**; (3:63, #123) **86**; (3:65, ##136-137) xix-xx
Isaiah the Solitary, *Guarding the Intellect*, (1:22, #1) 96; (1:24, #12) 286
John Cassian, *Eight Vices*, (1:80-81) **193**
*Holy Fathers of Sketis*, (1:96) 170
[John of Damaskos], *On Virtues & Vices*, (2:337-338) **84**; (2:339) **183**
John of Karpathos, *For the Monks in India*, (1:315, #71) **193**; (1:317-318, #83) **197**
Mark the Ascetic, *Letter to Nicolas*, (1:153) **74**
*On the Spiritual Law*, (1:113, #36) 232; (1:119, #138) **74**; (1:119, #139) **74**; (1:119, #140) **74**; (1:119-120, #141) **74**; (1:120, #151) **74**
*Righteous by Works*, (1:138, #152) **74**; (1:139, #160) **74**; (1:145, #224) **74**
Maximos the Confessor, *For Thalassios: C2*, (2:143, #25) 183; (2:145, #31) **197**; (2:147, #39) 292-293

On Love: C1, (2:54-55, ##17-19) **197**; (2:56, #35) 58; (2:62, #83) 81, **82**; (2:62-63, #84) **82**; (2:64, #94) 262
On Love: C2, (2:67, #16) 58; (2:70, #31) **82**; (2:72, #39) 120; (2:75, #55) xvi; (2:75, #57) 116; (2:79, #84) 261
On Love: C3, (2:90, #47) **191**; (2:93, #67) 117
On Love: C4, (2:109, #72) **188**
On the Lord's Prayer, (2:287) 116, 161; (2:292) **187**; (2:297) 161-162
Various Texts: C1, (2:173, #45) **188**; (2:176, #58) 59; (2:177, #60) 59-60
Various Texts: C2, (2:199, #58) **189**; (2:201, #67) 287-288; (2:202-203, #73) 16; (2:206-207, #90) 95-96
Various Texts: C3, (2:215, ##24-25) **198**; (2:216, #28) **198**
[Maximos the Confessor], Various Texts: C1, (2:178, #63) 163; (2:185, #92) 231-232
Various Texts: C2, (2:203, #75) 288

Nikiphoros the Monk, *Watchfulness & Guarding*, (4:194) 131; (4:204-205) 130; (4:205) 131
Nikitas Stithatos, *On Spiritual Knowledge*, (4:147, #29) 176; (4:148, #31) 163; (4:148, #33) 164; (4:155, #53) 292
*On the Inner Nature of Things*, (4:121, #51) **199**; (4:121, #50) 171; (4:124, #61) 284; (4:125, #64) 175-176; (4:137, #100) 183-184
*On Virtues: 100 Texts*, (4:94-95, #60) **187**

Peter of Damaskos, *Book I, Introduction*, (3:76) 120-121; (3:77-78) 251-252; (3:84) **190**
*Book I, Obedience & Stillness*, (3:108) **185**
*Book I, Seven Forms of Bodily Discipline*, (3:89) 175; (3:151) 117
*Book I, Spurious Knowledge*, (3:201) **186**
*Book I, The Bodily Virtues as Tools for the Acquisition of Virtues of the Soul*, (3:103-104) **199**
*Book I, The Difference between Thoughts and Provocations*, (3:207) **80**
*Book I, The Seven Commandments*, (3:93) **185**; (3:94) **186**; (3:94) **187**, (3:96) **187**; (3:96) **188**; (3:97) **189**; (3:97) **190**; (3:98) **190**; (3:98) **191**; (3:98) **192**
*Book I, The Sixth Stage of Contemplation*, (3:135-6) 13
*Book I, The Third Stage of Contemplation*, (3:115) **190**
*Book II, VIII. Mortification of the Passions*, (3:231) **192**; (3:233) 118
*Book II, XXIV. Conscious Awareness in the Heart*, (3:277) 141
Philotheos of Sinai, *Forty Texts on Watchfulness*, (3:17, #3) 127; (3:23-24, #19) 244; (3:26, #26) 127; (3:29, ##34-36) **79**; (3:29, #35) 58

Symeon Metaphrastis, *Paraphrase of Makarios*, (3:285, #2) **189**; (3:296, #30) **187**, **200**; (3:308-309, #55) **86**; (3:329, #100) **185**; (3:329, #101) **199**; (3:337, #116) 245
Symeon the New Theologian, *On Faith*, (4:18) 169-170
*Practical & Theological Texts*, (4:39, #73) **189**; (4:42-43, #87) 283
[Symeon the New Theologian], *Practical & Theological Texts*, (4:53, #126) **189**
*Three Methods of Prayer*, (4:70-71) 128-129; (4:71) **185**; (4:72)

**190**; (4:72) **192**; (4:73-74) 139

Thalassios the Libyan, *For Paul: C1*, (2:310, #56) **198**
*For Paul: C3*, (2:320, #22) 232
Theodoros the Great Ascetic, *Spiritual Texts,* (2:17-18, #19) **85**; (2:19, #28) 182; (2:22, #46) 182; (2:33, #86) **188**
[Theodoros the Great Ascetic], *Theoretikon,* (2:43) 178; (2:43-44) 12; (2:47) 179
Theoliptos, Metropolitan of Philadelphia, *On Inner Work,* (4:180-181) 232
*Texts,* (4:189, #3) 171